"This book is an ax for the frozen sea of the heart."
—**Chris Chivers, BBC**

"Likely to change the way you view the world, and the impact you can make in it." —**Mia Farrow**

"A superb and superbly written book about the wars young Americans fight, and the ones we can prevent at a sliver of the cost."
—**Tom Ricks, former defense correspondent, *Washington Post***

"Barcott's memoir documents . . . what Kenya taught him about waging war, building peace and listening across cultures."
—**Jina Moore, *Christian Science Monitor***

"An incredible story."
—**General Bernard E. Trainor, author of *Cobra II***

"*Three Cups of Tea* meets *One Bullet Away* in this extraordinary story of courage, compassion, giving a damn, and making a difference. Rye Barcott is a smart, compassionate counterinsurgent; *It Happened on the Way to War* demonstrates that deep knowledge of the world's people is critical to winning the wars of today and preserving peace for tomorrow. If you read only one book this year, read this book."
—**Lieutenant Colonel John A. Nagl, author of *Learning to Eat Soup with a Knife***

"Barcott's book is important for leaders to read for a unique perspective on duty and service and as a window to viewing the new security environment." —**Butch Bracknell, *Marine Corps Gazette***

"Rye Barcott is one of those rare people who can bridge the widest divides. This book is a gift."
—**Nathaniel Fick, author of *One Bullet Away***

"Read this book. You'll be hooked after the first page."
—**Adi Ignatius, editor in chief, *Harvard Business Review***

Endorsements from Educators for *It Happened on the Way to War*

"A must-read for students looking to make a change in the world and wondering how to get started. It is an inspiring, exciting, and humbling account of how our young leaders can make a big difference, and that's why I am so pleased that Rye Barcott's book has been embraced and adopted as course material at SUNY campuses."

—**Nancy Zimpher, Chancellor, State University of New York System**

"This splendid story of self discovery and the critical importance of public service distinguish this remarkable book. I hope it is read by this generation of young people, especially to learn that one life can and should make a lasting difference."

—**William Friday, President Emeritus, University of North Carolina System**

"A fascinating story of the reconciliation of the irreconcilable—the melding of the dispassionate warrior mentality with that of the compassionate citizen seeking a better humanity through sustainable self-improvement. It is a story of people with emotions bared and deficiencies highlighted, including Rye's own. In short, it is a story of humanity at its best and its worst, and it is especially suitable for summer reading programs."

—**Erroll B. Davis, Jr., Chancellor, University System of Georgia**

"This is a great read. Few books illustrate the convergence of hard and soft power as well as *It Happened on the Way to War*."

—**Joseph S. Nye, Dean Emeritus, Harvard Kennedy School; author of *Soft Power***

"This true story of emerging and consummated passion is as raw and riveting as it is informative and important, especially now at a time when young people have unprecedented opportunities to make an immediate impact in the world. Every student should read this book."

—**Phillip Clay, Chancellor, Massachusetts Institute of Technology**

It Happened on the Way to War

A MARINE'S PATH TO PEACE

Rye Barcott

B L O O M S B U R Y
New York   Berlin   London   Sydney

Published by Bloomsbury USA, New York

All papers used by Bloomsbury USA are natural, recyclable products
made from wood grown in well-managed forests.
The manufacturing processes conform to the environmental regulations
of the country of origin.

LIBRARY OF CONGRESS CATALOGING-IN-PUBLICATION DATA

Barcott, Rye.
It happened on the way to war : a marine's path to peace / Rye Barcott. — 1st U.S. ed.
p. cm.
ISBN: 978-1-60819-217-5 (hardcover)
1. Kibera (Kenya)—Social conditions. 2. Social service—Kenya—Kibera.
3. Community development—Kenya—Kibera. 4. Slums—Kenya—Kibera.
5. Poor—Kenya—Kibera. 6. Carolina for Kibera. 7. Barcott, Rye. 8. Volunteer
workers in social service—Kenya—Kibera—Biography. 9. Volunteer workers in
social service—United States—Biography. 10. United States. Marine Corps—
Officers—Biography. I. Title.
HV446.5.B37 2010
362.5'56092—dc22
[B]
2010030544

First published by Bloomsbury USA in 2011
This paperback edition published in 2012

Paperback ISBN: 978-1-60819-431-5

1   3   5   7   9   10   8   6   4   2

Typeset by Westchester Book Group
Printed in the U.S.A. by Quad / Graphics, Fairfield, Pennsylvania

To Tabitha Atieno Festo

&

Salim Mohamed

Talent is universal; opportunity is not.

Contents

KEY LOCATIONS

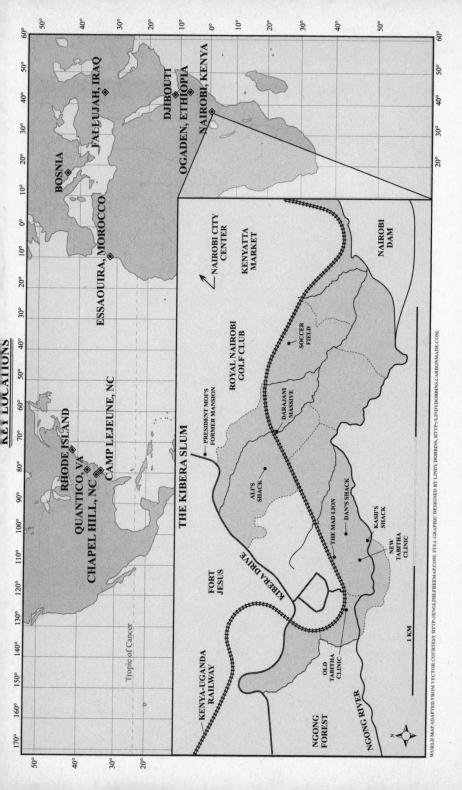

RHODE ISLAND

QUANTICO, VA

CHAPEL HILL, NC   CAMP LEJEUNE, NC

BOSNIA

FALLUJAH, IRAQ

ESSAOUIRA, MOROCCO

DJIBOUTI

OGADEN, ETHIOPIA

NAIROBI, KENYA

Tropic of Cancer

THE KIBERA SLUM

NAIROBI CITY CENTER

KENYATTA MARKET

NAIROBI DAM

PRESIDENT MOI'S FORMER MANSION

ROYAL NAIROBI GOLF CLUB

SOCCER FIELD

DARAJANI MASSIVE

ALI'S SHACK

THE MAD LION

DAN'S SHACK

KASH'S SHACK

NEW TABITHA CLINIC

FORT JESUS

KIBERA DRIVE

KENYA-UGANDA RAILWAY

OLD TABITHA CLINIC

NGONG FOREST

NGONG RIVER

1 KM

WORLD MAP ADAPTED FROM VECTOR COURTESY HTTP://ENGLISH.FREEMAP.COM. FULL GRAPHIC DESIGNED BY LINDY DOBBINS. HTTP://LINDYDOBBINS.CARBONMADE.COM.

Prologue

The Horn of Africa

November 2004

Tabitha liked to say that you have to sacrifice for success, and I was thinking about her and her strong brown eyes as we blazed into the Ogaden Desert. My interpreter and I were midway to our forward operating base somewhere near Somalia. We hadn't seen a living creature in hours. It was just the two of us in our Land Cruiser with an emergency supply of food and water, spare tires, an encrypted satellite phone, suitcases of counterintelligence equipment, a rifle, a shotgun, and a crate of grenades. I pulled over near a patch of thorny, sage-colored bushes. It felt more appropriate to whiz in a bush, even if we were in the middle of nowhere.

My urine evaporated as soon as it hit the cracked earth. I heard rustling as I zipped my fly. Something grunted. I reached for my pistol. A baboon bounded out from behind a bush up ahead. Another appeared, then another. Before I knew it, I was staring at a dozen miniature cavemen with arms that reached the ground.

It was a standoff. A headline from a government threat advisory flashed to mind: MAN CLAWED TO DEATH BY SAVAGE BABOONS.

I stepped back. The pack leader scampered forward. I stopped, switched the safety off my pistol, and took aim. The soft click of the safety carried through the desert air. The lead baboon hesitated. My hands shook slightly.

"Ergh, ergh." One of the baboons shuffled forward. "Ergh, ergh." It swayed like a boxer, knuckles to the ground, shoulders shifting.

One of them crouched, then sprang toward me. I jerked the trigger, turned to the Cruiser, and ran. As soon as I slammed the door shut, two baboons leaped onto the windshield, shining us with their hot-pink rear ends. I floored the accelerator. The hairy little men flipped into the air and into a cloud of dust behind us.

"Can you get a CAR for that, Lieutenant?" my interpreter, Hussein, joked.

The coveted Combat Action Ribbon was typically awarded for receiving and returning enemy fire. Hussein, a forty-year-old Ethiopian American who had previously worked as a manager at a luxury hotel in Georgia, had an impressive understanding of the Marine Corps and our martial culture.

Hours after the baboon ambush, the intense sunlight began to affect my eyes despite my dark, wraparound sunglasses. My sensitivity to light was a symptom of the laser eye surgery the military had given me the previous year. Hussein took the wheel, slid in *Ray Charles Greatest Hits*—one of my girlfriend Tracy's favorite CDs—and gunned it. I resisted my instinct to slow him down. I wanted to get to our destination as much as he did, and I assumed he knew how to handle the roads.

We sped toward a bend on a rocky ridgeline. Ray was singing "Georgia On My Mind," and I was thinking about Tracy, her long, strawberry-blonde hair, almond eyes, and southern grace. We had been dating since the end of my senior year of college. I missed her, and I was only halfway into my nine-month deployment. Suddenly, a tiny deerlike creature appeared in the middle of the curving road motionless, staring at us. Our rear wheels began to skid. Hussein hit the brakes, throwing the vehicle into a tailspin. We careened off the ridge and flipped over. The Land Cruiser slid into a boulder, crushing the roof above our heads like tinfoil.

I WAS TWENTY-FIVE and hanging upside down in a Land Cruiser in Ethiopia's Ogaden Desert. Dust layered my khakis. This was not what I had imagined when, at seventeen, I signed an eight-year contract with the Marine Corps in exchange for a college scholarship. I had seen myself in an infantry battalion covered in camouflage and face paint. I knew it was dangerous. That was part of the attraction. If I died as a Marine, I envisioned an honorable death, a death in combat. I never imagined losing my life in a car wreck, or to a pack of baboons.

"Hussein, you all right?" I couldn't see his face.

"Yes, sir." His voice trembled.

Ray Charles crooned:

> *Georgia, I said Georgia*
> *A song of you*
> *Comes as sweet and clear as moonlight through the pines*

"What the hell was that?"

"Dik-dik."

"Dik-dik?" I had only a fleeting recollection of seeing deerlike dik-diks on safari in Kenya as a young teenager.

"Yes, sir."

Gasoline fumes filled our vehicle. We needed to get out and secure our gear. I flipped the thumb release on my Spyderco knife, sliced the seat belt with the half-serrated blade, and pulled myself out of the shattered window. Hussein crawled out of his side. We stashed our gear and surveyed the damage.

"I should have just hit it," Hussein observed.

Damn right you should have, I thought to myself, bottling my anger. *Why didn't I tell him to slow down?*

My blood pressure rose as reality set in. I was responsible for a team of five highly trained Marine human intelligence specialists on the frontiers of the Global War on Terrorism. I always told my team to drive safely, and there I was standing in front of a crumpled $40,000 vehicle, our mission stalled and our lives having faced unnecessary danger.

I was pushing too hard in more ways than one, and I dreaded the conversation that I would have with my boss back at our headquarters, an old French Foreign Legion outpost in Djibouti called Camp Lemonnier. My boss, a gruff Marine colonel, ordered me to report to his command post as soon as we returned.

———

"SIR, LIEUTENANT BARCOTT reporting as ordered, sir." I walked into the colonel's tent and locked my body at attention. He was the senior human intelligence officer in our Horn of Africa task force.

"At ease, Lieutenant."

I relaxed, locked my hands behind my back and widened my stance. "Sir, I need to apologize. There's no excuse. I was in charge. I screwed up. It won't happen again."

"Lieutenant, that's right. You screwed up. But we have a mission to accomplish. Learn from what happened. Press on. Got it?"

"Yes sir." I popped back to attention, the Marines' way of saluting superior officers when indoors.

"Carry on, Lieutenant. Carry on."

I left the colonel's tent and changed clothes. I needed a run to clear my mind. It was noon. The thermometer read ninety-five degrees Fahrenheit. My Marines thought I was too gung ho for running in such heat, but I preferred it. In twenty minutes, I could get a workout that would take an hour in a gym.

The sandy, three-mile trail behind our base's flight line stretched toward the sea like a long pier. There were two signs at its entrance: the first warned of snakes and scorpions, the second advised jogging with a buddy. I wasn't opposed to the idea, but I could never interest anyone in joining me. Most runners hit the trail at dawn or dusk. Every now and then I passed a bearded man running solo at the hottest time of day. "SF," our Special Forces operators, were the only ones who wore beards to conceal their military identity on missions. I didn't know any of them well enough to propose a buddy run.

My stopwatch set, I took off with my shirt in one hand and cell phone in the other. When my Marines or an intel source needed to reach me, it was often urgent.

A musty breeze swept in from smoldering pits of garbage in Djibouti's largest dumping grounds, a landfill located adjacent to Camp Lemonnier. My conversation with the colonel spun on repeat in my mind. While it troubled me that I had messed up, the colonel's words were also comforting. I could still prove myself. We were human intelligence collectors. We were Marines. My team could ramp up our already intense pace, and I would set the example by personally taking on more. We would out work the old man's expectations.

I sprinted the final hundred-yard stretch. Dizzy and dry heaving, I stumbled to the cooler, pulled out a two-liter bottle of water, and doused my throbbing head. A faint ring rose above the sound of the wind. It was my cell phone with a call from Kenya.

None of my Marines were in Kenya. The call was from someone at Carolina for Kibera (Key-bear-ah), the nonprofit I cofounded three years earlier with the nurse Tabitha Festo and the community organizer Salim Mohamed. A microcosm of the world's problems, Kibera was Nairobi's largest slum. There, more than two hundred thousand people lived in an area the size of New York's Central Park. The United Nations projected that up to one fifth of the world could live in "mega slums" like Kibera by 2020. I had first traveled there as a college student to do research on youth culture and ethnic violence, and for the adventure. Over the years, however, Kibera became my second home. It wasn't easy to balance my Marine Corps responsibilities with service in Kenya, and it was becoming more challenging as Tabitha and Salim grew our organization from a small clinic and sports program reaching hundreds to a movement that empowered thousands of young people.

"*Habari*," I answered, "Hello."

"Rye, it's me. How are you?" It was Tabitha. While I called Tabitha from time to time to touch base, she never called me. It was too expensive, and she was conscious of my commitments as a Marine.

"Good, *mama*, how are you?"

"Oh, not well." Her voice cracked.

"What is it?"

"It's not good. Perhaps you can come?" Her phone beeped three times and cut off. I couldn't get through when I tried to call back.

Tabitha rarely asked for anything, and she never complained. If she was reaching out to me, she needed me. I called Salim. He told me Tabitha was "really sick." He thought it would be good if I could come to Nairobi.

Suddenly the two worlds that I worked so hard to keep in their own compartments were colliding. It was abrupt, and the timing couldn't have been worse. I needed to prove myself to the colonel, not ask him for a favor. Yet, I had to ask. Even though we shared neither blood nor skin color, Tabitha was family.

TABITHA AND I had first met in 2000, when I spent five weeks living in Kibera during the summer of my third year in college. She showed me around the slum after we had been introduced by her best friend, Jane Atieno. Tabitha wanted to welcome me to her home for chai, Kenya's staple drink, before I returned to the States.

We reunited the day before I left near Jane's ten-by-ten-foot shack, her "ten-by-ten." I recognized Tabitha immediately from her oversized black leather coat. Her hair was pulled back in short, tight braids, and her brown eyes conveyed strength and wisdom. She wore a dark green, conservative skirt. If it weren't for her leather coat, which appeared to be designed for a man, I might have thought she was a no-nonsense librarian. Later, I would learn that she was only thirty-four and widowed with three children.

We crossed the railroad track and made our way into Kibera. Tabitha, in flip-flops, walked as if she was on a mission. I struggled to keep up as mud sucked against the soles of my boots. Women greeted her deferentially with smiles and the Swahili words for nurse and doctor: *nass, daktari*.

Old-school reggae music thumped from the Mad Lion Base, a small shack with a bad reputation. The face of a lion with fiery eyes was spray-painted on its tin wall. The lion's eyes appeared to be aimed at us.

"Me, I hate this place," Tabitha whispered.

We were in a part of Kibera known for the wrong reasons. She pointed to charred remains on the ground: a patch of clothing, a half-burned shoe, and a head-sized rock stained with dried blood.

"Thief." She shook her head. "Mob justice."

The Mad Lion sold moonshine for twenty shillings, about a quarter per shot. The moonshine was illegal, though police rarely crossed the tracks to patrol the area. The corrupt police were hated in Kibera and they knew it.

A lanky man stumbled out of the Mad Lion toward us. Tabitha stopped. The man's eyes were as red as the lion's. He pointed at me, stumbled, and slurred, "*Mzungu* [white man], you give me something. You give me . . ." His arms flailed over his head and he collapsed. One of his hands splashed into the foul muck of a sump, an open sewer. A dozen young men watched with hard eyes.

Tabitha placed two fingers on the man's neck. She gently folded his eyelids back and inspected his eyes. The man remained unconscious as she lifted his arm out of the sump.

"Okay." She straightened her back. "Let's continue."

We walked toward Darajani Massive, the Massive Bridge. It arched over the tracks on one of the only dirt roads that cars could navigate into the slum. Weeks earlier, Tabitha had overheard a group of young men talking outside a shack near Darajani Massive. She referred to them as "hardcores." She had said that they called me Van Damme and were "plotting" against me. It was the first and only credible threat I had received in Kibera. I didn't know what "plotting" against me meant, and Tabitha hadn't been able to clarify.

Nevertheless, I took any threat seriously. Security was always on my mind. I varied my routes, never flashed money, befriended local thugs, and identified myself by an African name. After a couple of weeks, I picked up some Sheng, a language of the youth that mixed Swahili, mother tongues, and gangsta rap lyrics. It had no formal rules, evolved rapidly, and was unintelligible to elders. Sheng helped me establish my bona fides in a way that I would never have imagined.

A gang of men hanging out at Darajani Massive looked at me curiously. A white man walking in Kibera without an entourage was uncommon. My dark sunglasses concealed my eye movements as I studied their midsections for weapons. Widening my stride, I tried to look cool and confident. My heart slammed against my chest. The hardcores needed to think I knew more about their lives and Kibera than I actually did. I moved my hand to my pocket and fingered the waffle grip of my Spyderco knife.

The biggest, meanest looking guy was at least six feet tall, with biceps the size of my neck. He snarled at me and gnawed on a piece of wood, a *toothbrush kienyenji.*

"*Vipi beshte. Napenda toothbrush kienyenji yako. Wewe una meno kama simba,*" I greeted him in Sheng and Swahili: "What's up friend? I like your traditional toothbrush. You have teeth like a lion."

The gang burst out laughing.

"*Mzungu* knows Sheng," someone chuckled.

A man with calloused hands stepped forward. The rest of the group fell silent. "*Wewe ni soldja wa mtaa. Karibu,*" he said: "You're a soldier of the streets. Welcome."

I thanked him with a *gota*, a fist bump. *Soldja* was a term of high respect, a title that had to be earned.

"Nice job. You're an interesting one," Tabitha said as we walked away.

Her compliment was reassuring. Though I didn't know her well, I sensed that she was slow to praise.

It began to drizzle. The mud grew thick. We ducked down a narrow alley that twisted into a dizzying array of turns. By the time we reached Tabitha's house, I felt as if I were in the middle of a labyrinth. The thought reminded me of a Marine Corps recruiting advertisement in which a square-jawed warrior battles his way out of a medieval maze, slays an evil statue that magically comes to life, and transforms into a Marine in full dress blues with ribbons and a glimmering Mameluke sword. Silly as it was, I loved that ad. I first saw it when I was fifteen, and it had reinforced the calling I felt to be a Marine. "It is a test," the ad's only words conclude in a baritone voice, "Not just of strength, but of the power of the mind. And if you complete the journey, you will be changed forever. The few, the proud, the Marines."

Illuminated with a paraffin lamp, Tabitha's ten-by-ten was sparsely furnished and clean. I left my mud-caked boots on a step outside the front door. An outdated calendar hung on a wall with an advertisement for margarine; a small plastic cross hung on another wall. I sat down on her sofa while she disappeared behind the colorful *kanga* sheet that divided her shack into two parts: living room, and kitchen/bedroom. The sofa pillows were as hard as wood.

Tabitha emerged with two plastic cups, a thermos of chai, and a tin with brown sugar. She had no money and only a handful of earthly possessions, but she had enough to make chai for a visitor in her home.

"How many do you take?" She pointed to the sugar tin.

"One, please."

Tabitha dropped a heaping spoonful of sugar into my cup, then dumped four spoonfuls into her own. She removed a note card from her purse and slid it across the table. It was one of the cards I had used in my life-history interviews with Kibera youth. The card had four questions:

- What are your greatest problems?
- Are there NGOs (nongovernmental organizations) doing anything about your problems?
- What are your aspirations?
- Were you in Kibera during the ethnic violence?

"You left this card behind when we first met. You always ask the youth about their problems. But you never asked me about my problems. You want problems?" Tabitha said softly but firmly, fingering her plastic cup of chai. "I'll tell you problems."

Rarely had I been confronted in such a way. I asked Tabitha if I could turn on the tape recorder that I carried for my research.

"It's okay."

I placed it on the table.

Tabitha took a deep breath and began, "Now you can imagine the problems I've been having. Okay, I'm jobless. Staying the way I'm staying. Initially I used to work, yes, to help my children little by little. But then, you know, I lost my job. Now we're just hanging. I'm almost at the street children level, the way you're seeing me. And I'm educated. I'm a registered nurse. Imagine. Now, there are too many unemployed nurses. Once, I dreamed of starting a clinic for my own, but I've no savings. Do you think it's easy to bring up children with no husband, no job, no business?"

"So how do you make your payments—your rent, food, and things?"

"My rent? For me to pay, even at the time I'm talking to you, I'm having an outstanding balance of four months. I usually rely on friends and relatives. If I go to somebody, maybe sympathizers, I say, 'Give me something little,' I pay the rent."

"Where are your children?"

"I've got the firstborn in the house. There used to be two others here. But when we can't manage, they just got out and went back to their grandmother's." Tabitha referred to her "motherland," her rural home in Nyanza Province near the shores of Lake Victoria. Every year thousands of people moved from the rural areas to the slums of Nairobi in search of greater opportunity.

"They're not in school?" I asked.

"They're not in school, even now."

"So why do you stay in Kibera, *mama*? Why not return to your motherland?"

"I don't have any land. We're just pushing, you see. My husband was the firstborn in the family, but he died. I'm poor, but they [relatives in the rural areas] still think I'm the one to provide for them. Yet I've nothing to give." She gestured to the mud wall with the old margarine calendar.

Her sense of urgency was arresting. Tabitha's problems were so vastly different from my own. Yet I'd felt a strong connection to her ever since she had warned me of my first threat.

"Now I'm doing nothing," she continued. "I tell you I'm doing nothing because I don't have money. If you want to sell *sukuma wiki* [collard greens], you have to have money."

"You want to sell *sukuma*?" Collard greens, cabbage, and tomatoes were staple vegetables. They could be purchased for a pittance at nearly any turn in the slum.

"Yes, I can, if I can get money to start purchasing the *sukuma*."

"What would your plan be?" It struck me as a bad idea to become another seller in such a crowded market.

"I can't compete in the slums. Here they won't pay. If you have the money, you go to different areas. You know, Kibera is a slum. Once you have a little money, there is Eastleigh, Huruma. You can choose such areas where residents, they have a little bit of income. Isn't it?" Eastleigh and Huruma were lower-income areas notorious for their high murder rates and levels of gun violence.

"What would you do?" I asked. "Purchase a place to sell it? That might cost as much as seven thousand shillings." It was about $100 at the time.

"Even that's too much. You know me, the life I'm living, you can't talk of such money."

"If you had fifteen hundred shillings, how would you do it?" In my time in Kibera I hadn't given out any money, but I wanted to do something for her and with her.

"Then I choose the place. Like now, a sack of *sukuma* is twelve hundred. Now if I go and purchase this one sack, I know I'd have a balance of three hundred. Now this three hundred, let me assume that fifty shillings is for the people who carry it from one place to where you sell it. And then I keep the rest for transport to Eastleigh."

"You think it can work in Eastleigh?" I was impressed by her detailed understanding of costs.

"Yes, it can. Obviously I'll do it, because there are people who have money and there the police don't come down on you for not having the hawker's (vendor's) license. You know that thing, I can't afford. A hawker's license can cost you five thousand. So if I go to Eastleigh with my plans, obviously I'll succeed. I'll sell my *sukuma*."

"Have you talked with anyone who's succeeded?"

"I've known many, very many," her voice rose. "What we're crying out for is money."

"So you could start off tomorrow if you had money?"

"If God gives me today, tomorrow, the twenty-ninth of June in the year of our Lord 2000, I'll be on the track."

"The track to success."

"Yes, I'm telling you the track to success."

Spontaneously, I unzipped the secret holding area in my canvas belt and pulled out two folded-up thousand-shilling notes, $26. "Then the track begins today."

Tabitha looked at me and took a deep breath. "God bless you. I know I'll work with it and it'll be something. I'll even mail you. I'll tell you how my business is going."

"*Sukuma wiki!*" I pumped my fist in the air.

"I'll push the *wik*," she responded, laughing for the first time that day. *Sukuma* means "to push," and *wik* is an abbreviation of *wiki*, or week. Residents joked about "pushing the week" when they could only afford to eat collard greens.

I had purchased eleven *kangas* as gifts for friends in the United States. The brightly colored sheets with Swahili aphorisms were used as dresses, sachets, baby wraps, wall decorations, and room dividers. I reached into my bag and handed one to Tabitha. The *kanga* was deep purple with bright orange splashes and crisscrossing, black and white lines. Tabitha unfolded it and held it in front of her, inspecting its rich colors and crisp texture. She gasped as she read its aphorism, which was in a deep Swahili that I didn't understand until she translated it:

"*Mawingu ya dunia ufanika wajane.*" The clouds of the earth cover the widows.

"It is a lesson," Tabitha explained. "When you have a husband, people respect you. If your husband dies, you're looked down upon. People start hating you. And you know, you are not the one who killed him. If you're married, you have a cover; even if you have a husband who is abnormal, you have that cover. So now this *kanga*, it's telling me my cover is in fact the clouds of heaven. Oh, I think it is a good day for me!"

Tabitha refolded the *kanga* with great care, reminding me of my military color guard detail in college, when we slowly lowered our flag and folded it into a tight triangle for the night's watch. It was a good day, and I admired Tabitha. I doubted that I could live with such strength and dignity if I found myself in Kibera, alone, with no job and three children.

We shook hands. Tabitha didn't seem to be the hugging type. She walked me to a hill overlooking a portion of Kibera's sea of rusted tin roofs. We parted ways. When I looked back, she was standing on the hill with her hands folded behind her back like a sentinel. I didn't know if I would ever see Tabitha again, or what would become of the $26.

THAT FIRST FAREWELL with Tabitha was on my mind as I walked through the sultry air at Camp Lemonnier to the colonel's tent, his command post. I'd spoken to him only hours before. Inside me, in my chest, I felt a terrible strain. I imagined my insides as a rubber band, bending and stretching, latched onto two fingers pulling apart. *How far could it stretch before it snapped?*

It was rare to show up without an appointment, but the colonel could see from my face that we needed to talk. He was only vaguely aware of the work we were doing in Kibera. Although they were different worlds, I wanted to believe that my work in Kibera made me a better Marine.

I stood at attention in front of his desk, swallowed hard, and said, "Sir, I have an unusual request for you."

"Stand easy, Lieutenant. Tell me about it."

I explained Carolina for Kibera, our organization, the difference it was making in the community, and how personal it had become. I poured my soul into it. I told him about Tabitha. She was sick and I needed to see her. I laid it all out. When I stopped, there was a long silence. Marines usually shunned such emotional appeals. I could feel my neck pulsing. My palms were sweaty. The colonel pulled his dog tags out from under his fatigues. A small silver cross dangled between the two gray tags. We had never discussed our faiths. The colonel pinched the base of the cross with his thumb and his index finger. He closed his eyes for a moment.

"Well, what you are doing, Lieutenant, is God's work." He took a deep breath, "I think there's something we can find for you in Nairobi for a few days."

I almost lost my bearing and gave the old colonel a big bear hug. "Sir, thank you, sir."

It was December 2004. I stepped out of the tent, packed my dad's olive-green duffel bag from Vietnam, and caught the next bird to Nairobi.

Part I

CHAPTER ONE

The Grenade

West Greenwich, Rhode Island

My father was the main reason I was a Marine. He was a warrior, and the war that defined his generation lived on with a vividness and an immediacy that I neither realized nor had the capacity to comprehend as a child. He barely slept and would grunt when I tiptoed to the bathroom in the dead of night. After a neighbor's home was robbed, Dad added dead bolts to the doors and created barricades with two-by-fours and metal hooks. He positioned a baseball bat next to each door, formed a neighborhood watch, placed lights on automatic timers, and rotated our clunker cars through different locations in the garage and front yard. When we walked through the woods behind our house, he spotted details I rarely noticed: animal droppings, faint footprints, feathers, and hunting stands hidden in the evergreens. He taught me to shoot, to hunt, and to fight at a young age. He warned me to be careful and to anticipate danger when I least expected it, and he was the most defensive driver one could imagine. At least once every five minutes he laid on the horn, flashed the high beams, and shouted names at drivers that my friends found hilarious, such as "gumball," "dipstick," and "swineherd."

My father made decisions and then charged into them until he finished the deed or became exasperated, in which case he quit as dramatically as he had started. As a sociology professor, he valued rigorous and rational thinking. Yet at times his mood changed so abruptly that he appeared impetuous and put everyone except his battle-hardened friends on guard. Dad, whose firm Prussian appearance was accentuated by a thick black mustache, often came across to others as confrontational when he didn't mean to be. Yet as intense as he was, and as outraged as he could feel at perceived injustices, I never saw him become violent. He always managed to contain his frustrations, often releasing them through competitive, injury-inducing sports. While my father may have had many of these characteristics before Vietnam, I believe the war cemented them and made them more salient.

Few military artifacts were in our home, but the ones I discovered captured my imagination at an early age. Dad's dress blue uniform hung with its Bronze Star and Purple Heart in a storage closet next to his Mameluke officer's sword. The faded olive-green duffel bag was tucked away in another closet. A plaque from the Third Reconnaissance Battalion hung near the entrance to his basement den with the inscription Swift–Silent–Deadly in Latin and the image of a skull punctured by a tight triangle of bullet holes.

And then there was the smoke grenade. Coated by a heavy wax preservative, the rusty, old grenade blended into a bookshelf behind the plywood desk where my father graded term papers and wrote research articles. Its cylindrical body had once held a fuse and a firing pin. A bullet hole through its core prevented it from ever detonating. When I first discovered it as a boy, I tried to visualize my father at twenty-four, leading a platoon through a Vietnamese jungle. When the ambush happened, the smoke grenade strapped to his flak jacket in front of his heart intercepted a Vietcong bullet. At the same moment, a bullet tore through his cheek, and another ripped into his leg.

That rusting grenade exerted a force over me. When I ran my finger over the shredded exterior, time seemed to stop. I closed my eyes and was transported to a still place of light without sound. The force had a dark quality that would take decades and a war for me to sort out. I never spoke with Dad about the grenade or the darkness behind the light. As much as I loved and admired my father, he was intimidating, and I could never figure out a way to talk about it. Though it was a filter for many of his judgments, Dad never said much about his war.

My father's response was subdued when in high school I accepted a full Reserve Officers' Training Corps (ROTC) scholarship to our nation's oldest public university, the University of North Carolina at Chapel Hill (UNC), in return for a four-year active-duty and four-year reserve service obligation in the Marines. His lukewarm reaction bothered me until I realized that it came back to the Vietnam War, a war that he believed was so misguided by generals and politicians that it was criminal. His combat experience made him eternally skeptical of any institution's ability to protect the best interests of individuals, and he was especially conflicted about the Marine Corps. My father was glad he had served our country, and he had formed his deepest friendships in the Marines. His best friend included me in his inheritance after he passed away. Lieutenant Colonel R. J. O'Leary, his former ROTC commander when Dad was a midshipman at Miami University in Ohio, landed me my first real summer job in high school as a hand on a cattle ranch in Wyoming. These relationships were things to live for, and they happened because of the Marines. Yet at the same time my father chided the hubris of the brotherhood, and he believed that many militaries throughout history too often destroyed more than they protected. He thought American foreign policy was excessively militarized, and he distrusted war-prone politicians who had never served a day in uniform. More personally, he knew the horrors of combat and dreaded the possibility of my death or severe injury pursuing a service he had encouraged, however subtly.

My mother was far less ambivalent in her views about the Marine Corps. She believed the military squelched the type of reflection and critical thinking that was so important in her own profession as an anthropologist and professor of nursing at the University of Rhode Island. She detested violence and the possibility of killing. Mom, whose easy smile and gentle appearance led some people to underestimate her, believed our military did more to incite violence than to deter it. Her entire body shook with anger when we listened to pundits on the evening news praising new weapons systems and military tactics in the Gulf War. And yet she never openly discouraged me from joining the Marines. That would have been against her deep-rooted values of freethinking and free choice. She was less judgmental than my father, and I knew that she would support any career decision I made so long as I was kind to people and did my best to help others.

Mom first encouraged me to study Swahili when I went off to college.

She knew that before I graduated I wanted to return to the continent that had helped me get on the right track when I was floundering through adolescence. I didn't know where in Africa I might end up. I simply knew that I needed to go, and that I would probably conduct some type of research in order to "give back." My mother, who rarely gave strong advice, told me that I should prioritize Swahili if I intended to return to Africa. She believed it was essential for anyone who wished to conduct research in a foreign country to know some of the local language. Research, she warned me, could be seen as being simply extractive, and it was essential that it be approached with humility. Learning a language was a sign of genuine commitment. It needed to start there.

THE FIRST AND only trip I had taken with my parents to Africa was far more transformative than we had anticipated. On graduation day from junior high school in 1993, as a fourteen-year-old, I had held a camping party in the woods behind my house. Unbeknownst to my parents, my buddies and I stashed bottles of hard liquor at the campsite. One of my friends drank so much gin that he went into seizures and had to be emergency evacuated in the middle of the night while I was lying in a pool of vomit. My parents had saved for many years so that the three of us could take a monthlong trip that summer that would culminate with two weeks on safari in Kenya. After the camping fiasco, they grounded me for the summer and contemplated canceling the trip.

"Maybe he'll realize how lucky he really is if he sees other parts of the world," my father finally concluded.

When our airplane touched down at midnight in Nairobi, we were disheveled and sleep-deprived. If our body language didn't tell people that we were tourists, our outfits certainly did. Mom, who kept her wavy, dark hair back in a ponytail with an elastic band, carried a dog-eared copy of Isak Dinesen's *Out of Africa*. She wore scuffed-up hiking boots and a fanny pack stuffed with travel documents. My father carried a Swahili phrase book and a backpack. His gym shorts exposed his massive calves, calves so thick he had to cut the elastic band from his athletic socks to prevent loss of circulation. On his suggestion I brought a copy of Hemingway's "The Short Happy Life of Francis Macomber," a story of big-game hunts in the Masai Mara that instantly captured my imagination. We would soon be

on safari in the same exotic lands Hemingway had written about. It didn't
dawn on me then that I was not dressed for the bush. I wore Nike Air
Jordan sneakers, a dirty white Boston Red Sox baseball hat, and a T-shirt
that draped like a skirt over my baggy jeans.

After a short ride in a beat-up taxi, we arrived at the Norfolk Hotel
and parked behind a Bentley. A dozen tourists sipped gin and tonics on
the Lord Delamere Terrace, a perch at the entrance of the hotel named in
honor of one of the most famous white settlers and land barons in Kenyan
colonial history. Legend had it that the Norfolk was a favorite watering
hole for Hemingway himself. Colonial times, however, had long passed, and
Nairobi had developed a criminal reputation. *Nai-robbery*, some expatriates
called it.

Had he been aware of its reputation, my father would not have suggested the following morning that Mom and I take a stroll to the Masai
Market while he made the final plans for our safari. By the time we found
our way on foot to the market, the place was bustling with hawkers ped-
dling colorful beadwork, clothes, and ebony carvings from small open-
air stands. Our attention turned to the spectacle at the bottom of the hill.
There before us was a scene like no other.

Hundreds of cars clogged the arteries and battled each other to get
ahead in one of Africa's largest roundabouts, a place called the Globe.
Matatu minibuses flashed neon lights and thumped American hip-hop and
African ghetto rap. Drivers laid on their horns; sirens sounded. A *matatu*
jumped the sidewalk to get ahead, nearly sideswiping a pedestrian. The
patch of dirt the size of a small park in the middle of the roundabout appeared to be a dump with fires smoldering on top of heaping mounds of
refuse. Small creatures glided between the burning pits. We walked down
the hill for a closer look.

The burning garbage released a sour odor that mingled with diesel
fumes and the nauseating stink of sewage. Dozens of soot-coated children
camped inside the roundabout's circle. They picked through the garbage
with plastic bottles hanging from their mouths like pacifiers, feeding their
lungs the fumes of toxic industrial glue. There were no adults. A small girl
with an infant swaddled to her back in a colorful *kanga* wrap darted up to
cars stuck in the roundabout's enormous jam. A glue bottle bobbed from
her mouth. The infant on her back appeared to be crying. I had never
witnessed such wretched squalor.

"Mom, I'd like to give this to that girl," I removed my wallet and took out some cash that I had earned mowing lawns.

A group of teenage boys paced toward us with bottles in their mouths and yellow, frozen eyes.

"We better go now," Mom said hastily.

She led me quickly back through the market. The teenagers trailed off. Afterward, Mom consoled me. "It's okay," she said. "It's natural to feel bad. There's a lot of pain in the world, and it's good to help when you can."

By the time we returned to the Norfolk, I was overcome by profound sadness. I thought that I might have felt better if I had been able to give some money to the girl with the infant on her back. At least I would have been able to help in a small way. Yet I wasn't able to do anything, and the feeling of powerlessness in the face of desperation was something that I didn't know how to process. That night, lying sleepless in the plush confines of the Norfolk, I thought about that girl and the infant, and for the first time in my life realized how fortunate I was to be an American.

THE FOLLOWING DAY we went on safari in the Masai Mara at a camp called Rekero, far from the diesel-choked streets of Nairobi. We delighted in seeing the wild animals of the Great Rift Valley, the tectonic fault line that reaches from Mozambique to Lebanon and hides many clues to evolution's puzzle. We watched lions stalking and dik-diks grazing with zebras and Cape buffalo. We drove alongside galloping giraffes and stampeding wildebeests, absorbing their thunderous energy and marveling at the beauty of the land. It was exhilarating. Somehow, though, I had anticipated these sensations. What I didn't foresee was my interest in the local people.

On our last day our Masai guide Jackson Ole Looseyia invited us to his village, where he welcomed us into his house, a smoky mud-and-wattle hut. I was amazed by his austere lifestyle. Looseyia told me about his culture and patiently answered my many questions. Afterward, while my parents took a nap, Looseyia led me with his long, rhythmic strides up a steep path to the escarpment behind the main camp. I was panting by the time we reached a slab of granite jutting into the air like a tilted tombstone. Looseyia stepped to its edge and surveyed the landscape below.

I caught my breath and asked Looseyia about his ambitions. He looked at me curiously and replied that it was a very American question. After a pause, he told me that he wished to guide for the rest of his life because it was his main talent, and because he respected the tradition of passing knowledge on to others.

"And you, what do you want to do?" he asked, facing me.

In the third grade we had an assignment to identify whom we wanted to be like when we grew up. Every night my parents and I watched the evening news with Tom Brokaw. Brokaw reminded me of a friendly uncle, and I liked that he had an impact on how people viewed the world. I wrote an essay on being a news anchor and appended a glossy photograph of Brokaw in the newsroom. However, explaining who Tom Brokaw was to Looseyia seemed out of place, so I told him the truth.

"I don't know. I want to do something significant."

"Everything we do matters. Don't take what you have for granted. You can do something significant. But you know who makes that possible?"

"What's that?"

"It's your parents."

"Oh, yeah, of course," I replied.

"No, you're not getting me. You have more opportunities than I can even dream. You have these because of them. You should treat them with more respect."

I was at a loss for words. What he was saying resonated deeply. I had taken a lot for granted.

The following morning Looseyia accompanied us to the dirt airstrip. I gave him one of my baseball hats and we exchanged addresses. It had only been four days, yet it was difficult to say good-bye. My father handed Looseyia his cane in an impromptu gesture of appreciation.

"For me?" Looseyia asked in disbelief.

"Sure."

"Really?"

"Of course," Dad said. "We're grateful for all you've done for us."

"In our culture a man's walking stick is the most significant gift. It's given from a chief before he passes to the next chief, or to his son."

"Well, I don't plan on croaking anytime soon, but I do hope you'll be a chief." My father laughed, though I could tell he was deeply moved by the meaning his gift conveyed. He asked Looseyia to join us for a final family photograph.

As our plane lifted off, Looseyia stood on the savanna holding the cane above his head. My father, peering out from his window, saluted him.

FIVE YEARS LATER I was in my first of four Swahili classes at UNC. The language had a smooth sound and a rhythmic flow, and I enjoyed studying it even though the class itself was one of the most polarized I had ever been in. A dozen male athletes and a few guys looking to complete their foreign-language requirement with as little work as possible sat in the back rows. Separated by a no-man's land of barren desks, the rest of us, about eight students, sat in the front.

It wasn't a classic geek-jock divide. The students with me in the front rows were an eclectic and adventurous group. A friend to my left studied the plight of child soldiers in Uganda. The student on my right aspired to be a missionary in Tanzania. For those of us in the front, Swahili directly connected to our life plans.

Professor Alphonse Mutima did the best he could teaching the bifurcated class. With his stocky build and infectious laugh, one could easily have mistaken him for a man who had lived a comfortable life. But few comfortable lives came out of the Democratic Republic of the Congo, and his was not one of them. Professor Mutima didn't speak about his upbringing in class. He was reserved and didn't want to feel pitied. We captured only glimpses of his former life when he explained certain words with unique cultural meanings and applications, such as *kanga*s, the colorful wraps that hung on walls or were worn as skirts, baby carriers, and shawls. When Professor Mutima spoke of such things, the elevated, engaging tone in his voice conveyed the longing he felt for the home he had never returned to. I found him to be fascinating and often walked with him across our wooded campus after class.

Professor Mutima devoured what little news came from press coverage of Central Africa. When we came to difficult subjects, he made light of the ironies that emerged from insecure lives, such as the absence of obesity in many parts of Africa. His laughter veiled a pain and anxiety so deep it would cripple most men. Professor Mutima dealt with the boys in the back rows, but he had little respect for them, or for anyone who he believed took the great gift of a university education for granted.

With time, Professor Mutima told me about his home in Goma, a city perched on an active volcano at the Rwandan-Congolese border. Goma earned notoriety as home to the largest refugee camp in the world after the 1994 Rwandan genocide. Professor Mutima recommended I read a book about the genocide by a writer named Philip Gourevitch, and he pointed out a vivid excerpt from the book that described Goma as "one of the most bewildering spectacles of the century," where "bulldozers had to be brought in to dig mass graves and plough the bodies under. Picture it: a million people, shifting through the smoke of cooking fires on a vast black field, and behind them . . . the Nyaragongo volcano had come to life, burbling with the flame that made the night sky red."*

I had also been told about the book by an army officer who served on a humanitarian assistance mission to Rwanda. The officer predicted that my military career would be dominated by American responses to ethnic conflicts that threatened to destabilize entire regions, as had occurred with the Rwandan genocide.

For winter break that year my mother and I took a short vacation together. I spent the first two days engrossed in Gourevitch's book. Its cover featured an intriguing photograph of a lawn chair in front of a foggy lake, and its title was the longest I had ever seen: *We Wish to Inform You that Tomorrow We Will Be Killed with Our Families*. The author's photo was equally striking. He looked off to the side with a devilish smile, heavy bags sagging beneath his dark eyes, his hair whisking up from his forehead as if he had just stepped off a motorcycle.

I vigorously circled and underlined entire passages of the book. It was a habit of interactive reading that I had learned from my father. Returning to some passages a half dozen times, I read many excerpts out loud to my mom. It was baffling. In Rwanda more than eight hundred thousand people were killed in one hundred days. I recalled watching the evening news as a fifteen-year-old when a segment aired with footage of a group of Rwandan boys murdering a wounded man. They used machetes and clubs spiked with nails. This was my first realization of humanity's capacity for great evil, and I found it and my reaction to it as fascinating as it was repulsive.

---

* Philip Gourevitch, *We Wish to Inform You that Tomorrow We Will Be Killed with Our Families: Stories from Rwanda* (New York: Picador, 1998), 163–64.

I wanted to battle the forces that created such horrific frenzy, and yet, at the same time, the darkness itself held some attractive power that I didn't understand but could not deny.

How and why genocide happened were the obvious questions, and they went unanswered. They were disturbing enough, though beyond them, a more personal question lingered. If I had been born in Rwanda and was confronted with the ultimatum of killing an innocent person or being killed, would I kill? While I wanted to say that I would resist, in truth I didn't know, and that uncertainty made me all the more curious.

Gourevitch's book with its lucid meditations reawakened these thoughts and emotions. As enlightening as his writing was, so many elemental questions about good and evil remained. By the time I put down his book, I knew I wanted to go to Rwanda to understand for myself the elements of darkness that I could one day be called on to battle as a Marine.

During our last night of vacation, I told Mom about Swahili class with Professor Mutima. We talked about anthropology and her former academic adviser at UNC, James Peacock, a beloved anthropologist with long, salt-and-pepper eyebrows and a kind, unassuming presence. I had reached out to Professor Peacock after growing bored with my first semester of freshman classes. He had invited me to his office in Alumni Hall, the building on campus where my parents met as graduate students in 1969. I was anxious about the meeting until I walked into his office and found him sitting cross-legged on top of his desk, shoes off, listening to Indonesian hip-hop. After our meeting, Professor Peacock had let me join his graduate-level anthropology seminar on globalization. The theory was over my head, but I had enjoyed the small group discussions. When I chose to write my term paper on the Masai in Kenya, Professor Peacock had introduced me to a graduate student named Jennifer Coffman. Jennifer focused her fieldwork in southern Kenya and generously helped me navigate my first major research paper.

Mom listened eagerly as I told her about how Professor Peacock's class and my conversations with Jennifer had opened my mind to anthropology and the power of ethnography.

"I'm so glad to hear this," Mom responded. I could tell that she was relieved that I had shaken my teenage apathy.

"But, Mom, there's something else." Unsure how she would respond, I had saved it for the end. I had enough to keep me busy with a demanding course load and ROTC commitments. Yet I felt that I needed to do more. I needed to go to Rwanda.

"Rwanda?" Her voice cracked.

"Yes, Mom, I want to go. I need to go."

"Oh, my." She paused. "Are you sure?"

I had wanted to return to Africa, and Rwanda seemed to be the right fit. I explained to my mom that I could learn about ethnic conflict there, develop my Swahili, and make a real contribution with research. After an hour or so of discussion, my mom told me that she understood and would support me. Although I had anticipated her support, her words felt great to hear. Mom, too, was an explorer. As a young nurse she had lived alone for a year in a village in Peru. She knew about the drive to go to places where many others would not venture. It was part of my inheritance, as was my middle name—Mead—in honor of the legendary anthropologist Margaret Mead.

Mom and I spent the rest of the night talking about Rwanda. She helped me think about how to get there safely and in a way that would not jeopardize the security of the local population. Weeks later, she sent me a handwritten note with one of her favorite Margaret Mead quotes: "Never doubt that a small group of thoughtful, committed citizens can change the world. Indeed, it's the only thing that ever has."

"Change the world." It sounds cliché to me now, but it didn't back then. The phrase spoke to me throughout college and, before that, adolescence. It had connected with me ever since one day, as a boy, when I fell through the ice into the pond behind our home. Something extraordinary happened that day. I was with Peaches, our golden retriever whom my parents had named after their favorite tree in our backyard. Peaches was my most loyal playmate. She slept in a hay patch in our barn, and I could often tell where she was by the jingle of the miniature cow bell that my parents hung from her collar. That day we were playing catch with her favorite tennis ball when the ice gave way beneath me. Engulfed by the frigid water, my head smacked a piece of ice when I tried to come up for air and escape. Trapped, I panicked. I thought I might die.

Kicking violently, I inhaled a gulp of water. Not until my head collided with another piece of ice did my body relax, and I detected rays of light filtering in through the hole that had swallowed me. I swam to it, hoisted myself out of the water, and gasped for air. Peaches barked then licked my face.

Although Peaches often ran ahead of me, that day she stayed by my side. I shivered back home across frozen fields and collapsed into the shower with my clothes on. The steaming water cascaded over my head, slowly replacing the bitter chill with a numb, tingling sensation. As my body warmed, my mind expanded with euphoria. I had survived. I had faced death, and it was exhilarating.

Curious to return to the spot where the pond ice had collapsed beneath me, I trudged back out over the snow with Peaches that afternoon. A thin layer of ice had formed over the hole by the time I returned. When I raised my walking stick to break the ice, Peaches barked. She dropped to the ground, paws out. Her cow bell stopped jingling. The wind died. I froze and looked around for an animal or a person approaching us. There was nothing, and then, suddenly, there was everything.

The force swept me into its embrace. It felt like I was floating outside of my body. I heard no words and saw no form or shape. All I could see was light, just as when I had touched the grenade that saved my father's life. This time, however, the light lasted longer and came with a sense of clarity. It was warm and glorious. I was a believer, but never before had I felt God. Never before had we communicated directly.

That day at the pond made me realize that life could be cut off at any moment. I don't really know why, but I started believing that I wouldn't live past thirty years old. When I told some of my closest friends about my premonition, many of them thought it was a morbid idea, a death sentence, a noose. But I found it to be liberating. I didn't think about having a career in a profession that would take me years to learn. I didn't imagine getting married or having children. From that point forward, I had a new sense of purpose and time, and there was an awareness that I was alive for a reason that was larger than myself. What I sought was a short, intense life that would make a bold impact and live beyond me.

———————

YEARS LATER, AT some point near the beginning of high school, I realized
that my greatest fear was an ordinary life. The Marine Corps was the
answer, and although I had been groomed and guided to it implicitly by
my father and his closest friends throughout my childhood, it felt like a
revelation.

With my mind made up, I started wearing a USMC T-shirt, cut my hair
into a high-and-tight, and bought an American flag for the antenna of my
old Ford Ranger pickup truck. Football became my sole sport, and I used
my off-season to lift weights and bulk up so that I could compete as a defensive tackle against linemen twice my size. I watched war movies such as
Platoon and *Full Metal Jacket* so many times that they influenced my language. "Take the pain!" and "What's your major malfunction, numbnuts?"
were among my favorite lines.

Acquaintances often looked surprised when they first learned of my
career choice. Rhode Island was such a liberal place that many people I
knew in the affluent community of East Greenwich, where I attended
public high school, thought that only kids from disadvantaged backgrounds
chose the military. "Why would you do such a thing?" I was often asked.

"To serve my country," I said, using the common refrain without any
real understanding of what it meant.

My career choice changed the way I viewed the world, and it gave me
a greater sense of purpose in school. In American-history class, I argued
that "might makes right." In English, I read *The Red Badge of Courage*
multiple times in search for clues to how I might respond the first time I
faced enemy fire. I imagined artillery applications in precalculus home-
work. Chemistry offered insights into the capabilities of enemy weapons
of mass destruction. Spanish could be a tool to communicate with Latino
Marines. I was becoming a better, more engaged student.

Unfortunately, my improved performance in school came too late for
the Naval Academy, which turned me down. The rejection stung. My
grades were strong but not stellar. I barely ranked in the top 10 percent
of my high school class and had underwhelming SATs. A lot of valedic-
torians, SAT aces, and captains of varsity teams were applying to the same
schools. I lacked those accolades. My only recourse, I assumed, was to
work harder. So I threw everything I had into my ROTC scholarship
application, spending weeks preparing for my interviews, rewriting essays, and training for the physical fitness test. The final question in the

application asked, "What word do you feel best describes you?" I wrote, "Determined."

IT HAD WORKED out. I had made it to UNC with a full ROTC scholarship, and by the time I was in my third semester of Swahili, I knew that I wanted to go to Rwanda. But I was struggling with how to get there. One day Professor Mutima brought in a former student named Ted Lord. A thin, young guy with a marathon runner's physique and a serious face, Ted stood at the front of the room and patiently waited for the chatter in the back rows to stop. Once it did, he began speaking in Swahili, a Swahili that was as smooth and as fluent as Professor Mutima's. Had I not been looking directly at him, I would never have guessed that Ted was a *mzungu*, a white guy who grew up in Baltimore.

Realizing that our comprehension was limited, Ted transitioned to English. In a calm, low-key manner, he told us briefly about the year he'd spent in Tanzania. He explained that he had received a Burch Fellowship, an award that any UNC undergraduate could apply for so as to have "a unique life experience." Ted used his fellowship to work as an apprentice to world-renowned door carvers on Tanzania's Zanzibar island. My mind raced with possibilities as he spoke.

Professor Mutima proudly announced that Ted had arranged for a set of Zanzibari grand doors to be installed at the entrance to the new UNC Honors Office. When he opened the floor to questions, I asked, "How did you do it?" It was a clumsy question, but Ted sensed what I was getting at.

"Once you know what you want to do," he explained, "start sending e-mails, making phone calls. You've got to be flexible, be persistent. Reach out to a bunch of people and eventually a few, maybe five percent, will give a damn. That's enough, though. When they respond, you can follow up and start pulling it together."

I couldn't pay attention during the rest of the class. I was thinking about Ted's apprenticeship and his contribution of grand Zanzibari doors to the university. Ted pulled it together as a sophomore. I was a junior. "Reach out to a bunch of people and eventually a few will give a damn."

That afternoon I returned to my dorm room, finished the one-page proposal to study the Rwandan army's invasion during the genocide, and sent it to two dozen people.

"Sir, I am in the Marine Corps ROTC program at UNC and am learning Swahili," I wrote to the author Philip Gourevitch, hoping that he would be one of the 5 percent. "Your book inspired me to focus my university studies in Rwanda. I know you are busy but I would appreciate it if you would give me your thoughts on this brief one-page proposal attached." I included a few of my reflections about his book and clicked SEND.

THE FIRST PERSON to respond to my e-mail blast was a USAID officer who had worked in Rwanda. We met at a national security conference that I had helped organize at UNC. Unlike many of the conference participants, she was approachable. She suggested that I forward my proposal to her ex-husband, a diplomat named Peter Whaley.

"Give his e-mail to no one," she said, "and tell him I recommended you be in touch."

With Ted's advice in my mind, I relentlessly pursued every lead. A week later, I had a meeting lined up with Peter Whaley and a few military officers who had worked in Africa and were based in the Pentagon. Fortuitously, my mom was in Washington that week attending a conference. Whaley left me a voice mail two hours before we were scheduled to meet. "Come to 20/20 K at seven," he said, his voice sounding too highstrung to conform to the James Bond impression I had of him. "I'll be at the bar. Hope you like calamari."

My mother dropped me off at 20/20 K at a quarter to seven. The lacquer on the oak bar reflected the soft light from hanging lamps with green shades. A balding man in a pink dress shirt sat at the end of the bar closest to the exit, hovering over a heaping plate of calamari with a martini glass close at hand. He had a small potbelly, and his legs were so short they may not have reached the brass footrest at the base of the bar.

"Mr. Whaley?" I asked, trying to make my voice sound deep.

He didn't look up. "You're younger than I thought. Here, have some calamari. Ya like calamari, right?" He spoke quickly with a strong New York accent. "How old are ya?"

"Twenty, sir."

"None of that sir stuff on me, and none of these for you." He tapped his martini glass with his fork. "Sorry."

I ordered tonic water.

"Good colonial drink," Whaley remarked, launching into long digressions about the history of tonic water as an antimalarial and his favorite preparations for cooking calamari.

The waiter handed Whaley another martini, "dirty, shaken not stirred."

"So were there any good calamari joints in Rwanda?" It was an awkward transition, but Whaley liked it. He slapped the bar and roared with laughter.

"That's why I had to leave. No goddamn calamari and too many dead bodies." His face turned as pink as his shirt. Then he started. He didn't eat another calamari or touch his martini for the next hour.

"Whaley's War, that's what they call it," he said, adding that he hated very much to have a war named after him. I had heard about Whaley's War from another source and assumed it had something to do with the violence that spilled over from Rwanda into the Congo after the genocide. Whaley's own explanation didn't help much. He spoke of Tingi Tingi and other obscure places that I had never heard of. He took me deep into battle tactics, drawing on a napkin with forceful movements: fat arrows for the armies, R for rebels, ovals for the "thousands of civilians." Balls with T's on top represented air assaults. He pushed so hard on his pen that he ripped into napkins and had to start over multiple times. Sweat formed on his brow. I didn't know where he was going, but I knew I couldn't stop him. I could only feed him follow-up questions and propel him to the next story. Each battle ended with Whaley slashing an X across the ovals and tearing the napkins to shreds with his ballpoint pen.

At nine P.M. my mom walked in, put her hand on my back, and greeted us in a soft voice. She said she would be having dinner in the back of the restaurant, and she left before Whaley could engage her in conversation.

Whaley looked down at his pile of destroyed napkins and appeared to be puzzled. We hadn't spoken about my project all evening. I sensed I had an opportunity before losing him to another war story.

"So, what do you think of my proposal?"

He looked at me as if it were a foolish question. "I'm meeting with you because it's important. It's a story that needs to be told. You've read Gourevitch, right?"

"Yes, of course." Gourevitch had even responded to my e-mails, though it seemed unlikely that the famous writer would help me apart from answering a few questions about his book. I didn't know at the time that Gourevitch had lived in Whaley's house in Rwanda. They were friends.

"Well, if you read Gourevitch, then you understand that the RPA [Rwandan Patriotic Army] story needs to be told."

I nodded and waited for Whaley to offer some advice or perhaps even make a gesture to help me. Instead, he turned back to the Congo, and I sat there listening for another hour. By the end of it my mind was spent. The names of people and places twisted my brain into knots, reminding me again of how little I knew. I had stopped my part-time job bouncing at bars in Chapel Hill to focus on Rwanda, but a few meetings and a few months of extracurricular reading could get me only so far. As Whaley destroyed more napkins, I began to wonder if our meeting was a waste of time. Then, at precisely ten P.M., Whaley stopped, flagged the waiter, and placed his credit card on the table. I offered some cash but he waved me off and made a remark about remembering what it was like to be poor and in college. When he stood up, his demeanor suddenly shifted. Lowering his voice, he leaned forward and said, "Tomorrow I'll introduce you to a man. He works for the president of Rwanda, and he'll help you. Tell no one that I introduced you two, and call him as soon as you get my e-mail."

I had spent three hours for a ten-second offer of an introduction that might be able to take me where I needed to go.

BEFORE I COULD proceed with my plans to go to Rwanda, the Marine Corps had to sign off on my proposal. I had a good relationship with Major Boothby, my Marine commander, and I was about to test the strength of it with my proposal. The major could shut me down for any number of reasons, not the least being that I would need to spend the second half of my summer in Quantico, Virginia, at Officer Candidates School (OCS), the Marine officer's equivalent of boot camp.

It was an unseasonably warm January day. My armpits were sweaty and my chest was tight as I walked across our campus greens passing students in flip-flops tossing Frisbees and laying out beach blankets. By the time I reached the major's office in our handsome brick armory, my armpits felt like a swamp. I pounded his hatch with my fist and announced my presence as he had trained us to do.

"SIR, MIDSHIPMAN BARCOTT REPORTING AS ORDERED, SIR."

"Enter, Barcott. Good sounding off. Stand easy."

"OOHRAH, SIR," I barked.

Major Boothby didn't need a briefing. He had already read my written proposal. "Barcott, can't you do anything normally?" He swigged black coffee from a mug with the inscription MARINE CORPS SNIPER. "Most midshipmen will spend the month and a half before OCS physically and mentally preparing themselves. You want to go attach to an army in Rwanda?"

"Sir, it's good training. Plus, I'll be a better Marine if I understand the ethnic fighting in a place like Rwanda."

Hands locked together, Major Boothby sat in silence for a moment before concluding that he would send my request up the chain of command because I had taken the time to study Swahili and had performed well in ROTC. "And because you've got guts," he added, "and it takes guts to make stuff happen. Marines have a bias for action. In life, you have to take risks. In the Marines, you take even greater risks. Understand what I'm saying, Barcott?"

"Yes, sir. Thank you, sir." I popped to attention.

Major Boothby stuck his trigger finger out at me, "Just make sure you pass OCS."

THE BURCH FELLOWSHIP Selection Committee awarded me a $6,000 grant to travel to Rwanda that summer. Everything seemed to be falling into place until one morning when I woke up at five A.M. for an ROTC run. Before heading out of my dorm, I quickly checked my e-mail. To my surprise, there was an e-mail with a blank subject line from Whaley's contact in the Rwandan Office of the President. I had not heard back from the man after our initial phone call, when he pledged to personally support my proposal. "Anything for Peter Whaley," he had said. His e-mail, however, contained only one, cold sentence:

"You are no longer welcome in my country."

There was no salutation, no signature block, and no additional explanation. I stared at the e-mail in stunned disbelief before forwarding a copy to Whaley with a request that he call me.

One of my ROTC buddies who knew about my Rwanda plans detected something was wrong after we finished our run through the quiet trails surrounding the campus. When I told him about the e-mail, he smiled and whacked me on the arm like my father would do. "Semper Gumby, devil dog," he said, making a play on the Marines' motto, *semper fidelis*. Always faithful, always flexible. The ability to adapt to rapid change was a touchstone of Marine Corps "maneuver warfare." Most setbacks were temporary if you approached them with the right attitude.

My phone was ringing by the time I returned to my dorm room.

"Rye, Peter Whaley here. I'm not surprised by the e-mail. It's bad in the Congo right now and the Rwandan army needs to focus there. I'm sure you understand." He was direct as ever. The security situation had changed and the Rwandan military didn't have time to take responsibility for a Marine-in-training on a research project.

"So it's a dead deal?" I asked.

"Yes."

"No other channels?"

"No. But you'll find something else, and when you do, let me know. I may be able to help."

I needed to consult with my other advisers. Out of convenience and familiarity, I went to Jennifer Coffman first.

"*Hujambo*, Rye," Jennifer greeted me in her office as she prepared for an African-civilizations course that she was teaching later that morning.

"*Sijambo*, Jennifer." She was one of the few teachers I called by her first name, though it still didn't come naturally. She had to correct me at least a half dozen times before I adopted the habit. In ROTC, even upperclass midshipmen went by *Mr.* and *Miss*.

Jennifer's office was small, windowless, and warmly draped in *kangas* and colorful artwork from her fieldwork site in Kajiado, a windswept expanse of land east of the Masai Mara. A brick propped the door open. She drank chai from an old jelly jar that sat next to a photograph of her husband and two young children.

I told her about the e-mail.

"Well, that's *great* news!" She clapped her hands. "This way you'll be sure to stay alive, and you'll just have to go to Kenya."

"Thanks, Jennifer, but I really wanted to go to Rwanda."

"Why?"

"Well, you know."

"Yeah, but tell me again."

"I'm going into the Marines and wanted to study ethnic violence."

"Well, have you heard of Kibera?"

I shook my head. Jennifer explained that she hadn't heard of Kibera when she first traveled to Kenya as a Duke University undergraduate in 1989. The only slum in Nairobi that was talked much about then was Mathare. By the time Jennifer began her doctoral research at UNC, however, Kibera had grown exponentially and become the largest slum in Nairobi. It had a history of ethnic violence and a far more ethnically diverse population than Mathare. Jennifer offered to put me in contact with a family she knew with a house near the slum.

I didn't have much time, and I didn't have any other options. I thanked her and returned across the quad with the peaceful, giant poplar trees to my room at Old West Dorm. There were fewer than a dozen hits when I typed *Kibera* into Google. The first link took me to a BBC article about ethnic clashes between Muslim and Christian groups in 1995. The article identified Kibera as a "tinderbox," and the largest slum in Africa. Off to the side was a photograph of a man lying in mud with a machete gash across his head.

Tinderbox was a strong word, and the slum appeared to be a fault line between ethnic groups. If Kibera erupted into more violence, it could destabilize the entire country, and possibly even the region. This argument was implied but not drawn out in the BBC article. As soon as I realized it, I started a new proposal and the search for the next 5 percent who would give a damn.

CHAPTER TWO

Big *Gota* (Fist Bump)

Kibera, Kenya

MAY 2000

THE FLIGHT FROM LONDON TO NAIROBI covers forty-two hundred miles in eight and a half hours. During the early colonial days in the late 1800s, when the British first started landing by ship in the port of Mombasa, the trip took weeks. With the exception of traveling via London, I didn't think I shared much in common with the old colonialists. They had arrived in Kenya to exploit resources. I was there to learn and to give back by "producing knowledge," a heady phrase that my parents liked to use.

According to my watch, it was five in the morning back on the East Coast. I had stayed awake all night, gripped by anticipation. It had happened so fast since the moment I had walked into Jennifer Coffman's office. Kibera felt like a mystery. I viewed my research as an adventure to find and sort pieces of a neglected puzzle. During my final month in Chapel Hill, I had gathered more information. A librarian had tracked down an old doctoral dissertation from the 1980s that portrayed Kibera as a cauldron of corruption, cronyism, and competing tribal interests. A medical doctor at UNC who had conducted a public health assessment in Kibera had advised me that "it will forever change what you think of resilience."

Most of my conversations had been phone calls with Kenyans living in the States. Few of these Kenyans had ever been in Kibera, though they all knew it as "Africa's largest slum." Their descriptions of Kibera conformed to ghetto stereotypes. In their minds, the slum was a no-go zone of filth, thuggery, and ignorance. One Kenyan had described Kibera to me as a "cesspool," where the people "swim in their own shit." Another Kenyan had advised me to travel with at least a case of hand sanitizer. The stuff was cheaper and easier to find in the United States, he had said, and in Kibera "you'll need a ton of it."

These Kenyans with whom I had spoken knew little about Kibera and never mentioned the slum's history of ethnic rioting. When I had asked about this volatile dynamic, most of them downplayed the events as squabbles among the poor. It was a point of pride that Kenya was a peaceful country, and they had objected to my suggestions that ethnic violence in Kibera could spill across the country. If I mentioned the Rwandan genocide, most Kenyans became outright defensive. Kenya would never go the way of Rwanda, I was told, because Kenyans "loved peace so much." I didn't know much, but I knew enough to be skeptical of this peaceful-culture mythology.

Everyone with whom I spoke agreed that Kibera needed a lot of help. Where was the government? It was one of my first questions, and I was shocked to learn that the president himself, Daniel arap Moi, lived in a mansion less than one hundred yards above the slum. I found this hard to believe, and most of my Kenyan contacts laughed about its absurdity, as if to say, "Good luck figuring it out, kid."

A Kenyan businessman sitting next to me on the flight from London seemed intrigued by my research proposal and its focus on youth. He managed a hotel in Nairobi, and he suggested that job creation was the key to fighting poverty and violence. When I asked him if he employed residents from Kibera at his hotel, he replied hesitantly, "You know the problem there is trust, not skills, trust. You see?"

I could understand a businessman's concern about trust in his workforce, but his attitude struck me as discriminatory. Did poverty alone make people less trustworthy?

My attention shifted to the work ahead. It was a daunting to-do list. With five weeks on the ground I needed to identify at least a dozen youth leaders who would participate in life-history interviews, piece together

Kibera's past, and determine what organizations, if any, existed to help youth and prevent ethnic violence. I hoped to spend my nights in Kibera because living there could help establish my credibility.

This action-oriented plan presupposed answers to two questions: Could I handle it? Would the community accept me? Deep down, I didn't know the answers. Nevertheless, I felt an intoxicating sense of possibility that stemmed from the idea that I could help make sense of what appeared to be a forgotten part of the world. My research could make a real difference.

"*JAMBO, BWANA*. You military?" A Kenyan customs officer pointed to my dad's olive-green duffel bag. Faint traces of black ink remained where his rank and service were once stenciled: FIRST LIEUTENANT, USMC. I viewed that old duffel as a talisman, a force that would help keep me safe when I faced danger.

"Yes, sir, I'm a student in military training," I said in Swahili.

"Oh, that's good Swahili. You're welcome." He waved me past without inspecting the bag.

By the time I landed in Nairobi, I had only one solid point of contact near Kibera, a woman named Elizabeth. Elizabeth was the acquaintance of Jennifer Coffman's who lived with her husband, Oluoch, in a housing development adjacent to the slum called Fort Jesus. Elizabeth and Oluoch welcomed me on my first night with a feast of beef stew, a maize meal called *ugali*, and *sukuma wiki*, collard greens.

"*Karibu* Kenya." Oluoch greeted me with a firm handshake. "I am your father. This is your mother."

They certainly didn't look like my parents. Oluoch, who coordinated homestays for an American study-abroad program, was built like an ox. His thick neck blended into his shaved head. Oluoch might have made a great lineman on an American football team had it not been for his age, which I assumed was about forty-five, and his beer belly. His aloof attitude contrasted with Elizabeth's natural warmth. Her vibrant blue and yellow gown and *kanga* wrap draped elegantly off her body. She was full figured like the patrician women of Renaissance paintings. A Montessori nursery school teacher at a private school, she and Oluoch earned enough income to fall into the lower end of Kenya's thin middle class.

We squeezed the *ugali* like putty and dipped it into the savory beef broth. Elizabeth began asking me about my parents. "Oh, sorry," she said when I mentioned I was an only child. Although I joked that I had given my parents enough work as an adolescent so that they were content with one child, neither Elizabeth nor Oluoch seemed able to comprehend that some parents could want to have only one child. Apart from that awkward moment, we made easy and natural conversation. Elizabeth spoke about her daughter studying at an American university. Oluoch told me stories about attending conferences at universities in the United States and asked about UNC and our famous basketball team. He was impressed that many of our players studied Swahili.

"No wonder they're such a good team," he said, laughing.

As we finished dinner, Oluoch commented on my research proposal. "We read your thing. Very interesting. You know, these people, you'll meet some of them down there." He waved his hand toward the wall. "They live like animals. They have nothing."

Oluoch's condescending tone bothered me, but I withheld my impulse to say something. I was a guest in his home, and I needed his help. Oluoch was going to arrange a meeting at the Ministry of Education through a personal contact to fast-track my research permit. He also offered to introduce me to Dan Ogola, a youth leader in Kibera who could show me around. He trusted Dan because Dan had once helped an American student who was lost in Nairobi's Uhuru Park, a place notorious for muggings. Dan had escorted the student back to Oluoch's house in Fort Jesus and never asked for anything in return.

"But more important"—Oluoch raised his finger—"the boy is a Luo. And you, you are a Luo. When were you born?"

I was sure I was a white guy from Rhode Island, but I went along with it. "Nineteen seventy-nine."

"No, no. What time of day? When?"

"Six A.M."

"Ah, yes, I should have known. You are Omondi."

Elizabeth clapped her hands. "Ah, Omondi!"

"It's a good Luo name," Oluoch said. "And because you are our son, you're a Luo. You are from Ugenya. That is our home in Nyanza Province near Lake Victoria, where we eat a lot of fish. We like fish. This name,

I can see it on you. You have ambition. Omondis, they can be ambitious. This is a good thing."

"Yes, it's true. Yes, they can!" Elizabeth cheered.

"The nickname for Omondi is Omosh," Oluoch continued. "Luo names always start with an *O* or an *A*. So now you know how to identify your brothers and sisters."

It felt special to receive an African name. I didn't know that it was a common offering from host families to young college students.

"Thank you, *Mama, Baba*," I said with a smile, using the Swahili words for "mother" and "father."

"My son Omosh." Elizabeth clapped her hands together. "Omosh of Kibera."

My FIRST NIGHT was miserable. Wide awake with the excitement of being in a new country, my mind raced and my body fought to resist jet lag. When I did finally fall asleep, the mefloquine pills that I was taking to guard against malaria filled my brain with hallucinogenic dreams. I would have stopped taking the drug had it not been for all the Vietnam War books that had imprinted my mind with vivid images of death and suffering caused by malaria.

Cluck, cluck, cluck, coookooo. A rooster in the small courtyard sounded off at four A.M. I cursed the bird, flipped on the light, and started scribbling down reflections, including my reaction to Oluoch's description of Kibera as "down there." I needed to go there. I needed to go where I wasn't comfortable. That had always been part of the attraction, whether it was Rwanda, or Africa's largest slum, and I was impatient. Fort Jesus might be considered a ghetto by American standards, but the living seemed to be easy. I needed to find someone who could show me the ropes and help me locate a few places to stay in Kibera. If Dan was as large and as imposing as Oluoch, he might make a perfect confidant.

After a half hour of writing, I turned to Tom Mboya's *The Challenge of Nationhood*. Jennifer Coffman had recommended the book to me with a comment about how his death was a loss to the world. The book, part of a series edited by the legendary Nigerian novelist Chinua Achebe, identified Mboya as a chief architect of Kenya's independence, a friend of John

F. Kennedy's, and a politician "widely regarded as the most likely succes-sor to Jomo Kenyatta as President." I was taken by Mboya's voice, and noted a few of his passages about political manipulation of ethnic identi-ties. In one passage, Mboya concluded, "Perhaps the most crucial factor during this period is the role of personality of the men at the top—those who head the governments of the new states."

Writing in March of 1969, six years after Kenya's independence, Mboya warned that if the first generation of African leaders, such as Jomo Kenyatta, did not stop rewarding their own ethnic groups at the expense of the nation, the "second generation leadership would inherit a frame-work that is so dependent on personality that it cannot survive the person on whom it depended. This could bring with it a phase of deep political problems—tribalism, personality cults, foreign intervention and even mil-itary coup."* Four months after those words were published, assassins gunned down Tom Mboya on a busy street in Nairobi's city center. He died at age thirty-nine, a father of five children, and a martyr for the demo-cratic ideals he espoused.

THERE WAS A knock on the door shortly after I put down the book. I rose to meet Jane Atieno, Elizabeth's maid and house helper. *"Mimi ni Omosh,"* I greeted her.

"Wacha!" she exclaimed. "Omosh, you? No." She shook her head back and forth as if it were the first time she had met a white person with an African name. Her hair was short and shaped like a pancake with a part down the middle. She had wide hips, strong arms, and an unforgettable, breathtaking smile.

"Aye, you're up early. Students, they don't get up so early. It must be true you are an Omosh."

"Yes, I was born early in the morning. I'm a morning person." I was proud to have a chance to show off a nugget of new knowledge. "And you, what time were you born?"

"Let me tell you, *atieno* means 'night.' I was born in the night. But I have to wake up early, and so that's what I do."

---

* Tom Mboya, *The Challenge of Nationhood* (Nairobi: East African Publishers, 1993), 9.

We made small talk as Jane heated milk and prepared a tray with bread, jam, and margarine. Her English was spotty, so I transitioned to Swahili. She pointed out corrections as I stumbled through sentences. When I moved to the sink and started cleaning dishes, she protested. "Oh, no, Omosh, this work I need. If you want to take my work then you can lift that bag there."

A cloud of soot exploded into my face when I dumped a bag of coal into the storage trough. Jane pursed her lips and waited to gauge my reaction. As soon as I smiled, she burst out laughing. "Oh, Omosh!"

Roused by the commotion, Oluoch stepped out of his room, belched, and walked through the courtyard bare-chested in a towel and flip-flops. "Hot water," he barked at Jane.

"Mornin', Oluoch," I said.

"Oh, you're up. Our meeting with the Ministry of Education is delayed a day. We'll go together tomorrow. But the boy will come by this morning to show you around."

Oluoch continued to the bathroom as Jane heated a can of hot water for his shower. I assumed that Jane was not from the slum since Elizabeth had not mentioned her when we had spoken about my interest in meeting residents from Kibera. "Do you live near Fort Jesus?" I asked.

"Me, I'm from Kibera slums. That is my home, down there." Pride resonated from her voice.

"Wow, you're the first person I'm meeting from Kibera. What's it like?"

"Let me tell you, I love Kibera. You know, life is hard. I can say it's not easy. But Kibera is home, and me, I love."

Love was the last word I was expecting to hear in reference to life in Kibera. "Well, I'd like to hear more about that. You know, I'm here to study in Kibera."

"In Kibera?" Jane eyed me curiously. "But you're a *mzungu* [white guy]. *Wazungu* [white guys] don't go to Kibera."

"Why not? Is it dangerous?"

"I can say it's not so-so dangerous. We don't see many *wazungu*, though. You're welcome anyway, only at night it's not good."

"Thanks, Jane. You mean to your place? Can I come see your home during the day?" After only a short time together, I felt that I could trust her.

"Aye, Omosh, you ask such funny questions." She looked over her shoulder as if she were worried about someone overhearing. Elizabeth was in her bedroom and Oluoch was still making noises in the bathroom. Jane lowered her voice, "A *mzungu* has never been to my place. Maybe it can be possible."

I was curious about Jane's apprehension to the suggestion of my visit, but before I could ask her another question, Dan showed up. Baby-faced and slender with small, square-framed glasses and a buttoned-up appearance, Dan looked nothing like Oluoch. Oluoch had referred to Dan as "the boy from Kibera." Although *boy* was frequently used by old African men to refer to younger men, Dan could actually have passed for a boy. He certainly looked much younger than his twenty-two years.

"*Habari. Mimi ni Omosh.*"

Dan slapped his knee. "Omosh, you? No!"

He joined me for toast and chai and removed four pages of meticulously handwritten notes from his plastic briefcase. Dan had composed the notes after Oluoch gave him a copy of my research proposal. The top of the page read:

DANIEL OGOLA (DAN)
ETHNIC CONFLICT AND YOUTH IN KIBERA
I. YOUTH MOST PRESSING PROBLEMS
A// INADEQUATE FOOD

- Partake of starvation diet, usually *sukuma wiki* and *ugali*
- Inconsistent meals
- Effect: quarrels which provoke youths to violence or going on the street to panhandle

B// SHELTER

"And you live in Kibera?" I asked. The depth and organization of Dan's analysis easily matched my own skills.

"Of course. Kibera is my home. I can show you."

WE FINISHED OUR breakfast and left Fort Jesus. It was still early in the morning. People poured out of the slum to go to work or search for jobs.

There was a vibrant energy on the streets. Hawkers peddled goods from rows of roadside stands. Music blared. *Matatu* minibuses honked their horns to part the waves of people. Pedestrians stopped and stared at me as I wove through the foot traffic with Dan. Never before had I been so conscious of how different I looked. It wasn't simply the stark contrast of my skin color. I was larger than most of the men, and I was poorly dressed. My father would have said my six-pocket pants, dirty boots, and dark short-sleeve shirt looked "ratty" in comparison to the dress of so many of the men wearing suits. It was an uncomfortable, awkward feeling. While I would never blend in, the worst part was the sense that I was being judged by strangers in ways that I didn't understand.

Dan didn't seem to notice the attention we were attracting. He continued to walk swiftly, weaving through the waves of oncoming pedestrians while commenting on various topics as if he were a safari guide. On our left he pointed out a shack where I could "top up" on cell phone credit. To our right was the shoe shiner Dan used when Kibera became muddy. Up ahead was his church, a simple, unmarked tin shack that was a branch of Jehovah's Witnesses.

"*Jambo*," I greeted men staring at me as I passed. None of them responded.

"What's that all about?" I asked Dan.

"I don't know, but they probably don't like *jambo*."

"Why?"

"You know, *jambo* is like what you say to little kids, or to foreigners. Actually, you never hear it here. Even the little ones in the slum speak Sheng."

"Speak what?"

"Sheng, the language of the youth."

"Do you speak it?"

"Yes, a little." You had to know some Sheng to survive as a young man in Kibera.

"*Vipi*, Ogola?" a man greeted Dan.

"See, that's Sheng for 'What's up?'" Dan explained. "There are a lot of greetings like that among the youth. And that's my last name, Ogola. I'm a Luo, like you."

"So what should I say in return?"

"*Poa*. It means 'cool.' And sometimes they like to bump fists, like this."

Dan extended his fist. We tapped knuckles. "*Gota* [goat-tah]." He laughed. "They call that *gota*."

We stepped onto a mud path, passed a dozen more stands, rounded a bend, and there it was. Kibera looked like a large brown salamander speckled with dots of silver and green. It dipped and rose, a sea of dirt and rust spotted by new roofs shimmering in the sun. Blue gum trees stood like flags above the frozen waves. The green-gold savanna of Nairobi National Park stretched far off in the distance. It was staggering to behold. The sheer density and size of Kibera was difficult to imagine even as I stood looking at it. Its population estimates ranged absurdly from two hundred thousand to more than one million. No one knew how many people lived in Kibera.

Railroad tracks separated us from the shanties. More than simply marking much of its northern boundary, the railroad connected Kibera to the heart of Kenya's colonial history. The Kenya-Uganda Railway, once the largest overseas engineering project in the British Empire, stretched hundreds of miles to connect Uganda to the port of Mombasa. Allegedly the British chose Nairobi as the capital because it was one of the only spots near the midway point of the railway line with a mild climate and access to water. I would have never guessed from their appearance that the tracks had played an important role in shaping the region's history, nor could I imagine that just prior to the railway construction this region had been sparsely inhabited. Strewn with trash and lined by foot-deep sumps of frothy sewage, the tracks doubled as a walkway for tens of thousands of residents who commuted by foot each day out of Kibera. Rickety stands offering all manner of commodities had been cobbled together within five feet of the steel rails. It was a wonder that even slow-moving trains could pass through Kibera without destroying things and killing people.

A mob of about fifty men had gathered around a dirt mound next to the tracks. "NDP! NDP!" the mob cheered, fists in the air.

"Politics," Dan whispered. We were approaching the local pulpit for politicians and preachers, where a rally was being held for the largest opposition party to the government of President Moi. By mid-2000, after twenty-two years of rule, Moi's iron grip on power appeared to have permanently cracked. Nowhere was the African "big man" more detested than among the Luos in Kibera.

We crossed the tracks.

"*Mzungu*, you are welcome!" the speaker on the mound bellowed into his megaphone.

I swung around and was startled to see the mob looking at me. A few of the men flashed me a thumbs-up. I reciprocated, throwing my thumb up into the air. The mob exploded with applause and fist pumps. "NDP! NDP!" they shouted.

"What was that?" I asked Dan.

"Oh, good work." He laughed. "You gave them the thumbs-up. That's the NDP sign. Now they know you're a Luo." I was too stunned to realize that on my first walk into Kibera I had taken sides in the political posturing that threatened to rip the place apart.

The smell of garbage and excrement made me gag. It was everywhere, as was the commotion. Every tin shack along the main alleyway sold something: haircuts, water, used clothes, machetes, traditional medicine, manual labor, cassette tapes, charcoal, sex, rotting fish heads, and vegetables. Vendors shouted like auctioneers. Rap music and Congolese Lingala clanked out of squeaky speakers. Women wrapped in colorful *kanga*s sat quietly hawking vegetables. Babies cried.

A small girl beneath a jagged overhang of a tin roof pushed a toy wheel, a plastic cap connected to a piece of coat hanger. She drove her wheel around some bumps in the mud and into a sump, a moat of brown-black waste slugging toward Kibera's southern boundary, the Nairobi River.

Dan tapped the girl's head and guided the wheel out of the sewage. "Push it here, not there."

"*Mzungu, mzungu!*" The girl looked up and pointed at me with delight. "White person!"

I spotted a shack selling coffins. Among the simple plywood structures, there were miniature wood boxes. It took a moment for me to realize that they were baby coffins. My chest tightened. I had never thought about what it must be like to be a parent, or to lose a child. But at that moment, it was all I could think about.

Dan marched on, seemingly unaware of the effect that the slum was having on me.

A man named Baba Chris welcomed us to Dan's compound, a two-building "plot" with about sixty people in seventeen ten-by-tens. Baba Chris offered us chai in his shack. It was not good form to refuse such a gesture of hospitality, but I was too tired. I needed to lie down. "Thank you, but next time please." I shook his hand and begged his pardon.

Dan's room was neat and furnished with a wood bed, sofa, small table, paraffin stove, and a cardboard box with some cookware. A handful of clothes hung from a piece of twine on the wall. The sun hammered the tin rooftop, creating a sauna inside. I stretched out on the bed as Dan left to purchase sodas. Shutting my eyes and relaxing my body, I took in the sounds. A boy shouted. A dog barked. A man coughed. A wood door slapped shut. Water splashed and a broom whisked across cement. Far off in the distance, pickaxes pinged like chimes. Music rattled off stereos, stretching for high notes out of reach. Then there was the breeze, that cool breeze that moved over the rippled rooftops with a soft whistle. My head was pounding. I wanted to capture the breeze and pour it into my face. I was exhausted, disgusted, and overwhelmed, and it was exhilarating. *This* was exactly what I wanted—to be pushed to my limits, to go somewhere and do something risky, important, and complicated. At last, I was where I needed to be.

Dan returned with sodas and began to tell me about his life. As he spoke, it dawned on me that while he might not look tough, Dan was stronger than I could imagine. Raised by a single mother who brewed moonshine out of her home in the rural Nyanza Province near Lake Victoria, Dan first arrived in Kibera as an eighteen-year-old high school graduate in search of opportunity. He rented a shack with his brother and held odd jobs in Nairobi's Industrial Area, to which he commuted by foot for two hours each day. Dan's eyes were severely burned in an accident at a chemical manufacturer, and the company refused to cover his medical expenses. With persistence, skill, and luck, he recovered and eventually met a businessman who helped him pay for an accounting course. After acing the course, Dan found work as an office assistant in Nairobi's city center. It was his first full-time job in the formal sector, though he had much larger ambitions. Dan wanted to be a surgeon. He viewed Kibera as a rung in his ladder of socioeconomic advancement.

"A surgeon? Have you ever met a surgeon from Kibera?" I asked.

"Not really, but that doesn't mean it can't happen." His attitude was amazing. Later in our conversation he surprised me again by offering his house as a place to stay. I thanked Dan for his generous offer and told him that I'd appreciate crashing at his place as soon as I secured a research permit with Oluoch.

"What, do you think they'll arrest you?" Dan laughed.

"I don't know, perhaps."

"No, the police, never. They never come down here. Closest they'll come is the railways. They're afraid, you know."

"Afraid of what?"

"Afraid they'll get lost, and maybe even beat. You know, the community, we deal with it ourselves. Mob justice. A thief steals from you here, the community will respond. And if they catch that thief, it'll be the end of him. Beat him and burn him."

I cringed.

"Here we have a saying," Dan continued. "You would rather cross a thief than a policeman on the tracks. Why? Because the thief will just take your stuff. The police, they'll take your stuff *and* throw you into jail."

"Dan, should I be concerned about thieves? I mean, would I be endangering you if I stayed at your place?"

"No, no Omosh. Me, I'm okay, and this is a good compound where we look after each other. We have a lot of good people here. But maybe don't tell a lot of people where you're staying. And keep doing that *gota* thing. The thugs, they like that."

I laughed, thinking about how the universal fist bump might become my best defense. My ROTC commander Major Boothby would have enjoyed my exchange with Dan and referred to the information he provided as an example of "local intelligence."

"Big *gota*, Dan," I extended my fist.

OLUOCH AND I struck a deal that night back at Fort Jesus. I could keep my gear at his house and have access to a bed and a meal whenever I needed it without giving advance notice. In return, I would pay him a thousand shillings a day, about $13, and I would hire his nephew as a research assistant for another thousand shillings per day. Despite having graduated with honors in political science from Kenya's top university, the University of Nairobi, Oluoch's nephew was still searching for work.

The following day, Oluoch took me downtown to meet his contact at the Ministry of Education. Oluoch wasn't much of a conversationalist. He stared out the window until I asked him about the official we were going to meet to fast-track my research permit.

"He's a Kamba. They like sex."

"Who?" I asked, taken aback.

"The Kamba, they like sex. They are loose, not serious people."

"So is the official like this?"

"Of course, he's Kamba, like I said. The Kikuyu on the other hand, all they care about is money. They are businessmen or thieves, or both. Never trust a Kikuyu."

Oluoch continued, unfazed by the strangers surrounding us: Luhya were submissive and best suited for simple jobs such as watchmen and cooks. Nubians were lazy because most Nubians survived simply by renting out a few plots in Kibera. Kalenjin, the ethnic group of President Moi, were fast runners but slow-minded.

"And the Luo?" I preempted him. "What are my relatives known for?"

Pleased by my question, Oluoch responded, "We are stubborn and smart. We are smart because we eat so much fish."

That was it, the ethnic taxonomy, cut-and-dried. It was absurd. Had a teenager mentioned the same stereotypes to me, I might have lectured the kid about bigotry. Yet Oluoch aired them as if they were science.

By the time we reached Jogoo House "B" in the city center, it was mid-afternoon. It was a tired, grim high-rise. None of the lights worked and half the elevators were busted. Men wore dark suits. Women avoided eye contact, and no one smiled. I was wearing my classiest outfit for the occasion: a seersucker blazer, khaki pants, and my Timberland boots.

A faded bronze nameplate on the office door read PERMANENT SECRETARY. I assumed the permanent secretary was a mid-level bureaucrat, a paper pusher. After a half-hour, his assistant escorted us into his office. A handsome maroon carpet covered the floor. Photographs of men with serious looks lined the walls.

The permanent secretary rose from behind his large desk and greeted us in English.

"*Vipi mzee?*" I said, figuring I would lighten it up a bit. "What's up, old man?"

He furrowed his eyebrows.

"Big *gota*." I offered my clenched fist over his desk.

Oluoch shrugged his shoulders. I kept my fist extended and then shook it slightly to signal that he was leaving me hanging.

"Yes, yes, very good." The permanent secretary, who I would later learn was the second highest-ranking official in the Ministry of Education, laughed and touched my fist with his flat hand, as if he were tapping the head of a small child. He lifted a folder with the three-page application Oluoch and I had prepared. "So, Kibera. Tell me, young man, what is it you want to do down there?"

In broken Swahili I told the permanent secretary that I wanted to live in Kibera and talk to young people about their lives. Before I could mention the part about studying ethnic violence, he interrupted, "So, you're into reggae? Discos?"

"Um, sure."

"And you like African women?"

I didn't see that coming. "No, no, bwana, it's research," I backpedaled. "You have amazing women here. I mean, I love them. I love them all. But I have a girlfriend." It was a bit of a fib. I hadn't had a steady girlfriend for months. The last one I had had dumped me for working too much.

"Hmph." The permanent secretary didn't believe me. Understandably, he saw me as a young, clueless college student in Kenya to have a good time, and that was fine by him as long as I paid my $400 research-permit fee.

"There you go *gota* man." He laughed and passed me the permit. "You're welcome to Kenya."

Oluoch wasn't too pleased by my actions, and he had a right to be upset. My big *gota* to the permanent secretary was a stupid, juvenile move. Oluoch looked as if he was about to explode as we boarded a bus back to Fort Jesus. His attitude prompted me to fiddle with my cell phone. Texting was not yet popular in the States. I decided to try out my first text with a note to Dan. My message started off with a simple "What's up?" until it dawned on me that I had no interest in spending the night at Oluoch's. I changed the note and shot Dan a request: "Can I crash at your place tonight?"

"No prob. *Unajua* the way?"

I wasn't sure if I remembered the route to Dan's place, but I didn't want to inconvenience him. It seemed like a good challenge of my Marine navigating skills.

"*Hakuna matata*," I thumbed out the line made famous by *The Lion King*. "No problem."

———

It was dusk and thousands of residents were returning to Kibera for the night, the daily tide rushing back to sea. Within minutes of having crossed the tracks, I was thoroughly lost, and the mud alley ahead of me looked like a firing line. Gangs of young men hung out on each side of it surveying the foot traffic, looking bored and mean. There were too many men to give fist bumps, and it was getting dark. Jane had warned me to be careful at night, when the thugs came out to prey on the drunks and *washamba*. *Mshamba* translated to "farmer," but it meant anyone new to Kibera, a rookie without a clue. I was a big white *mshamba*, though I tried my best to look cool and confident. I couldn't afford to show them how lost and afraid I really was.

Deep reggae rumbled from within the only painted shack on the alleyway, a forest green ten-by-ten with an orange sheet draped over its entrance. MAD LION BASE the main wall of the shack read above a painting of a lion's head that looked like something out of a comic book. The beast's salivating mouth was frozen between a smile and a snarl. Its fiery red eyes appeared to be watching me.

Men smoked joints on a wooden bench. The bass thumped, rippling the orange sheet and rattling the thin tin walls. One of the men took a drag and pointed at me like a target. Heads turned.

I walked on, sweating, wondering why I had been so foolish to have walked into Kibera alone on my second night in the slum. My father would have been furious with my judgment, as would Major Boothby.

"Mister Omosh," a voice said.

I spun around but didn't see anyone.

"Mister Omosh." A young boy half my height was standing at my legs.

I crouched down and gave him a *gota*. "Hey, buddy, how do ya know my name?"

The boy was a relative of Baba Chris, the man who had offered me chai at the front gate to Dan's compound. As relieved as I felt about now having a guide to reach Dan's shack, I didn't know what to make of the fact that the news of my presence was spreading so rapidly. *Would the community awareness protect me, or would it make me more vulnerable?*

By the time I arrived at Dan's shack, he had finished cooking the maize meal *ugali* and *sukuma wiki*, collard greens. Baba Chris joined us for dinner.

He was sick and wanted to make some small talk to take his mind from the pain. We spoke about English Premier League soccer, then we turned to politics, which Baba Chris seemed to follow as if it were a sport. Baba Chris was particularly enthused about the prospects of his tribe's most famous politician, Raila Odinga. Odinga, the Luo son of Kenya's first vice president, was the member of Parliament for the district of Nairobi that included Kibera. He was also the leader of the NDP, the opposition party that had been rallying at the dirt pulpit near the tracks.

Eventually Baba Chris brought the conversation to his illness. Sweating and shivering, he had lost his appetite and was in too much pain to ignore it. A friend of his who was a nurse thought he had malaria. The cost of the medication was about $7, which was more than he could afford. A week earlier he had spent his meager savings on school fees for his children. Without other options, Baba Chris intended to wait it out. If his wife made enough money selling some "small things" in the local markets, they might be able to pay for the medication in a few days. I didn't ask what was on my mind: *Was Baba Chris going to die?*

Later that night, as Dan slept soundly, I tried to process the blizzard that had been my first two and a half days in and around Kibera. I knew so little about the place, and it was so vast. Yet I was meeting good people: Jane with her unforgettable smile and infectious laugh, Dan, and Baba Chris. The only reason Baba Chris brought up the cost of the malaria medication was because I had asked him. He never asked me for assistance, and I wasn't sure how I would have responded if he had asked for help. I told myself that as a rule I wouldn't give out money in Kibera. It was a safety mechanism that my father had suggested. The color of my skin made people suspect that I had a lot of money, and I couldn't afford to confirm those suspicions if I intended to spend my nights there. Yet I wanted to help Baba Chris. I admired his strength, and I felt that I knew him even though we had just met. I could give him some of my mefloquine pills. However, to the best of my knowledge the pills were designed to prevent malaria, not treat it. *Perhaps I could give Baba Chris some money through Dan?*

People shouted in the distance. The noises never stopped in Kibera. Images of small coffins swirled in my head. I had come to study youth and ethnic violence. Now I was thinking about what it must be like to be Baba Chris, to have a family and be stuck in this place. My mind was so far away from research. Ethnic violence seemed like a remote problem relative to day-to-day survival.

I could remember only one other time in my life when my world had been suddenly turned upside down by a place. It was that time at the roundabout before our safari, when my mom and I saw the small street girl with an infant on her back and the bottle of glue in her mouth. I was fourteen years old, and I wanted to help that girl and the infant. Afterward, my mother had told me that my instincts were right. "It's natural to feel bad," she had said. "There's a lot of pain in the world, and it's good to help when you can."

Kibera was unbelievable. It was as if I was imagining it even though I was there in a tin shack with my back against a lumpy mattress. It wasn't simply the side effects of the mefloquine that left me questioning reality. It was everything about the place—its magnitude; its deprivation; its raw pain. Kibera was wrong. In our world of plenty, people shouldn't live like this. How was it possible that a father might die of a disease that could be treated for seven dollars? I paid more for my haircuts.

CHAPTER THREE

The Present and the Future Leaders

Kibera, Kenya

JUNE 2000

FOR TWO WEEKS I had been staying in Gatwekera, one of Kibera's eleven villages. I switched every other night between Dan's place and other locations. Guys with shacks never seemed to object to adding another friend or relative. It was one of the unwritten rules of Kibera: To survive you pulled together. If you had the means, you shared, because you never knew when your time of need might come. It was easy to lose every physical possession when you had little and the threats were many: fire, theft, sickness, injury, unemployment, or just a string of bad luck. For many residents, the community was their only insurance.

We packed together like sardines, positioning ourselves head to foot so people of the same size didn't lie next to each other. Otherwise, you slept next to a friend's gnarly foot and got kicked in the face all night. In the mornings, I handed my host fifty shillings, about seventy-five cents. It was slightly more than the cost of my water, chai, dinner, and access to a *choo*—a pit latrine. I never returned for an overnight if my host asked for more, and I often commented about being a broke college student. I didn't want people to think I carried much money. I had learned about the danger of cash in a place such as Kibera from one of Dan's neighbors, a middle-aged man who was attacked one night by thugs with machetes.

The man believed that the thugs had followed him from the market after he accidentally flashed two thousand-shilling notes while purchasing some food. They had crashed through his door, sliced him across the chest, and demanded precisely two thousand shillings. He had almost lost his life for $26.

There was another reason to be cautious about money. Money threatened to further complicate the relationships that I was navigating with my sources, many of whom were becoming friends. Most of these young men had unrealistic expectations about how I might be able to help. One young man asked me for a month's rent; another asked for an American wife. I tried to be straightforward and direct about my own limitations, though it was difficult because once they opened their lives to me, I felt an obligation to do something more substantial. I wanted to help them, but I didn't know where to begin. The need was so colossal in proportion to my resources, and I didn't want to create dependency.

The young men I interviewed represented each of Kibera's five largest ethnic groups, with one exception. In my initial two weeks in Kibera, I didn't meet one Nubian. My sources told me that the Nubians, who were also known as Nubis, were combative and kept to themselves. They had a reputation for being insular and guarded after enduring years of encroachment by other ethnic groups migrating into Kibera.

Fewer than thirty thousand Nubians lived in Kibera. They resided in only four of Kibera's eleven villages, and Gatwekera, where I spent most of my time, was not one of them. Yet the Nubians defined Kibera. Their presence made it the only slum in Nairobi where residents had legitimate claims to land dating as far back as the colonial era. The Nubians of Kibera descended from Sudanese and Ugandan soldiers who fought with the British Empire's King's African Rifles. Their British military commanders regarded them as "a better class" of warriors with "a capacity above that of the ordinary African."* In return for their service at the turn of the twentieth century, the British granted them severance pay and rights to settle on the fringe of Nairobi with their families. The Nubian settlers

---

* The Kibera survey report by Deverell and Colchester, Kenya National Archives RCA (MAA)—2/1/3 ii, 1944, p. 2, as quoted in Johan de Smedt, "Kill Me Quick: A History of Nubian Gin in Kibera," *International Journal of African Historical Studies* 42, no. 2 (2009).

called their new home *kibra*, a Nubian word for "bush," because it was so heavily vegetated. That was the beginning of what less than one hundred years later would become one of the largest slums in the world. As far as the Nubians were concerned, the four villages in Kibera belonged to them.

From rural farms to slums to city life in an "estate" such as Fort Jesus—or maybe even a house in a posh neighborhood such as Woodley, where the president lived—that was the dream of Dan Ogola and so many young people who had migrated to Kibera. By contrast, I had heard that many Nubian young men sought a life in Kibera, even if they eventually had the means to move out. For many of them, Kibera was not a transitory stop on a dream of upward socioeconomic mobility. They were proud of Kibera in a way that was distinct from the attitude of other ethnic groups. I needed to meet them and hear their story.

I RETURNED TO Oluoch and Elizabeth's compound in Fort Jesus once a week to shower, consolidate my field notes, and get five hours of uninterrupted sleep. During these evenings, I enjoyed talking with Elizabeth. Each conversation took us deeper into her own vision to create a Montessori-method nursery school inside the slum. She had given it a lot of thought, and she appreciated hearing some of my observations. As much as Elizabeth wanted to help, she didn't know the slum well. Fort Jesus was less than three hundred yards from Kibera, yet it was a world away.

When I told Oluoch about my need to talk to Nubian youth, he commented between swigs of Tusker beer, "I don't know many of those people. Muslims, they are lazy and don't do much. But I do know this one. Taib he's called. He owes me a favor."

Oluoch explained that Taib was a former councillor, a member of the ruling KANU political party who had lost his last reelection bid as one of Kibera's three representatives on the city council. Taib wanted to run again, and Oluoch thought he would be interested in meeting with a *mzungu*. He drained his Tusker and called Taib. Within two minutes, I had a meeting scheduled.

The following day, Taib met me with a firm handshake at the door to his office on Kibera's north end. His curly gray hair receded from his high forehead. He wore short, faded jeans that revealed a couple inches of skin above his ankles and bare feet. I placed my mud-caked Timberlands by the door and joined him on a thatched mat.

"So you're here on research, is it?" Taib asked.

"Sort of. I'm talking with youth and staying in a shack near the river."

"Really, a *mzungu*, down there?"

"Yes, Gatwekera."

"Gatwekera?"

"That's right."

"It's dirty there." His line caught me off guard. The Nubian villages in Kibera allegedly had higher standards of living than the parts of Kibera closer to the river. However, we were still in the slum. The houses were made of mud. The sewage ran in open sumps.

A striking, elegant woman dressed in black and gold entered the room. She offered us the most common snack in Kibera—white bread and butter—and Nubian-style strong tea without milk.

"So the Nubians were warriors?" I asked Taib as the woman poured a steaming shot of tea, stopping precisely at the rim of the glass.

"Ah, yes, so you know some of our history. I bet they don't teach that in North Carolina." Taib chuckled. "Let me tell you about the Nubians, young man."

For the next hour Taib took me on an accelerated history of the Nubians in Kibera. It was the narrative of a disenfranchised people. After military service with the British King's African Rifles, the Nubians carved out an exclusive and highly lucrative business selling "Nubian gin," an illicit moonshine. Perceived by many Kenyans as old colonial loyalists, the Nubians were largely excluded from the euphoria of Kenyan independence in 1963. Once a charismatic Nubian lost his seat as the area member of Parliament in 1974, the Kibera land grab began in full force. Marginalized from political power, the Nubians had little recourse as migrant families flooded into Nairobi's slums hoping to escape the grueling, monotonous struggle that characterized rural existence for many Kenyans. Mwangi Maathai, the ex-husband of Nobel laureate Wangari Maathai, was elected as the area parliamentarian. According to Taib, Maathai worked in concert with corrupt lower-level politicians and political appointees, the district officers, councillors, and chiefs who granted construction permits in return for bribes that sometimes included claims to future cash flows from rent collection. Kenya's political and economic elite were one and the same, and they were profiting from the growth and perpetuation of the slum.

Taib claimed that Kibera received no government services, and that city council maps identified the land as simply belonging to the "Office of the President." He argued that he had little power to bring resources to the slum when he had served as councillor, though he continued to battle for land-tenure rights, which the Nubians never possessed. Over the years, Nubian claims to Kibera decreased in acreage as the land sky-rocketed in value. Initial claims to more than 4,000 acres had diminished to as little as 450 acres, an area larger than half the size of the modern Kibera slums and potentially worth tens of millions of dollars to developers and politicians anxious to gentrify the area.

Despite all of this, the Nubians aligned with the reigning political party, KANU. For much of Kenya's postcolonial history, they had no other viable option. The Nubians were too small a constituency to put up a fight from the outside. Taib owned the building we sat in, and he had decided to make it a KANU field office when he ran for councillor in 1993. He hoped its branding would generate more resources for his campaign. "But it led to nothing," he snapped.

When I shifted the conversation to youth development, Taib claimed, "No one has done more for youths in Kibera than I have. I've really tried to rehabilitate them. The problem with youth idleness is a big one."

One of my core areas of research was to determine what organizations existed in Kibera for youth, and whether any of those organizations helped prevent ethnic violence. Most of my sources believed that only a handful of organizations in Kibera involved youth, and none of these organizations appeared to be well regarded. One organization from another slum in Nairobi, however, frequently came up in conversations as an example of a great youth program: the Mathare Youth Sports Association, or MYSA. I heard about MYSA so much that I was curious about its model of using sports to promote youth leadership. "Do you have any success stories in Kibera, like MYSA?" I asked Taib.

"MYSA," Taib exhaled. "Everyone knows MYSA. But the fact is here we have KIYESA [Kibera Youth and Environment Sports Association], and we were around before even MYSA. We just never had a *mzungu* to fund-raise for us."

I assumed the bitterness in Taib's voice came from a place of envy, or some other backstory of personality clashes and politics that I might never understand. Regardless, it was surprising to hear about KIYESA. The organization that Taib had cofounded in the early 1980s hadn't come up once in my interviews with youth. Taib explained that KIYESA held soccer tournaments each year and then launched into a tirade about NGOs, the typically international nongovernmental organizations. He accused NGOs of existing simply to perpetuate the relatively luxurious lifestyles of their staff.

"They keep their offices outside of Kibera and drive nice cars. The money goes here," he slapped his stomach. "Not here," he stomped his foot on the ground.

Taib's comment struck a chord. I was dismayed at the level of waste and ineffectiveness I had witnessed when I visited one large NGO in Kibera that was managed by outsiders. I was beginning to discover that most large NGOs had a similar approach. They were top-down and entered the slum with preconceived ideas of what was wrong and how to fix it. They didn't seem to ask or involve the local population. The people these NGOs purported to serve needed to be included in more of the decision making. Although the term was so frequently used that it could sound clichéd, the residents needed to be "empowered."

"Even right here you have an example of a community-based group. These are the ones the *wazungu* should support, not the big NGOs. You've seen Gange?" Taib pointed toward the door.

"The trash pit?"

"No, no, the car wash, in front of the trash."

"There's a car wash there?"

"Come."

We stepped out of his office door. A few tough-looking men washed cars with sponges in front of a rotting heap of garbage with street children and slum dogs scavenging through it. A small metal sign read:

GANGE YOUTH SELF-HELP GROUP

PROJECT NO. 1

REHABILITATION CENTRE

"I got these youths their space," Taib said, and led me to a few men sitting on a bench. *Youth* in Kenya could refer to anyone under the age of forty.

"*Salaam alaikum.*" The oldest member of the group stood up and greeted us. He was wearing a tank top.

"Ali, I want you to meet Omosh." Taib introduced me.

Ali laughed. It was a deep, hearty laugh like my father's. He looked like a soldier. He kept his hair cropped short. His upper body was so lean and muscular that it appeared to be chiseled.

"You're strong. Do you lift weights?" I shook Ali's hand with a firm grip.

"Mmmm," he groaned.

"I like weights. Maybe we can get a lift in later?"

"Mmmm."

THIRTY YEARS OLD, Ali Khamis Alijab was the chairman of the Gange Youth Self-help Group. I befriended him, and days later he led me to a friend's gym to lift weights. The gym was a humble creation of welded bars and slabs of cement. Between sets I asked Ali about Gange. He told me that he had spent too many years causing trouble. He cofounded the self-help group to provide employment opportunities and improve his community after the birth of his daughter Khadija six years earlier. Ali and his two dozen friends pulled together funds for projects from dues of typically less than $4 per year. In this way, they self-funded the start-up costs of their car wash. Although Gange's second project, a community garden, didn't generate income, it had a special importance to Ali, who loved flowers and trees because they "reduced stress."

After our workout, I joined Ali for strong tea in his ten-by-ten. A bumper sticker stuck to his door read ALLAH GIVES AND FOR-GIVES. MAN GETS AND FORGETS. His place was the most humble one I had come across in Kibera, where gradations of poverty could be measured by the presence of certain luxuries, such as a cement floor, electricity, a clean communal latrine, and space. Ali lived with none of these things. His caked, cracked mud shack contained a box-spring mattress, two chairs, and a chest of drawers. A drawer with a lock held Ali's most cherished possessions: the Koran, a 1993 *Muscle & Fitness* magazine, and photographs of friends and family. He kept a friend's detached keyboard on top of his chest of drawers. Fascinated by the Internet, Ali viewed typing as the key to a mysterious new world of possibility. He practiced every evening by candlelight.

Three hundred yards from Ali's front door, Kibera's largest tree, a blue gum, towered above the shanties, with wide branches, evergreen leaves, and gnarled roots that wove heavy knots into the earth. The Kenya-Uganda Railway ran beneath the blue gum, demarcating Makina Village from the rest of the slum. This was Darajani Massive, the area named after the large bridge. Days earlier, Jane Atieno's best friend Tabitha had warned me that "hardcores" around here called me Van Damme and were "plotting" to ambush me. I didn't mention the threat to Ali.

As we strolled toward Darajani Massive, idle young men with serious faces nodded to Ali deferentially. "*Salaam alaikum*," he greeted them as we passed. I nodded. If those men had been targeting me, they would have to think twice after seeing me with Ali.

Ali stopped at the base of the majestic blue gum tree and tilted his head toward its rustling leaves. "See, Omosh, no stress." Even in such crushing, dense living conditions, one could find tranquility. As I stood silently with Ali beneath the tree, my mind drifted to a spiritual place.

ONE NIGHT I stayed at Ali's shack. I intended to stay for three evenings, but a burning itch engulfed my body. It was nearly as unbearable as the prickly heat I developed later in the Marines when I wore the same sweaty shirt squeezed under body armor for days at a time and felt as if an army of red ants were burrowing into my back. My eyelids swelled, my skin burned, and I began to sneeze uncontrollably.

"Ali," I finally asked, sitting up on his box-spring mattress, "what's happening to me?"

"Ah, yes," he said calmly, "*kiroboto*."

Kiroboto, the barely visible African bedbugs, bred in mud and filth. One of the few ways to cleanse a home of them was to burn all of the bedding. Ali never asked me for anything, though he once remarked that if he could save enough money, he would buy new bedding and rid his home of the maddening *kiroboto*.

I tried to stick to Ali's diet. Eating the same meals gave me a better sense of life in Kibera. Plus, I wanted to challenge myself to see if I could actually do it. I was self-conscious about having grown up comfortably and wanted to prove that I could defy the stereotype of the soft, pampered middle-class kid.

Ali drank a cup of strong tea in the morning and then went all day until his first and last meal, which generally consisted of *sukuma wiki* and *ugali*. It was as if Ali fasted all year. For the first time in my life, I experienced insatiable hunger. My stomach ached for food. The hunger was all-consuming, and I ashamedly gave up on Ali's diet after two days.

On another night, Ali's best friend and Gange cofounder, Kassim, joined us for dinner. Few people in Kibera were as tall as Kassim, and his black leather train conductor's cap added an inch to his appearance. Kassim walked with long, slow strides and exaggerated arm swings. His charisma was infectious, and he appeared to be both feared and admired by other young Nubian men. After dinner, I asked him about the ethnic clashes from 1995. Dozens of Nubians had fought in those clashes, and I had heard rumors that Kassim helped lead them into battle.

Kassim gave me my first full overview of the clashes. They began with the decapitation and castration of a Nubian teenager whose body was dumped early one morning near the blue gum tree at Darajani Massive. At the time, the Nubians, long allied with the ruling political party, posed one of many threats to the presidential ambitions of Raila Odinga, Kibera's incumbent member of Parliament. By Kenyan constitutional law, a candidate had to be an elected member of Parliament to run for president. According to Kassim, Odinga and his ethnic constituency, the Luos, felt threatened by the Nubians, many of whom served as landlords in Kibera's predominately Luo villages. Kassim explained, "In the ghetto, people act according to perceived strength and weakness. Nubians, we're weak in numbers. What would happen if the whole of Kibera turned on us? Probably that would be the end. That boy's death was like an act of war. Nubians, we own a lot of the houses that Luos live in. Since most of us don't have jobs, that rent collected is our life, and you see how we live. It's pathetic, but it's enough. What would happen if we did nothing? Some Luos might stop paying rent. They could try to challenge us on our rights to this land. I hate bloodshed. It's stupid. But we had to seek justice. We had to defend our community."

Although it wasn't clear who threw the first stone, two days of bloody clashes ensued. Shanties burned. Dozens of young men were injured or killed. Eventually the Government Service Unit, President Moi's feared Special Forces, rolled into Kibera in fatigues and full riot gear. Like the president himself, the Government Service Unit was above the law.

They quelled the rioting like a barbarian horde on a medieval battle-field.

The *kiroboto* bedbugs swarmed about Ali's ten-by-ten. I clawed at my hair in a futile attempt to rip them from my scalp. Seeing my discomfort, Ali led us outside to the frame of an abandoned sofa on a mound of dirt next to a *choo*, a pit latrine. Craning his head to the sky, Kassim pointed out constellations that he had learned as a boy on scouting trips in the Ngong Forest adjacent to Kibera. It was one of the few forests in the world that existed within a city's limits, and in it Kassim claimed he had once spotted a leopard. I looked out across Kibera. A half-moon cast a dull white glow off a thousand rooftops. The stench from the *choo* was awful.

"So are there any organizations for youth that are bringing Nubians and Luos together?" I asked. "I mean, you said it yourself, Kassim, the violence is stupid. It shouldn't happen."

"Yes, that's right, Omosh, but organizations for youth in Kibera are not so many. We don't have something like MYSA."

There it was again, the Mathare Youth Sports Association. "MYSA, I've heard a lot of youth here talk about it. Does it also bring ethnic groups together?"

"You know, Mathare slums are mostly Kikuyu," Kassim said, referring to Kenya's largest of more than forty ethnic groups. "But MYSA is good because you know it creates role models, and in the slums, that's what we need."

Ali appeared disengaged from our conversation. He sat with his legs crossed and his chin in the cup of his hand.

"What are ya thinkin' about, Ali?" I asked.

"He's meditating," Kassim replied.

Slowly returning to the conversation, Ali responded in his baritone voice, "I'm just thinking, Omosh. Khadija, she always says, 'Daddy, I'm going to Standard One [first grade] next year.' I can't let her down, Omosh. That's what I'm meditating about, that and this *choo*."

We laughed, deep, long, and from the gut. Hard life can inure one to many things, but not the stale stench of an overfilled *choo*.

I NEEDED TO stay focused in Kibera, but MYSA had come up too many times. One day I caught a *matatu* minibus to Mathare to see the organization for myself. Although it was the only road into Mathare, where more than 150,000 people lived, I expected a less perilous ride. But Juja Road defined mayhem. Even Iraq's Route Ethan, one of the most dangerous, destroyed roads through downtown Fallujah, where I would be stationed years later, offered a smoother ride—provided a bomb didn't explode.

Juja Road had once been paved. Head-sized chunks of asphalt jutted out of the dirt like errant cobblestones. Yet vehicles blazed down the road as if they were ambulances en route to emergency rooms.

The gangsta rap inside my *matatu* masked a cacophony of horns outside as vehicles swerved to avoid head-on collisions and craters big enough to swallow small cars or slice tires from their axles. One crater was so immense locals joked that it could hide an elephant. Our driver threw on his wipers to clear a layer of grime from the windshield. All the while, a grandmother sat next to me, dozing.

I shouted, "MYSA," twice to the driver, whose cheek was full of *khat*, a highly addictive stimulant that causes loss of appetite, sex drive, and sleep. I wasn't sure he heard me until he slammed on the brakes and pointed at the door.

An assortment of half-constructed cinder-block multistory buildings lined the roads. Up ahead the MYSA building stood out with its trademark forest green and yellow gates. As soon as I passed through the gates I felt as if I had entered a different world. A couple of youth wearing MYSA soccer jerseys practiced tricks with a soccer ball made of twine and plastic bags. A dozen girls were doing calisthenics in the main hall next to a wall that read Giving youth a sporting chance. In another room a young man sang a Swahili verse while mopping the floor. As I walked around, a few young people greeted me but didn't stop what they were doing. It was a good sign. In Kibera, a lot of young people dropped what they were doing when a *mzungu* showed up.

I poked my head into an office. A slender man with a thin black goatee and a Muslim skullcap spoke with a boy in a soccer uniform. The man sat next to his desk with the boy's chair facing him. He glanced up for a second to see if he recognized me, then continued to give his full attention to the boy. The boy seemed to hang on his every word. When they both stood up, I realized the man was not much taller than the boy. Only then did the man look up at me and introduce himself as Salim Mohamed. He had light brown skin and close-cropped, black hair. I assumed he was Somali because of his Muslim name and angular features.

I handed the boy one of the Creme Savers hard candies from my pocket.

"That's interesting," Salim commented.

"What?"

"You carry those candies."

"Sorry, I usually keep them for kids." I reached into my cargo pant pocket and pulled one out for him.

"No, no thanks, mista. I'm not a kid." He laughed.

I took out a bottle of hand sanitizer and offered him a squirt.

"No thanks." He grimaced. "You know, us, we find that a bit offensive, like why do you need to clean your hands every time you touch a kid."

"Good point. I should have used it before I touched the kid. Obviously I'm the dirty one."

Salim laughed, and I began what had become my typical spiel. I was Omondi, but people called me Omosh. I stayed in Kibera, in Gatwekera Village, near the river. "Do you know Kibera?"

"What kind of question is that? You know, when you're in the ghetto, you know all the slums. I can go to any slum in Nairobi and feel at home." I instantly felt a connection to Salim because he pushed back. When I asked him if I could record our conversation with my tape recorder, he slapped his desk and laughed. "Mista, what are you gonna do with that?"

"It's for research. I'm an undergraduate at the University of North Carolina, the home of Michael Jordan. You know Jordan?"

"Of course I know Michael Jordan. I'm not a *mshamba*," he said, using the pejorative that translates to "farmer."

"A *mshamba* like me." I pointed to my muddy boots and cargo pants.

"Yes, yes, that's it. That's a very funny outfit you're wearing, by the way."

"It's good for me because it has a lot of pockets for my tapes and stuff."

Salim's face grew suddenly serious. "You know, I also know research. People in Mathare, we're tired of research." I admired the pride in his voice, and I was beginning to harbor misgivings about my role as a researcher. I would get a senior honors thesis out of it, but what would Kibera receive? I opened up and told Salim that I wanted to do more but didn't know where to begin. I didn't want to cause dependency. "Money can cause more problems," I said.

"Okay, Omosh. What you're saying is actually what I believe, so you can record. But only if you send me what you write. I'd like to read it."

We had a deal. I placed the silver machine on the table. As Salim took me through the background of MYSA and his role as a founding member, I tried to turn the conversation back to him. There was a natural flow because several of the most formative experiences of Salim's life paralleled the development of MYSA from a twenty-team soccer program to a world-renowned pioneer of youth development programs with a professional soccer team called Mathare United. However, when I asked questions that were too personal, such as how he spent part of his childhood with his grandmother on the streets, Salim stopped and asked me about my own upbringing.

For security reasons I made a habit of concealing my identity in Kibera. News of who I was and what I was doing traveled quickly in the slum, and I thought it would be safer if casual acquaintances didn't know too much. While I didn't usually go so far as to create cover stories, I was often deliberately vague with information or said preposterous things in Swahili that made people laugh and distracted them from their own questions. Yet something about Salim and his quiet confidence was reassuring. I felt I could trust him. Plus, I was in Mathare, not Kibera. So I opened up. I even told him my most guarded secret about training to be a Marine.

"I hate war," Salim cut me off.

"Me, too." He looked intrigued as I explained how I believed that the military fundamentally promoted peace. Salim didn't ask follow-up questions, though as our conversation progressed he made allusions to a sense of suffering from hunger and other physical duress to which he assumed I could relate because of my chosen profession.

We had been talking for more than three hours and gone through three double-sided miniature cassettes when Salim finally exclaimed, "Okay, enough, mista!"

"Just one more question, please?"

"What?"

"Can you tell me about Mama Fatuma? Is she alive?" She was the founder of the well-known children's home that had adopted Salim.

"She passed away in 1997. Man, I really loved her. She was tough. She walked with a cane, but if you did something to upset her, she would drop that cane and run to get you. She liked me because, you know, I'm social. If she didn't see me one day, she would ask where I was."

"How'd she find you?"

"When the police cracked down on hawkers, we were separated from my grandmother. I was processed through the courts, and my grandmother, she was forced to let me go. She really hated it, and she fought. But how can a hawker fight the courts? The courts processed me to Mama Fatuma Goodwill Children's Home, and my grandmother, she didn't know how it was."

"You became Muslim when you went there?"

"That's right, but you know it was my choice. Mama Fatuma, she didn't force that on me."

"She sounds amazing."

"She was. Let me tell you, she was amazing and tough. One day she interviewed me. I remember she asked me these funny questions. One question was 'What is it you want to do with your life?' I told her I wanted to find a home for all the kids in the streets."

"That's a big goal. How old were you then?"

"Around ten years."

"Wow," I had fallen through the ice at my pond and dreamed of doing something with lasting significance when I was around the same age.

"Yes, and I still want to do that thing."

"In Mathare?"

"In Nairobi."

"How about Kibera?"

"Kibera, too, but that's a conversation for another day." He laughed.

I had walked into Salim's office without an appointment and taken up his afternoon. "Salim, I'm sorry, man, but please, just one more question?"

He sighed.

"Why's there no MYSA in Kibera?"

"Good question." He shrugged.

"Maybe we can do something?"

"Maybe. Sure." He glanced at his watch. "If you come back, I can help."

"So you'd be interested?"

"Maybe, but now I'm tired, mista, so forgive me if I have some work to do."

SALIM AND ALI struck me as men of integrity whom I could trust, perhaps because of their deep faith, about which I didn't know much but respected. They were somehow able to stay on righteous paths. I wanted to befriend them, to help them, and to learn from their wisdom. If I were in their situations, I doubted I could remain focused on anything except myself. Yet, they were making significant contributions to their communities. Through them and others I was beginning to realize that residents in places such as Kibera and Mathare had sustainable solutions to the problems they faced. With a few opportunities, many of which I had grown up taking for granted, young people could rise above even the most desperate situations.

As I returned to Kibera that day, another of Salim's comments from our long interview kept surfacing in my mind. We had been talking about Kenyan politicians, and I had remarked with the platitude that youth are the future leaders. "No," Salim had objected, "Youth aren't the future leaders. They're the present and the future leaders."

CHAPTER FOUR

"Because I can"

Kibera, Kenya

June 2000

ALONE IN DAN'S TEN-BY-TEN, I CLENCHED my buttocks and prayed for the sensation to go away. If only I could hold on until morning. Then I would have daylight to help me navigate the muddy path, and I wouldn't have to wake Baba Chris, my neighbor at the front of the compound who kept the key to the *choo* and was recovering from his bout with malaria. I might even make it to Fort Jesus to use Oluoch's commode. I dreaded the *choo* I shared with Dan and his fifty neighbors and always tried to time my long calls to occur when I was outside Kibera.

The sensation mounted. It could have been diarrhea, perhaps caused by bacteria in the lukewarm chicken I had for lunch earlier that day at a roadside shack. If I had diarrhea, it wouldn't wait until morning. I reached for the roll of toilet paper and slipped on my flip-flops. Boots would have been preferable, but I couldn't risk bending over to lace them up.

I knocked on Baba Chris's door. "Sorry, *choo* please." It was almost midnight. The door cracked and a naked arm hung out, dangling the key.

The treacherous forty-foot journey took me less than twenty seconds. It felt like a Slip 'n Slide, and I barely made it without falling. I unlocked the padlock and hung my paraffin lamp on a hook in the ceiling. I was so pressed that the noxious fumes didn't affect me, nor did the flies or the

cement floor covered by feces that had missed the head-sized hole. I squat-
ted on two cement steps above the hole and felt an incredible sensation of
relief as my body expelled its liquid waste. Diarrhea.

Flies circled around my rump and landed in uncomfortable places. My
flip-flops lost traction as I swatted at them. I thumped onto the floor.
Other peoples' feces squashed into my bare butt. Horrified, I shouted and
vomited into my lap. I wiped myself maniacally, churning through the
entire roll of toilet paper, then raced back to my shack to wash. Along the
way, I slipped and fell in the mud. My pants were so nasty that I took
them off and left them crumpled outside the front door to Dan's shack.
With a sock and a bar of soap, I scrubbed myself raw in a plastic bucket of
cold water. By the time I returned to bed I was freezing and traumatized.
It might have only been sixty degrees Fahrenheit, but the damp, wet air
seeped through my skin. All I could think about was being caked in feces.

My ROTC training taught me how to pack lightly, and I had fit all of
my clothes, including three pairs of cargo pants, into my dad's old duffel
bag. I had already tossed one pair of cargo pants in a dump after having
slipped and fallen into a sump of sewage. When I told Salim about the
incident, I expected him to laugh at the thought of a *mzungu* slipping into
a sump, but he didn't. Instead, he told me in a serious voice that I should
have cleaned the pants and given them to a street child if I was too squea-
mish to wear them. I thought about the crumpled pants outside and decided I would clean them up later.

Too cold to sleep, I got out of bed, dressed, and made my way to the
Mugumeno Motherland Hotel at five A.M. with one thought on my mind—
hot chai and warm, deep-fried bread called *mandazi*, the East African
doughnut. Hotels in Kibera were for eating, not sleeping. The Mugumeno,
a tin shack on the main alley above Dan's place, opened well before dawn. I
sat in my favorite spot, a bench next to the hole in the wall that served as
the only window. It was an overcast morning, and I thought about rain.
Rain made Kibera all the more miserable.

A handful of patrons sat silently sipping chai. There was only one breakfast option. The matron, a large woman with a wide gap between her two
front teeth, greeted me with a warmth and familiarity that reminded me of
Southern hospitality. "Good morning, Omosh," she said glowing, handing
me a cup of hot chai and a plate with two steaming *mandazi*.

The chai soothed my shivering body. I dipped a *mandazi* into it and devoured half of the triangle-shaped doughnut in one bite while reading hand-painted signs that decorated the walls. At first, the signs reminded me of bumper stickers. They were prosaic, funny, and seemingly random offerings. However, with time, I saw that they revealed insights about life in Kibera:

OUR CUSTOMERS ARE SPECIAL, SERVICE IS FREE.

KUKOPESHA NI KUPOTEZA WATEJA

(TO GIVE ON CREDIT IS TO LOSE CUSTOMERS).

BEHOLD, NOW IS THE ACCEPTED TIME,

NOW IS THE DAY OF SALVATION.

Later that morning I traveled to the other end of Kibera for a meeting with Jumba, the founder of one of the few locally led NGOs, a micro-credit program called Ghetto Credit. A gangly man, Jumba had two swollen scars shaped like fingers that sliced down his cheeks. We met at his office near Kenyatta Market, a cluster of ugly, cream-colored multistory buildings with an open-air marketplace famous for its *nyama choma*—roasted meat.

Jumba was one of my most talkative sources. He could speak for long stretches without interruption. He began our meeting that day with a long-winded monologue about why he believed access to credit was a human right. By midday I could smell the savory *nyama choma* wafting through the window. On my suggestion, we carried our meeting into the marketplace. As we sat down at a butchery that doubled as a restaurant, a waiter slid us a wooden chopping board topped with chunks of roasted beef, diced tomatoes, onions, cilantro, and a small pile of salt. Kenyatta Market's reputation was well deserved. We tore into the *nyama choma* as a butcher chopped at a fresh carcass. Not a word passed between us until we had devoured the meat.

Finished with our feast, Jumba began talking me through the basics of micro-credit. I was intrigued by the concept of giving loans to small groups of residents without collateral and then holding those groups accountable for repayment. Jumba charged 10 percent interest to cover administrative costs, which sounded reasonable. He explained that his organization gave most of its loans to groups of older women in Kibera because women were generally more responsible than men.

While targeting older women for loans made sense, my research was focused on youth and ethnic violence. Jumba told me that he had dreamed for many years of starting a micro-credit program for youth. He quoted the adage "an idle mind is the workshop of the devil" and suggested that creating jobs was the most effective way to prevent ethnic violence. I hadn't given that perspective much thought before I arrived, though the longer I stayed in the slum, the more intrigued I became by it.

At the end of our four-hour meeting, Jumba told me that he would be interested in piloting a micro-credit program for youth if he could access start-up capital. I assumed that running a pilot project would cost a few thousand dollars. To my surprise, Jumba said he could do it for as little as $400. It was such a small figure. *Perhaps I can help him raise that money?* I thought to myself as we parted ways.

The rain held off that afternoon while I walked along the railroad tracks from Kenyatta Market to Dan's shack. The forty-five-minute walk offered views of many of Kibera's eleven villages. I stopped to photograph one of Kenya's most jarring contrasts, where a ten-foot cinderblock wall separated Kibera from the Royal Nairobi Golf Club, the city's oldest golf course. Every day, tens of thousands of residents walking to work passed this two-hundred-yard stretch of manicured lawn with its dapper golfers. A playground for Kenya's elite, the course came with a sweeping view of extreme poverty. Its sprinklers sprayed the fairways while Kibera's residents paid more than five times the city council rate for water that was often contaminated.

I had come to Kibera with the belief that knowledge and awareness could make an impact. Surely if people knew about this place things could change. If I could help expose Kibera to the world, I thought the world would respond. Yet, Kenyan elites were aware. I snapped a panorama with my disposable camera and walked on, remembering that I still needed to clean my filthy pants. It was the last thing I wanted to do.

My pants were nowhere to be seen by the time I returned to Dan's shack.

"Excuse me," I asked my first neighbor, a mother with four children, "I think I've lost my pants. Do you know where they are?"

The woman tried to contain a giggle. "Sorry, Omosh, I don't know."

I stepped to the next shack and I received the same reaction. Little did I know that the expression to *lose your pants* was also a popular way of saying "gone nuts."

The last shack was in the least desirable location. It sat adjacent to a small area used by all of the compound's residents to shower and urinate. I was curious about who lived there. A neighbor had told me there was a fourteen-year-old girl named Vanessa, though I had never seen or heard her. Whoever lived in this final room was unlikely to know where my pants were, but I knocked anyway.

An old, wrinkled grandmother cracked the door open. She stood a little over four feet tall and had a thin patch of curly white hair. Her face looked like leather. She didn't move as I greeted her and explained my predicament. After a long pause, she opened the door fully and gestured for me to enter with a slight movement of her hand.

The grandmother's ten-by-ten was even barer than Ali's shack. Two faded *kangas* divided the space into halves. My half had nothing but a stool and a paraffin lamp.

"Vanessa cleaned your pants," the grandmother said in Swahili. "The pants, they are here."

When she pulled back one of the *kangas*, I thought I was seeing a ghost. A girl stood motionless with my folded pants in her stick-thin arms. She was missing chunks of hair. Her skin clung to the bones in her face as if she were a skeleton. A dark, sleeveless slip hung between the bend in her slight shoulders and slender neck. The grandmother took the folded pants from her and handed them to me.

"*Nimeshukuru sana*," I said. "I'm grateful."

Vanessa slowly lowered her arms.

"I'm Omondi but people call me Omosh."

Her mouth twitched as if she wanted to smile but couldn't. I extended my hands and took a step forward, cupping her palm into mine. Her skin felt like a hot iron. Every movement must have caused her pain. I didn't want to be the source of any more discomfort, though I had to ask why she did it. Why did she go out of her way to clean my pants? What motivated her?

The words came softly. Her lips hardly moved. "*Kwa sababu naweza.*"

It knocked the wind out of me. "Because I can." Vanessa didn't expect anything in return apart from perhaps the good feeling of having done something that was appreciated. There were no more words. I fought to hold back tears as I stood there looking into her beautiful eyes, eyes that conveyed everything as they rose unnaturally from her sockets—the fear and the pain, the love and the hope, the hope, the hope despite it all, the hope despite her body losing a battle against a silent thing they called *dudu*, "the bug." It was an invisible curse that she did nothing in her short life to invite, that no child ever did, but that came and could not be stopped.

"Because I can," she had said.

A week later Vanessa died of AIDS. Her body was removed from Kibera in a wheelbarrow and buried in a communal grave in Nairobi.

That night after Vanessa's body had been taken away I sat on the edge of Dan's lumpy mattress and tried to ignore the sounds of Kibera: piercing ululations of night funerals, rats squeaking, babies crying, coughing, wheezing, snoring, the wind whistling. I was wearing the pants she had cleaned. My head throbbed. The rubber band sensation pulled my chest apart. I cried. I craved silence.

At dawn I made my way to the Mugumeno Motherland Hotel. I needed to warm my body with chai. I was an emotional wreck. The normally jovial matron was subdued. She poured my chai and slid me a plate of *mandazi* without saying hello. A drunk man stumbled through the door.

"*Mzungu, mzungu.*" He pointed and wobbled my way. "Give me something small."

It was always what they asked for, *kitu kidogo*, something small. A blast of rage shot through my body. Who was he to beg? Vanessa didn't beg. She asked for nothing.

"He's not a *mzungu*." The matron stepped up and smacked the man across the face. "This is Omosh from Gatwekera. Now you get out of here." She shoved him out the door. It was rare to see a woman with the audacity to assault a man in public. The matron nodded at me. "Sorry. That man, not a good one."

That was when it struck me. I was in Kibera for only five weeks, but I was there, and I had unique access to remarkable people such as Ali, Dan, Taib, Jane, and Jumba. These people impressed me with their actions as much as their words. I approached many of them as sources, but they could be partners, too. No other white people were spending their nights in Kibera. I was lucky to have been born with great parents and in a land abundant with opportunity. I could do something. I could reach out and support those who were stronger and wiser than I was.

THAT EVENING I returned to Fort Jesus for a shower. Elizabeth invited me to dinner. Oluoch was at a pub. With a week left in Kibera, I wanted to spend the night alone sorting out my thoughts about how best to act on my research. However, Elizabeth's beef stew smelled good, and I welcomed the rare opportunity to speak with her alone.

As we ate, I told her about Vanessa. Fighting to stay composed, I stumbled through the story about her unexpected act of kindness.

"I'm sorry," Elizabeth responded with tears in her eyes. "Those, those are the ones I wish to serve at a nursery when they're younger."

"Please, tell me about it, your dream."

"You see," she explained, "education begins in nursery school. Excellence begins early. These children, born to a single mother or maybe without parents, they deserve it, too. They can succeed, but we must start early. That's what I believe, anyway, and if you can help, it could be a great thing."

So began a long conversation. Elizabeth told me more about her career and how Montessori schools functioned, which I found interesting in part because I had attended a Montessori as a five-year-old. She spoke passionately about breakthrough learning moments with children she had taught over her twenty-year career.

"Omosh, will you help me?" Well-timed, she asked directly.

"Yes, I'll help raise the funds," I responded reflexively, though I had the wherewithal to add the caveat, "I have no idea what this will mean. I don't know how much money I can raise, but I'll try." Although Elizabeth didn't have a budget, I assumed it would be relatively cheap to rent a room and launch a nursery school. Those details could be sorted out later. The important thing was her vision and her dedication to creating something extraordinary.

"Oh, Omosh, thank you, thank you *so very much*!" She embraced me. It was a more enthusiastic reaction than I had anticipated, and it felt good.

It felt good until I thought about it. I had a limited amount of time and resources. While I trusted Elizabeth and was sure that her initiative would be a worthwhile endeavor for Kibera, a nursery school had nothing to do with my research in violence prevention and youth development. It was a good gesture on my part to try to help fund-raise, but that was it. It wasn't taking research to action. It wasn't empowering leaders, or doing anything particularly innovative. I wanted to do something unusual and with consequence for people my age in Kibera whom I admired. And I wanted to battle the things that I hated.

Near the start of my final week I scanned my list of more than seventy sources and decided to meet with ten of the most promising ones, including Ali, Taib, Dan, and Jumba. I planned to ask each person if they had any ideas for new projects or businesses. My focus was still on preventing ethnic conflict, though I decided that I would remain open to different ideas as long as they came from community leaders. The talent was within Kibera, and I felt that engaging it would be the best way to fight extreme poverty and prevent violence.

That was my plan. Unfortunately, I fell ill and the plan collapsed. At first, I felt nauseated and lost my appetite. Hours later, dry heaving began, followed by cold sweats. I assumed it was food poisoning. Hunchbacked, I made my way to Fort Jesus and collapsed on my bed. I had been telling people that I was living in Kibera. But I never "lived" in Kibera. I always had the option of a quiet night in a warm bed with a hot shower and a flush toilet. I could always escape.

Jane helped remove my boots. She brought me water and checked on me throughout the day. Elizabeth returned in the evening and encouraged me to go to the hospital. It was a good idea, but the thought of a bouncing taxi ride and the hospital's fluorescent lights and polished halls turned me off to it. Plus, if it was just food poisoning, all I needed to do was take the pain. I spent the night in the fetal position shivering so forcefully that I imagined my teeth shattering.

The next morning, Jane brought me some small black tablets that she said would help my stomach. Her best friend, Tabitha, was a nurse and had told her about the tablets. Tabitha was one of many people who had taken time and graciously showed me around Kibera during my first couple of weeks. I remembered her mostly because she had tipped me off to the rumor that the hardcores at Darajani Massive were planning to ambush me.

It was a threat that seemed to have disappeared after I walked the area with Ali.

"Jane, what is this?" I asked holding up one of the tablets.

"*Makaa.*"

"Charcoal? Like burnt wood?"

Jane nodded and explained that it was a traditional remedy for ailments ranging from upset stomachs to malaria. Desperate for relief, I popped the charcoal tablets into my mouth and tried to lie still. Every movement caused pain.

The second night of the shakes was the worst because the cold sweats were interspersed with extraordinary heat. It felt like I was trapped in a sauna, then suddenly submerged in ice water. The hot-cold cycle spun through the night. No amount of clothing made a difference. Hours passed. I curled in the bed, clenching my muscles, grinding my teeth, and cursing the invisible thing that ravaged my body.

Surprisingly, I regained some strength by morning and was able to eat a piece of toast. As Jane washed some clothes in a bucket, she spoke with me about her struggles raising five children in a ten-by-ten with her husband, who was an underemployed carpenter.

"How did you do it then, before you worked for Oluoch and Elizabeth?" I asked.

"I can say it was not easy."

"You're so strong."

Jane laughed. "Us, we are survivors."

"Survivors."

"Yes, survivors." Jane explained that Tabitha had befriended her as a neighbor, even though Tabitha was educated. When Jane's children fell ill, Tabitha had purchased medicine and cared for them. She had never asked for anything in return. "And she is strong. Let me tell you, strong. Stronger than me." Jane looked up from the soapy water. Every day she spent hours bent over buckets, scrubbing vigorously.

Tabitha was a survivor, too. Shortly after she lost her nursing job at a hospital when the government cut its health-care expenditures, her husband, a metalworker, passed away. By Luo custom, Tabitha was supposed to marry her late husband's brother, move back to her rural homeland in Nyanza Province, and become a second wife. But Tabitha refused because she didn't respect the man. "He was not a good one," she had told

Jane, who could not fathom how Tabitha mustered the courage to defy Luo marital customs.

Ostracized by her family and widowed with three children, Tabitha joined Jane in a search for work. For three months they worked together without pay as house help for an Indian man. When they found the job at Fort Jesus with Elizabeth and Oluoch, Tabitha insisted that Jane take it. Tabitha remained with the Indian man, working for room and board until he refused to feed her children, at which point she quit and returned to Kibera. That was two years ago. She had been searching for work ever since.

"And, Omosh," Jane finished, "Tabitha, she still wants to meet you. You said you would meet with her before you left, so Tabitha, she could show you her house and make you chai. You are not forgetting, are you?"

The day before I left Kibera I met Tabitha near Jane's ten-by-ten. She was wearing her oversized, black leather coat. Her hair was pulled back in short, tight braids. Tabitha immediately detected that something was wrong with my body. When I told her about my symptoms over the previous nights, she said that it sounded like a mild dose of malaria. It was mild, she explained, because I seemed to be recovering and was still taking my antimalarial mefloquine pills. Typically mefloquine prevented malaria, although it could be overwhelmed by large doses of the disease through multiple insect bites, such as the many that had covered my shoulders and back after having traveled to Lake Victoria for a weekend and sleeping without a proper bed net.

Tabitha made me chai, answered some questions about her life, and then confronted me. "What we are crying out for is money," she said, locking her strong brown eyes onto mine. Earlier that summer I had passed Dan $7 to give to Baba Chris for malaria medicine. In part for my own safety, I hadn't given out any other money in Kibera. But Tabitha had a plan, and there was something about the conviction in her voice. I handed her two one-thousand shilling notes, the equivalent of $26.

I didn't think I would see Tabitha again. As I said my good-byes to Jane, Dan, Elizabeth, Ali, and other new friends, I hoped that I could one day return to Kibera. But I didn't know if it would be possible, and my attention was turning to Officer Candidates School, OCS. My orders to the Marine Corps boot camp for officers instructed me to report to Quantico, Virginia, in a week. "Just make sure you pass OCS, Barcott,"

Major Boothby had warned. Up until then I hadn't worried about passing the six-week gut check, as my father referred to it. I knew plenty of friends and colleagues who had passed OCS. If they could do it, I could do it. However, if Tabitha was right, and I had a mild dose of malaria, then my odds of passing OCS were suddenly in question. The disease was among the world's biggest killers, and Tabitha had warned that my recovery might take weeks. I didn't have weeks. In less than seven days I would be reporting to duty.

If I didn't pass OCS, I would be the laughingstock of my ROTC unit. It was agonizing to even imagine drill instructors shouting in my face like something out of *Full Metal Jacket*: "WHAT'S YOUR MAJOR MALFUNCTION, NUMBNUTS?"

The thought was unbearable. Even soft sounds sent my head ringing with bolts of pain. *What the hell had I got myself into?*

CHAPTER FIVE

What's the Key?

Quantico, Virginia

August 2000

"Get up my rope, Schwartz," Sergeant Instructor Staff Sergeant Sweeney shouted, sounding like a fire alarm. Although I grew up using Barcott as my last name for convenience, my true name was Schwartz-Barcott, and it was so long that my uniform nametape couldn't fit all fifteen letters. For the first time in my life, I became known simply as Schwartz, the name made famous by *Spaceballs*, the 1980s parody on *Star Wars*. "I see your Schwartz is as big as mine," so goes the famous line. I'm all too familiar with it.

"SCHWARTZ," Staff Sergeant Sweeney bellowed.

My head throbbed. It was the end of week three, the halfway point, and it had been a long three weeks. I had to keep taking mefloquine after I returned from Kibera, and the drug never stopped screwing with my mind. My nights were miserable blurs of bizarre hallucinations. Even though I was exhausted and on the verge of collapse, I slept horribly as my body battled the remnants of the malaria that had struck me weeks earlier in Kibera.

My eyesight had deteriorated from years of heavy reading in Chapel Hill's dark coffee shops. Contact lenses were forbidden at OCS, so I had to wear military-issue glasses with oversized brown frames and lenses so thick they resembled bifocals. The glasses appeared to have come out of an old World War II supply depot. We called them "BCGs," short for birth-control glasses. A fellow candidate told me that I looked like a reject from a horror movie.

"SCHWARTZ!"

My BCGs fogged up as I strained to hoist myself up the rope. I knew the secret to rope climbing was form, but I always muscled my way up with my arms. Now I was only three quarters of the way and stuck.

"SCHWARTZ. SCHWARTZ. SCHWARTZY-SCHWARTZ!" He drew the attention of two dozen candidates waiting to move on to the next exercise.

Staff Sergeant Sweeney was one of the two drill instructors for our fifty-man platoon, and he had targeted me since the first run. I had finished the three-mile race near the top of the class of two hundred candidates in under eighteen minutes. Along the way, however, my bowels kicked in. The lingering effects of malaria robbed me of my control. Stopping the run to relieve myself wasn't an option. I reached into my Skivvies and pulled the blob out. It had the texture of Jell-O, and I was far enough ahead of the pack so that no one saw me. Sprinting by the commanding officer's building, I tossed it under a bush and finished the run with my soiled hand clenched in a fist.

Staff Sergeant Sweeney stood at the finish line with his arms crossed. Avoiding his eye, I made a beeline to the barracks.

"Schwartz, stop. You come here, you."

I turned and ran to him. "Yes, Sergeant Instructor Staff Sergeant Sweeney."

"What's in your hand, Schwartz, huh, what's in your hand?"

I hesitated.

"I SAID WHAT'S IN YOUR HAND, SCHWARTZ? ARE YOU TESTING ME? ARE YOU GETTING CUTE WITH ME YOU SHITBIRD?"

"I shit myself on the run, Sergeant Instructor." I opened my fist and revealed the residue.

"That's disgusting, Schwartz. Get out of my face, you disgusting candidate. Go clean yourself."

Six other candidates were on Sweeney's hit list. Within the first week he had determined that we were the "assclowns and bottom-feeders," the lowest 10 percent of the platoon that needed to be weeded out first. He made it his personal mission to see that we would "never lead Marines." Three of the targeted candidates were thrown out of OCS in the first two weeks for a variety of stress-induced infractions. Another candidate was caught passing a note during a class and lied about it. There was no discussion when it came to integrity violations. The candidate was immediately jettisoned and lost his $80,000 college scholarship.

I had my fair share of screwups. On day ten, I neglected to tuck in my bed sheets properly. "Why, look here, Schwartz." Staff Sergeant Sweeney's voice rose. "Candidates, eyeballs. Candidate Schwartz has given us another example of what not to do. For his disregard to attention to detail, everyone pays." He belted out orders as I stood at attention and the rest of the candidates ran around in a frenzy stripping and remaking their racks.

Did I belong here? For the first time in my life I felt ostracized from a group that I badly wanted to be part of. For the first time I was at the bottom of a class trying to battle against a horrendous first impression. I was failing at something that mattered. Even without malaria I would have had a tough time. I was often a klutz and forgot simple things. I spent a lot of time in my own head, thinking and observing. I didn't consider myself to be a natural leader, though I wanted to lead. I wanted to be part of something with historical significance, to feel what the military historian John Keegan had called the mask of command. I wanted the burden, the challenge, and the responsibility. What I didn't realize was that the adversity I faced at OCS was deepening my commitment to military service. The calling could not be beaten out of me.

Other people I knew who had passed OCS came to mind: the upperclass midshipmen at UNC, my father, and a high school friend. I thought about Kibera and how the living conditions there were so much more arduous than OCS, where we returned to air-conditioned barracks each night and always had clean water, flush toilets, medical care, and food. I gave myself a pep talk. The stress of life in Kibera was real. The stress at OCS was artificial. If I could make it through Kibera, I could make it through OCS.

"SCHWARTZ!"

My hands locked onto the rope. I couldn't muster the strength to pull myself to the top.

"GET THE HELL UP HERE, SCHWARTZ, YOU TURD," Staff Sergeant Sweeney shouted from his perch on the adjacent rope.

I threw my arm up and went for another attempt. The rope tore into my calluses as I slid down it and collapsed in a mulch pit. Sweeney pounced on me, pressing his finger into the bridge of my nose. "You're a quitter. God hates a quitter."

A quitter? I had been called many things but never that. I loathed the sound of it. Although my instinct was to fight back, that rope gave me self-doubt.

A candidate named Sean Gobin from Rhode Island approached me in the barracks after I had fallen from the rope. "Sha-watz, I'll help you get up that rope, man," he offered. We had thirty minutes of down time each evening. That day, Gobin gave his time to me. He took me to the ropes and taught me the right form, which involved using legs more than arms. By the end of his tutorial, I had it down. I scaled the rope, slapped the wood beam, and sounded off with the word that accompanied our group exercises—"*KILL.*"

It was a silly ritual, and saying it felt odd at first. But I took it for what it was. It was part of the acculturation into a service rooted in violence. OCS was the test. Most exercises ended with full frontal assaults where we charged targets head-on, running into a blaze of make-believe gunfire. There was little discussion of discretion in combat or ethically gray areas such as missions that could endanger civilians. That would come later, if we made the cut. Behind the scenes, we joked about it. Our own morbid sense of humor developed as we started to cope with the reality that our avocation might call on us to take the lives of other people. After a buddy of mine broke his wrist on the obstacle course he looked at me and groaned, "Kill."

I laughed. I conformed. I convinced myself that my mind was still open and independent, and that ends could justify means. Sometimes we had to kill to reestablish peace.

When we walked back to the barracks that evening, I thanked Gobin for his lesson and made some comment to the effect of "I don't know how I'll repay you."

"Sha-watz," Gobin stopped me, "I'm not lookin' to be frickin' repaid. Just graduate. Maybe we'll fight together someday."

The following morning we ran the obstacle course again. Staff Sergeant

Sweeney had me run it twice to see if I could get up the rope the second time when I was tired. With the right form, it was a breeze. I launched up the rope, smacked the wood beam, and shouted, "KILL."

Gobin had taught me an invaluable lesson in leadership. He had taken the initiative and reached out when he saw a way that he could help. He had given of himself to better the unit. I respected that and began to emulate his style. In so doing, I made fewer mistakes because I was less focused on myself.

SOMETIME DURING WEEK five our platoon went on a three-day field exercise in the forested hills behind the school. I had finished my final dose of mefloquine and was sleeping better at night. We carried thirty-pound packs and M16s without ammunition for ten miles in the first movement of the long exercise. It was so humid it felt as if we were walking in a steam room. We hiked for fifty-minute intervals separated by ten-minute breaks to change socks and drink water. During the breaks, candidates were instructed to knock back two full canteens of water so that we didn't become heat casualties. I pounded my two canteens and envisioned the lukewarm water entering my body and running straight out of its pores.

A Humvee putted behind our formation with a water buffalo, a steel tank of water so large it needed its own trailer. It was a luxury for us to have all the clean water we could drink at no cost. I imagined the column of candidates balancing thirty-pound jerricans of water on our heads like the women in Kibera. The thought entertained me for a while and helped keep my mind off my blistering feet and chafing crotch.

We finished the ten-mile hike at a small clearing in the woods by a rocky road, staged our gear, and prepared to patrol in squads for the rest of the afternoon. We patrolled without packs, moving quickly and without direct access to the water buffalo's seemingly endless supply of water. We were trained to be always on the alert for heat casualties, which could cause serious, long-term injury, or death. That afternoon, two candidates collapsed from dehydration. As soon as they fell, our navy medic, the "doc," removed their pants and inserted a rectal thermometer. It was a procedure known as the silver bullet. Candidates who received it had to wear a large *H* on their shirts for the rest of OCS to indicate their increased susceptibility to heat injuries. It was the Marine Corps' scarlet letter. At the time, I was convinced that I would rather die than receive the dreaded silver bullet.

None of us looked forward to the night exercise. Some candidates became cranky and complained when the drill instructors were not within earshot. We were told the exercises would go on for an undetermined period of time. Staff Sergeant Sweeney appointed a stocky football player named Miller to be our squad leader.

Miller delivered a crisp set of orders for our first mission, a long tactical movement to a resupply point. He was a top performer but had trouble with night land navigation. He led us through a swampy bog and into a jungle of green briars. Shortly afterward, Miller fell and badly twisted his ankle. The squad stopped and formed a circle around him. No one knew what to do as Staff Sergeant Sweeney stood off to the side in the shadows, quietly observing us. I followed an instinct and took charge.

"Our objective has changed. We need to get Miller back to the bivouac." I paused to gauge the reaction from the squad. There was no response. I told our most capable navigator to guide us back. Since we didn't have a stretcher, we would have to carry Miller with one man under each arm. The most important thing was balance. I identified the largest candidates and told them to carry Miller out.

"The rest of us will be on security," I instructed. "We'll move in a wedge formation around Miller."

"No, no." Staff Sergeant Sweeney emerged from the shadows, "You need more security. You can only have one candidate hauling Miller's ass at any time."

Miller weighed over two hundred pounds. No one wanted to carry him. Tensions began to rise. I told the group I'd take the lead and that we'd take turns alphabetically by last name. Being in charge motivated me to carry Miller much farther than I had initially anticipated, and the squad became more energized as we progressed. Soon other candidates were volunteering to carry Miller.

When we arrived at our bivouac site, Miller leaned over and grabbed the back of my neck. "Thanks, I owe ya."

I couldn't see his face well, but he seemed to be getting emotional. An ankle injury could threaten his graduation from OCS and his chances of becoming a Marine officer. I leaned forward and said to Miller, "You owe me nothin'. The doc will take care of your ankle and you'll graduate. One day we may fight together."

As WE ENTERED our final week of OCS, we began administrative outprocessing and had more time to think. We still marched everywhere we went. Candidates took turns calling cadence. One afternoon a candidate called cadence with a ditty I had first heard when I joined ROTC as an incoming freshman at UNC. "LEFT-RIGHT, LEFT-RIGHT, AND WHAT'S THE KEY?" the candidate sounded off, emphasizing each word to the rhythm of our boots on the asphalt.

"CON-FI-DENCE," we replied.

The ditty had bothered me when I first heard it as a freshman. It sounded corny, and it was different from the macho hunter-killer stuff we were used to hearing. But my bigger issue with the ditty was conceptual. At the time, I confused confidence with arrogance, and I thought both words characterized a disregard for life's complexity. History was rife with cases of supremely confident leaders who made poor judgments that caused tremendous harm. The word also reminded me of a comment my father had once made about hubris, the quality of excessive pride that was the tragic flaw of so many of the classic Greek heroes. "Hubris," Dad had proclaimed while we watched a Marine give a press conference during the first Gulf War, "is the greatest threat to the Marine Corps."

Hearing the cadence at OCS, however, clarified things. After all, no one wants to follow people who are unsure of themselves. Confidence could be a great enabler. It was the foundation that made it possible to lead Marines into dangerous places, even when the one leading was a twenty-two-year-old with a college degree and little life experience. It was also one of the key qualities that first attracted me to Salim, Tabitha, and Ali. It took confidence to make an impact in places that others viewed as hopeless. I needed to embrace it as one of my strengths and trust that my education and upbringing would keep hubris at bay with a questioning mind and a humble heart.

We formed a phalanx on the steaming asphalt parade deck for graduation day. Friends and family congregated in a row of bleachers, fanning themselves with the ceremonial programs. I had finished in the lowest

third of the class. Disappointed by my lackluster performance, I was glad
that my parents had another commitment and couldn't make the trip.

The ceremony was uneventful. We marched around in a square and
then stood locked at attention with our bootheels melting into the parade
deck as a Marine general officer gave a long-winded speech over speakers
that were so squeaky they could have come out of Kibera. The only thing
I remembered from his speech was the ending: "Congratulations, future
Marine officers." We were no longer candidates.

Before we broke formation, Staff Sergeant Sweeney held us at attention for one more long, sweaty minute. "Marines move toward the sound
of guns," he said in a calm, methodical way. "They aren't looking to you
to be their friends. They don't need you to be a friend. They need you to
lead them."

A handful of us without family present headed back to the barracks to
pack our gear. In the larger scheme of things, all we had done was pass a
six-week mini-boot-camp through which hundreds of candidates churned
each year in hopes of being Marine officers and, possibly, if their timing
was right, finding themselves in a position of responsibility on missions
that mattered. Nevertheless, in the moment, the experience felt much
more significant. As we walked together toward the redbrick barracks, we
realized that it was the first time we had moved across the parade deck as a
group and not been marching. It didn't feel right. So we shifted into a small
formation. Miller stepped out to call cadence. He had wrapped his severely
sprained ankle every morning and grunted out the last two weeks of OCS.
He kicked us off with a ditty, driving his heels into the burning black
asphalt.

"LEFT-RIGHT, LEFT-RIGHT, AND WHAT'S THE KEY?"
We shouted back as one, "CON-FI-DENCE."

MY CLOTHES, CAMOUFLAGE, and other gear from OCS filled two duffel
bags. I tossed the new duffel in the back of my old Dodge Caravan, the
Green Bean. I stowed my other duffel, the one with my father's name still
faintly stenciled on it, up at the base of the passenger's seat. It reminded
me of a rare moment when Staff Sergeant Sweeney had shown me some
respect. He was chewing me out for the length of my nose hairs when he
spotted my old duffel.

"WHAT THE HELL IS THIS, SCHWARTZ?" he shouted. "WHY IS THIS DUFFEL FADED AND MARKED UP? ARE YOU TOO CHEAP TO GET A NEW BAG?"

"Sergeant Instructor—"

"AND WHAT DOES THIS WRITING SAY ANYWAY? 'FIRST LIEUTENANT.' YOU THINK YOU'RE A LIEUTENANT ALREADY? YOU'RE A CANDIDATE. YOU'RE NOTHING."

"It's my father's."

"He was a Marine?"

"Yes."

"Pogue?" Sweeney asked, using the pejorative for Marines not in combat-arms specialties.

"No, infantry, recon."

"Combat?"

"Vietnam."

"Very well, Schwartz. Now go take care of your nose hairs. You look nasty."

"Aye aye, Sergeant Instructor Staff Sergeant Sweeney," I said and jogged to the head to tear out my nose hairs.

Around the same time as the incident with my dad's duffel, I had questioned my decision to go to Kibera. Now that my body was back in shape and I had passed OCS, I no longer had doubts about that decision. I did, however, have a better appreciation of the risk that my ROTC commander Major Boothby had taken. Had I been badly injured in Kibera, or if I had failed OCS, Major Boothby would have shouldered responsibility for supporting my request. It was a decision that could easily strike a more conventionally minded Marine Corps officer as reckless. My request had clearly spelled out my intent to live in one of the world's largest slums and then, less than a week later, attend one of our country's most intense officer candidate courses. Yet Major Boothby took a chance on me. For that he earned my fiercest loyalty and respect.

The sentries at the main gates stood at attention as I drove past. I was heading back to Chapel Hill for my senior year. Euphoria rushed to my head as I gunned the Green Bean down I-95. I had done it, and now I was going back as a senior, a big man on campus. I was no longer a Marine candidate. I was a midshipman first class, soon-to-be "second lieutenant of Marines." I loved the sound of it. My dream was coming true.

I called home to share my happy moment with my parents. Dad was out but Mom was there. I told her some stories about OCS: the rope, the night patrol, and the incident with Dad's duffel. I spoke quickly, lacing my sentences with Marine jargon, hyperbole, and words such as "outstanding," "motivating," and "absolutely." Mom enjoyed hearing about my experience, though her response was subdued by her distrust of militarism and military bravado. When she offered me a warning about culture shock, I thought she was shifting the conversation back to Kibera. However, she was referring to the Marine Corps as well. "You've just been in two intense cultures," she said. "It's like dual culture shock."

I hadn't thought about my summer in such a way, but Mom was right. One of the things that most impressed me about Kibera was the spirit of community and its strong identity. There was a defiant pride associated with being from the slum. The Marine Corps was also an extremely close-knit, proud community. Both worlds had their own languages. The Sheng of Kibera didn't translate in other parts of Nairobi; the jargon of the Marine Corps was challenging my mother's ability to understand what I was saying. It wasn't simply that they were different cultures. They were both extraordinarily strong cultures with high barriers of entry and elaborate rites of passage, rituals, and myths. In three short months, I was indoctrinated in each of them. Each place had pushed me to my limits, then accepted me in its own way. In Kibera, the community welcomed me. In the Marines, the command deemed that I was worthy of the title. I had stepped into two worlds with identities so forceful they could border on kinship, blood bonds. They were two worlds where I could make a difference, two worlds that mattered.

My mother offered me some advice for how to deal with the "dual culture shock." As an anthropologist, she understood the issue from personal experience and a lifetime of scholarship. "It takes time," she said. She spoke about how it was important to realize that I was adjusting, and to accept that. She cautioned me to find outlets for my energy and not to get upset when I saw things that bothered me. It was natural to feel frustrated, she said. She was giving me great advice, and I was committing it to memory. I knew culture shock was powerful. I needed to be ready for it. I needed to face it.

"And you need to slow down. You need time to think. Go slow."

Her final words stunned me. I didn't know what to say.

"Rye, did you hear me?"

"Yes, Mom."

Yes, I had heard my mother, and it felt like the one thing that she could have said that was impossible. I was always a bit fired up as a kid, high energy and high maintenance. However, college, Kibera, and the Marine Corps gave me a sense of urgency like none other. I didn't know exactly where I was running, but I was running, and I wanted to go faster, not slower. Slow down? How could I slow down when it was just the beginning?

Part II

CHAPTER SIX

Doers

Chapel Hill, North Carolina

FALL 2000–SPRING 2001

THE DUAL CULTURE SHOCK MY MOTHER warned me about didn't hit me until after I returned to Chapel Hill for my senior year. When it arrived, it landed hard. I felt like a foreigner in the comfortable, pampered world of the university. Little things bothered me: empty classrooms with their lights on and air conditioners roaring, half-asleep campus security guards, rich kids in fancy cars, the cost of a cup of coffee. I stopped going to the school cafeteria because I couldn't tolerate the waste on people's trays. My friends were my age, but I felt much older.

One night during my first week back on campus, a student who looked as if he had just stepped out of a country club mistook me for someone else and confronted me at a college bar called Four Corners. At first, I tried to de-escalate the situation, but he was obnoxious and we were drunk. After he tossed his beer in my face, I head-butted him and began choking him until a buddy ripped me away. Had I not known the bartenders from my days working there as a bouncer, I might have been arrested and lost my opportunity to be a Marine Corps officer.

That was my wake-up call. I stopped going out and barreled into my work. The work was addictive and focused on two areas beyond my normal course load and ROTC training. The first area was an opportunity to teach a self-structured class for one hour of pass/fail credit to under-graduates during the spring semester of my senior year. Still searching for a greater understanding of ethnic conflict, I decided to teach a course on "ethnic cleansing and genocide." I spent a lot of time reading grue-some, heartbreaking accounts of man's inhumanity to man. Professor Peacock, the anthropologist who had once taught my mother, served as my faculty adviser. He had a hands-off approach and treated me more like a colleague than a student. Together, we coauthored a statement on ethnic cleansing for the American Anthropological Association, which he had previously led as its president. I viewed Professor Peacock as my first mentor in college, and I treasured the relationship we had developed over three years.

My deep dive into the subjects of ethnic cleansing and genocide com-plemented my main area of focus, which was to write a senior honors thesis on ethnic violence and nongovernmental organizations in Kibera. Professor Richard Kohn, a military historian, served as the chair of my thesis committee. I had taken two classes with him. Although he wasn't an anthropologist and had no ties to Africa, his wisdom from a lifetime studying armed conflict was invaluable, and as a historian he helped me connect the key events in Kibera's past. Most important, he took a hands-on approach with my work.

Early in the fall semester Professor Kohn encouraged me to apply for a Rhodes Scholarship. He had once served as the chief historian of the U.S. Air Force, and he knew that a handful of Rhodes scholars were se-lected from the military service academies and ROTC programs. I didn't know much about the Rhodes, which provided two years of fully-funded graduate-school education at Oxford University, but I enjoyed a good competition and was flattered by his recommendation. I pulled together an application and put my name into the arena.

By the time I arrived at the North Carolina State finalist round, I knew much more about the prestigious scholarship and assumed that my chances were slim. My assumption was confirmed by the other finalists. They were students who had already made significant contributions. They were activists, athletes, and entrepreneurs. They were doers. One of the students had launched an educational-software company from his dorm room that generated more than a million dollars of annual revenue. A young woman aspiring to be a doctor created a nonprofit to distribute high-quality, used medical equipment destined for Dumpsters to clinics in the developing world. These students were like Ted Lord, the door carver and aspiring medical doctor who had spoken to our Swahili class. They took initiative and made things happen. I was disappointed but not surprised when I wasn't selected as one of the two candidates to advance to the next round.

One of the other finalists suggested that I speak to her friend Kim Chapman because of my interest in youth development in Africa. Kim was a recent UNC graduate who had produced a documentary on youth and AIDS in South Africa. I followed up and met Kim in her office later that week.

Five feet two inches tall with short, curly blonde hair, and a silver stub nose-ring, Kim ran marathons and played rugby. She impressed me with her high energy, sharp mind, and good nature. She had twenty minutes before her next meeting, and in that short period she gave me a synopsis of how and why she produced a film that would later be shown at the annual International AIDS Conference. As we finished the meeting, Kim asked me briefly about Kibera and told me that I should give her a call if I decided to "do something, besides research, of course."

"Research." There it was again, the albatross. I had convinced myself that research was important because it created awareness and could help give voice to the poor. But my conversation with Kim reminded me that research was the beginning, not the goal.

RETURNING HOME FOR Christmas break, I avoided reaching out to my high school football buddies, who were reuniting at the bars to relive the glory days. I turned off my cell phone and set up in my mom's office, a ten-by-ten at the University of Rhode Island's College of Nursing. It was quiet and isolated, just what I needed to finish the first draft of my thesis.

Most of my writing that week focused on two chapters on nongovernmental organizations in Kibera. Many of the NGOs that I had encountered were led by expatriates or elite Kenyans who spent comparatively large sums of money on comfortable offices, Land Cruisers, and other perks. The more time I spent studying these parts of the development industry, the more frustrated I became with it. In most cases, large international NGOs seemed to take the wrong approach. Instead of asking the target communities about local needs and context, these NGOs brought in highly educated foreign experts with their own solutions to problems that they didn't really understand.

It was a bitterly cold, gray New England day. Everything outside appeared dead. Kim Chapman, Ted Lord, and the doers whom I had met during the Rhodes competition were on my mind, as were Major Boothby's words about Marines having a "bias for action." I took a break from the computer and started pumping out sets of push-ups on my mom's office floor. My contacts with Salim, Taib, Jumba, and Elizabeth were sporadic, although they each seemed eager to have me return. They had captivating stories, big visions, and a lot of talent. An idea finally took shape in between push-ups: *I could do something in partnership with these Kenyans that would be larger than raising money for Elizabeth's nursery school. Together, we could develop young leaders and make change in Kibera. I could start an organization, raise a small amount of money, and invest it in community leaders.* It was simple, but I viewed it as a radical departure from the way most aid worked. In fact, it struck me as so powerful and right that I didn't think much about the possibility of failure.

Fund-raising was on my mind as I typed an e-mail announcing the birth of the organization. It didn't seem all that daunting at the time. In fact, I assumed it'd be easy. We lived in a supremely affluent country, a country where the cost of the ink for my printer could feed a family in Kibera for two months. *It could have been the other way around. We, too, could have been born with nothing.*

I figured I could get some support from the university and our alumni. A Rhode Island "Tar Heel Club" had thrown a send-off party for the three of us in the state who were heading to Carolina. About twenty alums showed up for the party. They treated us like we were heroes, as if we were already part of the tribe, and they loved the university. They loved Carolina and Carolina basketball with a passion. UNC had Tar Heel Clubs in nearly every state in the country. It was a rabid fan base, a large pool of potential donors. Surely they would want to help? The name flowed from that assumption. Carolina for Kibera, CFK.

My Palm Pilot had a hundred contacts in it. I pulled a list of three dozen people who I thought would be interested and able to help CFK: family, friends, Peter Whaley, and my closest professors at UNC. Most of the recipients were obvious additions. However, I deliberated heavily about including Major Boothby on the e-mail. Some old advice from my father came to mind. Dad always cautioned me to have important conversations in person whenever possible. I didn't know much about what it would take to start an NGO, but I knew that I couldn't get back to Kibera without Major Boothby's support. I decided to wait until I was back in Chapel Hill and had a more thorough plan before I approached the major.

Once the e-mail was ready, I paused and took a jog through the empty halls. What I was doing wasn't rational. With my thesis, teaching the ethnic cleansing seminar, graduating, and getting ready for the Marines, I had more than enough to do. Yet CFK was such a good idea, and if we didn't do it, who would? I returned to Mom's office, stood over her old Apple computer and took the plunge with the click of a mouse.

Practically every recipient of that first e-mail wrote back to me. Each response felt as if I were opening a gift. Professor Peacock, who never wrote more than a line in his e-mail replies, sent back one word—"Good." Jennifer Coffman wrote a note saying, "Go for it!" The responses were encouraging from everyone except Whaley, who asked, "Are you sure the world needs another NGO? You're better off just giving the money away."

"It takes more than giving away money," I replied. "We'll invest in local leaders and learn in partnerships with one another."

For the rest of winter break I ignored my writing and immersed myself in the details of starting an organization. I charted out a timeline that included a long to-do list. A fair amount of my time was spent learning the language and jargon of the nonprofit community. One of my first hurdles was to obtain 501(c)(3) status as a U.S. tax-exempt organization so that charitable contributions could be deducted. After I read a few pages of the dense Internal Revenue Service application, the need for an attorney to help me navigate the process was clear. Unfortunately, the average attorney charged thousands of dollars.

My parents were surprised but supportive of my decision to launch CFK. They believed in the idea of taking research to action and much of their own work had been practically focused on real world needs. Mom, of course, brought me back to the Margaret Mead quote about never doubting the power of a "small group of thoughtful, committed citizens." My father, who enjoyed being contrarian, reminded me of a quote from Karl Marx: "The philosophers have only interpreted the world, in various ways; the point, however, is to change it."

After I vented to my parents about the more prosaic challenge of legal fees, Dad suggested that I talk to his old friend George Levendis, a former infantry officer and Vietnam veteran who had become a partner at one of Washington, D.C.'s, most prominent law firms, Patton Boggs. I forwarded Mr. Levendis a copy of the CFK e-mail and followed up with a phone call. He cut me off ten minutes into my fervent spiel about NGO waste and the importance of youth empowerment.

"Okay, okay, I got it." He sounded preoccupied. It was midmorning on a workday, and I would later learn that his law firm calculated client billing in fifteen-minute increments. "I think we can make this happen. I'll be in touch."

It didn't much matter what kind of nonprofit it was. As long as it was well intentioned, George Levendis would help the son of his friend and fellow Marine. A week later, Patton Boggs committed to providing thousands of dollars' worth of free legal expertise. *Semper fidelis.*

FOLLOWING MY FATHER's advice, I briefed Major Boothby in person about my hopes for CFK as soon as I returned to Chapel Hill from Christmas break. At the time, the Marine Corps appeared to have more officers than it knew what to do with and needed midshipmen to volunteer to delay our start date at the Basic School, the six-month course at Quantico that marks the beginning of every new Marine officer's career. Major Boothby didn't see a problem getting my request approved for three months of unpaid leave to return to Kibera, and when I told him about our overarching goal to use sports and youth leadership development to prevent ethnic violence, he said my work there could teach me a lot about unconventional warfare. His only caveat was that raising the $20,000 that was needed would be a considerable challenge. This surprised me because I still assumed that $20,000 would be fairly easy to generate for such a noble cause. Major Boothby decided that I needed to raise half before he would sign off on my proposal and send it up the chain of command.

My first priority was to establish a Web site. It was the age of the Internet and no serious organization existed without a site. I envisioned setting one up, securing our 501(c)(3) status, then watching the donations roll in online. Unfortunately, I quickly learned that building a Web site required knowledge of a computer language called HTML. I needed to build a team, and I didn't have much time. I worked around the clock, spending most of my evenings on my laptop in dark corners of coffee shops on Franklin Street, Chapel Hill's main drag. I drank so much coffee I could no longer sense the effect that caffeine had on my mind.

One night at the Carolina Coffee Shop, I noticed a big white guy with short, matted black hair laughing loudly in another corner of the room. *"Baadaye,"* he said into his cell phone. "Later." He wore a silver stud in his nose and looked comfortable in his baggy, six-pocket shorts, flip-flops, and untucked collared shirt.

"Vipi?" I walked over and asked him after he hung up his phone. "What's up?"

"Poa, sema," he replied. "Cool, speak."

It had been a while since I had had a casual conversation in Swahili with a stranger.

"I'm Omondi, but people call me Omosh." I stuck to the introduction I had given hundreds of times in Kibera.

"Omosh?" He burst out laughing, a deep laugh like the ones I used to receive when I dropped the same intro lines to disarm the hardcores. "I'm Nate," he replied in Swahili, "but people call me Nate dog."

"Nate dog?"

"Yeah, with a double *g.*"

"Nate dogg, I like it." We bumped fists.

Somehow we started talking about Gourevitch. His book *We Wish to Inform You That Tomorrow We Will Be Killed with Our Families* had had a similarly profound impact on Nate, who had just returned from a semester study abroad with the School for International Training in Tanzania. Nate was graduating with me that semester and didn't know what was next. I knew he was looking for an adventure, though, because he told me he was reading Che Guevara's *Motorcycle Diaries* and thinking about backpacking from Cairo to Cape Town.

"Have you heard about Kibera?" I asked. "It's on the way."

"Kibera?"

"Yeah, it's a large slum in Nairobi, one of the largest in Africa." I spoke about the promise of young people there, CFK, and my hopes to get resources directly into the hands of local leaders rather than NGOs with no real connections to the community.

"*Hatari sana, na poa sana,*" he said with a spark in his eye. "Very dangerous, and very cool."

Nate and I became fast friends. We hung out at the coffee shops and lifted weights together. Nate knew the power of grassroots, community-based development because he had seen it firsthand when he lived in a Masai village in Tanzania for a month. After Nate helped recruit an acquaintance of his to set up the CFK Web site, I tossed out the idea of our going to Kibera together. I knew the probability was low. I hadn't raised any money and planned on leaving immediately after graduation. Nate, like me, didn't have any savings from which he could pull to cover his travel expenses. It would take a leap of faith.

"I'm in," he responded without hesitation, gripping my hand as if we were about to arm wrestle.

"*Tuko pamoja.*" I stuck my fist in the air. "We are together."

AMONG MY TOP priorities was to build a local board. Professors Kohn and Peacock were the first to join as members. Both men accepted our offer even though they sat on many other boards and had hectic schedules. Additionally, I reached out to Dr. Alan Cross, a professor of social medicine who had conducted a public health assessment in Kibera. After I invited him to our board, Dr. Cross asked a question that made me cringe: "So when are you going to ask me for money?"

I was uncomfortable with asking people directly for money, and I especially disliked the notion that I had read in a fund-raising book that "donors may be buying *you* more than the organization." I wanted people to appreciate what we were building for the merits of the work we would do on the ground, not simply because of a personal affinity for me, UNC, or the USMC. Unfortunately, in the initial months of CFK, most people were "buying me," or, as one businessman put it, "betting on the jockey." That reality felt awkward and in conflict with my values.

"Well, sir, I wasn't going to ask you for money. I'm just thankful you can serve on our board."

"Rye, stop. Do you believe in this?"

"Absolutely. With everything I have."

"Well, then you need to treat fund-raising like a military mission." Dr. Cross had once served as an Army physician. "You're the conduit to

Kibera. People need to believe in you, and you need to ask them. They won't take offense. If they do, we don't want their money anyway. Some people think fund-raising is a game. It's not a game. What you'll do with the Kenyans in Kibera matters, and think about that when you ask people to open their wallets and purses. But, you have to ask, directly."

WITH FEWER THAN three months left until graduation, I attended the annual Reserve Officers Association midwinter conference in Washington, D.C. A man with a patchy beard, reading glasses, and a flannel shirt approached me in the lobby of the Washington Hilton. "Excuse me, I'm sorry to bother you. My name's Andrew Carroll. I live across the street and was curious about what was going on here?"

If he hadn't asked so sincerely, I might have just directed him to a booth with brochures. Instead, I explained the conference.

"Thank you for what you're doing." His gratitude was authentic but felt out of place. I had not served anywhere and was enjoying a full ride to college. When I asked about his own work, Andrew explained that he was an author and was editing a book of unpublished war letters that would honor the legacy of veterans and send its proceeds to nonprofits.

"That's great. I just started a nonprofit." I gave him a quick overview of CFK.

"Good stuff and especially meaningful that you're doing it as a Marine. I'll send you a check. What's your address?"

"Really?" I fumbled through my bag for a brochure.

"Of course. I know how it feels to start something from nothing." He took my brochure and left me standing in the lobby wondering if I would ever hear from him again.

I had handed out over a hundred brochures while I was in D.C. To my dismay, only one letter was waiting for me when I arrived back at Chapel Hill. The return address read, "The American Poetry and Literacy Project."

"Good to meet you and good luck," Andrew Carroll had penned in hasty handwriting.

I pulled out the check and wondered if I was counting the zeros correctly. CFK's first check was for $1,000 from a five-minute encounter with a soon-to-be-famous writer in a distant city.

ANDREW CARROLL'S CHECK made me optimistic about the prospects of raising a large chunk of the $20,000 from our first letter campaign. Nate and I built a spreadsheet with about 150 folks: fifty professors, fifty friends and family, and fifty "others" who included wealthy UNC alums and people with ties to Africa and business addresses that we could find from Google, such as Michael Jordan and Bill Gates. On "launch night," Nate bought a bottle of Old Overholt rye whiskey and joined me in my dorm room with another friend, a tireless women's rights advocate named Alison Beckwith, whom we had met in an African-studies class. We were giving out titles like candy, and she became CFK's "press manager." While we didn't have any press to manage, it sounded important, and she was interested in a career in public relations. The three of us stuffed envelopes and penned handwritten, personal notes into the wee hours of the morning. Nate wrote the note to Michael Jordan:

> Dear Mr. Jordan,
> Jambo from Chapel Hill. You would be surprised by the athletic talent in Kibera.
> We use sports to prevent ethnic violence and promote community development, and we'd be honored to have your support.
> *Tuko Pamoja* (We Are Together),
> Nate

Donations trickled in from the fifty "friends and family" group: $10, $20, the occasional $50. We received only one check from a UNC professor, and no one from the "other" group replied. The lackluster response dampened my spirits and was followed by a rejection letter from the public-service scholarship program at UNC that had supported Kim Chapman's South African AIDS documentary with one of its $5,000 grants. We had worked hard on that grant proposal and expected to be selected. The rejection stung. *What were we doing wrong?*

Nate and Jennifer Coffman helped coach me for what I viewed as one of our last shots at receiving a major grant. The Burch Fellowship Dinner was an annual event with the patron of the fellowship that had first enabled me to travel to Kibera, Lucius Burch III. After the dinner, I had five minutes to deliver a presentation about my fellowship experience. I was nervous until I began the performance and felt the audience moving with me as I took them into Kibera and told them about the untapped leadership ability of young people surviving on less than $1 a day. "We'll do what other nonprofits don't," I announced, chest out, "we'll get resources directly into the hands of local leaders because they have the solutions. We don't."

My eye contact focused on four people spread throughout the room, including Lucius Burch and an impressive-looking gentleman with neatly combed, sandy brown hair in the front row. I mixed jokes into the intense material and concluded with a crowd-pleaser—a photograph of a Kenyan in Kibera wearing a #23 UNC basketball jersey and giving a big, happy thumbs-up to the camera.

"And, yes, we wrote to Michael Jordan."

After the presentation, the strong man with sandy brown hair approached me. "Matt Kupec, good to meet ya. That was great. Darn good. Darn good job. I think I've got something for you. Can you come to Georgia in a month and talk to a group I'm pulling together for Carolina First? It's a place called Reynolds Plantation."

It took me a moment to make the connection. Carolina First was the university's capital campaign, and Matt Kupec was the vice chancellor for university advancement, a former star quarterback who led the efforts to bring in millions of dollars to the school each year. I squeezed his hand and looked him in the eye. "Yes, sir. I'll be there." Whatever commitments I had could be rearranged.

Working hard had its perks, and I took advantage of many of them, especially the invitations to events with free food. One day I received a particularly fancy letter to attend a university public service gala and formal dinner. When I asked Nate if he'd like to go, he reacted strongly. "No way," he said. "We have two months left on campus. You need to take a break from CFK and get yourself a real date. This thing's perfect. Girls love guys in public service. You got a real opportunity here. Don't screw it up."

Nate's advice prompted me to reach out to Tracy Dobbins, a gorgeous woman with long, straight, strawberry-blonde hair; almond eyes, and an elegant European look. We had met two years earlier in a small seminar. When the professor called on her, Tracy made brilliant comments in an understated Southern accent. Her poise and quiet strength drew me to her. I prepared more for that seminar than others with the hopes that my comments would impress her. However, I never discovered whether she noticed. I was shy about asking women out, and I suspected she was too sophisticated for my rowdy military and fraternity friends. Although she had graduated the previous year, she was still living in Chapel Hill, and we had recently been reconnected over e-mail through a mutual friend.

Tracy accepted my invitation and joined me for the gala. We started dating afterward. The first place we went was Pepper's Pizza, where the host named Moses welcomed me by name and asked Tracy what she was doing with such a "dude." Tracy experimented with my favorite dish: fresh gazpacho, a salad with "Dijopi" dressing (honey Dijon and poppy seed), and a slice of "Slaughterhouse Five." I had eaten more meals at Pepper's than at any other restaurant in my life, and I was happy and relieved that Tracy liked the place, even though it was staffed by tattooed crazies blaring heavy-metal music. As graceful and as intelligent as Tracy was, she was also down-to-earth and easygoing. We enjoyed each other's company for what it was. We didn't talk about what would happen when I graduated and left for Kibera and the Marines.

A DAPPER CHAUFFEUR'S sign read MIDSHIPMAN BARCOTT. REYNOLDS PLANTATION. The chauffer insisted on taking my bag and led me to a black Mercedes in a special parking deck at Atlanta's airport.

"How long to the plantation?" I asked, with images of Rhett Butler and Scarlett O'Hara in my mind. A "golfer's mecca," Reynolds Plantation was located on a private preserve once called Cracker's Neck.

"'Bout an hour," the chauffer replied in a thick drawl. "What'll ya be drinkin' this evening, sir?"

"Oh, you have drinks in here?"

"Yes, sir, full bar."

"Tonic please."

"Vodka or gin?"

"Just tonic, thanks." Anxious, I took out my notes to fine-tune my presentation.

"No drink, work on the ride over. You must be staff." The chauffeur turned around and inspected me as if I worked for him.

"Somethin' like that." I laughed. With less than $2,000 raised for CFK, my presentation had to work. Matt Kupec offered me only one piece of advice in preparation: "Wear your uniform. They'll love that."

I was uncomfortable with the idea. I was going to Georgia to talk about CFK, not ROTC. Although a large part of CFK's mission was to prevent violence, it didn't feel right using my military identity so flagrantly as a fund-raising tool. I consulted Major Boothby on this, too.

"Fund-raisin' ain't as easy as you thought, is it, Barcott?"

"No, sir, but we're not quitting."

"I know, and that's a good attitude. Now you need this money for humanitarian work in Africa, right?"

"Yes, sir."

"And you need to raise half of it, a total of ten thousand dollars, before I endorse your request to take unpaid leave as a new second lieutenant and spend the entire summer in this African slum, right?"

"Yes, sir."

"Well, that's a noble mission. So wear your uniform and do us proud."

MY UNIFORM WAS "shit hot," and that was a good thing. I had spent hours preparing it. Its khaki creases were razor-blade sharp. The ribbons and rank insignia were precisely aligned. My shoes were so thoroughly spit-shined that they looked like glass, and I had surgically cut out even the smallest of Irish pennants from my shirt and heavily starched, teepee-shaped garrison cap. The shirt stays, elastic bands that connected our socks to the bottom of our collared shirts, were so tight they rubbed the back of my legs raw. They were perfect. It was perfect. I was locked on and ready to go.

"Two billion dollars." A donor announced the goal of the Carolina First capital campaign.

My jaw dropped. No one before had mentioned the amount of money the university aspired to raise. The audacious amount followed with a dazzling performance where donors stood up and made multimillion-dollar pledges. The room exploded in applause. It felt like a high-stakes auction. Resentment began brewing inside me. How could it be so hard to raise a few thousand dollars for Kibera when such mind-boggling sums of money could be raised for buildings with rich people's names on them? Little did I know that most of the money raised went toward scholarships to support students like me, and endowments to recruit and retain professors such as James Peacock and Richard Kohn.

Confidence replaced my anxiety as a professor of physics delivered a persuasive PowerPoint presentation on nanotechnology. Before I knew it, the chancellor was introducing me and describing CFK's work as a great example of UNC undergraduate initiative. I delivered my presentation on a slide projector and concluded with an appeal. "So if you are inclined, please send us some support. A little bit goes a long way in Kibera."

Upon returning to Chapel Hill, I learned that one of the donors had publicly pledged $2,500 and encouraged the rest of the room to follow suit. His self-initiated action meant a lot to me, and it helped generate about $7,000 from the Georgia trip. However, we were still $11,000 short of the $20,000, and I needed to reach Major Boothby's $10,000 target within the next week or I would miss the deadline to submit my summer-leave request.

Until that point, I had still not asked an individual directly for money. With Dr. Cross's advice in mind, I mustered the courage to call Lucius Burch. I assumed the prospects of getting some additional support from him were high.

Mr. Burch, a venture capitalist from Tennessee, had a gruff voice. I tried to lighten him up with some small talk, but he was clearly preoccupied. I told him about my fund-raising for CFK and asked him for "some support." I didn't have the guts to name an amount, though I had planned on asking for $5,000.

"I won't give anything else," he said, "Out of principle I only give once."

Stunned, I thanked him for the fellowship in his name that first took me to Kibera, then I went for a cinder-block run through the rolling, kudzu-draped trails around campus. I had learned the workout at the Marine Corps' Mountain Warfare School. As I pounded the sandy trails with my cinder block in my hands, I realized that I was more upset with myself than Mr. Burch. I should have made a more persuasive case.

There was only one more donor on my list whom I thought I could call and who had the means to make a sizable donation. I finished my run, stashed my cinder block under a bush, and prepared for fifteen minutes. Alston Gardner, an affable middle-age entrepreneur from Atlanta who had made a small fortune when he sold his consulting company, had been at the Reynolds Plantation. We had met through Professor Peacock. Alston congratulated me on my performance at the plantation.

"Thank you, sir. Sir, we really need your help for Kibera," I said with confidence.

"First of all, call me Alston. Second, how much do you need?"

"Five thousand."

"I'll send you twenty-five hundred."

For the first time I directly asked someone for money for CFK, and it worked. It put us over the halfway mark.

"Thank you. Thank you so much. Thank you, sir. I mean, Alston." I hung up and jogged to Major Boothby's office, leave request in hand and ready to return to Kibera with our team of doers.

CHAPTER SEVEN

The Sword

Chapel Hill, North Carolina

May 2001

MENTORSHIP WAS A WORD THAT I RARELY used when I first entered college. It had a heavy sound and a formality that made it inaccessible. I wasn't sure what it meant or how it related to my life. Four years later, as I prepared to graduate, be commissioned, and return to Kibera, I viewed mentorship as the single most important factor in my journey. I was fortunate to have an extraordinary group of mentors. These older, more experienced men and women were life advisers who formed a support network, a council of elders that remained invested in my development as long as I did my part to keep in touch.

My good fortune with mentors started when I was a boy. At the time, I didn't know what to call the attention my father's Marine friends gave to me when they asked me questions about life and coached me on how to be a man. Years later, I asked one of my first mentors why he had taken so much time to guide me when he had a large family of his own and a busy career. Lieutenant Colonel R. J. O'Leary, a combat veteran of three wars, replied, "Because that's what Marines do, and I know you'll pay it forward."

There was an important difference between my childhood mentors such as Colonel O'Leary and those I found during college. My father's friends had taken the initiative to reach out to me. In college, I had to seek mentors out and earn their trust and respect. It took me a while to figure this out. Fortunately, I had met Professors Peacock and Kohn during my freshman year.

Professor Kohn served as my thesis committee chair, and Professor Peacock was a reader. Their approaches were as different as their personalities. Although Professor Kohn acknowledged a connection between ethnic conflict and economic development, he encouraged me to sharpen the focus of my thesis on young men and ethnic violence instead of poverty alleviation. On the other hand, Professor Peacock helped me flesh out the more abstract framework of participatory development to explain why so many nonprofits were ineffective at engaging youth and preventing violence. He encouraged me to think of CFK as a test of participatory development and a way to take research to action.

My father, much like Professor Kohn, thought that the most interesting issue to research in Kibera was the cause of ethnic violence. He seemed to see CFK as a diversion that could detract from my preparations to lead Marines. Distractions could have lethal consequences in combat, he warned. My father wasn't opposed to international aid. But he saw the intervention we were aspiring to achieve through CFK as just that—aid, a little good in a place that needed a lot. Although my father's ambivalence frustrated me, it also deepened my resolve to make CFK successful.

My mother, on the other hand, was one of CFK's greatest ambassadors from the very beginning. Her support meant a tremendous amount to me. Just like Professor Peacock, Mom was often theoretical. She saw participatory development as an idea worth spreading, a framework that could lead to systemic change and make the world a better place. Mom's enthusiasm connected to her experiences as a young nurse in Peru, where she worked in a small hospital with impoverished nursing assistants. After a year in a remote desert town, she had left behind relevant skills that could be used to help address some of the community's needs.

Up until college, I had taken my parents' active involvement in my schoolwork for granted. From primary school through high school they had read and critiqued nearly every paper I had produced. What they had done was remarkable, and I wanted to honor them. "Dedicated to Drs. T. P. and Donna Schwartz-Barcott," I wrote after the cover page of my thesis. "For twenty-two wonderful years of constant support, encouragement, and intellectual partnership."

Nate laughed when he read the dedication. "Sounds like a light read?" he said. Tracy giggled when she saw it. "I wonder what kind of 'intellectual partnership' you were having as a toddler," she joked.

Professors Kohn and Peacock forwarded the thesis to an external review committee of three other professors with a recommendation for highest honors. I had poured my heart and mind into that thesis, and I was eager to hear the committee's decision. Never before had I worked so hard for so long on a single project. Days later, the committee awarded the thesis highest honors. The recognition bolstered the credibility of what we were about to do in Kibera, and that credibility ended up being more important than I had initially imagined.

Although UNC had provided us with considerable support and let me present my proposal to some of its top donors at Reynolds Plantation, the university legal counsel raised liability concerns about UNC affiliating in any way with a grassroots organization in a "dangerous Third World slum." Professor Peacock had managed to marshal $6,000 of grant money to support CFK. However, the funding had to be routed through the university, and the pushback from the legal counsel threatened to prevent us from accessing it. We needed that grant to reach our $20,000 goal, and the thesis enabled me to build a mini-coalition of senior professors who were willing to lobby the legal counsel on our behalf. With less than a week to spare before graduation, the counsel relented. We were fully funded and ready to go.

NATE AND I sat together in Kenan Stadium at graduation. Looking out into the bleachers of thousands of fellow students in shiny Carolina blue caps and gowns, Nate joked that we looked like an "army of Smurfs on cell phones." Four years earlier I never saw a cell phone on campus. Now it seemed as if every student had one.

The ceremony began and most students continued to chat on their phones, toss beach balls, and wave to their parents as if nothing were happening. The dual culture shock that my mom had warned me about had never quite worn off. My classmates on their phones were being disrespectful. If a beach ball bounced my way, I planned to pop it with my Spyderco. We were adults and all of this pomp and circumstance, which came with a price tag, was for us. The chatter and ball bouncing continued as the main speaker stepped to the podium. Even if we couldn't hear him, we should have shut up. I was waiting for one of those beach balls to bounce my way when Nate tapped my shoulder.

"Interesting speech, huh," he said with mock sincerity. "Really inspiring stuff here."

He cracked me up.

"She's hot," Nate said, looking down the bleachers.

"Who?" All I could see were caps and gowns.

"That one, *safi sana* [very nice]." He pointed to a blow-up doll bouncing with the beach balls. "Wanna ask Tracy to a double-date?"

Nate always knew how to bring it back to earth. He had shaken my sour mood. At the end of the ceremony, James Taylor's "Carolina In My Mind" was playing, and I began to feel nostalgic.

> *In my mind I'm goin' to Carolina*
> *Can't you see the sunshine*
> *Can't you just feel the moonshine*

As excited as we were about CFK, I didn't want to leave Chapel Hill. So many of the clichés about college I had found to be true. It was a place of seemingly unlimited possibilities with communities of thinkers and doers tackling some of the world's largest problems. I loved being a part of it, and I loved being a Tar Heel. Steeped in Southern traditions, UNC inspired a sense of identity that at times felt as intense as what I had experienced in Kibera and in the Marines. Not until my final month, however, did I begin a true immersion in the South by dating Tracy, whose family had been in North Carolina for centuries.

In fact, although I didn't want to admit it, Tracy was the real reason I wasn't ready to leave Chapel Hill. I was falling in love, yet I feared the commitment and the trappings of what I perceived to be an ordinary life. I saw myself as "expeditionary," just like the Marine Corps, our nation's "expeditionary force-in-readiness." It was a point of high pride for me that I could fit my life's belongings into the back of the Green Bean, sleep anywhere, live with little, and be always on the move. I didn't want a relationship to hamper my autonomy. I didn't want it to change my identity.

There was something else, too, something deeper. I was still influenced by my near-death experience as a boy at the pond. I didn't have

career horizons, and the last thing I thought I wanted was marriage or a
family. I knew from my mom and dad what it took to be great parents. I
couldn't imagine that I would ever be ready to make such sacrifices, and
I certainly didn't want to be responsible for a fatherless child. I thought I
could make far greater contributions to society as a roving soldier with
things like CFK on the side than as a father or a husband. If my premonition played out and I was dead by age thirty, my time was running out.

Nine months earlier, when I was driving out of OCS, my mom had
warned me to slow down. It wasn't until I met Tracy that I did. Tracy's
presence alone allowed me to step back, reflect, and enjoy life more completely. No one had ever had such an effect on me. It didn't matter what we
were doing. Even when we were doing nothing—taking a nap, driving
somewhere, walking across the campus greens, sitting in silence—we were
content. We were happy just being together. This attraction transcended
the physical and brought with it a new sense of belonging that I didn't
know how to interpret, and couldn't resist.

Tracy's strength was reflected in her own life journey. When she was
sixteen years old, she decided that she was going to be a clinical psychologist after reading about the profession in magazines. Ever since then she
had pursued her goal, graduating as valedictorian of her high school
class, earning Phi Beta Kappa at UNC, and enrolling in a Ph.D. program. She had a large, loving family, though her parents were somewhat
disengaged from her work. She never complained about money and often
offered to split expenses when we went out. Yet she was so saddled with
debt that she could have qualified for food stamps.

One night after some hard drinking Nate asked me to describe Tracy in
one word. I thought about it for a moment and replied, "Angelic." Drunk or
sober, I had never used that word to describe a person. Nate raised his eyebrows skeptically. Seeing the sincerity in my face, he withheld judgment
until meeting her the following weekend. Afterward, he advised me to "do
whatever it takes to hold on to that *msichana mrembo* [beautiful girl]."

I was torn. A part of me was saying let it go, and I suspected Tracy had
similar feelings. She knew I grew up dreaming of being a Marine, and
she didn't want to become attached to a guy whom she would never see.
Yet the attraction between us was too powerful to ignore or cast away, and
in the end it didn't feel like a choice. We had to try. We agreed to give
it a shot, and the more I thought about it, the more I tried to convince

myself that it was possible to have it all. If I could be based at Camp Lejeune, North Carolina, as an East Coast Marine, then we could still see each other on weekends when I wasn't deployed overseas. And maybe the deployments wouldn't be that difficult. It was peacetime after all.

OUR MARINE CORPS commissioning ceremony contrasted sharply with our large, distracted graduation. It took place on a cloudless, Carolina-blue day. The dome-shaped Old Well, our university's icon, stood to our side flanked by beds of pink and white azaleas. My uniform was so tight I walked with my stomach clenched. My neck pulsed beneath the midnight blue choker-collar. My mother, Tracy, Major Boothby, and the friends and family of the two other soon-to-be second lieutenants formed a half-moon around us as my father read me the Oath of Office.

"I, state your name, do solemnly swear . . ." Dad stated in his booming bass.

"I, Rye Barcott, do solemnly swear . . ." I stood at attention in my dress blues, eyes fixed on the jagged scar across my father's cheek. Thirty-five years earlier a bullet from a Vietcong machine gun entered and somehow exited without chipping a tooth.

We continued, my father, then me, stating the verses passed down by legions of Americans who had served in uniform. As I repeated my father's words, I felt a new responsibility to carry on that martial legacy, the legacy that stretched from the Revolutionary War to the Persian Gulf. It was the legacy of men and women of arms who gave up some of their freedoms to safeguard those of their countrymen and -women, born and unborn.

" . . . that I will support and defend the Constitution of the United States against all enemies, foreign and domestic; that I will bear true faith and allegiance to the same; that I take this obligation freely, without any mental reservation or purpose of evasion; and that I will well and faithfully discharge the duties of the office on which I am about to enter.

"So help me God." My father whacked me on the shoulder, smiled, and pulled Mom and me into his embrace. When the cameras finished clicking, we joined a conversation with other parents. All three fathers in the group were Marines, and each father led his son in the oath. One of them, a lieutenant colonel, shared his swearing-in story with us, when decades earlier he had walked into a captain's office in civilian clothes, raised his hand, and read the Oath of Office. That was the extent of it back then. The colonel said he was pleased that our own swearing-in ceremony was so much more personal by comparison.

Afterward, my parents hosted a small lunch reception as a graduation gift. It was a gracious way of expressing appreciation to a handful of my closest advisers from the Marine Corps and college. One of my mentors, Colonel T. C. Greenwood, drove down from Washington to make the event. We had met through my dad, who had served with Colonel Greenwood's father in Vietnam. An infantry officer, Colonel Greenwood had a scrappy Irish look and the special blend of toughness and compassion that was the hallmark of great Marine officers. In his current assignment, he was a director at the White House National Security Council. He was the first active-duty Marine to encourage me to learn about nongovernmental organizations (NGOs), which he called "nonstate actors." Colonel Greenwood believed that NGOs had important but often misunderstood relationships with the military. He thought that CFK would make me a better and more informed officer.

As my parents stood and offered a toast, I looked around the room and thought about how lucky I was to have such a group of mentors. It dawned on me that I had received far more than I had given. I hadn't begun to "pay it forward," and I doubted I could ever give back anywhere close to the amount of wisdom and love I had received from these men and women. First and foremost in that group were my parents.

It wasn't until we were back at the hotel that my father approached me in the parking lot next to a forest of Southern pines. Mom was taking a nap. Dad opened the cargo hatch of the woody, my parents' aging wood-paneled Dodge Caravan, and turned to me. I braced myself for a lecture. Instead, he told me that it had been a special day for him, and that he hoped I would be able to keep a critical mind, wherever the Marine Corps took me. He hoped that I wouldn't allow myself or my men to be taken advantage of by others, no matter their rank or powers of persuasion.

As he turned to remove something from the cargo, a line from the Oath of Office flashed to mind: *I will support and defend the Constitution of the United States against all enemies.* Our oath pledged allegiance to a body of ideas and a way of government, not to an individual or an ideology.

With Mom and Peaches (as a puppy) at home in Rhode Island.

With my father and Lieutenant Colonel R. J. O'Leary, a combat veteran of three wars who was one of my first mentors, on the Padlock Ranch in Wyoming, 1990.

With Looseyia, my parents, and Dad's cane at the Rekero Camp, Masai Mara, summer 1993.

Ali Khamis Alijab giving Mom her first tour near the west end of Kibera, with the Ngong Forest in the background, summer 2001.

In Dan's shack with my dad's duffel bag, June 2000.

Baba Chris's daughter at the entrance to the compound where Dan's shack was located (*Jason Arthurs*)

Nate "Otis" Nelson making friends in Kibera, summer 2001.

Rashid Seif (far left) at CFK's first war on trash, summer 2001.

CFK's first soccer tournament in Kibera, where thousands of residents crammed along the sidelines to watch, summer 2001.

Change of command with Captain Mike Dubrule (bottom left), battalion commander Lieutenant Colonel R. E. Anders, and Captain Joe Burke on the field outside our company in Camp Lejeune, June 2005.

On patrol in Fallujah, February 2006.

With Second Lieutenant Peter Dixon and Salim at Peter's commissioning ceremony in Chapel Hill, May 2006.

Kash, 2002.

Tabitha (third from right) on a home-based care visit to a patient's shack, 2003.

Salim welcoming then senator Obama to CFK in Kibera, August 2006.

The beautiful bride,
Tracy Barcott.

Left to right: Kim Chapman (CFK board chair,
2002–2008), CFK volunteer Aaron Charlop-
Powers, Salim, and Professor Jennifer Coffman
(CFK board chair, 2009–present) at our wedding
at the Peacocks' home, Chapel Hill, July 2007.

ith Salim on the top floor of the new Tabitha Clinic after the ethnic clashes of 2008.

ith Tabitha's oldest son, Kevin, and Tabitha's best friend, Jane Atieno. The new
bitha Clinic rises up behind Kevin, March 2010.

Tabitha Atieno Festo, 2002. *(Brenda Sizemore)*

I interpreted my father's advice as a way of saying that the nation commissioned us as officers to think and to be discerning with our leadership.

Dad faced me holding his Mameluke sword, palms-up, the flat edge of the blade resting against his heavily calloused hands. Derived from sabers of Ottoman warriors, the sword's silver blade glistened in the late afternoon light. I fingered its flat edge as a flood of emotions swelled over me. My father was not a warmonger. He even disliked the word *warrior*, which he considered to be "belligerent" and "self-inflating." But I viewed him as a warrior. He was a warrior who loved peace and knew about unnecessary wars after having fought in one of them. Flawed leadership, however, did not take away from the need for a strong defense in a volatile world. Peace had to be guarded with a sword and citizens who would willingly put their lives on the line.

Dad's mouth was twitching the way it did the only two times I ever saw him tear up. He gestured to me with a nod, turned, and walked away into the forest of tall Southern pines. I sheathed the sword. He had done his part, and now it was time to do mine.

CHAPTER EIGHT

Things Fall Apart

Kibera, Kenya

MAY 2001

WE WERE ON OUR FLIGHT TO KENYA. Nate and I sipped gin and tonics, told tales, and toasted Hemingway, Kibera, and our future partners—Taib's KIYESA, Jumba's micro-credit program for youth, and Elizabeth's nursery school. We had funding, a board of directors, an office at UNC, business cards, and tax-exempt status from the IRS. We had a vision and a plan. We were good, I thought to myself, and flagged the stewardess for another round, real good.

"Ya know what? We need a motto," Nate suggested on his third or fourth drink flying somewhere over the Sahara.

"Yeah, a motto. Good call. Maybe something in Swahili, like *tuko pamoja*, or somethin'." I had liked that phrase, which translates to "we are together," ever since the time I first heard it during one of my research interviews.

Nate wasn't feeling it. "It's okay, but how about somethin' edgier."

"What do ya mean?"

"I mean, somethin' that describes what we're about, but with a punch to it."

I leaned back and thought about Nate's challenge. What words could characterize what we were doing?

"Participatory development." I laughed.

"Yeah, that's horrible. Good vision, bad motto."

"Youth empowerment?"

"Lame." Nate rolled his eyes and faked a yawn.

The stewardess delivered another round. *What if the motto was based on our style, the way we rolled, our "battle rhythm," as we called it in the Marines? What words could capture that?*

"I got it, man," I came back after a minute of hard concentration. "I freakin' got it." It was a phrase I had heard at OCS.

"Yeah, what?"

"This is good. You ready?"

"Well, you've set a pretty low bar so far. Send it."

"Speed and intensity."

"Hah! I love it." Nate slapped his knee, "It's perfect. That's exactly it. Speed and intensity. It's like the story of your life."

"Our life."

"No, definitely not."

"Well, for the next three months."

"Yeah, okay, I can dig that." He threw me a *gota*.

That was it. We had three months. At the moment, it sounded like a while. If we could do all that we had accomplished in the United States as students, I could only imagine how much we could get done with full-time "speed and intensity" in Kibera. At that point, the plan was simple. As I had done the previous summer, we would stash our gear at Oluoch and Elizabeth's place in Fort Jesus and use their house as a fallback when we weren't sleeping in the slum. After a couple days catching our bearings, we would reconnect with Taib and Jumba. We'd provide advice and a small amount of funding and help them develop their inter-ethnic youth empowerment programs. On the side, we could provide some funding to Elizabeth as she built her nursery school, which she decided to name the Carolina Academy. That was it. At the end of our three months, CFK would go away in Kenya and possibly remain as a small organization with an office at UNC to fund-raise for additional support for our Kenyan partners.

BY THE TIME the gin wore off we were in Fort Jesus. The first twenty-four hours on the ground was like déjà vu. Elizabeth and Oluoch prepared a feast of *ugali*, *sukuma wiki*, and beef stew. They asked Nate about his family, and they updated us on the soap opera of Kenyan politics. Only one politician ever did anything right in Oluoch's opinion: Raila Odinga, whom Oluoch called the leader of the Luos. By that time, Raila, who was known by his first name, had been the member of Parliament for the constituency that included Fort Jesus and Kibera for nine years. Oluoch sounded defensive when Nate asked if Raila had done much for Kibera: "Of course. A lot. They've even named a village after him."

"A village?"

"Yes, that's what I said. A new village across the river. They call it Raila."

"Across from Gatwekera?" I asked in reference to the village where I had spent most of my time the previous summer. I recalled seeing a few houses on the other side of the river, though it sounded as if they must have multiplied dramatically over the previous year. Each "village" in Kibera housed tens of thousands of residents.

"Yes, yes, that's right."

"Have you been there?" Nate asked. "To Raila Village?"

"No, of course not. I've no need to go down there." He swung his arm out toward the direction of the slum. Oluoch wasn't aware of how much his comments bothered me. I was having the same visceral reaction to him and his patronizing attitude as I had experienced the previous summer. I shifted the subject to soccer, which Oluoch always liked to discuss. We ended the evening without an incident.

The next morning we met Jane as she arrived to work. Jane hugged me as if I were a long-lost friend. "And this is Otieno. People call him Otis," I introduced Nate.

"Then you're my brother," Jane smiled, wide and full. "I'm Atieno, Jane Atieno. Welcome, Otis. Welcome to Kibera."

"It's been too long, Jane. How's Kibera?" I asked.

"Kibera is Kibera. Not much has changed, but I can say we're pushing. Oh, it's good you've returned home. Omosh, you know, me, I knew you'd come back. Will you be staying with us down there again?"

"Of course."

"It is good!" she exclaimed, reminding me of the visit I had taken to her ten-by-ten shortly before I left during my first summer. Her shack was neatly furnished, the walls covered by sheets. It had some luxury items, too, such as a black-and-white television, which was tuned to the World Wrestling Federation when I had stopped by. I had seen far poorer conditions in Kibera. Yet I was floored that Jane and her husband managed to raise four adolescent sons and a daughter in such a small space. In classic Kibera understatement, Jane acknowledged that it was "not easy" when I asked her about it. Then she laughed. Somehow, Jane could always laugh. There was something deeply uplifting in her spirit, something marvelous.

As we walked to Dan's house, Nate reflected on our brief encounter with Jane, "That smile of hers, it's unbelievable. She's unbelievable. I don't know her and I already love her." His words captured the way I had felt when I first met Jane, and it was a feeling that would only grow stronger with time. Sometimes you can just tell when you're in the presence of a special soul.

Eyes followed us up Kibera Drive toward one of the slum's largest entry points. Adrenaline blasted to my head. I transitioned to my old style, quickly finding a groove: exaggerated arm swings, long strides, Sheng greetings to strangers. Nate was a natural. After a few minutes he, too, was in the rhythm. We were a duo. We didn't stop until we reached the entry point, and there, suddenly, Kibera was in front of us, the big brown salamander, a sea of humanity. I assumed my reaction would be different the second time around. It wasn't. I stood there with Nate, silent for a moment, awestruck by the sheer magnitude of the place.

"Wowsers," Nate reacted, "there it is. It's even bigger than I imagined. This is nuts."

"What do ya mean?"

"I mean, what we're doin' is crazy."

I had never thought about it in such a way. Yet at that moment I felt the same sense of apprehension that I had experienced the first time I stepped into Kibera with Dan. What we were doing was not smart. Maybe I was just lucky to have made it out of Kibera in one piece during my first summer? We stood there, dumbfounded, looking like *washamba*, "farmers" in the big city.

"Nate"—I turned and looked him in the eye—"you ready for this?"

"Can't turn back now."

"Let's do it."

We stepped across the tracks, throwing out *gotas* and Sheng as I traced the route back to Dan's shack. The main routes hadn't changed, though the side alleys had shifted as new shacks swallowed old walkways.

I was feeling a high until I spotted the coffin maker.

Nate saw it too. "Is that what I think it is?"

"Yeah, man."

"The coffins are so small." He reacted.

"*Watoto.*" It was easier to identify in Swahili the chilling reality that building coffins for kids was a good business in Kibera.

In a sump of sewage a short distance from the coffin maker, we spotted what appeared to be a bloated baby with bluish white skin. We stopped in front of it, stunned. On closer inspection, it was a dead puppy floating in the waste. Not far away a little boy played with a plastic bottle cap in the mud. I looked at Nate. His face had lost its color. We didn't say anything. Kibera. I hadn't expected to be so affected again, but there I was torn by a maelstrom of emotions: happy to finally be back, sad for the children, disgusted by the filth, and angry at the injustice.

We walked on, quiet and somber until we approached the Mad Lion Base. Snapping back into my Kibera act, I fist-bumped my way down the alley saying mindless things in Sheng with Nate by my side. The lines worked invariably: to the men hanging out in front of a butcher shop, "*Tu-napenda nyamchom ya punda*" (We like roasted donkey), to the *mama* selling vegetables, "*Tunakula kichwa ya samaki tu*" (We only eat fish head), to the kid shouting "*Mzungu! Mzungu!*" (White guy! White guy!), "*Si wagoso. Sisi ni charlie wa mtaani*" (We aren't whiteys. We are Charlies—homeboys—of the street). Even the hardest, most drugged-out men laughed. Many of them, we would later learn, pitied us and thought we were insane.

Baba Chris welcomed us with a warm embrace at Dan's old plot. As soon as we entered Dan's shack, Nate and I collapsed on his sofa.

"What the hell just happened?" Nate asked.

"Yeah, I know, nice job. That was intense."

Nate sighed. "Is that what it's always like?"

"Pretty much."

"It's like we're actors, only our lives are on the line. I mean, I'm pumped, and at the same time I'm totally exhausted."

Dan smiled as we spoke about our walk. He looked good, and he had reason to be upbeat. Dan was about to get married. He was earning enough money in his accounting job to "afford a wife" and move out of

Kibera. After five years in the slum, Dan had stepped into a new economic class. He had held on to the shack, but he now lived in a ten-by-ten in Fort Jesus. It was a different world. He paid taxes and had running water, legal electricity, hard walls, and relatively quiet nights. Dan was the Kibera dream. He had moved to Nairobi as an eighteen-year-old in search of opportunity, and through hard work, luck, and skill, he was making it. Many youth had Dan's strengths, but few had his good fortune. Most never escaped the grind of hand-to-mouth existence.

Dan didn't forget his roots. He continued to lead a small community group to help other young leaders in Kibera, and he gladly offered to help Nate and me get started with CFK. It seemed like a good setup. Dan had secured his shack so Nate and I could spend the summer there for $13 a month, fully furnished. I knew the area and could trust the neighbors such as Baba Chris, although many were new, including the people in the shack at the end of the plot where Vanessa had lived. No one seemed to know what had happened to the stoic grandmother who had cared for her. One day she just disappeared, and a new family moved in.

Nevertheless, the familiarity of the place made it feel like the right fit, if only there were enough space. Nate, I learned on the flight over, was a loud snorer. Really loud, "like Homer Simpson," he joked, referring to the legendary cartoon character whose snores rattled the walls. We couldn't sleep in the same shack. We needed to find a separate place for him, preferably with a youth leader we could trust and who didn't mind snoring. Dan recommended we meet up with an acquaintance of his, John "Kash" Kanyua, a twenty-two-year-old soccer star who lived in a shack near the river with a make-shift gym where youth liked to work out. Dan mentioned that Kash coached an under-twelve soccer team, had a good reputation in the community, and might know of a place where Nate could stay. Dan proposed that we meet Kash for chai at the Mugumeno Motherland Hotel the following morning. However, Nate and I were eager to get a workout.

"Let's just meet him at his gym," Nate suggested.

Dan looked at us skeptically. He wasn't a lifter, so he didn't understand that there was nothing like a good lift to bond new acquaintances.

"*SUKUMA*, PUSH. *SUKUMA*, PUSH." Nate spotted Kash the following morning.

"Humph-humph. Er." Kash exhaled and forced the homemade bar with four slabs of cement off his thick chest. He had close-cropped hair, a chiseled jaw, and Hollywood looks.

Nate reached for the bar to guide it back to the rickety rack. It was Kash's tenth rep with more than two hundred pounds. Kash foiled Nate's attempt to relieve him, lowering the bar evenly back down to his chest for a final rep.

"*Pata kubwa!*" Nate shouted. "Get big!"

Kash strained and struggled, his back flat on the chipped wood bench, slowly pushing the bar up until his elbows locked. He didn't need help. He racked the weight and rose with a grin.

"Your turn, Omosh."

I squeezed by him and took his place on the bench. There was not much room in Kash's gym, a tiny triangle of dirt next to a flooded *choo* swarming with flies as big as thumbnails. A strand of rusted barbed wire separated the gym from another row of mud shacks. One of Kash's dozen neighbors had installed the wire when he had discovered that people were sneaking into their *choo*. There were more churches than *choo*s in Kibera, Kash observed. The poorest of the poor defecated in plastic bags and tossed them into open sumps. Called flying toilets, the bags resembled miniature parachutes and slowly made their way to the river and the Nairobi Dam, a cesspool at the far east end of Kibera that once supported the docks of the colonial Nairobi Sailing Club.

I hit my max on eight reps. I was surprised I couldn't match Kash's eleven. Nate bested me with nine. Pleased with his performance, Kash stacked the concrete slabs and metal bars so that they wouldn't block the way for someone dashing to the *choo*. He escorted us around the corner to his ten-by-ten.

"How many people do you sleep with?" Nate teased Kash about the size of his bed, which was draped with a silky pink comforter.

The bed fit four people, Kash said, but his shack was in such an undesirable location near the river that friends rarely stayed at his place.

"It's the only bed in Kibera big enough to fit Nate," I joked. "And pink's his favorite color."

"Yeah, pink, it's nice. Reminds me of flowers. You're welcome to stay here by the way. Me, I don't mind," Kash offered.

"Kash, do you snore?" I asked.

"'Cause my snores rattle the walls." Nate laughed.

Kash wasn't a snorer, though he seemed strangely intrigued by the challenge of sleeping next to one.

"If I move in, I'll have to help you decorate this place Kash, ol' buddy," Nate slapped him on the arm and gestured to the walls, which were barren with the exception of a small mosaic featuring a Siamese cat. Not much else was in Kash's shack apart from his big bed, battery-powered radio, and dog-eared French textbook. Kash sounded upset as he explained that he once had more furniture.

"I had more stuff before the rains came." He pointed to his tin roof. "When the rains come, it's very loud. It covers the sound, you see. Nobody wants to be in here then. The rains bring mud and thugs."

Kash's comment reminded me of a lesson from a military exercise, when I attempted to lead a squad of midshipmen through a forest at night. We were soaking wet and shivering when Major Boothby circled us up. Rain, cold, and night were the ideal conditions for Marines, he explained. The rain covered the sound of movement, and bad weather always brought out "the human factors of war." "Hit the enemy when their will to fight is at its lowest point," Major Boothby instructed. "Hit 'em when all they can think about is a hot meal and a warm bed."

Thugs had crashed into Kash's room in the middle of the long rains. They held him on his bed with the tip of a machete pressed into one of his nostrils, and they took everything he owned, except the bed and the French textbook. The fear was not the worst part, Kash said. It was the sense of betrayal. Kash only welcomed his closest friends into his room, and the thugs had known the precise locations of his two most prized possessions: a stereo and a soccer trophy.

"Man, that's intense," I reacted. "You sure it's safe here for Nate to stay?" Nate looked as if he had the same question on his mind.

"Yeah, it's fine man." Kash looked at Nate. "'Cause the rains are over and thugs, they won't know what to think of a big *mzungu*. They'll fear you."

"You found the thugs who robbed you?" I asked.

"No, but I haven't stopped looking."

"Does it ever make you regret your decision to come here?" Nate asked.

"What do you mean?"

"Here, I mean, to Kibera, to the slum." Earlier Kash had told us that he'd left his parents and came to Nairobi as a teenager in search of more opportunities.

"Depends. Life here sucks." He kicked a pebble across his dirt floor. "We live like animals. But it depends. It depends 'cause I don't know how the story will end."

Kash didn't have a formal job. He sold things periodically for income. It was vague, but I was familiar with how informal work ebbed and flowed, and I was captivated when he explained how he taught himself French. Kash studied the language every night from his textbook in hopes that he could one day qualify for a job as a flight steward with Air France. The benefits of such a job sounded so great they were difficult for him to comprehend: health insurance, paid vacation, salary, and a pension. In addition to his airline ambitions, Kash dreamed about soccer. It was his passion, and like most serious players, he aspired to one day compete in a stadium with thousands of fans. He also realized the power of sport to organize and inspire youth. For that reason he spent much of his free time coaching a team of boys called the Slumtotos.

"Do Slumtotos compete in KIYESA?" Nate asked.

"What?"

"KIYESA, you know, Taib's thing."

"Oh, yeah. It doesn't do much."

"But Taib says it's the only tournament," I interjected.

"Taib's full of shit," Kash reacted. "There are lots of tournaments like his, and they all charge the fees. They're money making. My kids, we can't afford."

"Fees?" Taib had never mentioned fees to me.

"Yeah, few thousand shillings per team." It was the equivalent of $30 to $50.

"Figures," Nate grunted, as I asked myself if I could still trust Taib.

"You guys don't need Taib," Kash challenged us. "Just do it yourselves."

A COUPLE OF days later Nate and I met at the Mugumeno Motherland Hotel to brainstorm over a steaming plate of pilau, our favorite Swahili dish, rice cooked in a seasoned broth with bits of beef. We had been in

Kibera for less than a week. The news that Taib might not be respected by the youth in the community surprised me more than Nate. A politician was a politician in his book, and he assumed every Kenyan politician was corrupt. He was probably right, though I remained hopeful that some government leaders took the high ground and put the public interest above their own narrow ambitions.

"So what do you think of Kash's idea?" Nate asked.

"Which one?" I shoveled a fistful of pilau into my mouth.

"To start our own thing."

"How would we?"

"With leaders on the ground like Kash." Nate's observation struck a chord. The whole reason we formed CFK was to empower local leaders. KIYESA could only bring different ethnic groups together to prevent violence and create new role models if it was well led. We decided we needed to gather more information by talking to youth individually and holding a couple of focus group discussions about sports and development.

Perhaps I should have spoken with Taib about our efforts and directly raised some of the concerns we were hearing in the community about KIYESA. We hadn't written off working with him. We still thought the greatest impact we could have in our short time with our limited funds would be to help build the capacity of a preexisting organization, not start something new.

Taib called Oluoch to express his displeasure when he learned that we were back in Kibera and had not yet consulted with him. Oluoch maintained a transactional relationship with Taib. Although I didn't realize it at the time, it was in Oluoch's interests to have KIYESA dropped from our agenda so that we might spend more time and resources on Elizabeth's Carolina Academy. The day after we had arrived, Oluoch had asked me for a $1,500 loan to purchase a used minibus. He intended to start a busing business. Although the business would not be connected with the Carolina Academy, Nate and I had assumed Elizabeth knew about his request. We trusted Elizabeth and didn't want to potentially damage our relationship by saying no to Oluoch. Shortly after his request, I lent him the money with a handwritten agreement that pledged repayment within a month.

"What's that *mzungu* doing?" Taib allegedly shouted at Oluoch over the phone, "I run soccer in Kibera. Nothing happens without me!"

Trusting Oluoch's summary of the conversation, we thought Taib sounded like a hothead, not what we were hoping for in a partner and community leader. We decided that we needed to keep our distance.

SIX MONTHS BEFORE Nate and I had arrived in Kibera, I had sent $400 to Jumba to launch Jumba's junior credit scheme. It was the easiest $400 I would ever raise. My mother had given it to me for Christmas. We now wanted to see the results of the investment. Yet every time we brought it up in conversation, Jumba detoured to discuss macroscopic issues about poverty and economic development. As a college student, I had enjoyed hearing his wide-ranging opinions on such topics. But now we were trying to get something done. Just when Nate and I began to question if we should continue to work with Jumba, he introduced us to one of his field officers, a community organizer who helped us mobilize a dozen youth representatives for our focus group discussions on sports and youth leadership in Kibera.

Every one of the youth representatives knew the word *development*. It conjured up a mix of notions ranging from wealth, privilege, and corruption to jobs, education, and health care. We told the youth representatives that we had no money and wanted to "brainstorm." Most of them were familiar with that term too. It was another favorite word of the development community, and Kibera was a source of no small supply of community-assessment surveys for well-heeled NGOs. Most residents assumed nothing would come of these surveys, though were often content with them as long as participants received some type of simple compensation—sodas, lunch stipends, something.

We didn't want to be the white faces leading the project. If CFK was going to work, it would have to be locally led. We tried to convince Kash to lead the workshop, but he refused for reasons that weren't clear. I should have realized that if Kash was apprehensive to lead, others would be as well. Kash was one of the most self-assured guys I had met in Kibera. It was part of what had attracted us to him as a prospective leader.

THE FOLLOWING MORNING we held our focus group discussion on a hill overlooking Kibera. The first few youth representatives showed up looking shy and hesitant. One of them walked away as soon as he heard that we didn't have sodas. The other representatives sat quietly on the short grass around our flip chart. They laughed at our Swahili and silly jokes as we made introductions.

"How can sports be improved in Kibera?" I asked.

No one said a word. I called on Kash for his opinion.

"We need more fields and supplies." A few of the participants nodded in agreement, then silence returned. The group never warmed up. Nate and I had to solicit every response.

We felt dejected as we walked back through Kibera. We had nose-dived into something we knew nothing about. Nate had read a lot of Malcolm X and Che Guevara. I had once worked in a soup kitchen in Rhode Island. Neither one of us had studied social work, let alone had any real expertise in it.

We knew we weren't being patient enough. Community organizing took time. Yet we only had three months. The first meeting with youth leaders took up the better part of a day, not to mention the time that went into planning it. Hustling up and down Kibera recruiting youth representatives had consumed much of the previous week. We didn't know what to do next. Perhaps we might get some assistance from a community organizer named Semaj Johnson who was about to join us? I had met Semaj through a mutual Kenyan friend, and, after a dozen phone calls, he had agreed to spend a month with us that summer before he started a new job in the South Bronx.

"Let's just table the sports until Semaj gets here and focus instead on the Carolina Academy and Jumba's youth micro-credit program," I proposed to Nate.

"You think Jumba will work?" he asked skeptically.

Nate had a good point. We needed to find out for sure what had happened to the $400. We decided we would press Jumba to see his books the next day.

"AH, YES, THE books, they are here." Jumba stuck his index finger in the air as if he had made a profound point and added his trademark pause in between thoughts, "Ehhhh."

"Well, can I see them?" I asked.

"Sure, that I can arrange. Why don't we get some chai, ehhhh?"

"Now?" Nate asked. "Can we see them right now?"

"Yes, yes, my assistant she can arrange while we have chai." Jumba appeared unaffected by the directness of Nate's question. Jumba was either a really good liar, or he had the books and had been too busy to pull them up previously. Most of his accounting records were kept in the adjacent room in hard copy. Jumba had an old Apple computer like my mother's. It didn't have a basic spreadsheet program, and we were only talking about a $400 initiative in an organization that we believed disbursed tens of thousands of dollars of loans each year. Maybe we just needed to cut Jumba some slack?

We braced ourselves for another long meeting as we ordered our chai and Jumba launched into a soliloquy on development. We tried to direct him back to the plans being made to ramp up the junior ghetto-credit scheme.

"What size loan would be most appropriate to start with for youth?" Nate asked.

"Well, you see, that one, that one's a tricky one, ehhhh. It will require some studies. I can't be sure precisely the amount but I do know this thing, this thing will create jobs, much needed jobs. You've seen it, isn't it? Kibera needs, ehhhh, jobs."

Around and around we went. We were there nearly two hours. Finally I asked him about how he would target youth for the program. Jumba launched into a tangent about a group of youth who ran a program inside the Nairobi Dam.

"Inside the dam?" Nate interjected. We must have misheard him. Clogged by tall reeds of hyacinth, the Nairobi Dam was Kibera's cesspool. No one could run business inside that rancid, disease-infested swamp.

Jumba, however, didn't pick up on our surprised expressions. He went on talking about a youth group running businesses and a fitness club inside the dam. Exasperated, Nate pressed his palm to his forehead as Jumba carried on for another hour. We never saw the books or got to the bottom of the $400 mystery.

"He's full of more crap than the Nairobi Dam," Nate concluded as we waited for a *matatu* minibus to take us back to the other side of Kibera. "At least we never have to meet him again."

I had quoted Jumba in my honors thesis. I had trusted him. Jumba dressed modestly and lived in Kibera, or so I thought. I should have pressed to see his books much earlier, and I should have visited his home. Home visits always told me a lot about a person. It was another rookie mistake, and Nate was right. We couldn't keep investing time and energy in someone we didn't trust.

FEELING DOWN, WE returned to Fort Jesus for dinner to talk about Carolina Academy with Elizabeth. Oluoch was at his favorite bar, a tin pub called Garage. To that point, we hadn't spoken much with Elizabeth about details, such as costs and timelines. In the back of my mind, the school was the third priority. Although it would be the first Montessori nursery school in Kibera, it was the least innovative of the three projects, and I believed it was the easiest to complete. It was a one-time start-up investment. We simply needed to help Elizabeth build a school and then let her run it.

We had assumed Elizabeth would be ready as soon as she had the capital. We imagined she had a plan with the same depth and detail as the outline Dan had prepared in advance of meeting with me the previous summer. We were wrong. I was wrong. Elizabeth had nothing, and the only thing she seemed to have thought about was who to hire as the school's housemaid and cook. It was as if Elizabeth was still waiting to see if I was serious, and her reticence actually made sense when I thought about it. *Why bet on a college kid delivering on a promise to help?*

While I tried to understand her perspective, I couldn't help but think about how Elizabeth watched television for two hours every night after dinner. *Why wouldn't she use this time to do something productive?* The question gnawed at me. I didn't consider that I was young, energetic, and in the middle of an adventure. I rarely felt the need for downtime. Elizabeth was old enough to be my mother and worked all day in the same routine she had followed for thirty years.

Brushing aside my frustrations, I proposed that the next step would be to make a timeline and a budget to spend $4,000 of CFK seed capital to build the Carolina Academy. Elizabeth smiled and started speaking affectionately about her vision to offer high-quality education to "the little ones." I could feel her goodness and warmth as she spoke. Yet I couldn't help question if I had made a mistake with Elizabeth too. *Did she have what it took?*

IT WOULD'VE BEEN good if Nate and I had spoken more after dinner that night. Instead we stepped off to return to Kibera. The slum's character changed with the sunset. By nine P.M., most residents locked themselves into their homes. By ten P.M., the thugs were out en masse, roving the alleyways for targets. It was nearly eleven.

We moved quickly and didn't speak, our hearts thumping inside our chests. I kept a hammer in my backpack with the zipper pulled down slightly so that I could remove it quickly.

Kash met us midway, near the Mugumeno Motherland Hotel. We exchanged *gotas* and he escorted Nate down the steep, slippery path toward his shack by the river. I dropped down a narrow alley and pounded on the thin sheet-metal door for Baba Chris to let me into the compound.

"*Omosh hapa,*" I repeated until he rose from bed and unlocked the gate.

"Welcome, Omosh," Baba Chris said with a smile and sleepy eyes. A wave of relief came over me. I was safe.

This sense of relief vanished as soon as I unlocked Dan's shack and thought about the day's events. I doubted Nate shared my frustration. He maintained a more realistic outlook of the probabilities that CFK could succeed. He had come to Kibera for many reasons: to make a difference, adventure, our new but strong friendship, and because he didn't have anything else lined up. He didn't know what he would do for full-time employment when he returned to the United States, and we didn't talk about it. I had no doubt that Nate would figure it out. He was one of the most perceptive friends I had. His gentle soul and big heart enabled him to connect with youth no matter how shy, tough, or afraid they might be. His presence lifted spirits.

I sat on Dan's hard bed with my head in my hands. The tin wall was thinner than a book cover. It shook with sound. Pressure mounted inside my head. Again, I craved silence and thought about slapping the flimsy wall and shouting at the crying baby next door.

Please, baby, please be quiet.

Everything was falling apart. KIYESA and Taib. Jumba. Probably even Elizabeth. They were all disappointments. I was a disappointment. I thought I was a good judge of character; I thought I knew enough about Kibera to identify the most promising programs and leaders. That, after all, was the entire premise of CFK. Find local leaders fighting problems and support them. Yet within two weeks our team had collapsed.

Why hadn't I seen through Jumba and Taib during my first summer? If I screwed up with them, how could we ever hope to find the great leaders in Kibera? Was it even possible?

Nate and I would never be a part of the community. We were young *wazungu*. Residents spoke to us through a kaleidoscope of hopes, dreams, fears, and motivations that we could never fully comprehend, no matter how long we "lived" in Kibera. A toxic thought entered my mind: Maybe we should just quit. We could spend the rest of the summer looking for one good community-based group, give them a chunk of money, and return home.

At one level, the idea of downsizing CFK's ambitions was liberating. It was also excruciating. We told a lot of people in the United States about the vision. Many of those people had invested in its promise as much as they had invested in me personally. I felt a commitment to our donors that was more powerful than I ever imagined given the relatively small amounts of money they had given. Yet their actions mattered more than the amounts.

I could hear Staff Sergeant Sweeney shouting in my face after I fell from the rope at OCS: "God hates a quitter." Marines don't quit. I was ashamed I was even considering the idea. I thought about what my father might say. He would want to know the facts. He would ask me about our overall objectives. Then I suspected he would tell me to stick to it, if for no other reason than the fact that Nate and I still had two and a half months in Kenya.

The thought of my father prompted something more profound: At the core of our philosophy was the conviction that some of the poor have the solutions to the problems they faced. Many youth in Kibera were eager to seize opportunities and lead the fight against poverty and violence. In the end, it was their fight, not ours. But we could help. If we quit, we failed them and we failed the vision.

"Youth are the present and the future leaders."

A Kenyan youth leader, someone I respected, had told me this. I shut my eyes and tried to remember who had said it. It bothered me that I couldn't remember who it was. It was someone I admired, someone with whom we needed to consult immediately. It was someone who could restore my faith in what was possible.

CHAPTER NINE

Messiahs

Nairobi, Kenya

JUNE 2001

"YOUTH ARE THE PRESENT AND THE FUTURE LEADERS."

It took me the entire night to remember that those words belonged to Salim Mohamed, the charming, gritty, engaging leader who ran the information and communication department at MYSA, the Mathare Youth Sports Association. Our contact had been sporadic since the previous summer. When I had mentioned KIYESA in e-mails months before returning to Kibera, Salim had rebuked me. "Oh, that politician thing. Not for me," he had written. The subtext I had missed in his response was that KIYESA didn't exist for the youth. Young people in the slums quickly learned to size up the self-interest behind individual actions. It was a survival mechanism, a skill honed on instinct.

It had been two weeks and I hadn't yet reached out to Salim. I was worried that he might not be eager to meet. Although I still felt a bond from our first meeting when I had revealed that I was a Marine in training, I doubted Salim remembered me as anything more than another idealistic foreigner, a *mzungu* visiting MYSA to learn something more about the world and himself.

At eight A.M. I punched Salim's number into my cell phone as a hot cup of chai from the Mugumeno Motherland Hotel warmed my other hand.

"Hallo. Who's speaking?"

"It's Rye, Rye Barcott with Carolina for Kibera, but people call me Omosh."

"Omosh, I've been waiting for your call."

"Really?"

"Of course."

"That's great! I'm here with my friend Nate, who goes by Otis. Can we meet up?"

"Omosh and Otis, that's a funny one. Sure, we can meet. When?"

"How about today?" I didn't expect it would work on such short notice, but Salim said that he would be in the city center. We could meet for afternoon chai.

I set up two more meetings in the city center to fill the day, then walked down to Kash's shack, handing out a few Creme Savers hard candies to kids along the way. A handful of residents shouted, "Omosh!" The recognition felt good, though I still wondered whether it enhanced or jeopardized our security.

Nate and I had many contrasts, including our sleep patterns. Nate preferred late nights and late mornings. The military had conditioned me to early nights and early mornings. I rarely needed an alarm clock. Unless I was completely exhausted or operating on less than three hours of sleep, I woke up at five A.M. or earlier. Our rhythm worked well. I enjoyed spending my early mornings in Dan's shack writing in my journal, making plans, and sending letters to friends, family, and donors. Nate preferred to stay up late and have important conversations with Kash and other youth. His late night conversations often provided the greatest insights into the lives of young people in Kibera. During one of these conversations, Kash told Nate about his dream to go to college. Kash said that after taking the SATs and scoring well with a 1090, a soccer coach at an American college had expressed interest in recruiting him with a full scholarship. Impressed by his initiative and SAT scores, Nate pledged to help Kash craft his college applications.

Nate's distinct, chain-saw snores reverberated through the tin roof as I approached Kash's shack. Kash opened the door looking well rested.

"How can you sleep through that?" I asked, pointing to Nate conked out on top of the silky, pink comforter, mouth open.

"*Hakuna matata.*" Kash shrugged. "No problem."

Nate woke up and I told him the exciting news about Salim.

"Oh yeah, MYSA. Awesome." He yawned, recalling MYSA from my thesis. When I turned to Kash, I saw a puzzled look come across his face.

"What's wrong, man?" I asked.

"Nothin'." Kash shook his head. Before I could press him to tell us what was on his mind, Nate cracked a joke about cuddling with Kash the previous night. We laughed hard and swapped snoring stories. I shared a story about Marines sprinkling soap shavings into a snorer's mouth one night. The experience was so unpleasant that the snorer, a young Marine, allegedly never snored again. Kash wasn't impressed. He said in the Kenyan army they would have saved the soap and just beaten the snorer.

We got in a quick lift with Kash before heading downtown. Over the summer, Nate and I would have meetings with more than fifty people in search of allies among Nairobi's local elite, few of whom had ever ventured into the slums. Most of these meetings were dead ends. The three meetings that day, however, were consequential.

Our first meeting was with Ben Mshila, an executive at General Motors East Africa who had hosted Jennifer Coffman in Kenya when she was a study abroad student in 1989. Jennifer thought Ben could make a great board member, and she had made the connection. Nate and I were impressed by Ben's easygoing nature and his genuine interest in Kibera, which, unlike many affluent Kenyans, he had visited numerous times to assist other nonprofits. When Ben asked us how our programs were going, Nate responded, "Well, it's still early."

Nate had something else to do in the city center, so I went alone to see Chris Tomlinson at the Associated Press. A colleague of Peter Whaley's, Chris was a war correspondent and looked the part. He wore a goatee, combat boots, and a safari shirt with half rolled sleeves. We immediately drew a military connection. Chris had served as a signals intelligence specialist in the U.S. Army and was impressed that the Marine Corps allowed one of its second lieutenants to live in a slum and launch a nonprofit. I clarified that I had taken unpaid leave and was recently commissioned.

"Doesn't matter," Chris said. "You're still a Marine. You get kidnapped or killed, and it's the Corps' ass on the line. Good on 'em for taking the risk."

Chris was sharing a story with me about Rwanda and his friendship with Philip Gourevitch when a call came in about a breaking story on Somalia and cut our meeting short. I handed him my business card and invited him to Kibera.

"Unfortunately I've only covered the bad news in Kibera," Chris sighed, "If it bleeds it leads, you know? When you guys are ready for a piece, lemme know. We're always lookin' for good human-interest stories."

NATE AND I linked back up before our meeting with Salim in Barclays Tower, a glassy skyscraper with an Internet café called E-world. E-world had the fastest connection we knew of in Nairobi, though it was still agonizingly slow. It froze all the time and took twenty seconds to load an e-mail. We ordered ginger sodas called Stoney Tangawizi and turned to the computers. I finished an e-mail to Tracy and felt a light tap on my shoulder.

"Hey, mista."

There he was, Salim Mohamed. Short and slender, he wore a Muslim skullcap, jeans, sneakers, and an untucked Liverpool soccer jersey. His canvas satchel was similar to one that Nate carried.

"Nice man-purse," Nate joked, comparing his satchel to Salim's.

Salim laughed. "This is a bag, mista."

We caught up with some small talk before transitioning to CFK. We were brutally honest with Salim about our shortcomings. We told him about Taib and Jumba and what a flop the first focus-group discussion had been. Salim shook his head, as if to say, *And what did you guys expect?*

Nevertheless, Salim was intrigued by what we were doing. It impressed him that I had actually come back after that first summer, and that Nate and I knew some Swahili, slept in Kibera, and tried to meet youth leaders directly.

Salim spoke passionately about the power of community-led organizations to create role models and support local solutions to problems. He was a natural leader, calm and confident. He spoke straight and had bona fides. I wanted to latch on and learn from him. Fortunately for us, he agreed to lead our next youth-representative meeting in Kibera. We offered to cover the cost of his transportation from Mathare.

"No thanks," Salim replied, "I'm not doing this for that. But you agree we have this sort of contract. When I come to Kibera with you guys, we're going to do things my way, not yours. And it'll start with the soccer but end with the community."

"You got it, man, that's what we need." I extended my fist for a *gota*, the Kibera form of a contract.

"That guy's amazing," Nate said as soon as we left the meeting. He had no reservations about Salim. I felt like perhaps my own judgment was being restored.

THE FOLLOWING EVENING Kash asked what happened at the meeting with "the Mathare guy." I figured Nate could handle the debrief with Kash, and I left to get some pilau at the Mugumeno Motherland Hotel. As soon as I stepped out of Kash's room, the stench of rotting flesh hit me and extinguished my appetite. I decided to try to find a different route back to Dan's old room. Marine instructors at Mountain Warfare School during my sophomore summer taught us the importance of keeping multiple "avenues of approach." The surest way to get wiped out in combat, they warned, was to telegraph your movements. I had been walking the same route from Kash's house to Dan's old shack every night. It was the main route, wide and busy during the day, dark and empty at night. Dozens of blind spots made for ideal ambush points. I needed to learn every twisting alleyway that could lead me to Dan's room, and the only way to do that was by trial and error.

The sun began to fall, casting a pink-orange light across the big sky. I was thoroughly lost by the time I spotted a woman buying *sukuma wiki* at one of Kibera's thousands of makeshift kiosks. The woman wore a chipped black leather coat that was at least two sizes too large. The sleeves of the coat draped over her hand such that I could only see her fingertips as she reached for a plastic bag of chopped collard greens.

She turned around and her jaw dropped. I didn't recognize her. "Omosh," she gasped.

She took my hand and began speed-walking up the garbage-strewn path. It was unusual for women to walk at such a fast pace, and her purposeful stride jogged my memory.

"Tabitha?"

She looked over her shoulder with a faint smile.

It was Tabitha Festo, Jane's best friend, the nurse to whom I had given two thousand shillings, $26, to buy vegetables. I had handed her the money and a *kanga* the previous summer, a day before returning to the United States to begin OCS. I didn't know then if I would ever see her again.

Tabitha led me into a ramshackle compound with a square, dirt court-yard and three long corrugated-steel shacks. To our left, the compound's tin walls were painted in a cream color with something written in red paint, a sign of some sort. My eyes glanced over it.

Tabitha released my hand and pointed at the writing on the wall.

RYE MEDICAL CLINIC. SACRIFICING FOR SUCCESS.

I stood in stunned disbelief.

"You see, I told you I would do it." She smiled, wide and full. She rarely smiled, but on the occasions when she did, it was like Jane's smile. It was amazing.

I was numb.

"I told you, Omosh. You, you didn't want to hear. But I told you, and then you gave me that money when I was at rock bottom, just holding on, and see."

The building had six rooms separated by a narrow cement walkway. Tabitha rented two rooms, one for her family, the other for her clinic. It was one of the only clinics in Kibera open twenty-four hours a day.

"I keep it open because, you know, here we have to sacrifice. People, they don't stop getting sick when the night comes." The clinic room was neatly organized, clean, and sparsely equipped with a wood table, a stool, and a cabinet with some generic medicine and bandages.

"I started this bare-handed." She turned to me. "In fact I can say that it was with the bare of my hands. This place, it is meant to deal with people like me."

Tabitha led me back to her room. It was chai time. I was still in shock. *Was this for real?*

A baby boy named Ronnie played on the bed next to Tabitha's older daughter. When I tickled his feet, he laughed and bounced his little arms against the bed. I assumed he was a neighbor's son. Tabitha looked at Ron-nie and explained that it had taken her six months of selling vegetables before she had enough savings to start her clinic. Shortly after she started, she had discovered a package wrapped in a *kanga* at her doorstep. At first she thought the package was a bundle of vegetables from a patient who could only pay in kind. Then the bundle moved. It was Ronnie.

"I picked him up and he was very cold," Tabitha remembered. "He was outside for too long you see. I was worried about that other thing, too." She leaned over, placing her hand on Ronnie's head.

"What thing?"

"HIV." A sad look was in her eyes as she said the three letters.

"Is he positive?"

"I don't know. He has to be eighteen months. That's when the test can be reliable." She turned to a chest of drawers, removed a tightly folded *kanga*, and read its beautiful Swahili aphorism: *"Mawingu ya dunia ufanika wajane."* It was the *kanga* I had given her the previous summer. "The clouds of the earth cover the widows."

Holding the *kanga* in front of her, Tabitha said that it affirmed God's presence as her savior. God created the clouds that protected her, and Ronnie was a gift from heaven. She would do her best to care for him and anyone else who showed up at her clinic ill and in need.

As I sat in front of Tabitha drinking my day's sixth cup of chai, the shock slowly dissipated and I realized I wasn't dreaming. I thought about my mother. She was a nurse and an anthropologist. She had taught me how to listen. She had taught me to help people when I could. I was in Kibera because of her, and I imagined Mom there with me seeing Tabitha's clinic for the first time. It was Tabitha's clinic after all, not mine. I was honored by the clinic's name, but it made me uncomfortable as well. My mom would have felt the same way. All I had done was hand Tabitha $26 after she'd spent two days walking me around Kibera and shared part of her life story with me.

Ronnie crawled onto my lap, gripped my thumb with his little hand, and cooed. "He's a good one," Tabitha said with a faint smile.

Swept up in the moment, a tear trickled down my cheek. Salim had reaffirmed my faith in youth leadership, and now Tabitha was proving that it was possible. It was possible to change Kibera.

CHAPTER TEN

Harambee

Kibera, Kenya

JULY 2001

"HARAMBEE!" Beach Bum stood and stammered the Kenyan national motto—"We all pull together!" It was the beginning of the first major fund-raiser for Tabitha's clinic. Beach Bum, a distant relative of Tabitha's, was tall with disproportionately large hands and a drooling problem. He showed up drunk in a purple T-shirt that bore his nickname. beach bum the shirt's bubble letters read above a cartoon sketch with half-naked white kids and a clutter of toys. *"HARAMBEE!"* he shouted again and stared at Nate and me with a frothy mouth.

Though I didn't know Beach Bum, I had already passed judgment on him. I saw him as a large part of the problem in Kibera—one of many older men who spent their time in a perpetual drunken haze, leaving their wives to raise their children, take care of their house, and generate income by selling vegetables or by other hand-to-mouth jobs. Tabitha wasn't bothered by his presence. It was an important day for her and she knew how to handle him. Beach Bum was a relative, and for all his misgivings, he was there because he wanted to be supportive. When she gestured to him with a firm look, Beach Bum quietly took a seat on one of the short stools.

Tabitha looked sharp. Her hair was pulled back in a bun and she was dressed in her Sunday best. Nate called it her pilgrim outfit: white-collared shirt under a boxy black dress with a top that resembled overalls. She carried herself as if she were running a hospital. Meanwhile, reggae music echoed from the Mad Lion Base, the den of crime, drugs, and moonshine two plots behind us. Tabitha never knew when patients would arrive. Her doors were always open, even to the hardcores at the Mad Lion.

There weren't many of us, and Nate and I didn't know any of the other eight older men, each of whom was dressed in a suit. We felt out of place in our six-pocket pants and untucked collared shirts. "At least Beach Bum is here," Nate quietly joked.

Tabitha had set the goal of the *harambee* at seventy thousand shillings, nearly $1,000. I didn't know what she was expecting from us. Regardless, it was a large step up from the $26 for vegetables the previous summer. Before the *harambee*, she showed me her books, which were meticulously kept in handwritten ledgers. Running a sustainable clinic was daunting. Medicine alone was expensive, and most residents couldn't afford to pay more than $2 per visit. Tabitha was searching for suppliers of low-cost, high-quality medicines. I thought we could help by tapping into our networks and using our American identity and affiliation with UNC to open doors otherwise closed to a nurse from Kibera. Nevertheless, Tabitha needed funds to expand the clinic, and she was counting on us to help. She had already located a building near Jane's house with seven rooms and a pit latrine. Tabitha thought she could get the rent down to as low as $150 per month for the entire building.

Nate and I had to make some hard decisions in advance of the *harambee*. CFK's focus was on preventing ethnic violence through youth development. Tabitha's clinic didn't quite fit with our plans. We were just getting started with what we hoped would become a youth-led soccer and community service program directed by Salim and modeled after MYSA. That needed to be the focus of our efforts. But we wanted to find a way to support Tabitha. Nate suggested that high-quality, locally led health care wasn't too much of a stretch if we took a more "holistic" approach.

Professor Peacock had introduced me to the concept of holism, and I had used the idea frequently in my thesis to argue that the most effective efforts to prevent violence addressed all of its causes and weren't focused on one line of assistance. After all, youth had to be healthy to grow into leaders who could one day break Kenya's culture of corruption. This way of thinking had enabled us to justify support for Elizabeth. Although nursery school was only the first step in the education pyramid, it was the starting point. We hoped her efforts could inspire others. While Tabitha didn't exclusively focus on youth, half of her patients were under twenty years old, and she was a role model for other women. We decided that Tabitha's clinic fit into our evolving model.

We had enough money to cover the full $1,000 *harambee* target, but that would have defeated our larger purpose of community participation. We decided instead to make a challenge grant and match any money raised up to a total of seventy thousand shillings. This challenge created an opportunity for Tabitha to double her target.

AN EMCEE IN a three-piece suit kicked-off the *harambee* once Beach Bum sat down. "Now Bwanas Omosh and Otis have put before us a big challenge, a very big challenge. For every shilling that we bring to the lady, I say for every shilling raised today, they will"—he paused—"they'll match it!"

The audience erupted in applause. "So now the challenge is with us right here in this room," he continued. "I can say it is on us now, us here in Kibera. Otis and Omosh, they have done their share, and thanks to them for that."

The show had begun. I assumed it would be a short skit that would last maybe a half hour. I didn't know that *harambee* performances were steeped in ritual and protocol. Before each initial donation, a donor stood and told a story about his connection to Tabitha and his rural motherland. The men were all Luos from the same region on the shores of Lake Victoria. With the exception of one man who remained quiet, they all lived in the predominately Luo villages of Kibera. By the two-hour point, every man except the quiet one had donated. Together, they had come up with an impressive twenty thousand shillings, about $300. Even Beach Bum had made a generous pledge.

A wail and a pounding sound interrupted the *harambee*. Tabitha sprang out of her stool and met a distraught man shouting in Luo at the front door. "It's okay," she said, leading him to the other room. The man clutched his arm as blood dripped from his sleeve. Tabitha cleaned the wound and bandaged his arm. I would later learn that the man was one of the hardcores from the Mad Lion. When Tabitha returned thirty minutes later, her pilgrim outfit was speckled with blood.

"*Panga*," she said with a somber look. "Machete."

"See! There it is." The emcee raised his voice. "She turns no one away. I can say she's like the Red Cross, here in Kibera, where you know even the Red Cross, it is afraid to come. Yes, yes, we can do more to support this lady, this amazing lady."

He squeezed another five thousand shillings from the group before his attention turned to the quiet man, the only one who had not contributed. Apart from the emcee, he was the best-dressed man in the room. He identified himself as Charles Amolo Mbidha, a former resident of Kibera who worked as a manager at the Magnate security-guard company in the city center. Charles spoke softly, and with great affection about Tabitha's nursing him when he was bedridden many years earlier and couldn't afford to pay. He delivered this eloquent speech while referencing a note card. Toward the end of it, he mentioned his son and choked up. He was too emotional to continue. Tabitha, who was often stoic, appeared to be on the verge of tears. Something terrible must have happened. Charles stopped talking and removed an envelope from his breast pocket. Tabitha opened it slowly. We sat in silent anticipation as she slowly counted the stack of brown shilling notes.

"This man, this good man, has given us a great gift." Tabitha made eye contact with each person in the room before she continued. "Only to me it's more than that. I can say that to me it's a gift from God. He has given us thirty thousand shillings. May God bless you."

"It's incredible!" The emcee was elated. "Incredible! And Omosh and Otis will be matching it."

"Yes," I interjected, "but not us. It's CFK. CFK will be matching it." I didn't like the sound of Nate and me being given recognition for the donation. It wasn't our money. Those funds belonged to our organization, which we assumed wouldn't exist in Kenya once we returned to the States later that summer. The *harambee* was triggering new ideas: *Maybe CFK should stick around? Maybe Salim and Tabitha could lead it?*

"That's right, Caroleena. Caroleena for Kibera," the emcee enthused. "This is the beginning of a blessed thing for Kibera. One day I believe this clinic will be a hospital, a hospital I tell you. Isn't it? What I'm doing is predicting that one day there will be doctors, doctors here, here in this community." He stomped on the floor.

"And from the community," Tabitha said. "If God is with us, the doctors, they'll one day come from the community. Imagine."

Yes! I thought to myself. *Yes, that was exactly it. That was the vision. One day there would be doctors from Kibera.* In a place where many residents had never seen a doctor, one day it would produce them.

SHORTLY AFTER THE *harambee*, which raised more than $1,500 with CFK's contribution, Tabitha opened a bank account and began negotiations with the building's landlady, a Kenyan woman who lived in a posh part of Nairobi near Kibera and drove a Mercedes-Benz. Somehow the landlady had caught wind that *wazungu* were involved and had informed Tabitha that the rent was now twice the amount of her initial offer of $200 per month.

It infuriated me that this lady would pull such a move. *Why should affluent Kenyans be landlords in a slum where no one has land tenure rights?*

Tabitha speculated that the lady had political ties. Every structure built in Kibera had to be sanctioned by the area chief, the lowest-level political appointee in the Office of the President. The landlady was profiting from Kibera. Our funds were for improving life in her own backyard, her country, her continent, and she was trying to take us for a ride. I could hardly contain my rage.

Tabitha tried to calm me down. "This one, let me handle," she told me. I backed down, but days passed and Tabitha didn't seem to make any progress with the negotiations. We were losing precious time. We needed to open the new clinic before we left in two months. An opening event could build momentum and possibly even raise funds in Kenya.

I wanted to go with Tabitha and confront the landlady. Fortunately, Jennifer Coffman talked some sense into me. Jennifer had become a professor at James Madison University, and she was in Nairobi conducting research. She advised me to let Tabitha take care of it. She was right, and I would return in the future to this conversation whenever I came across a particular passage from none other than Lawrence of Arabia. Marine commanders frequently quoted this passage from Lawrence's famous "27 Articles" to illustrate the right approach to counterinsurgency:

"Do not try to do too much with your own hands. Better the Arabs do it tolerably than that you do it perfectly. It is their war, and you are to help them, not to win it for them. Actually, also, under the very odd conditions of Arabia, your practical work will not be as good as, perhaps, you think it is."*

What Jennifer told me that evening, and what Lawrence of Arabia put into writing in a very different context, struck at the heart of participatory development. I couldn't do it "perfectly" in Kibera. I couldn't even do it well. If I had negotiated with the landlady on my own, it likely would have exploded and further complicated Tabitha's life.

Jennifer reinforced her advice when she visited us in Kibera. She was the first American to visit and her opinion meant a great deal to me. After a long meeting with Tabitha in her ten-by-ten, Jennifer reacted, "I love her. She's amazing, so unassuming, so strong. My God, that woman is strong. Count me in for support. Donations, sure, but I want to do more."

TABITHA EVENTUALLY BROUGHT the landlady down to $150 per month. I felt like a fool for having questioned her negotiating abilities, and from that point forward I never inserted myself into the details of running the clinic.

After Tabitha finished the rent negotiation, she asked Nate and me to help her think about whom to invite as the guest of honor for the opening ceremony. I proposed U.S. ambassador Johnnie Carson. One of my advisers at UNC was a retired ambassador and an old friend of Mr. Carson's. Plus, our new colleague Semaj Johnson had arrived from the South Bronx and was working on a grant proposal for a few thousand dollars from the United States' Ambassador's Self Help Fund for Tabitha's clinic.

"The ambassador would be good," Tabitha reacted. I was surprised that she didn't sound more impressed. It would be a major coup if we could convince the ambassador to come to the opening of a small clinic inside Kibera that had no formal ties to the U.S. government. We also considered some prominent Kenyans who might be able to help us fundraise. However, it was difficult to come up with many candidates because the wealthiest Kenyans all seemed to be connected to public allegations of large-scale corruption. Toward the end of our brainstorming session, Nate threw out an idea in jest. "How 'bout Mama Omosh?"

* T. E. Lawrence, "Twenty-seven Articles," *The Arab Bulletin*, August 20, 1917.

"Is it possible?" Tabitha asked with uncharacteristic excitement. Since my mother did her own research and writing during the summers, she might travel to Kenya. Tabitha's enthusiastic reaction prompted me to ask.

My mother was thrilled when I asked her to fly to Nairobi for ten days to help Tabitha. I didn't ask her to be the guest of honor at the opening ceremony. That would have made her uncomfortable. We spoke about how we knew Dad would love to return to Kenya as well. Unfortunately, he was busy with his own research on the effects of a coalmine disaster in West Virginia.

Mom's security was heavy on my mind a month later when she arrived in Kibera. One morning toward the beginning of her visit, I spotted her walking alone near the clinic. I had just returned from a sports-program meeting with Salim, and I was on a part of the tracks that towered above Kibera on a steep, four-story-high slope.

"Mom, up here!" I shouted.

She couldn't hear me. A tall man staggered toward her. The man pointed at her. Mom stopped. He stepped toward her. I leaped off the tracks and bounded down the muddy slope. He stepped closer.

I barreled toward the man like I was back on the high school gridiron, shoulders lowered, fists clenched. Just before I could plow into his midsection, I slipped and skidded in the mud between them. When I stood up, his strong body odor and alcoholic breath made me gag. He stuck out his palm and slurred, "*Mzungu*, give me something small."

"Get lost."

"I am lost, *mzungu*."

He was probably harmless, but I was too worked up to laugh. As I escorted my mom back to the clinic, the man stammered in Swahili, "Something small. Something small. *Mzungu* has something small."

"Thank you, son." Mom put her arm around my shoulder. "You came to the rescue for Mama Omosh."

TABITHA HAD MOVED into the new, seven-room clinic beneath the railroad tracks, and Mom stayed in one of the empty rooms. Kash lived in the other spare room rent-free in return for security.

My father would have lost his temper if he had known about Mom's living arrangements. No security precaution in Kibera would've been strong enough to satisfy even his most basic safety requirements. After all, my mother may have been the first fifty-year-old white woman to have spent nights in Kibera. Although I thought she had one of the safest arrangements in the slum, it was not without risks. Even Salim and Tabitha differed in their opinions when I asked them separately for advice. Salim, the only person I knew who was as hyper-security-conscious as my father, thought it was too dangerous. "I don't recommend it," he said. "Anything can happen."

Tabitha, on the other hand, was confident that my mother would be safe as long as she didn't walk alone outside of the clinic at night. I shared both perspectives with Mom and left the decision to her. Not surprisingly, she wanted to give it a try. Mom still had an adventurer's spirit and a nurse's heart.

ON HER SECOND night in Kibera, Mom awoke to a clamoring noise on the tin roof above her room. She called Kash, who was sleeping in the adjacent room. Responding immediately, Kash inspected the premises with his machete and a hammer.

"*Hakuna matata*, Mama Omosh," Kash reported after a thorough search. "No problem. It's just a pussycat."

Mom laughed and went back to bed. She saw her stay in Kibera as a precious gift. She cherished her interactions with Tabitha, Jane, Kash, and the clinic staff. She spent a fair amount of time, as well, with the first Nubian I had met in Kibera, the cofounder of the Gange car wash, Ali Khamis Alijab. Ali offered to walk Mom around Kibera. He was older than most of the youth representatives Salim and Kash were mobilizing for the sports program, but he wanted to stay involved and was honored to welcome my mother to his community.

Ali still lived a Spartan life. He survived on a meal a day and put what little savings he generated from hawking used shoes toward school fees for his beloved daughter, Khadija. Over the past year, he had taught himself how to type with the scrap keyboard that he had borrowed from a friend. Mom and I helped Ali set up an e-mail account and send his first e-mail. We celebrated the event with lunch at a pizza place downtown. It was Ali's first taste of pizza. "*Tamu.*" He grinned and released a baritone chuckle. "Sweet." He ate one piece, boxed the remainder for Khadija, and insisted that we not purchase any more. "You have done enough. *Shukran*, Thank you."

Each night, Mom penciled pages of observations from her days in the clinic and her walks with Ali. She wrote in a yellow tablet notebook as Kash listened to Edith Piaf in the adjacent room. Ever the anthropologist, Mom recorded sights and sounds, events and conversations, and details about the people. It was the people that my mother found most compelling. She tolerated the living conditions out of respect for her new friends and colleagues. It was one way that she lived according to her conviction that all lives are fundamentally equal.

The work never stopped at Tabitha's clinic. Oftentimes the most urgent medical cases came late at night: babies to deliver, rape victims, wounds from fights, and late-stage complications from AIDS. The work did, however, ebb and flow, and Mom and I were with Tabitha during one late afternoon lull when she asked my mother the meaning of the name Rye. Mom explained that I was named after a scene in the book *Catcher in the Rye*, where the protagonist, Holden Caulfield, pictured himself standing at the edge of a cliff in a field of rye. He was there to protect the children playing in the field. Mom described it as a beautiful field with long wisps of amber-colored rye tall enough to touch Tabitha's shoulders, and stretching for as far as the eye could see.

"Oh, I see it. It is good," Tabitha reacted. "You're a guardian."

"No more than you are," I said.

"Yes," she replied, "that is what I hope to do here for the widows and the orphans."

"My!" Mom gasped, "this is unbelievable." Tabitha's insight was genius. Her observation was a link between my two worlds of Kibera and military service. For my mother, it was the first time she had thought of her profession with a word like *guardian*. She later told me that she remembered this as one of the most meaningful moments of her ten days in Kibera.

I knew my mother's trip would impact her, though I underestimated the profound cultural significance that her visit conveyed. Salim and Tabitha viewed her trip as an omen of CFK's potential to survive beyond that summer. Mom's presence cemented our long-term commitment. It was no surprise that Tabitha insisted my mother be the guest of honor for the new clinic's opening. Mom was uncomfortable with the arrangement, but she agreed to it so long as nothing special was done for her, and that she could continue to help Tabitha at the clinic after the formal ceremony.

The ceremony itself required substantial preparation. We needed to use it to build a broader base of support. Salim arranged for a youth group of drummers and dancers from MYSA to open the event, and we invited a number of people whom we thought we could recruit to a board of trustees if we eventually decided to keep CFK alive in Kenya. The invitees included Peter Whaley's friend Chris Tomlinson from the Associated Press, and Jennifer's colleague at General Motors, Ben Mshila. Reuters news agency offered to send a film crew from its television show *Africa Journal*, and an NGO called Pharmacists Without Borders agreed to provide Tabitha with low-cost medicine.

We gathered to the sound of drums in the clinic's triangle-shaped open-air waiting area. MYSA dancers swung into motion as drums thumped and the singing began. Nate spontaneously jumped out of his seat and started dancing with high knees and outstretched arms. People laughed at first, but soon we were all dancing. We were dancing with each other and with members of the community whom we had never met. Mom danced. Even Tabitha was dancing, though she was more restrained with her moves than others.

The only people who didn't dance were Salim and Chris Tomlinson. As confident as Salim could be in the community, he was often more withdrawn in front of larger audiences when his role was not clearly defined. As for Chris, he later told me that the only dancing he did was his native Texas two-step after at least a half-dozen shots of bourbon. I, however, had no problem embarrassing myself with my funky-chicken moves and absence of rhythm. Mom was happy, the sun was out, and Tabitha was about to launch a seven-room clinic. It was one of the best days of my life.

As the music died down we took our seats and Tabitha welcomed us with a speech. She was wearing her black leather coat and pilgrim outfit. She spoke softly as she referenced her note card. Her glasses were foggy and large, and reminded me of the glasses I had been forced to wear at Officer Candidates School. When she greeted "Mama Omosh" as the guest of honor, the audience gave a round of applause, which made Mom blush. Tabitha spoke about her vision to serve widows and orphans, and her dream of one day seeing a doctor who came from Kibera. She closed by talking about her motto for the clinic—Sacrificing for Success. Nate called it the "understatement of the century."

Tabitha's words were as modest as her delivery. After she finished speaking, I delivered brief remarks that I had memorized in Swahili. My main point was that although the clinic was named after me, it belonged to the community. That was what made it unique.

An assistant chief made the closing remarks. The chief had been fairly supportive of our work after he realized that we might make his life difficult if he continued to ask Tabitha for "something small." The chief said he knew that CFK was different from other NGOs because he had seen Tabitha, Nate, and me walking late at night "when even I don't like to walk. If I'm out then, you'll see me carrying my club."

One night earlier that summer, the chief had spotted me walking with my hammer in my hand. Late night in Kibera was no time for fist bumps and small talk. I had greeted him in Sheng and kept walking. The chief retold the story of this brief encounter. *"Wazungu hawa wana Kibich damu,"* he said, pointing at Nate and me and using the *Sheng* word for Kibera as the audience laughed. "These white guys have Kibera blood."

The ceremony ended and Tabitha began treating patients with a volunteer Kenyan medical doctor named Sarah Onyango. Nate, Semaj, and I sat back and observed as residents lined up for care. Semaj was impressed. He wasn't sure what he'd discover when he joined us after our first month. He certainly didn't expect to see international press coverage of a new clinic led by a local nurse.

"What's gonna happen to CFK?" Semaj asked. "I mean, we can't just go away now, can we?"

He was asking the pivotal question. Although Tabitha was making great strides, health care was never our primary focus. But there was something magical at that moment. If Tabitha could do all of this, why couldn't we do more in partnership, not only with her, but with the other Tabithas of Kibera?

THE U.S. AMBASSADOR didn't come to the clinic opening. In retrospect, it was a good thing. Tabitha wouldn't have been pleased if the ambassador had upstaged my mother. My outreach to the ambassador did, however, secure us a private meeting at his office. I planned to take the full team to the meeting: Salim, Tabitha, Elizabeth, Nate, Semaj, and my mother. Unfortunately, I was authorized to bring only three visitors to the meeting, each of whom would need a thorough background check. Security was a major concern at the embassy, where the memory of the 1998

Al Qaeda attacks on the U.S. embassies in Nairobi and Dar es Salaam was still fresh in people's consciousness.

Although Nate, Semaj, and my mom immediately offered to bow out of the meeting, I was frustrated by the limit on the number of visitors. I thought the embassy was overreacting to the threat of terrorism. If not for my father sending me e-mails to be on the lookout for signs of Islamic extremists, terrorism wouldn't have entered my mind. Dad repeatedly warned me to conceal my identity as a U.S. Marine, and avoid "tourist traps" and other "soft targets." He commented to me and his gang of old Marine friends that the terrorist Osama bin Laden needed to be the focus of U.S. national security. Dad rarely advocated for the use of lethal force, but he was uncompromising in his views on bin Laden. I didn't understand why at the time. I thought he was overreacting and discounted his warnings until we arrived for our first meeting and I witnessed the spectacle that was the U.S. embassy. Heavily guarded with high, cinder-block walls, stadium floodlights, and ribbons of razor wire, it looked like a maximum security prison.

There was one complication before entering. Tabitha had insisted on bringing Ronnie, her adopted, eight-month-old son. Sure enough, the Marine sentry, a sergeant, stopped us before we reached the metal detector. "There are only four people on the manifest to meet with the ambassador," the sergeant, a young hard charger, said in a crisp tone.

"My mistake." I took out my military identification card for the first time since I had arrived to Kenya and tried to make my voice sound deep. "Lieutenant Barcott, good to meet you, Sergeant."

"Sir." The sergeant inspected my ID and looked at me skeptically, "You're a Marine?"

"Yes, special assignment, Sergeant," I replied, thinking about the length of my hair. It had been four years since I had kept it so long.

"Well, sir, I'm sure the ambassador won't mind a baby."

"Oohrah, Sergeant."

"Oohrah, sir." He popped to attention as we passed through the metal detectors.

"What was that?" Salim asked.

"That's our greeting, *oohrah*."

"Sounds funny, and, 'sir'? I hope you don't start expecting us to call you sir in Kibera."

"No way, bwana. You're the sir."

"Don't even think about it," Salim shot back.

Ambassador Carson reminded me of the actor Morgan Freeman. Tall, handsome, and gray-bearded, he exuded a stately presence as he welcomed us into the sitting area of his office overlooking a swath of savanna at the edge of Nairobi National Park. Ronnie was an instant hit with the ambassador. His adorable, sleepy presence made for a natural lead into the story of the clinic. Tabitha spoke about her journey with characteristic humility and understatement, and I chimed in every now and then when she was being excessively modest. The ambassador listened with a calm, unaffected expression. I couldn't tell what his impressions were until he mentioned that he was amazed by what $26 in the right hands could create. He said he wanted to see the embassy doing more in Kibera, in part because the U.S. Centers for Disease Control and Prevention (CDC) was located right next to the slum near Jumba's office at Kenyatta Market and the Royal Nairobi Golf Club. I would later learn that the CDC headquarters in Kenya was among the largest CDC offices in the world, and that its pioneering work in disease surveillance and prevention had a global impact.

Tabitha's story was so moving that it could easily lead people to think that health care was our primary focus. The ambassador needed to know that our mission was to prevent ethnic violence and develop young leaders in a holistic way. As soon as there was a break in the conversation, I introduced Salim as my friend and colleague from MYSA. Ambassador Carson had a positive opinion of MYSA and believed in the power of sports to strengthen communities. Salim spoke about how our organization brought different ethnic groups together. To play in our soccer league, kids had to form interethnic teams, and they had to participate in community-service cleanups. "It's like you do something, we do something," Salim said as Ambassador Carson nodded in agreement. "You do nothing, we do nothing. Everything has to be earned."

"And you, ma'am?" the ambassador turned to Elizabeth, "Are you from Kibera?"

"Oh, no," Elizabeth recoiled, "I'm not from down there." The way she said "down there" didn't carry the same patronizing air as it did when Oluoch used the phrase, but I knew that it wouldn't sit well with Tabitha and Salim. Elizabeth was from a different class. She viewed her efforts to build a nursery school as charity for the poor, whom she pitied.

"And what happens after nursery school?" the ambassador asked.

The question caught Elizabeth off guard. She stumbled through a response about building a primary school, at which point I explained that part of our hope was to inspire others through our actions. The ambassador nodded, though he didn't seem to find my answer persuasive.

Despite losing momentum at the end of the meeting, the ambassador encouraged us to apply for a small grant from his self-help fund. Those were the words we needed to hear. It felt like a success as we walked out of the embassy. In fact, it felt like a major milestone, and I was looking forward to telling Semaj and my mother the news. They had already done a lot of work on the grant application.

We walked out of the embassy to our taxi and I proposed that we take a group photograph to capture the happy moment. As soon as our taxi driver snapped a picture, Kenyan security guards surrounded us. They confiscated my disposable camera and told us to leave immediately.

I should have known better. Of course the embassy wasn't going to allow photographs. That was a basic security precaution. The event forced me to ask myself if I had lapsed too far into NGO mode and out of the military mind-set that would soon define my career. It wasn't far away. My mother was about to return to the United States. In less than a month I would be back in Quantico training to lead Marines.

JENNIFER COFFMAN'S FRIEND Ben Mshila convened a dinner with Salim and Tabitha to thank my mother for her service. "To Mama Omosh." Ben raised his glass and toasted her. "Tabitha's motto is Sacrificing for Success. And this week, Mama Omosh, you have really sacrificed. In fact I can say that I was shocked when I learned you were staying in Kibera. You would be surprised, many of the Kenyans I know have never been to the slums. And you, you were sleeping there."

As Ben spoke, I thought about how Nate and I had spent almost the entire summer in Kibera without a serious security incident. I was beginning to underestimate the risks. The slum wasn't as crime-infested as many elites feared, but there were many dangerous places in Kibera and throughout Nairobi where outsiders would be foolish to venture without the right local guide.

The Somali neighborhood of Eastleigh where Tabitha had once sold her vegetables was one of the most precarious parts of the city. That evening after dinner I was planning to spend the night there at Salim's apartment. Located adjacent to the Mathare slums, Eastleigh was the next step up from the slums in terms of standard of living, and I was curious to see Salim's place. However, our dinner went longer than expected, and I needed to escort my mom back to Kibera.

"Rain check?" I asked Salim.

"Anytime, bro. My place is yours."

"But tell your friend that I'm sorry he felt like he had to find another place to stay tonight. Next time I can sleep on the floor." Salim shared his room with a deaf, mute friend from Mama Fatuma Children's Home.

"No problem, man."

The following day Salim missed a meeting in the city center and his cell phone appeared to be disconnected. Salim was extremely punctual and always carried his cell phone. We were seriously worried by the time he called me in the evening as I was escorting my mom to the airport. Salim sounded distressed and said something about being robbed before his phone cut out.

"Here," Mom said after I hung up. She handed me $200 in a roll of $20 bills.

"For what, Mom?"

"For Salim. I can't imagine he has insurance, apart from his friends and family."

Her gesture reminded me of the street girl with the infant swaddled to her back at the Globe Roundabout. "It's good to help when you can," Mom had said.

We arrived at the airport. I carried her suitcase to the terminal.

"Well, I wish I could stay," Mom said, looking worried.

"What is it, Mom?"

"Just stay safe, okay?"

We hugged. Words alone couldn't express how tremendous it felt to have shared those moments with my mother. It was the beginning of CFK, and Mom, more than anyone else, had inspired the journey.

SALIM'S BLOODSHOT EYES conveyed a rare depth of exhaustion when we met for breakfast the following morning.

"Dude, what happened?" I asked.

"Late that night, I was sleeping when they locked my neighbors' doors from the outside. My neighbors couldn't do anything when the thugs hit my door down." Shotgun to his head, flashlight to his face, they looted his home.

"It's just good you weren't there," he said, "because they would have demanded money from you."

"Or panicked and shot us."

"It's possible. Eastleigh people get worried when they see a *mzungu*."

"Man, I'm sorry. I even asked to stay with you."

"Why?"

"Because I endangered you."

"When you live in such a place, you're always in danger. I don't mind, but I'm also glad you weren't around. Definitely it would've been worse."

"Did they take much?"

"Rye, they took everything."

"Everything?"

"Yeah, everything that mattered. I still have my bed, some furniture."

"Oh, man"—I put my hand on his shoulder—"I'm so sorry."

"You know, it was somebody I know."

"What do ya mean?"

"It had to be someone who knew me well because the thugs left with my TV then came back minutes later for the remote. My TV was wired so that it could only be turned on with the remote. They must have been tipped off, you see. Only my friends ever came to my place. Only my closest friends knew about my remote."

"I've never been through such a loss, man. I don't know what to say other than I'm here for you. I'll help you in any way I can." I remembered my mom's gift. "And this, my mom wanted you to have this." I handed him the roll of bills.

"What for?"

"She was next to me when you called."

"Really?" He was tearing up.

"Really. Your mom would've done the same thing."

"No, she wouldn't."

"What?"

"You know my mom, she's in Mombasa."

"Oh?" I had assumed she was no longer alive.

"Have you seen her, your mother?"

"Yes, but not all that much."

"You knew her growing up?"

"No, in fact the first time I met her was when I was older and my grandmother, she introduced us. It was two weeks before my grandmother was killed, actually."

"Killed?"

"A bus hit her in the city center when she was on her way to her vegetable stand."

"Oh, man." A bolt of pain penetrated my heart.

"Yeah, it was bad, really bad. They took her to the hospital but the doctors, they were all on strike."

"And she had just introduced you to your mother?"

"Yeah, she did do that."

"I mean, what was that like?"

"Well, the thing is, I was older, like twenty years old. So for me it was more like the aspect of being good to meet her, but not having much to talk about. At one point it begins to be like we are punishing each other. It's not finding answers. At the same time just being together is good, because it's like we're moving forward."

"So your mother was there for your grandmother's funeral?"

"No, actually she was sick and stuck in Mombasa."

"Sick?"

"A stroke, or something." He sounded as if he was no longer comfortable talking about his mother.

"Your father, is he alive, too?"

"No, I don't know. The way I see it is, if my grandmother wanted for me to know my father she would have told me those things. She protected me from so much, you know. So that makes me not even wonder or explore it."

"She was such a great woman. I wish I would've met her." Although Salim didn't have a photograph of his grandmother, he had once described her hands. With skin leathered from the sun and calloused by the streets, they were the hands that had protected Salim. They were gritty and beautiful, tender and defiant.

"Yes, she was great. My grandmother and Mama Fatuma, they're my role models. They taught me honesty and working hard. If you live with integrity, it's that integrity that sets you free. If you're honest, then why fear? Those are the things they taught me, and, you know, both of them, they weren't literate."

"Was your grandmother buried here in Nairobi, or up-country. Because if she's here in Nairobi, maybe I can visit her, if that'd be okay with you?"

"My grandmother, her home was Nairobi, not up-country, and so it was really good that she was buried here in Nairobi. She's here in Langata Cemetery." Langata Cemetery sat on a hill overlooking Kibera. "Someday maybe we can go."

"You went to the funeral?"

"Of course."

"Did you help organize it?"

"Not really. These relatives from up-country showed up. Actually it was not good for me. At Kikuyu funerals, we wear this white patch if you are a relative of the deceased. When I went to get a patch from the basket, a guy stopped me and said, 'We don't know you. There's no Salim Mohamed in this family.'"

"Did you know him?"

"Aye, never. Never had I seen him. My name was changed when I went to the children's home. My grandmother, she didn't mind that I was Salim and had become a Muslim. She still called me by my Kikuyu name, but, you know, she accepted that thing. She loved me for being a Muslim. I was so pissed at that guy and the others. They didn't know my grandmother. They let her live on the streets. Anyways, the other hawkers were there and came to my defense."

"Was there a fight?"

"Believe me, I would have fought those people. But they knew it and so they stepped aside and I took the white patch. The other thing is that it's important to pour dirt on the grave. At first those people, they didn't want me to do that thing either, because again it's for the family."

"They tried to block you?"

"They tried but they couldn't. I forced my way in. Nothing would've stopped me."

"God, I'm sorry you had to go through that." I placed my hand back on his shoulder.

"It's okay, actually. I forgive them."

"You do?"

"Because that's the only way. You know, when I returned to Mama Fatuma's from the funeral, I was so angry. I told my brothers and sisters at the children's home what had happened, and we had a special bond that we all pull together. The thing is, our family, it was us. Mama Fatuma and my grandmother taught me that aspect of love. They had sacrificed for me and I just had this feeling that it was time to go beyond. We were on our own. But we were lucky, too."

CHAPTER ELEVEN

War on Trash

Kibera, Kenya

July 2001

As we entered our final two weeks in Kibera, Nate, Semaj, and I sat down to think about a plan for CFK beyond our short time on the ground. There was too much to do and we needed to prioritize what we could accomplish before leaving. At the top of our list was leadership. The three of us agreed that CFK could survive in Kenya only with Salim, who was still employed by MYSA, as the leader. Tabitha was too focused on the clinic, and Salim was the only other person we trusted who also had the necessary community focus, management expertise, and street credibility. While we were sure that Tabitha would support Salim as the head of CFK, the relationship between Salim and Elizabeth was on less certain ground. Elizabeth was aloof in Salim's presence, and Salim questioned Elizabeth's level of commitment and community awareness. In addition to executive leadership, our list of top priorities included forming a local Kenyan board and securing enough new funds to cover at least six months of operational expenses.

We decided to focus on pulling together CFK's grand finale. It would involve the final match of our first major soccer tournament and a major community cleanup. The grand finale would actually be a beginning, and it would help CFK establish its presence and identity in the community. We agreed that this cleanup was the most important event.

Cleanup, however, just wasn't the right word. A cleanup was what Nate and I occasionally had done in our dorm rooms. In Kibera, our community cleanups were battles. They were among the most physically demanding group activities in which I had ever participated. They were the ultimate Kibera gut check. At CFK, a cleanup meant going knee deep into the sumps of sewage, waste, and dead animals and hauling out tons of garbage in pushcarts that became so heavy they required a half dozen men to shove them out of the slum.

On Salim's suggestion, we planned the final cleanup to take place the morning after the championship match so that we could encourage fans at the game to participate. The pressure was on. Word had spread in the community about Caroleena, as our sports program was called. We anticipated at least a thousand fans, and most of those people would be seeing CFK's work for the first time.

With our plan in place, we jumped back into action. The following morning, Nate and I went to Fort Jesus to meet with Elizabeth and review the Carolina Academy budget. About an hour after we arrived, Oluoch stormed out of the bathroom with a red *kanga* wrapped below his belly. "How many times do I have to say it? Put the toilet seat down when you're done!" he barked.

I apologized.

Elizabeth flicked her wrist as if to say, *Don't mind him.* I was getting frustrated though. I had loaned Oluoch $1,500 to purchase a bus for his own private business venture. He was a month past due in paying us back, and we needed those funds. Each time I spoke with him about repayment, the tension between us spiked. Oluoch expected me to conform to Kenyan cultural norms, including deference to age. I remembered the wisdom Looseyia had passed on to me in the Masai Mara as a teenager, and I tried to treat Oluoch with respect. Yet the longer I was around him, the more his insults to others seeped under my skin.

Elizabeth had made considerable headway with Carolina Academy. Weeks after we cut her a check for $4,000, she had secured a building in Kibera that would comfortably fit fifty schoolchildren. She had interviewed candidates for teacher positions, while Jane had identified twenty orphans who were ready to be enrolled. That morning Elizabeth voiced her support for Salim's leadership and suggested that we finalize our budget that evening with Salim over dinner.

Evidently, Elizabeth didn't inform Oluoch ahead of time that she had invited us to dinner. Instead of retreating to his sofa to watch television after dinner, Oluoch remained at the table as we dove into the budget.

We had been clear from the beginning. CFK could only commit $5,000 to the launch of the Carolina Academy. After our initial investment, Elizabeth needed to figure out how to cover the additional costs. However, Elizabeth looked shocked as we reviewed the numbers. To complete the construction and furnish the school would cost $7,000. Running the school for a year with fifty children would cost at least $10,000. Elizabeth either underestimated the costs, or she had assumed CFK would be the sole sponsor.

"You've only given her four thousand dollars," Oluoch interjected.

"Yes, that's right." Legs crossed, I tried to remain calm.

"You owe us five thousand dollars. Where is it?"

"I owe *you*?" My voice rose. "No, we owe you nothing."

"Is that what you think, boy?" Oluoch leaned forward.

"Oluoch, please." Elizabeth reached for his wrist.

He waved off her gesture and continued, "Boy . . ." I didn't hear the rest of his sentence. I hated when people called me boy.

"How about this, Oluoch? You pay the fifteen hundred dollars you owed us last month for our loan, and then Elizabeth will get the one thousand dollars."

"Did you just, did you just threaten me, boy?"

"Don't call me *boy*," I stuck my finger at him.

"You, you come into my house, eat my food, sit there with your crossed legs, and insult me. Who do you think you are? You think you can just come to my country and boss us around like a British, like we work for you? No!"

It was the first time a Kenyan compared me to a British colonizer. My emotions cooled for a moment as I objected to his accusation on rational grounds. Participatory development was all about empowering local leaders. It was the opposite of colonial conquest. "I'm not bossing anyone around. We're just volunteers. Salim, Tabitha, and Elizabeth run their own projects."

"Salim? Tabitha? Who are these people?" Oluoch shouted. "You bring these people into my house. You bring a Somali street kid, or Kikuyu, or whatever the hell he is, and some slum woman into my house eating my food."

Salim stood up and excused himself. Elizabeth apologized and asked him to stay.

"No, *mama*," he replied. "I understand. I must go."

"We'll wait outside," Nate said, and walked out with Salim.

"You put him at the same level as us," Oluoch continued, pointing his thick finger at my face, "I never want to see him in here again, you understand?"

"They are equal. That's the point. And you owe us fifteen hundred dollars."

Oluoch swatted at my legs with his hand. "Don't cross your legs in front of me."

I stood and faced him, fist clenched.

Elizabeth threw her full figure between us. "*Stop!*"

I should have walked out. "You want to fight, Oluoch? Come on. I'm standing right here."

Elizabeth pushed me out of the living room and swept the door shut. Oluoch shouted in Luo, one of many local languages that I didn't understand.

Salim and Nate were waiting for me outside. They had heard everything. Salim looked both sad and angry.

"Sorry," I said, putting my arm around his bony shoulder. "How ya doin', bro?"

"I can never work with that man."

"What about Elizabeth?"

"Can you imagine sleeping in the same bed with Oluoch?" Nate joked.

Salim turned to me. "I don't know. I don't want to think about it right now."

I didn't want to think about it either. We walked with Salim to the main road so that he could catch a *matatu* minibus to his home, the same room in Eastleigh that was ransacked weeks earlier. He was trying to decide whether or not to follow our advice and move closer to Kibera, where it was safer. Just about any other place in Nairobi was safer than Eastleigh.

"*Tuko pamoja.*" Nate extended his fist to Salim. "We are together."

Salim smiled. "You guys, you guys are something else."

We bumped fists and Nate and I stepped off into the shadows, toward the railroad tracks and the shanties below.

WE WERE TOO busy to worry about Oluoch, and I still thought time and distance would help and that he would eventually repay the loan, at which point we could continue working with Elizabeth. Nate and Semaj thought I was naive for thinking Oluoch would ever make the repayment. I hoped they were wrong because I still admired Elizabeth and wanted to see the Carolina Academy succeed.

As for funding, my stress was tempered by my faith that if we communicated what we were doing in Kibera, we would get the funding we needed. I was especially optimistic about our one local lead—the Ford Foundation East Africa Office. Among the largest and most respected foundations worldwide, I assumed the Ford Foundation needed great grantees like us as much as we needed them, and I knew we had a compelling story. Tabitha had taken $26 and built a clinic. Our sports program engaged more than two hundred youth in our first tournament in less than two months. We were affiliated with a major research university in the United States, and we were a pioneer of participatory development, a smarter approach to aid.

Our "in" to the Ford Foundation's Nairobi office was Dr. Mary Ann Burris, a program officer who spoke fluent Mandarin Chinese and had spent much of her career in Asia. Mary Ann had arrived at the Nairobi office in 1996 and made one of her first grants to MYSA, where Salim became one of her primary points of contact. Salim spoke about Mary Ann with a son's affection. He loved her and had no doubt that she would support CFK. I responded enthusiastically and suggested we ask for a grant during our first meeting.

"I'll take the lead," Salim said, putting me in my place. "It's better to go slow with Mary Ann. She likes to get to know people."

If I had encountered Mary Ann in a different setting, I might have mistaken her for an artist. She had vibrant blue eyes and a striking, angular face. She was one of those people who seemed perceptive simply by the way that she moved, and when she spoke, I detected a faint Southern accent.

Salim handled the meeting as deftly as he ran CFK's youth forums. Their conversation occurred at multiple levels. In addition to bringing each other up-to-date on their lives, Salim mentioned CFK at opportune moments, and Mary Ann received updates about MYSA. She asked smart questions that struck at the power dynamics within the organization. Salim's responses helped me better understand why he might be willing to leave a relatively comfortable, high-status job to take a risk on a boot-strapped start-up such as CFK. Stymied by office politics, Salim craved more autonomy and more responsibility. He wanted to lead.

Mary Ann paid no attention to me at first. Hers was an office for the oppressed and the forgotten: orphans, street kids, battered spouses, prostitutes, homosexuals, and teenage mothers.

"So, you, Rye, nice to meet you. Where do you come from?" she asked toward the end of our meeting in a cool, slightly detached tone.

I mentioned UNC and her face filled with the color of familiarity. Mary Ann, too, was a Tar Heel, and her parents still lived in North Carolina. I relaxed and let the conversation flow, which it did until Mary Ann asked if I would be in Kenya full-time with Salim.

"No, ma'am. I'm a Marine. I need to return to service."

"'Ma'am'?" Mary Ann cocked her head, "Do I look that old?"

"Sorry, I didn't mean it like that. It's just what we say."

"Now why would you be going into the military?" I suspected that she had another unasked question that was often on the minds of Americans I had met who had little connection to the military: *Aren't you better than that?*

"It's another form of service. You get a lot of responsibility at a young age."

"Do you believe that about the service? Do you believe the U.S. military does the world a service?" The questions could have come across as hostile, though Mary Ann asked them in a genuine way, as if the thoughts were so antithetical to her worldview that they had never come to mind. I assumed then that Mary Ann was a pacifist and rejected war and the use of violence for political means based on her moral principles, many of which my mother probably also shared.

Salim looked eager to see how I would respond. We had spoken a lot about ourselves, though he had never asked me such direct questions. I knew he was also deeply skeptical of militaries, partly because so many African armies kept crony governments in power and committed ghastly human rights abuses. I didn't know if Salim was a pacifist, though he had confronted so much cruelty as a child that I assumed he shared my view about the necessity of a common defense in a violent world.

"Yes, I believe militaries do service. I think some wars are just and nations need strong militaries." Before Mary Ann could object, I added, more emphatically, "Do I think we're over militarized? Yes. Do we waste a lot of money on weapons? Absolutely. But I hope to understand it before I can influence it, and I think militaries can do more to prevent conflict. That's why I'm in Kibera now." I was covering a lot of issues in a broad and clumsy way, lumping together complicated ideas that I was still trying to figure out in my head.

"And you could die doing it?"

"Um, yes." I had never been asked such a direct question.

"And you could kill?"

"I hope it doesn't come to that."

"What if you don't believe in a war?"

"Well, that's a tough one." I laughed, and then she laughed, and the laughter punctured the tension. I had answered her honestly, and that was enough for the time being. Mary Ann skillfully shifted the conversation back to CFK and left me feeling as if I had survived a short interrogation.

At the end of the meeting, Salim invited Mary Ann to Kibera for our final soccer tournament, and I offered to set up a meeting with Tabitha. Mary Ann pleasantly thanked us for our offers but remained noncommittal. She hugged Salim, shook my hand, stepped back, and concluded, "Well, you two certainly make an odd couple."

I didn't know what to think of the meeting. Salim, however, was upbeat. He was certain that Mary Ann would support us, so certain that he agreed to leave MYSA and focus on CFK full-time. It was huge news. With Salim and Tabitha, we could move ahead with our plans to build an organizational structure on the ground, register as a Kenyan NGO, and form a formal governing board chaired by Jennifer's friend Ben Mshila.

GAME DAY CAME before we knew it. Although the average level of education in Kibera was low, much of the population possessed basic reading skills. The Ford Foundation let us use their photocopier to produce a thousand flyers with write-ups of the two competing soccer teams, a description of CFK, and a copy of our "fair play code," which established our core values and began with the line "For those who want to win on and off the field."

Thousands of residents showed up and crammed onto the dusty side-lines at one of Kibera's only two soccer fields, a patch of rutted dirt lined by sewage sumps in the middle of the slum. The turnout far exceeded our expectations, and we ran out of flyers well before the match started. I spent most of the game with Nate moving up and down the sidelines with our youth representatives spreading the word about CFK. During halftime, Kash set up a public address system he had borrowed from another organization and encouraged all of the fans to join the two competing teams the following morning at our community cleanup in Makina Village.

The tight, well-played match came down to a shoot-out with the team from Makina Village winning by a goal. Thousands of fans rushed the field and kicked up a tornado of dust. Ben Mshila presented the trophy and team award to Rashid "Kapii" Seif, the captain of the winning Zulu Youth Football Club. Unlike other tournaments, we decided against giving cash awards. Instead, we offered a set of uniforms and soccer balls from a large supply of used soccer equipment that we had received in a shipment from an Eagle Scout candidate in the United States. Salim knew that the team would appreciate the award. Uniforms and soccer balls were often prohibitively expensive. Most teams trained with "Kibera balls"—plastic bags wrapped in twine and squashed into small spheres slightly larger than a man's fist. Kibera balls typically lasted less than a week in the dirt and rubble fields. Rashid tossed the two soccer balls from Ben Mshila to his jubilant team and hoisted the trophy above his head. The crowd exploded with another round of applause.

I hadn't spoken to Rashid before that day. Most of my time with CFK was spent with Salim, Tabitha, Kash, and youth representatives. These were the leaders of the organization. Young men like Rashid, though, were whom we intended to serve most directly. After the celebration, I approached him and made some small talk in Swahili. I was struck by his composure and the confident, eager look in his eyes. Rashid carried himself like a leader, and he was only fifteen.

RASHID AND HIS team were among the first people I recognized in the crowd of hundreds of residents who gathered for our final cleanup the following morning. His team, dressed in the yellow soccer jerseys that we had awarded them, stood in front with rakes, shovels, and pushcarts. The second place team was there as well, standing side by side.

"Looks like an army," Semaj said, reacting to the large gathering.

Kassim, Ali's charismatic friend and cofounder of the car wash, had helped mobilize a half dozen local women's groups to volunteer at the cleanup and lend us their equipment. "It's incredible," Kassim said, "an army of *mamas* and ghetto *soldjas.*"

At that moment it hit me. *"Vita vya takataka!"* I exclaimed. That was what we were doing. It wasn't a cleanup. It was a "war on trash."

"I feel it," Semaj said.

Kassim laughed hard. "Yes, yes. That's it precisely, *vita vya takataka.*"

Salim rolled his eyes. He wasn't thrilled with the use of the word *war,* and he was right. It was counterproductive to our higher aim of preventing violence. I was too embedded in Marine culture to even acknowledge the most egregious cases of my excessively militarized language. Salim saw that I was enthusiastic about my war on trash and didn't push back on the branding, in part because words were less important to him. Our actions mattered most, and that's the point that he drove home minutes later in his opening remarks.

Salim thanked the *mamas* for joining in the day's cleanup and noted that although we were starting with boys' soccer, one day we hoped to create Kibera's first girls' soccer program. The cleanup, he emphasized, was more important than the games the day before because at CFK soccer was a tool for community development. As he spoke, Tabitha stood next to him with her arms folded behind her back. She was there in her CFK T-shirt and a tweed skirt to participate in the cleanup despite having been up all night delivering a baby at the clinic.

Salim introduced Kassim, who briefed the crowd in his booming voice about the task at hand. Each team of ten to twenty people would work together unclogging sumps and hauling out trash. Teams were responsible for the equipment they borrowed and would work until they ran out of garbage bags. We would dump all of the bags at one point on the main road. We were told the Nairobi city council had only three dump trucks for the city's estimated three million residents. But we had been persistent. One of the trucks would be making a special trip to Kibera.

Kassim concluded with a rousing crescendo: "This is a milestone for

Kibera. *Mamas* and youth working together in this, the first CFK *vita vya takataka*! That's right, war on trash. One day you'll look back and say you were here, today, when it started."

Armed with pushcarts and wheelbarrows, we rolled out. I stuck with Rashid and his team, who took to the war on trash with the same vigor and sense of purpose they had displayed the day before on the soccer field. Rashid led by example. He was the first to step up to the foulest and toughest jobs, of which there were no shortages. Hours later my pants were covered in black sludge that had the texture of mucus and the smell of rotting meat. I was sweaty, sunburned, and exhausted. And for a little while, Kibera was a little cleaner.

Rashid joined me for a soda after we finished. We talked a bit about his life growing up in Kibera and his dreams of one day playing professional soccer. Rashid spoke about soccer with great affection. He referred to his team as his family, and he said that the sport was important in part because it helped keep kids out of crime and other temptations that arise from "idleness." When I asked him about his other family, I was surprised and saddened to learn that he was an orphan. Rashid didn't know his father, and his mother had passed away three years earlier. He was living with friends and struggling to pay for his education, having just begun his first year of high school. School fees at even the lowest-quality schools ran at least $50 a year. That was big money in a place where the average annual household income was under $500.

As I sat on a wood bench sipping Stoney ginger soda from a straw and listening to Rashid, I thought about purpose. We wanted to help young people like Rashid unlock their potential. We didn't have enough funds or organizational capacity to run a scholarship program, though one day maybe we would. With more resources we could do so much. We could be a rung in the ladders for hundreds of young people like Rashid, and that felt like more than just a worthy pursuit. It was more than a personal mission. It was a groundswell.

Part III

CHAPTER TWELVE

From Peacetime to Wartime

Quantico, Virginia

Fall 2001

What I wanted to write to the head of the American study abroad program that employed Oluoch appeared in my dreams one morning in September shortly after I had reported to duty in Quantico. I woke up at 0400 hours and tiptoed to the other side of our barracks room in my Skivvies. There, I didn't need to worry about waking up my three room-mates while I caught up on e-mails, letters, and calls to Kenya.

The letter was my last recourse with Oluoch, who still owed CFK $1,500. That money didn't belong to Nate and me. It belonged to the community, and in my mind Oluoch's refusal to pay was the equivalent of stealing from the poor. There was something personal too. It felt like I was being conned, and that was as embarrassing as it was infuriating. After Oluoch and I almost got into a fist fight in Fort Jesus, we had hoped that Elizabeth would force him to repay the loan and that we could then continue to help build the Carolina Academy. These hopes disappeared shortly after I returned to the United States and learned that Jane had quit her job with Oluoch and Elizabeth to work for Tabitha. Although Elizabeth knew that the two women were best friends, she felt betrayed by Jane's decision.

Until that point I had viewed Elizabeth as a compassionate person. When I had called and spoken with Jane, however, I discovered that Elizabeth had paid her merely $30 per month. That was less than half the average rate for employment six days a week, six hours a day. Furthermore, according to Jane, Elizabeth never stopped Oluoch from making frequent threats to fire her for "offenses," such as not making his bathwater hot enough. These threats had frightened Jane. Thinking she had no other option for employment, she had endured the low pay and abusive environment like an indentured servant.

"But they knew you have five children and your husband doesn't have a steady job?" I had asked Jane on the phone.

"Who? This Elizabeth? No, Omosh. Omosh, *no*! It's not possible. Elizabeth, she has never been to my house, never."

Elizabeth lived fifteen minutes from Jane's house. She had spoken so eloquently about wanting to help the orphans that I had mistaken her for a leader who could earn credibility in Kibera. Yet Elizabeth was more of an outsider to the slum than I was. I should've realized this after our meeting with the U.S. ambassador. In the eyes of the residents, Elizabeth was just another *mtajiri*, "a rich person." She was well-intentioned and wanted to do good, but she was trapped in the prejudices and fears of her class. Her outreach was from a place of pity, not respect.

"Sometimes we go with that hunger," Jane once told me after I had asked her about her most difficult moments in Kibera. "And when I can't give, I tell my children, 'Please, it's difficult now. We're really struggling, but please, be strong.' When I say this, they tell me, 'It's okay, Mama. We understand.' They go without the food. They don't complain. They're good ones."

As I pounded my keyboard in Quantico's morning stillness, I heard Jane's voice in my head and thought about how Oluoch often spent more on beer and bar food in a day than he and Elizabeth paid Jane for two weeks of work. My letter would accomplish nothing for CFK. In fact, it could make things worse for the community. If Oluoch lost his job, it'd be even more difficult for Elizabeth to create her nursery school. I knew this. Yet I couldn't rid myself of the urge to strike out, to punish Oluoch for Jane, for Salim, for everyone who had ever borne the brunt of his bigotry, and for myself. I was deliberating whether to send the letter when my roommates' alarms sounded off at 0530 hours.

————————

A WEEK EARLIER, my three roommates and I had arrived in Quantico as strangers. We had reported to the Basic School and joined a company of two hundred other lieutenants. My mind was still in Kibera. I wished Nate, Semaj, and I had had another month to build CFK with Salim and Tabitha. Regardless, I didn't have a say in the matter. The Corps gave me three months of unpaid leave to launch CFK, and that was it. I had followed my orders and begun my military career.

The Basic School was the starting block. In keeping with the credo "every Marine a rifleman," every Marine lieutenant, including the future pilots and lawyers, started his or her career with six months of training to learn the basics of being a rifle platoon commander. The initial week dragged as we waited for the course to begin. It seemed as if the staff were simply going through the motions. The school felt worn down by the legions of Marines who had preceded us. We were another company of peacetime lieutenants, one of at least six to cycle through each year. When I sent the curriculum to my father, he commented that it looked as though not much had changed since he went through the school in 1964.

We were training for war with lessons passed down from the generations before us, yet war of the likes of World War II, Vietnam, or the first Gulf War seemed unlikely. We would more probably deploy to peacekeeping operations, such as the one under way in Kosovo, or to embassy evacuations and humanitarian aid missions in places such as Haiti and Sierra Leone. These missions mattered, and I looked forward to them. In college I had written papers that supported our military intervention in Bosnia and excoriated the United States for not doing more to stop the genocide in Rwanda. While I realized that we needed to train for war first, the Basic School curriculum felt antiquated.

There was nothing to do until the course began. That morning we dressed, filled our mugs with coffee, and headed to a formation for a daily head count.

"All present," a lieutenant sounded off to a captain.

We took a morning run through the woods and returned to the barracks. At 0845 hours I booted up my laptop to check my e-mail. Salim and I were trying to get a shipment of used soccer supplies through Kenyan customs without paying a bribe.

My roommate turned on the television.

"Holy shit. Look at this."

"How the hell does a plane crash into the World Trade Center?"

"Maybe the pilot was drunk?" my roommate, the son of a New Jersey union boss, took a guess. Neither one of us imagined it was an attack. It was peacetime.

I called home.

"Yes, good morning," Dad answered in his deep voice. When I told him about the crash, he turned on his television. After a long pause he concluded, "This is an attack. We've been attacked."

"Lieutenants, on alert!" a thundering voice echoed down the barracks hall.

Doors swung open. I said good-bye to my father.

"Turn on your televisions!" someone shouted.

A few lieutenants jumped into our room to watch the coverage. Everyone thought it was a mistake. Then the second plane struck. Suddenly the room was quiet.

"We're under attack," a lieutenant said, breaking the silence. "This means war."

We were placed on high alert and training was suspended. But it didn't feel as if we were on alert. We sat in our rooms. The lieutenants who had completed the Basic School and were attending Infantry Officers Course received live ammunition and formed a defensive perimeter around the base. We were envious of them because we wanted to do something, anything, apart from watching television and wondering about our futures.

I stayed online and received dozens of e-mails with prayers and expressions of gratitude from friends and family, old and new. Rarely had I been thanked for choosing to join the military. When it did happen, I felt self-conscious about it. I hadn't done anything, and up until that day it seemed improbable that I would go to war.

Cell phone coverage remained unreliable. When I finally reached Tracy, it was nighttime. She told me that her family in North Carolina wanted to thank me for my service. As she spoke, I realized that the day's events meant we probably would have little time together in the years ahead. This thought brought with it a bundle of emotions. I wanted to spend more time with Tracy, but I had joined the Marines to be far out on the front lines of America's defense. September 11 shifted those front lines from peacekeeping missions to combat, which, at its core, is why the Marines exist. We saw ourselves as guardian leaders in a dangerous world, though there was more to it than this high ideal. While I told myself that I was content with being a peacetime Marine, a strong part of me wanted to experience war. I didn't fully understand that part and couldn't explain it to Tracy. There was a lot to it. It had to do with the desire to prove myself, the ecstasy of danger, and darker things that would come out with time.

"Marines move toward the sound of guns," Staff Sergeant Sweeney had told us with his final words the previous summer at OCS. That drive was so powerful that it felt like part of our DNA, and it was a large part of what distinguished us. We wanted to be on the front lines of righteous battles. We wanted to be at Ground Zero with the firefighters running into the breach saving lives. We wanted to be in whatever fight was to come, and for me that desire was as strong as the forces that had taken me to Kibera and had me falling in love long before I ever intended to commit to a relationship.

THE BARRACKS HUMMED with speculation. Within hours Bin Laden's name arose as the primary suspect. A small minority of the lieutenants mouthed off about what they believed to be a larger problem with Muslims around the world. No Muslims were in our company of lieutenants, and I would later regret not confronting them. At the time, I didn't want to alienate myself from my new peers, and I didn't know how to object to them in a way that would be constructive. Our emotions soared, and I, too, was angry and out for justice.

Salim sent me an e-mail around noon. "We keep watching planes crashing into buildings in New York and Washington. Where are you? Are you OK? What about Semaj?"

Semaj was back at work in the South Bronx as a community organizer preparing to attend Howard University School of Law the following year. I assumed that he was fine, though I hadn't been able to reach him by phone. I told Salim that I was worried about American reactions if the attacks had been perpetrated by Muslims. Until that point, we hadn't written to each other about faith. We began an unusually personal e-mail exchange that Andrew Carroll, the writer who was CFK's first donor, later published in his anthology *War Letters*. One particular e-mail from Salim revealed the depths and power of his faith:

> I wasn't born Muslim . . . Mama Fatuma was a Muslim. She didn't
> force Islam on us, but I got interested in it because she saved me.

Islam is really important to me. I like the comfort it provides and
discipline. In that way it is kind of like the Marines maybe. I found
after I became Muslim that I had a community that cared about
me. On the streets there was no one. The Marines helped you get
educated. Muslims like Mama Fatuma helped me get educated too.
So I feel a commitment and duty to Allah, praise be His name. I
think we are all here for a purpose. I believe that purpose is guided
by Allah. There is a lot of bad in the world. Allah I can count on to
show us goodness and peace and so I hope this war will end and the
terrorists will be stopped so that we can go back to goodness.*

Our training began days later with a renewed sense of purpose. We were
at war. We cheered when President Bush gave a speech at Ground Zero
and said into a megaphone, "I can hear you. The rest of the world hears
you, and the people who knocked these buildings down will hear all of us
soon." We would deliver that message in person and through the barrel of a
gun. Soon our brother and sister Marines would descend into the mountains
of Afghanistan. Soon it would be our time to join the fight. I hoped that I
wouldn't miss the largest battles because of the nine-month training cycle
that awaited me if I was to fulfill my dream of becoming an infantry officer.

Weeks later I hit my first major roadblock.

"DOUBLE-TIME, MARCH," a lieutenant sounded-off, kicking our
platoon into a jog down the rifle-range trail. Formation runs were always
like walks in the park for me. We ran as slow as our slowest man, and that
was never me, fortunately—until then.

"Yo, Barcott, you all right?" asked my roommate from Jersey, who was
jogging alongside me. I was falling behind. The pulsing pain in my hip
was severe. It had started after three or four weeks of heavy-duty after-
hours training for my first marathon. I was still wearing my old sneakers
with treads worn smooth from years of pavement-pounding in Chapel
Hill. Lieutenants at the Basic School had been given the special option to
run the Marine Corps Marathon in honor of the 9/11 victims, and I had
immediately signed up with twenty others.

"Barcott, I said, you all right?"

---

* Andrew Carroll, *War Letters: Extraordinary Correspondence from American Wars*
(New York: Scribner, 2001), pp. 445–446.

"Yeah, yeah," I grunted. I finished the run but felt humiliated. I had slowed the platoon down.

Afterward, I limped into the medic's office. When the results from an X-ray returned, the doc told me I had a broken leg.

"What?" I didn't believe him. There was no time for a broken leg.

He pointed to a thin white line in the X-ray. "Stress fracture, upper femur. If you keep on it, it may break clean, and you can say good-bye to your Marine Corps career." My recovery would take at least six months, the doc said authoritatively.

I had broken my leg because I was too cheap to purchase new running shoes and too thickheaded to listen to advice about how to properly train for a marathon. Spiteful and bitter, I finally sent my letter about Oluoch and his delinquent $1,500 loan. CFK was running out of money, and I felt like a failure for getting recycled to Mike Company, a holding ground for "broke dicks." I thought mailing the letter would feel good, but that too was disappointing.

THERE WERE TWO dozen lieutenants in Mike Company, and I wanted nothing to do with them. Their low morale was toxic. Fortunately, the commander assigned me to be a training officer for a company of new warrant officers.

The training-officer job was the most perfunctory work I had ever been given. Each morning I showed up at 0700 hours and collected rosters. I kept a captain informed of the numbers, then sat around all day in an office with a phone that never rang. My peers were heading into the field to learn land navigation, call for fire, and machine-gun handling, and I was at a desk in a job fit for a chimp.

It would've been depressing if not for CFK. Being a training officer allowed me to volunteer nearly full-time. I sent hundreds of e-mails to Kenya, pitched foundations for funding, and developed our U.S. board. In the evenings I hit the weight room and then returned to my barracks to work another six hours with CFK. The work was sedentary but surprisingly exhilarating. Our decisions each day directly contributed to the growth of an organization that I believed had wartime relevance. We were fighting some of the root causes of terrorism by empowering youth and reconciling ethnic tensions in one of the world's most volatile slums.

It seemed unlikely that my assignment as a training officer would change my life, and for a while my Marine Corps plans remained intact. I wanted to be an infantry officer and then go to a reconnaissance unit, as my father had done. I had even written about this career ambition in my high school yearbook profile. Infantry was the backbone of the Marine Corps, and recon was so elite you couldn't join as an officer until you'd served a tour in the infantry. I figured the combination of the two would give me the best chance I had to get into the fight. However, after September 11 there was a lot of talk concerning the need for more human intelligence (HUMINT) in Afghanistan. Each Basic School company had one or two HUMINT billets for which lieutenants competed. I searched for more information online about HUMINT but couldn't find much. The manual of military jobs described it in vague terms as a job for "people persons." None of my mentors apart from the State Department officer Peter Whaley seemed to know anything about it, and Whaley was cryptic when I mentioned it over the phone. "Be careful where you speak about that," he had said, and offered no additional advice. The absence of accessible information further piqued my interest.

Warrant officers dropped by the training office from time to time to check the schedule and make small talk. I figured one of the warrant officers who specialized in counterintelligence might know something about HUMINT. Apart from my father, Warrant Officer R.R. was the only person I knew who still smoked a pipe. One afternoon he offered me an overview. "Now, Lieutenant, nothing that we tell you here will be classified, but ours is a field of quiet professionals. So please keep it to yourself," he began.

Counterintelligence (CI) involved safeguarding sensitive information and deceiving the enemy. It was often defensive in nature. HUMINT on the other hand referred to the collection of information through human sources and was often offensive. In the Marine Corps, the two specialties merged into one field called CI/HUMINT. Marine HUMINT officers led small teams of highly trained Marines on missions with infantry battalions, Special Forces, and other government agencies. They led interrogations and developed networks of informants on the battlefield. The operational tempo was intense because it was a small field in high demand. "You'll be deployed most of the time," Warrant Officer R.R. advised. "Not easy if you have a family."

I thanked him and told him that I might compete for a HUMINT billet once my leg healed.

"Good," he replied. "If you do, and if you get it, you may join us in Camp Lejeune. You'll be attached to infantry units, so you need to learn those skills. But most important are your listening and writing skills, and asking questions. You need to know how to ask good questions. That's the real secret."

Warrant Officer R.R.'s final words set the hook. I knew from Kibera and UNC that I could listen and write well, and I enjoyed interacting with people from diverse backgrounds. Most important, HUMINT sounded like a field that could take me to the war's front lines, perhaps even more frequently than the regular infantry. I called Tracy that night eager to tell her the exciting news that I might have found a new calling in the Marine Corps. Describing the field to her in general terms, I explained that it involved interacting with people, collecting and distilling information, and writing time-sensitive reports.

"Sounds like what I do." Tracy was in her second year in her Ph.D. program in clinical psychology. "But what is it that you actually do?"

I was hoping she wasn't going to ask that question. I apologized and said that I couldn't give many other details.

"What? That's ridiculous. Do you just not know?"

"Babe, I can't."

"At least give me a clue."

"It has something to do with espionage."

Tracy paused. She didn't impress easily. "That's intriguing. It could be a good fit. I'm happy for you."

"Well, I need to get it first. It's really competitive, you know."

"Yeah, I'm sure, but you'll get it."

"I don't know."

"I do, but what I want to know is if you'll be gone a lot in this job?"

"Some, but I don't know how much. Depends." I couldn't bring myself to tell her what the warrant officer had said about the operational tempo, or that I was torn between my love for her and my need to prove myself on the battlefield.

"I see." I could tell from the sound of her voice that she knew there was much more to it, and that in the end each of us had only so much control over our destiny. Things had changed, not between us, I hoped, but around us.

CHAPTER THIRTEEN

Change and Continuity

Washington, D.C.

NOVEMBER 2001

MY MENTOR, COLONEL GREENWOOD, WAS STILL a director of defense policy at the National Security Council. Our fathers had served together in Vietnam, when mine was a lieutenant and his was a colonel. One day he invited me to lunch at the Army and Navy Club, two blocks from his office in the White House compound. I didn't have to mention the anxiety I felt about having my military career delayed eight months because of a stress fracture.

"We're hard chargers. Injuries happen," Colonel Greenwood said before I brought it up. He arched one of his eyebrows, grinned, and told me to keep my head up. He knew that I was worried about missing the fight. Every Marine understood that. However, from his vantage point Marines would be fighting long after I finished my training. Though I didn't know it at the time, and much to Colonel Greenwood's dismay, some of the neoconservatives in the administration were already planning to launch an Iraq invasion.

As for HUMINT, Colonel Greenwood thought it was an excellent choice of specialty. It was an essential part of any serious counterterrorism operation. Every day he read dozens of classified intelligence reports, including occasional reports with information collected by Marine teams at the forward edge of the battlefield. Additionally, he thought the field would be a good complement to my own interests. Colonel Greenwood was one of the few senior Marine officers who knew about CFK. When he asked me for an update, I gave him an overview: We had merged sports and leadership development with health care, and we would soon launch the first all-girls' soccer league. If the doctors and my command authorized my travel, I would return to Kibera for Christmas leave.

Colonel Greenwood commented that CFK reminded him of his deployment to Haiti as a battalion operations officer in 1994. His battalion had taken on a hybrid mission to establish security and provide humanitarian aid. Such missions embodied what the Marine Corps called the "three-block war." This was the idea that Marines needed to be prepared to face high-intensity combat, peacekeeping, and humanitarian aid delivery at the same time. The military was experimenting with noncombat operations that supported nation building, and Colonel Greenwood suspected I would be a part of this experiment.

There were downsides to these hybrid military missions. While Colonel Greenwood was proud of the work his Marines had done in Haiti, he acknowledged that his unit had left before he could establish any depth to their relationships with Haitians. The military's short deployment cycles resulted in a constant change in personnel. Knowledge was frequently lost in never-ending transitions. "We lack continuity," Colonel Greenwood said. "These places need long-term engagement. That's why it's like a revolving door for the U.S. in Haiti."

Colonel Greenwood believed this constant change and failure to develop cultural expertise was the Achilles' heel of the U.S. military. Marines typically deployed for six months in order to avoid burnout, which was a crucial consideration in high-intensity combat. However, if we wanted to do nation building, that work required long-term commitment. It required a paradigm shift in our way of thinking.

"What you're developing in Kibera is the continuity," he observed, which in his opinion was valuable for Kibera as well as for my professional development. "Do you intend to stick with it?"

"Yes, sir, with everything I have." There wasn't a doubt in my mind. Ever since the day I reunited with Tabitha and we went zigzagging through the alleys to her little clinic behind the Mad Lion, I knew I was in it for the long haul. Even at the lowest points, I had faith. Most of the others had shifted gears. Nate was back in Wilmington, North Carolina, bartending and thinking about a career as a high school teacher. He wasn't that involved with CFK apart from his mentorship to Kash, which was a considerable commitment. Semaj was busy preparing for law school. My mother doubted we would survive as an organization, though she never said that to me. Thus Tabitha, Salim, and I, perhaps for very different reasons, were the only three people resolute in our unbridled commitment.

A PORTION OF Kibera exploded with violence shortly after my lunch meeting with Colonel Greenwood. Fueled in part by careless remarks from President Moi, rent control riots displaced thousands of people within days. Salim immediately suspended the sports program and helped Tabitha focus on providing emergency care at the clinic. We spoke together on the phone once a day. Salim sounded calm and confident. He told me he drew strength from Tabitha, and that I shouldn't worry about their safety because the fighting was isolated to a different part of Kibera. His reassurance gave me some peace of mind, though I still found myself waking up at night thinking about Tabitha, him, and our team on the ground.

Colonel Greenwood called me before the first press reports about Kibera's riots emerged online. He wanted to arrange a meeting for me to give a private briefing to the president's senior adviser for African affairs, a former Harvard Kennedy School of Government professor named Jendayi Frazer. He offered to call the Basic School commander, a fellow colonel, to have me excused from duty for an afternoon. I thanked him for the phenomenal opportunity. I would figure out a way to be there whenever Dr. Frazer wanted to meet, but I asked Colonel Greenwood not to call my commander. It was easy enough for a buddy of mine to cover for me at the training office.

The grand marbled halls in the National Security Council were surprisingly quiet when I arrived thirty minutes before my meeting with Dr. Frazer. I wasn't particularly nervous. By that point in late 2001, I had presented dozens of overviews about Kibera and CFK. Nevertheless, for a moment I stopped in the middle of a hall and took it all in. There I was, a lowly second lieutenant in the White House compound about to brief the president's senior African adviser.

A gracious African-American political scientist with hair almost as short as my own, Dr. Frazer warmly welcomed me into her office with high ceilings and a view of the West Wing. I moved through my brief without notes, occasionally referencing a photo or map from my handout. After my briefing, Dr. Frazer thanked me for my military service and our work in Kibera. She suggested that I consider Harvard's Kennedy School when the time was right for graduate work. Her thoughtful personal advice caught me off guard. Graduate school was the last thing on my mind. However, I did have a goal-oriented thought as I briefed her—maybe one day I could work at the National Security Council. In a rather clumsy way I asked her what she thought of her job as she escorted me out of her office.

"It's great," she said. "A lot of fighting fires. Every day brings a new challenge."

Colonel Greenwood enjoyed hearing about her parting remark when I mentioned it to him after our meeting. She was absolutely right, he said. So much was happening on any given day, it was easy to become reactive. In this regard, Colonel Greenwood's time at the White House was similar to many of his military deployments. As Marines, we often moved so quickly that it was difficult to see the larger picture.

"That's why what you're doing in Kibera is important. It's all about continuity. You'll see the change you make over a course of years." That was Colonel Greenwood's parting advice. He had been overly generous with his time. His in-box was exploding with classified traffic that needed his attention. "You know, Rye, it won't be easy to do both, and obviously the Marines come first. But you should try to balance these two things, and your family. Don't forget your family. Some commanders will be more supportive than others. Hopefully you'll have good ones, for your Marines' sake, for your family's, and for Kibera's."

To RETURN TO Kibera for Christmas leave, I needed to route a formal request up the Basic School chain of command. The command had no particular reason to support my request. I hadn't built any meaningful relationships with the staff, and my travel could easily have been viewed as a risk without payback. Figuring that my best shot was to fully explain CFK in a written request and hope that it would appeal to my commander's humanitarian sentiments, I spent a day writing and editing a two-page justification that included references to credible outside sources. My strategy was full disclosure, so I included quotes such as this one from a United Nations report:

NAIROBI, 13 December 2001—After weeks marked by tension, violent clashes, killings, rioting and looting, residents of Kenya's biggest slum, Kibera, have slowly begun rebuilding their lives. But even as an anxious calm returned this week, deep-rooted tensions remain in the sprawling suburb, home to hundreds of thousands of people.*

To my surprise, my leave request sailed up the chain of command and was approved within days.

My Christmas plans went over less smoothly with Tracy, who wanted to introduce me to her family over the holidays. Our relationship had matured that fall, in part because we were able to spend most weekends together. Although we hadn't made plans about our future as a couple, visiting family was an obvious next step. The problem was the timing, and the fact that I didn't realize that our families valued holidays differently. Tracy grew up with a tightly knit extended family that lived close to each other and always spent holidays together. My parents were far removed from their families in Washington State and Pennsylvania. Holidays were not as special for us. We had some family rituals—Dad, Mom, and I played tag football and basketball games with anyone who would join us, and we'd take long walks together in the woods behind our house—but it wasn't a big deal every now and then if something else came up.

Tracy expressed her disappointment and left it alone. She certainly didn't give me an ultimatum. Her patience was a blessing because I was still torn between her and my desire to be independent. Once my military command gave me authorization, I had to go to Kibera. I wanted to be there on the ground with Salim, Tabitha, and Kash defending those who needed it. I was moving to the sound of guns.

From the outskirts around Fort Jesus, where Salim rented an apartment, everything looked normal. Not until I stepped into the clinic did the damage become visible. Patients' faces conveyed emotional anguish

---

* United Nations, IRIN Report, "KENYA: Focus on clashes in Kibera slum, Nairobi," December 13, 2001, http://www.irinnews.org/report.aspx?reportid=29122.

and physical pain. The "anxious calm" that the United Nations' report had identified was palpable. Even Tabitha wore an exhausted expression that I would years later come to recognize as a numbness from overexposure to trauma.

Patients trickled in with wounds from the clashes: infected, pus-filled machete gashes, diarrhea from wastewater, and victims of rape and abuse by riot-control police. In three weeks a few dozen people had been killed, many more had been raped, and perhaps as many as three thousand residents had lost their homes to fire or eviction.

Once the violence subsided our soccer players lobbied Salim, Kash, and our fourteen youth representatives to hold the final match of the CFK tournament before many families returned to their rural homes for the holidays. Salim saw it as the first great test for our interethnic soccer league. Could we help reconcile tensions, or would a final match backfire and explode?

"For the youth, soccer is more important than who's in what tribe," Kash reasoned. "It's not the players. It's the fans. Those are the ones I worry about." Salim and Tabitha agreed, and Salim gave Kash the go-ahead to begin planning a final match.

Kash was thriving. Still living at the clinic to provide Tabitha with security, he appeared to command the respect and admiration of the fourteen volunteer youth representatives who helped him pull together the CFK soccer tournaments and monthly wars on garbage. Nate helped Kash edit his college essays, and we were optimistic about his chances of being admitted to UNC provided that we found funding to cover his expenses. To secure the funding, we assumed that Kash needed to travel to the United States with Salim and meet some of our top donors in person.

Kash spent most of his time during the clashes in the clinic with Tabitha. He recommended that we spend an afternoon with Ali's friend Kassim to learn more about what had happened. I was glad to hear that Kassim and Kash had become friends. Before CFK, Kash, a Kikuyu living in a predominately Luo village, had practically no contact with Nubians such as Kassim.

We met one afternoon near the majestic blue gum tree at Darajani Massive, the bridge in the center of Kibera where Nubian youth had congregated before the Nubian-Luo clashes of 1995.

"Kash! Omosh!" Kassim greeted us and wrapped me into a powerful embrace.

"You look good, man." I pulled back and gave him a friendly forearm to the shoulder.

"Aye, no, you, you look good. An officer and a gentleman, a soldier and a scholar," Kassim laughed, recalling phrases from *The Marine Corps Officer's Guide*, which I had once lent him. During my first summer in Kibera, Kassim had told me that he had inherited his ancestors' martial spirit and dreamed of becoming a soldier. Unfortunately, the supply of potential soldiers in Kenya far exceeded demand, and Kassim didn't have the funds to bribe his way in.

Within minutes of twisting along narrow back alleys, I was completely disoriented as Kassim led us deep inside one of Kibera's eleven villages. The charred remains of mud-and-tin shacks appeared suddenly and stretched across an area as long as a soccer field. It was a miracle people were able to stop the blaze. Kassim explained that we were standing at one of Kibera's ethnic fault lines. The side we had come from was predominately inhabited by Nubians; the other was "Luo land." Kassim didn't know many details about the clashes. He did, however, have a strong point of view about its causes, which reached straight to the top of the government.

President Moi had made an unusual public appearance earlier that fall when he stepped into Kibera and called for landlords to reduce their rents. Moi made his pronouncement as a favor to Raila Odinga, the Luo politician who had agreed to form a coalition with Moi's political party, KANU, after Moi announced his intention to step down from the presidency in 2002. It was an unlikely alliance. Moi, who was a member of the Kalenjin ethnic group, had once thrown Odinga in prison after a failed coup attempt in the early 1980s. Nevertheless, if the KANU candidate lost the election, speculation was that Moi might be held accountable and brought to trial as a private citizen for corruption scandals of staggering proportions. "That's Kenya politics," Kassim said, "all for themselves. Big men eat big."

As soon as President Moi made his announcement for lower rents in Kibera, large numbers of Luo tenants stopped paying rent. Nubians owned an estimated 10 to 20 percent of the homes in Kibera, and rent collection was a primary source of income for many households. Both sides, Nubian and Luo, claimed the other initiated the fighting. The violence had escalated quickly and spilled into other parts of Kibera by the time Moi dispatched his brutal paramilitary unit. The fighting stopped, though the root causes of the dispute remained unresolved.

It was in this context that we planned our final CFK soccer tournament. Although we mandated that teams be ethnically diverse, one of the top two teams was predominately Luo, and the other was mostly Nubian. Kassim thought it was risky and suggested that we mobilize additional security on game day.

"Is there anyone who would want to disrupt the game because of who we are? Does CFK have any enemies?" I asked.

"There's Taib," Kassim remarked. I hadn't thought about Taib since I had sent my angry retribution letter to Oluoch's employer. KIYESA, the pay-to-play soccer league that Taib established before running for the Kibera councillor's seat, appeared to be defunct. "He's still pissed off," Kassim added. "He keeps bothering me and Ali about it, says this bullshit about *mzungu* betrayal."

"You think he can turn the Nubian community against us?"

"Argh," Kash grunted. "You know Taib is all talk. Don't fear him."

"The only thing is what he says about Salim being a street kid from Mathare," Kassim said. "Some of the youths, they hear that and they wonder why it is that CFK is led by a guy from Mathare when we have so much talent here."

I had heard rumors about a few people opposing Salim's leadership on such grounds.

"But," Kassim added before I could ask Kash for his opinion, "Taib doesn't know that no one could do this like Salim. Salim knows how organizations work. In a way I can say that he is above the petty tribal politics of Kibera because he's an outsider. I mean, he looks like, I don't know, like a Somali. And of course Salim has Tabitha, and Kash, too. Man, we're a powerful team."

We were a powerful team, though our bank account didn't look so powerful. We were running out of money. Our account had less than $1,500. I spent my own money on plane tickets, postage, and administrative supplies. Salim lived on his meager savings from MYSA, and Kash continued to work in the community for income. Tabitha paid herself a pittance—four thousand shillings, about $50 a month. It was the same stipend she gave

Jane, her two nurse assistants, and a Kenyan nurse named Dorine Okoko who could have chosen a better-paying, far-less-intense clinic but stayed with CFK because of Tabitha's leadership, the learning opportunities, and the spiritual gratification she received from serving the community.

I was concerned but hopeful about our finances, and I believe my optimism helped support Salim and Tabitha through one of CFK's most fragile moments. They could build and lead a community-based organization in an African slum. I could provide entrée to the vast resources of the United States. We could only do it together, and together we planned for our most significant meeting.

We still needed one large funder, a sponsor. We didn't have many prospects apart from Salim's mentor Dr. Mary Ann Burris. I suggested to Salim and Tabitha that we ask Mary Ann for a formal meeting and present her with a polished proposal. Salim countered with an idea that we re-invite her to Kibera for our final soccer match. It was a high-risk proposition because we were still worried about an ethnic riot breaking out during the game. We discussed it for a few minutes until Tabitha weighed in with one of her favorite lines: "In life we have to take risks. Let's invite this lady to come and see the work we are doing with our bare hands. I'll make sure she's okay."

MARY ANN MET Tabitha and me at the clinic on game day. Tabitha escorted her past a queue of patients including a handful of HIV-positive adults, typhoid victims, hungry street kids, and babies with distended bellies.

"So what is it like to run this impressive clinic while raising four children?" Mary Ann asked.

Tabitha replied matter-of-factly, "You know, for me I can say it's not easy. It's a hard life. But we have to persevere."

My cell phone beeped with Kassim's security updates from the soccer field: "All secure." "No problem." "In control."

By the time we reached the soccer field thousands of fans were crammed along the muddy sidelines. "How about girls?" Mary Ann asked Salim, referring to the field and the largely male audience.

Salim was spending a fair amount of time launching a girls' soccer league with our Nubian youth representative, Abdul "Cantar" Hussein.

Unfortunately, it was slow going due to the deeply entrenched gender bias in the community. "We really need a separate program for girls," Salim told Mary Ann. Although I agreed with him wholeheartedly about the need, we first had to figure out how to raise at least $30,000 to fund our next year of operations in Kenya before launching new programs. If the Ford Foundation supported us, we could pursue our plans to grow the soccer and leadership-development program to two thousand participants and help Tabitha double the number of patients she treated each year to roughly five thousand. Without Ford, we would be stuck and might need to downsize our ambitions.

The soccer game went off without a security incident. As the fans stormed the field and hoisted the winning team onto their shoulders, Mary Ann casually commented, "I think I can get you guys support. Let me know how much you need and we'll work on the grant together. It will take a couple months, but New York [Ford Foundation headquarters] has never turned down one of my proposals."

I contained my urge to shout *Oohrah*, our Marine battle cry. "Thank you, Mary Ann. Thank you for believing in us," I said with Salim. We had our sponsor.

BACK IN MIKE Company after Christmas Break, I was lucky to have more downtime as a training officer. CFK needed a lot of work in the United States, and I immersed myself in a swirl of activity with the help of a half dozen U.S. volunteers and daily contact with Salim. We published an annual report and raised $5,000, a vital bridge before the Ford Foundation grant came through. That money enabled Ben Mshila and the Kenyan CFK board to put Kash on the payroll and give Tabitha money to buy medicine and develop her home-based care program for HIV-positive widows. We prepared our books for our first tax filings in the United States and in Kenya, and we selected our first class of undergraduate summer volunteers to help Salim in Kibera.

More e-mail came in every day. Some of my replies evolved into prolonged exchanges that every now and then led to good things. A bedridden women's rights advocate e-mailing from her home in a forest in Maine had asked me about the Nubians. After many months of e-mail, I called her and told her about Ali and his love for his daughter, Khadija. For the next eight years, this woman, Mary Beth Crocket, sponsored Khadija through school with part of her disability check and the meager earnings her husband made driving tractor-trailer trucks. On another occasion, two recent college graduates who had participated in a study abroad program in Kenya with the School for International Training, Karen Austrian and Emily Verellen, e-mailed with a proposal to launch a girls' center that would create safe spaces and be led by young women from Kibera. Salim and Tabitha saw the tremendous need for such a center. With their support Karen and Emily joined CFK and won grants from Columbia University and American Jewish World Service. Together with a group of young women in Kibera, and a young Kenyan leader named Caroline Sakwa, Karen and Emily spent the next year creating CFK's Binti Pamoja (Daughters United) Girls' Center. It would become the first comprehensive leadership-development program for girls in the community.

One of my greatest concerns was building a stronger board in the United States. To that point, our U.S. board was hands-off and served more as an advisory council. The members included Professors Peacock and Kohn, Dr. Cross, and my mother. Each member was an older professional who cared about CFK but didn't have the time or the energy to get heavily involved. We needed a champion who could help lead CFK in the United States. I made a list of five doers who were about my age and had an interest in African development. Kim Chapman, the rugby-playing Canadian public health specialist who had graduated a year ahead of me, was at the top of the list. Although I didn't know her well, we had many mutual friends, and her office was located next to CFK's office in the international center that Professor Peacock directed. Kim had strong views about economic aid, which she saw as too often being top-down and paternalistic. She thought our model of participatory development was the right approach and agreed to take over as our first board chair shortly after we presented the offer.

Kim was a take-no-prisoners manager who was results-oriented, meticulous, and dependable. We complemented each other well. My organizational and management skills needed work, and she was less interested in networking and fund-raising, or, as she called it, being a "schmoozing salesman." Kim became a fierce defender of our scarce resources. She was a leader who didn't tolerate sloppy thinking or let selfish interests get in the way of serving the community.

Kim and I focused on pulling together a week of big events in Chapel Hill with Salim, Kash, Nate, and me presenting to student groups and prospective donors in March before my Basic School training began. In addition to the presentations, we planned to hold our first U.S. board meeting and a major fund-raising dinner after Professor Peacock's wife, Florence, graciously offered their home for the occasion. A professional opera singer, Florence had designed and built their home to accommodate musical performances. Everyone in Chapel Hill seemed to know and admire the Peacocks, and they understood the importance of our work, in part because they had lived together in an Indonesian slum in the 1960s when Professor Peacock was an anthropology graduate student at Harvard. It was during one of Professor Peacock's seminars that I first heard the adage that came to define our ethos: "Talent is universal; opportunity is not."

THE WEEK IN Chapel Hill was going well, though we had hoped to raise more money. Our dinner at the Peacocks' house was our last shot to land a pledge that would cover tuition and living expenses for Kash to attend UNC. An admissions officer had confided to me that Kash's chances were "optimistic" if we could secure a full financial commitment.

Salim felt conflicted. He considered Kash a friend and thought it was a great opportunity for CFK. At our core we intended to help cultivate a new generation of African leadership, and Kash seemed to be a shining example of that promise. Although he would lose the only employee in the sports program if Kash left, Salim thought he had a deep bench of talent from which to choose among the fourteen youth representatives. What bothered Salim was the amount of money Kash's UNC degree would require. The bill for four years of tuition and living expenses would be nearly $100,000, an amount that was more than three times the total CFK annual budget. Couldn't that money do more and for more people?

I too was torn about the large gulf between the amount we needed to raise for Kash and the CFK annual budget. Salim and I spoke openly about our feelings on the matter. In my mind, the two situations were not comparable. Our most affluent donors were far more likely to write large checks to support an individual whom they knew than to support programs. I hoped that the emotional commitment these donors developed to Kash would deepen their loyalty to CFK and advance our fund-raising for the organization. Salim begrudgingly acknowledged this logic and said he would support fund-raising for Kash because he trusted me, not because he agreed with the decision.

About seventy people joined us for our dinner at the Peacocks. Salim and Kash dressed in elegant gold African robes, and I wore my Marine Corps dress blues with my shiny "butter bars," the insignia of the lowest-ranking commissioned officers in the Marine Corps. Jennifer Coffman, Kim Chapman, Nate, and my parents all attended and helped us tell the CFK story during the cocktail hour.

The spotlight turned to Salim and me. We opened the formal presentation with the short Reuters *Africa Journal* video profiling CFK, then moved through our presentation, improvising with jokes here and there. When we spoke about our first meeting at MYSA, Salim said that I was asking him so many questions he would have said yes to anything just to get me out of his office. I laughed and told the story of our first meeting at the Ford Foundation, when Mary Ann had concluded the meeting by saying that we made an odd couple.

Kash was nervous. Salim had traveled to the United States on multiple occasions, including a trip as a teenager with Mary Ann and the Ford Foundation. This was Kash's first trip. Nate had helped him adjust to the culture shock, but the whole experience was overwhelming. Now Kash was about to be paraded in front of a group of people as a final act.

He stepped into the center of the room and stood still. There was a long pause. I took a deep breath. As I exhaled, Kash began speaking, and as he spoke, he became animated. Kash enraptured the audience with stories about his life and the power of soccer to provide hope and unity. He spoke about the lack of decent educational opportunities for his brothers and sisters, and he told us about his dream of attending college. As the energy in the room neared a climax, Kash declared, "We aren't looking for handouts in Kibera. It's not up to you. You can't solve these things. You can help, but we must do it ourselves."

I didn't see it coming. Kash was often as stoic and tough as Tabitha. All of a sudden, tears fell from his face. "Thank you," he mumbled. The room rose in a standing ovation.

Alston Gardner and another donor, Thomas S. Kenan III, approached me at the end of the evening. Deeply moved by what they had heard, they each offered to cover half of the cost of Kash's college expenses if he got into UNC. It took months of preparation, but in two minutes we had received pledges for $100,000.

Everyone was deeply impressed by Kash, especially my parents. Mom reminisced about her overnights in Tabitha's clinic and falling asleep to the sound of Kash studying French while listening to Edith Piaf in the adjacent room. My parents were delighted when I told them about the pledges.

"Oh my!" Mom exclaimed. "He will thrive at UNC. What a great, tremendous thing."

It was a great, tremendous thing. It was a long-term investment in Kibera. Kash at UNC would further deepen the continuity Colonel Greenwood had spoken about. Kash would be the ultimate ambassador for CFK on campus, and a role model for youth in Kibera and beyond. He embodied the vision.

Only one person appeared to have a different perspective. "I don't know," Jennifer Coffman said to me afterward. She was looking at Kash, who was talking confidently to another donor. "There's just something about him that I don't trust."

CHAPTER FOURTEEN

Spyderco

Quantico, Virginia

SUMMER 2002

MY STRESS FRACTURE HEALED AND I STARTED the Basic School course for a second time. The days were long and intense, and I needed to finish at the top of my two-hundred-lieutenant class to secure the one human intelligence billet. I wanted HUMINT too badly not to aim for it, but I also didn't want to let go of CFK. I convinced myself that I could do both if I worked harder and smarter. CFK would make me a better Marine, and the Marines would help me improve my leadership with CFK. Nevertheless, this decision came with a cost. There was no downtime. The only books I owned pertained to war and economic development, and I rarely had time to read them.

Tracy thought I was nuts. When I saw her on the weekends I couldn't keep my eyes open past ten P.M. But she was also tired from her research and clinical work helping children with developmental and psychological disorders. We spent our weekends together exploring Washington, D.C. Sometimes we were so tired on Sunday afternoons that we pulled the Green Bean over into parking lots, reclined the bucket seats, and took naps. "We're like eighty-year-olds in twenty-three-year-old bodies," Tracy observed, giggling as she reclined her bucket seat in a parking lot somewhere around Georgetown.

Things were going well for CFK since our fund-raiser with the Peacocks in Chapel Hill. I had reduced the amount of time I poured into the organization from more than sixty hours a week to about twenty. I kept out of the operational decisions on the ground, although Salim and I still e-mailed daily to work through plans and donor relations. Our biggest news was that UNC had accepted Kash to the undergraduate class of 2007. He would be the first Tar Heel from Kibera, one of just 53 international students in the incoming freshman class of 3,460. We were thrilled, and Nate spent countless hours coaching him in preparation for his arrival at the end of August.

By the time Kash was about to fly to the United States, I was four months into the six-month Basic School course and facing final practical-application exams that would determine a large part of our class standing. Ranked among the top five lieutenants, I couldn't afford to slip on any of the exams. The exam that concerned me the most was land navigation, a seven-hour test that 20 percent of every class typically failed.

I didn't need distractions. But when Kash landed at John F. Kennedy Airport in New York, armed immigration officials detained him. Kash was sobbing when my father answered his collect call. He told Dad that the immigration officer made a mistake and wanted to send him back to Kenya. My father dove full bore to Kash's defense, slicing through the bureaucracy with his deep, authoritative voice. I could hear his introduction: "This is Dr. Schwartz calling on behalf of John Kanyua. With whom am I speaking?"

My father soon reached a senior immigration official and received the full story. U.S. immigration had increased its security protocol substantially after September 11. Something in Kash's file triggered additional screening, which included a check of his SAT scores. The SAT check did him in. Evidently, Kash had falsified his scores and forged his high school transcript. UNC Admissions had assumed that the copies of his SAT scores and transcript were accurate. This oversight was attributable in part to CFK's credibility within the university and the excitement that we had generated around Kash's application.

He was deported back to Kenya the following day.

My head spun with questions. *How could we not have seen it all along? We had introduced Kash to two of the university's most generous donors. How would they respond? What else had Kash not told us?*

When we first began the process of bringing Kash to UNC we had to identify an American sponsor in Kenya. Chris Tomlinson, the Associated Press correspondent on our Kenyan board, was traveling at the time. However, his boss, Susan Linnee, had agreed to help Kash after holding a conversation with him in fluent French.

I thought Susan would be outraged by the news. Over the past three months, she had invested a lot of time helping to prepare Kash. She had put her own name on the line.

"Listen, don't beat yourself up. These things happen," she responded to my phone call, "He had an opportunity to study in the U.S. coming from Kibera. If you were Kash, would you've done anything differently?"

"But he compromised his integrity," I replied, surprised by her response.

"I know, but what does integrity mean in such a place?"

Kash didn't have much to say when I finally reached him. Groveling would have been out of character, but I expected to hear an apology. Kash made it sound as if nothing had happened. He said he intended to move back into Tabitha's clinic and continue working for CFK. I hung up before I said something I would regret.

My worlds were merging. The Marine Corps emphasized integrity as the paramount principle of leaders. If we accepted Kash back, we'd send a signal that we tolerated deception. I appreciated that desperate conditions often led to desperate measures. If ever given access to such a great opportunity, the average person in Kibera may have taken the same actions as Kash. Yet as an organization we could only do so much. We needed to be led by the exceptional young people in Kibera, not the average ones. The most difficult test of that type of rare leader was if he or she could live with dignity and morality in conditions that tested core values every day. That's what attracted me to Salim and Tabitha, and what we had missed with Kash.

On the surface, the decision was clear. Kash needed to go. Yet it was complicated because he was a friend. I still cared about him and wanted him to succeed. As a group, we were torn. Salim took a strong stance. "Man, he really messed it," Salim said, sounding exasperated, "and I don't think Kash can stay in CFK. We need to think about what this means to others."

Tabitha was more lenient. She suggested we suspend Kash temporarily but eventually let him return as a volunteer. After almost a year living at her clinic and providing security, she trusted him. Nate also wanted to give Kash a second chance. As shocked as he was by the deception, he was tolerant in a way that I struggled to comprehend, and he knew Kash best. He believed Kash could have succeeded at UNC.

I expressed my own view in an e-mail to the donors who had offered to cover Kash's $100,000 of educational expenses. "In the end I don't think Kash could have succeeded at UNC," I wrote. "Perhaps it's best that this happened now instead of later, but it should have never gotten to this point. I'm sorry it happened, though I remain grateful to you for your support and advice."

Salim and I agreed that Kash needed to leave CFK. Tabitha held firm to her position that with time we should consider inviting him back. My mother shared Tabitha's viewpoint, which wasn't a surprise because Mom often sought the middle ground. I was most concerned about how Nate would react. When I called and spoke frankly with him about my feelings and the trade-offs we had to weigh in our decision, Nate eventually told me that he was cool with it, though I sensed from the tone of his voice that our friendship was wounded.

What I didn't expect was that Kash's situation would also strain my relationship with my father. Dad thought we should "cut him some slack." My father's position, which he took with a characteristic hard-line, angered me. He was a Marine. He should've understood my position and supported me with it. I was too emotional to realize and appreciate that my father's protective instincts were far more important to him than his judgments on effective leadership. Kash was becoming a second son to my father, and therefore he deserved a second chance.

Too stressed-out to think clearly, I consulted with Tracy. Although she hadn't yet been to Kibera, she had met all of the key CFK people with the exception of Tabitha. Tracy told me that she knew it was a tough decision. She thought I should trust my judgment and speak with Kash directly about our decision.

Initiating that second conversation with Kash was, at that point, one of the toughest moments of my life. The friend in me didn't want to make the call. I wrote down some notes and thought about Kash throughout a long night of little sleep. In the morning, I searched for excuses to delay the call until I heard a Marine voice in my head saying something about the burdens of leadership. I picked up the phone and punched in the numbers before I could change my mind.

Kash was subdued. He knew what was going on as I read from my notes, my voice sounding scripted and stiff. I couldn't bring myself to break the barrier between leader and friend. It was a defense mechanism. Kash didn't say much of anything, even when I asked him direct questions. His silence wore on me. By the time I had made it through my notes and had nothing else prepared to say, though so much more to talk about, I was angry with Kash for not apologizing. Somehow it wouldn't have felt like such a betrayal if he had just said he screwed up and was sorry. Yet there was nothing on the other end of the phone. "Kash, integrity is everything," I offered as a parting shot, "I hope you can restore yours."

DAYS LATER I was on the land-navigation course trying to keep Kash out of my mind as I scoured the forests for my targets. One might think a bright red can the size of a shoebox on top of a three-foot pole would stand out. I backtracked twice, paced out the distance, and conducted a careful terrain analysis. I was certain from the map's contour lines that I was on the right hill. Where the hell was the red can?

Time was running out. I needed to find ten cans and was stuck on the eighth. I had been alone in the woods for six hours, beating back brush on a scorching summer day. My canteens were empty. Less than an hour was left.

The final land-navigation exercise counted for a substantial part of our grade at the Basic School. If I failed it, I wouldn't get the HUMINT billet. I recalled the words from my platoon commander that morning. He had warned us not to self-destruct on the exercise.

Something grumbled. It sounded like my father clearing his throat. I turned and a black bear was standing on all fours a short ways off. He stared at me curiously. With my unloaded M16 at the ready, I froze for what felt like a long time. The bear grumbled again and began to paw the ground. I moved my hand toward the Spyderco knife clipped to my pocket, stepping back gingerly. Slow, steady steps. When the bear's attention shifted to some brush at its feet, I sprinted down a draw and up the adjacent hill.

Lo and behold, the red can was there. I checked it off, found the last two cans, and completed the exercise with minutes to spare. An instructor graded my sheet at the finish line. I had hit all ten cans correctly. I was going to be a Marine Corps HUMINT officer.

MY BALANCING ACT seemed to be working. With the exception of the incident with Kash, CFK was on the right track. Our sports program grew to two thousand participants; Tabitha's clinic was on target to treat five thousand patients by the year's end; and our new Binti Pamoja Girls' Center was establishing roots in the community by engaging young women in health and rights training. The Marine Corps assigned me to the East Coast at Camp Lejeune, North Carolina, where I would see Tracy on the weekends. The last major hurdle I faced before reporting to Camp Lejeune was to receive a Top Secret/Sensitive Compartmentalized Information clearance. I didn't understand what the Sensitive Compartmentalized Information part of the clearance meant, and neither did any of my instructors. Most of them only had Secret-level clearances.

The security clearance application included a notoriously lengthy background investigation. In my case, this was complicated by my having daily contact with foreign nationals. I was particularly concerned about how the government review agencies would perceive my relationship with Salim. If any names triggered special screening, I assumed *Salim Mohamed* would be one of them.

The only way to deal with the concerns was to address them head-on and hope that my disclosure would give peace of mind to the intelligence agents determining my fate. Without a Top Secret clearance, I wouldn't be eligible for HUMINT. I prepared a twenty-page addendum detailing CFK in addition to the normal book-length paperwork. When an agent came to interview me a week later, she seemed to be impressed by CFK's work. Before she left, I thanked her and gave her a CFK brochure. Weeks later, the government granted me an "interim" Top Secret clearance while the rest of my background investigation was completed. With it, I packed up and prepared to report to my company in Camp Lejeune and begin my advanced training.

"HERE YA GO, sir." Mo, a bull-necked sergeant, handed me a Kevlar helmet and a Vietnam-era flak jacket.

"What's this for?"

"The game" He grinned. "Football for morning PT [physical train-ing], sir. Outside on the field there." Sergeant Mo pointed to a wide patch of grass.

"Good to go, Sergeant."

Having just received the Iron Mike Award for the highest physical-fitness score in my Basic School class, I figured the PT session would be no problem. I took the flak jacket from Sergeant Mo. Sweat-stained with salt lines and spotted with dried blood, it smelled like Kibera.

Marines moseyed out to the field across the street from our team house, a one-story, asbestos-infested brick building. Some of the Marines sounded eager as they speculated about the prospects for war in Iraq, "the sandbox." Our company was one of the few Marine units where the average age was over twenty-five, and the Marines came in many differ-ent shapes and sizes. Some HUMINT Marines ran marathons. Others were horribly unfit, such as one nicknamed "the pumpkin smuggler" be-cause from a distance it could appear as if he had a pumpkin in his pants and another beneath his shirt.

The game began. Full contact. I was the youngest man on the field, and I went all out. As the hits got harder, a couple of Marines dropped with twisted ankles and dislocated shoulders. One of my teammates took a hel-met to the mouth and had to be carried off the field, where he watched the rest of the game on the sidelines spitting blood and shouting obscenities at the opposing team.

I stepped up for a rotation as quarterback. We marched upfield with short completions: ins and outs, slants, a buttonhook. I dropped back into the pocket on one play and spotted a break in the line. Pump-faking, I tucked the pigskin under my arm and barreled forward. It looked like I had an open field to the goal until Sergeant Mo came out of nowhere and crushed me. My helmet's chinstrap unbuckled as I smacked the ground. Tiny white stars appeared in the sky, then I saw Mo's thick bronze face and flaring nostrils.

"Welcome to the company, sir." He hovered over me, extending his club of an arm to help me up.

The rest of the game was pure pain. I pushed through it to save face, showered, and limped to the office of the company commander to for-mally report for my first day on the job. Our commander, a Marshall

Scholar who'd finished first in his class at the Naval Academy and spoke Russian, was at a meeting at higher headquarters. I figured I would catch him later. Rumor had it he worked so hard and was so frugal that he lived out of his office. His executive officer, First Lieutenant Michael Dubrule, caught me at his door.

"Heard it was a hell of a game." Lieutenant Dubrule shook my hand with a firm grip. We were about the same size and build. "I'm sorry I missed it. Too many injuries, though. I was battling the battalion about this Iraq deployment. They want sixty Marines ready as soon as the balloon goes up."

We were America's force in readiness, first to fight and always on the move. True to form, Lieutenant Dubrule's cubicle looked fully "expeditionary," with no photos or decorations. Apart from a couple of stacks of paper and a laptop his desk was barren. A map of the world yanked out of a magazine was tacked to the wall. A wooden T-stand made of three two-by-fours supported his kit: flak jacket, load-bearing vest, KA-BAR fighting knife, and Kevlar helmet. He wore two silver pins above his heart. The scuba bubble indicated that he was a combat diver. An emblem with lightning bolts and a shield designated his former military occupation—Explosive Ordnance Disposal. In the years to come, those EOD units would suffer the highest casualty rates in the U.S. armed forces.

A veteran of the first Gulf War, Lieutenant Dubrule had served a decade as an enlisted Marine before graduating from Florida State University and earning his commission. He led me into the commanding officer's room to a whiteboard filled with acronyms. Each acronym represented a school or deployment. Our unit had one of the fastest operational tempos in the Marine Corps, with typically less than half of the company back at Camp Lejeune at any given time. The commander's whiteboard showed teams attached to Marine units, Special Forces, NATO, and other government agencies around the world in Djibouti, Afghanistan, Guantánamo Bay, the Indian Ocean, Bosnia, and elsewhere. Other acronyms denoted schools where we received additional training: FBI Counter-Surveillance; Jump School; Survival, Evasion, Resistance, and Escape; High Risk Personnel; and Bill Scott Raceway High-Speed Pursuit Driving. I felt like a kid in a candy store.

A natural leader, Lieutenant Dubrule was the number two officer in the unit. He spoke with competence and candor. When I left the office,

I took out my pocket-size pad and scribbled down everything I could remember from his brief orientation to the company, my new home.

LOCATED ON THE coast of North Carolina near the edge of the Outer Banks, Camp Lejeune felt like an ideal launching pad. It was close to Tracy in Greensboro and CFK's U.S. office in Chapel Hill, and it was on the ocean, the great blue divide across which we would deploy. It was important for me to live on the beach. The only problem was money. I didn't want to pay beach prices for a place. After a couple of weekends of fruitless searching, I began to lose patience. One day Lieutenant Dubrule remarked that if he weren't married with two boys, he would live on a houseboat or in a camper. His comment triggered my recall of Rogers Bay Family Campground, a nest of campers on North Topsail Beach.

Located twenty minutes out of Camp Lejeune's back gate, Rogers Bay had three campers for rent. I chose the least expensive one and moved in for a hundred bucks a month. It was perfect. Less than a thirty-second jog to the beach, my camper had walls so rickety thin that I could hear the ocean at night after my neighbor, a retired shrimper who drank Crown Royal whiskey mixed with Sun Drop citrus soda throughout the day, turned off his country-and-western music and went to bed.

As for the work, my responsibilities were minimal relative to what I would soon face. I was expected to learn as much as I could about our field and build relationships with Marines until the next class for basic HUMINT training began at a base in Virginia. That was it, and it was a blessing, although I met it at first with frustration because the company was preparing for another war. It was early October 2002, months before Secretary of State Colin Powell delivered his "Weapons of Mass Destruction" speech to the United Nations. Yet in Camp Lejeune it felt as though an invasion of Iraq was preordained. Even though I was skeptical of why we were about to make war in Iraq, I found myself worrying that I might miss the action.

OUR BATTALION COMMANDER authorized a long leave over Christmas and the New Year so that Marines could be with their families before the probable deployment to Iraq. With that decision, the stars were aligned for me to return to Kenya during what I believed might be one of the country's most historic elections. As far as my military command was concerned, I was one of the few Marines with expertise on East Africa. Lieutenant Dubrule joked that my trip looked like a self-funded opportunity for professional military development. My request to spend another Christmas in Kenya sailed up the chain of command.

Once again, however, my decision went over poorly with Tracy. "Are we ever going to spend Christmas together?" she asked over the phone one night as my neighbor at the campground sang along to David Allan Coe's "If That Ain't Country."

"And will you please turn down that terrible music," Tracy added with an uncharacteristically sharp tone.

"Babe, it's not my music. You know my walls are thin. Listen, I want to be with your family, but I really need to be in Kenya with CFK."

"CFK will always need you."

"Oh, come on." I was getting frustrated. It had been a long day. "The elections are coming. It'll be a once-in-a-lifetime opportunity."

"Do you know how many times I've heard that?"

"That what?"

"That, that 'once-in-a-lifetime,'" she said, raising her voice.

"Well, I can't help that."

"Yes, you can. These are *your* choices."

"But it doesn't feel like a choice."

"I know, I know. You say that all the time, too."

I held the phone in silence. She was right to be upset. If I were in her place, I probably would've quit the relationship long ago. *How much of this would she tolerate?*

"Just go. Go. But it can't keep being like this."

A WEEK BEFORE Christmas I arrived in Kenya to find a letter from the former councillor Taib waiting for me at the clinic. Evidently, he had postmarked a copy to my old dorm room months earlier. Salim knew that Taib was still upset about our initiative to create CFK instead of fund KIYESA. Over the past year, we had received a couple of e-mails from people claiming to live in Kibera and accusing CFK of taking advantage of the community. We assumed Taib was behind the letter and e-mails. As far as we knew he and Oluoch were CFK's only two enemies, and Oluoch had no real ties to the community. An excerpt from one e-mail read:

> WHO EVER YOU ARE!!!
> OMONDI BARKOT
> WE PARENTS HAVE FOUND YOU ARE SPOLING OUR
> YOUTH BY PRETENDING YOU ARE MAKING PLAY
> FOOTBALL. THE YOUTH ARE USED IN FETCHING
> DRUGS, MARIJUANA, BY YOUR ORGANIZERS IN TURN
> THE SAME YOUTH ARE USED AS PEDLLARS . . . WHEN
> YOU STEP HERE YOU WILL KNOW THE TRUE SLUM
> FEELINGS WHICH YOU WILL REGRET.

We took the e-mails seriously. Salim replied to each anonymous sender with requests to meet and discuss their accusations. Our fourteen youth representatives conducted community-based investigations. Although Taib's letter to me made no references to the anonymous e-mails, he concluded his three-page letter by accusing me of taking advantage of his hospitality. As I read the letter, I could hear Taib's shrill, high-strung voice shouting: "WHEN MY GOOD FRIEND OLUOCH FROM FORT JESUS INTRODUCED YOU AND HANDED OVER YOU TO ME, YOU WERE IGNORANT ABOUT KIBERA."

Taib concluded his letter with a demand and a carbon-copy list: "We want full explanation of the betrayal otherwise we will file court injunction to stop all your illegal activities in Kibera."

CC - Dean of the University of North Carolina—USA
   - Director of Social Services (Youth Development)
   - Area Member of Parliament
   - Area Councillor
   - His Worship The Deputy Mayor
   - CNN
   - BBC
   - ALJEZIRA Television
   - Local Print and Electronic Media

Perhaps Taib wanted some type of payout. He had introduced me to local leaders, and we had mentioned KIYESA and other organizations as examples of potential local partners in Kibera. Yet this in no way obligated CFK to fund KIYESA. If Taib did send the letter to his ridiculous carbon-copy list, I never heard about it. I suspected any person who read the letter would discredit it for being so haphazardly argued and full of factual errors, misspellings, and grammatical mistakes.

Tabitha reacted by saying that if Taib walked into her clinic, she would escort him out on a stretcher. It was the first time I had heard Tabitha voice a threat, and it struck me as out of character. When I mentioned it to Salim, he corrected me. "That's the Kibera in Tabitha talking. She won't just stand back. She'll fight. You know, even me, I wouldn't want to cross Tabitha when she's mad."

Salim was equally upset by Taib's letter and focused on the paragraph where Taib attacked him personally: "How do you call Salim Mohamed from other area, yet there are so many youths in the area who are conversant and capable than him. If he was the best why isn't he still with MYSA? He has never been with them either."

Much as I had never heard Tabitha make a threat, I had never before heard Salim swear. "KIYESA is nothing," Salim said. "This guy is shit."

Salim and Tabitha knew they could handle Taib. I took a copy of the letter to Cantar, CFK's Nubian youth representative. Sounding like a salty Marine sergeant, Cantar responded, "This guy is nothing. The community has no respect for him. Don't worry. We'll take care of it at our level, ghetto level."

APART FROM OUR conflict with Taib, which our team handled peacefully with the support of the community, our attention was focused on the historic event before us. A Kenyan constitutional mandate was about to replace President Daniel arap Moi. Salim suspended CFK's soccer activities in advance of the presidential election. Kenyan politicians often used soccer as a way to mobilize votes before elections, and Salim and Tabitha wanted us to stay far away from politics.

I found their viewpoints fascinating. Salim and Tabitha were change agents, yet they believed nothing would change at the highest levels of their government. Like many Kenyans, they had lost faith in their leaders. Although they both wanted CFK to be apolitical, they acknowledged that real change would require a generational shift in leadership, and that, at its core, was our mission. From a long-term view, everything we did in Kibera was political because it all served the larger purpose of creating leaders who would prevent violence instead of inciting it.

In the days following Christmas the Kenyan people released decades of pent-up frustration and elected the leading opposition candidate, Mwai Kibaki, in a landslide. A public inauguration ceremony was scheduled to occur two days later in Uhuru Park, an emerald stamp of land adjacent to downtown Nairobi. It was the same place where Nobel laureate Wangari Maathai staged her courageous protest against President Moi in 1989, when Moi had wanted to clear the park and construct a statue of himself and a skyscraper to house his party's headquarters. Flummoxed by her audacity, Moi declared that women should follow "the African tradition," respect men, and be quiet. His comment drew widespread outrage and forced him to abandon his construction plan, thus preserving one of Africa's great urban parks.

Initially, Salim had no interest in going to the ceremony, which was projected to draw a crowd of an estimated half a million people. He predicted it would be a "messy thing" that could become dangerous, and he felt little connection to the euphoria gripping much of the nation. I didn't understand his detachment because I was wrapped up in the public outcry. I blamed Moi for many of Kenya's problems, including the existence of Kibera. "A fish rots from the head down" goes the worldly proverb I had heard many times in Swahili. More than any other person, Moi embodied the "big-man" culture of graft and patronage politics. He had presided over what academics called the criminalization of the state. I wanted to see him go down in person, to be a small part of that historic moment, cheering and jeering with the masses in the arena, justice triumphing.

"TOSHA! TOSHA!" PEOPLE shouted as they descended on Uhuru Park. "ENOUGH! ENOUGH!"

There were more people than I had ever before seen at an event. Salim and I had arrived two hours before the scheduled start of the ceremonies.

He had begrudgingly agreed to accompany me after I suggested we play some pool later that night. Salim never grew tired of talking trash and cleaning my clock on the pool table.

"RAILA! RAILA!" others chanted in support of Kibera's very own Member of Parliament and incoming cabinet member Raila Odinga.

A crowd began rapping "*Unbwogable*"—the theme song of the opposition. It translated to "uncrushable."

The only other white people I saw were journalists and dignitaries far away near the stage. Salim nudged me with his elbow and gestured to two men staring at me. I turned and flashed a two-finger peace sign, the symbol of the opposition party. They shook their fists at me approvingly. "*TOSHA! TOSHA!*"

Hours passed. The mob grew restive. My heels burned in my boots as if I were at the end of a long forced march. My bladder swelled from the coffee I had drunk earlier that morning. Some men urinated on the handful of acacia trees throughout the park. Older people began to collapse from the heat. Women and children trickled out as more men tried to push their way to the stage. Every time a new entourage of dignitaries arrived, tens of thousands of people at the front lines surged toward the stage only to be bludgeoned back by an army of police on horseback swinging billy clubs. Over and over we swelled, waves in a sea of humanity. I wanted to get closer to the front. Salim held me back.

Men hurled mud at the stage.

"*TOSHA!*" we shouted.

After four hours of waiting, the official party still hadn't arrived, and Salim was fed up. "*Tosha*," he joked, and left to walk downtown to an Internet café.

I waited for another hour, pressing closer to the stage until my bladder felt as if it was going to explode. I couldn't bring myself to urinate on an acacia tree, and by that time I doubted that Moi and Kibaki would even show up. The U.S. ambassador had arrived and left after discovering that a seat had not been reserved for him.

"FREEDOM!" a man nestled in the flat-top limbs of an acacia tree shouted, and flashed a peace sign as I walked away. Shortly afterward, Moi and Kibaki arrived and performed a peaceful transition of power.

THE CITY CENTER was deserted as I walked toward the Internet café. Normally, such quiet would put me on guard. But that day a warm complacency filled my senses. I felt as if I was floating through a mystical place when an arm hooked me from behind. Startled, I jumped, then relaxed. I assumed it was a friend surprising me until the arm drew tighter around my neck.

A gang of boys circled in front of me. They began clawing at my cargo-pants pockets and swinging their little fists at my face. I kicked and grabbed the arm around my neck, gasping for air and attempting to eye-gouge the one choking me. It was a maneuver I had learned in hand-to-hand combat drills. As I started to lose consciousness, the boys yelled something, released me, and scattered.

Some Kenyan men who had witnessed the attack congregated in a group across the street. They had captured one of the assailants. I stumbled over, shirtless and bloody.

"Oh, I'm sorry, sorry," a man in the group consoled me. He was a Good Samaritan. They all were. They had come to my rescue and were now surrounding a boy who looked like he could be eleven years old. A man stepped forward and drilled his foot into the kid's stomach. The boy coughed and held up his hand, pleading with wide, frightened eyes. Another man stepped forward and slugged him in the face, cracking his nose. The boy shrieked.

"*Mwizi, mwizi,*" a man snarled. "Thief, thief." He leaned over and punched the boy in the face. I thought they might kill him. That's what residents did to thieves in Kibera. Mob justice.

Stepping forward, I lifted the boy off the ground and hoisted him over my shoulder in a fireman's carry. He was lighter than the gear I carried in my dad's duffel.

"Where you taking him?" one of the men asked me. "We're not through."

"Yes, you're through. Thanks."

Lifting the boy off my shoulder, I told him that we were going to visit a friend. He followed me sheepishly, blood dripping from his nose. When I asked him some questions in Swahili, the boy's answers were too soft for me to understand. It was difficult for me to view him as a thief.

Salim was alone in the Internet café. He calmly gestured to the boy to sit down. Within a half hour, Salim knew a lot about the kid's life. The boy happened to be from Kibera. Salim struck a deal with him: We wouldn't turn him in to the police, and he could go see Tabitha to take care of his injuries. In return, we expected him to come to CFK's next war on trash.

The boy nodded and shuffled out the door, head down.

"Ya think he'll show up?" I asked.

"Not really." Salim didn't believe the boy wanted to be rehabilitated. "You know, with life on the streets you can only be helped when you're ready to get the help. This thing, it's got to be in you."

It was another lesson, a reminder that as an organization, and as individuals, we could only do so much. There were two different approaches: reach many and risk being superficial, or invest heavily in the few who have the desire and capacity to lead. CFK deliberately chose the latter. While it was easy for me to appreciate this approach as a strategic decision and a practical reality, it didn't make it any easier to see the boy shuffling out the door without a safety net.

In the United States, I might have taken the boy to the police, who would have engaged the state and its social services for children in abusive environments. These services were often poorly funded and rife with problems, but at least they were there. At least there was some hope for rehabilitation, some level of responsibility that society accepted for its children. In Kenya, a trip to the police would simply mean juvenile detention, which left most kids more spiteful and traumatized.

"What'd they take?" Salim asked me.

I wasn't sure. I had packed a fair amount of stuff into the eight pockets of my cargo pants and the breast pockets on my shirt. The boys had torn off three of my four cargo pockets and made away with a fistful of Creme Savers hard candies, a notepad, and a digital camera. My shirt pockets had had a little cash, perhaps $10 worth of shillings. I looked at Salim and patted the upper two side pockets on my pants. Suddenly, I panicked. My Spyderco. They had taken my Spyderco Delica. It was the pocketknife that I had carried since junior high school.

"Sorry, man," Salim said, and handed me a short-sleeve, baby-blue, collared shirt that he was carrying in his satchel. I put the shirt on and told Salim about my Spyderco. It probably struck him as odd that I had such a strong attachment to a knife. However, he was one of my closest friends, and he could tell that I was distraught. It felt as though I had lost a part of me. I would've given those kids anything else: my belt with the hidden pouch lined with $100 bills, my muddy, scuffed-up Timberlands, sunglasses, and every piece of clothing on my body. They might have taken these things in exchange, I suspected, because my Spyderco had little street value. The pointed tip of its steel, half-serrated blade had snapped off. The waffle-pattern tread on the black plastic grip was smooth from a decade of handling.

Like a bad love story, my Spyderco was gone and there was no way to get it back. Yet I couldn't stop thinking about it, and as I deliberated why it had happened, something more disturbing came to mind.

I had let my guard down. All of the warning signs were in front of me: empty streets, eerie silence, and an unpredictable gathering of hundreds of thousands of people nearby. Yet for some reason I had become complacent and forgotten my situational awareness. This awareness was a hallmark of my military training going back to Major Boothby and ROTC. As one of the most obvious overlaps between my two worlds, it was one of the ways that my military experience added the most value to my work in Kibera. Now it was breaking down at what felt like the worst possible time. Soon I could be leading Marines into places where momentary lapses into complacency had lethal consequences.

The failure of my situational awareness had allowed an assailant's arm to wrap around my neck. Then it was no longer an issue of vigilance, but of instincts. I should immediately have resisted. Instead, I thought the person was a friend and lost split seconds when I could have fought back. My father, I believed, would instantly have resisted. He would never have assumed the assailants were friends, not for a moment. He would have drawn blood on both sides. I had become too naïve, too complacent. My instincts were wrong.

So it was that I had to revisit the essential question: Could I do both? I assumed all along that it was possible, and I wanted it to be possible. I wanted the best practices of each world to inform the other. As Colonel Greenwood and Major Boothby suggested, I thought Kibera would make me a better Marine, and vice versa. Yet maybe the two worlds were too much for each other, like oil and water, two elements that were in some way irreconcilable. I was trying to force them together through my life, but maybe they were meant to be apart.

CHAPTER FIFTEEN

Compartments

Kibera

TABITHA, SALIM, AND I WERE IN THE CLINIC on New Year's Day when I received an urgent text message from Camp Lejeune. I immediately called my commanding officer. He was unrevealing with the details. We were on an unsecure line.

"You need to get back here. We're pushing the course a month forward because of what's going down [the Iraq War]. It [the HUMINT course] will start in three days. Can you make it [to Dam Neck, Virginia]?"

"I'll do my best, sir. Will it be all right if I am a bit late?" Most military schools started with a couple slow administrative days.

"Unfortunately not. You miss this one, you'll have to wait for the next class. Where you callin' from anyway?" He had more important things to worry about than my current location.

"I'm still in Nairobi."

"Oh."

"Sir, I'll be there." I couldn't wait any longer to finish my training, not after my eight-month hiatus from the Basic School.

"Okay, keep me posted."

"Roger that, sir." I hung up, said good-bye to Salim and Tabitha, threw

my clothes into my dad's old duffel, and raced to the airport to catch the
night flight to London.

The moonlight reflected off my camper's rooftop as I pulled the
Green Bean into Rogers Bay. My neighbor's Confederate flags flapped in
the breeze. He was the only other person who lived in the campground
year-round, along with a family of squirrels that he had named and befriended. Bucky, a feisty critter who was missing a front tooth, was do-
mesticated to the point where he ate peanuts from my neighbor's mouth
and sometimes slept in his bed. I enjoyed my rugged bachelor's existence
with my neighbor and his squirrels. I was also proud that my camper only
cost a hundred bucks a month. The utility bill didn't amount to much
either. The air conditioner was busted and my water often froze in the
winter, forcing me to bathe in the ocean.

My body odor was noxious the night I arrived, but there was no time
for a saltwater swim. I had been traveling for sixty-five hours and needed
to report to duty no later than 0700. I pounded a Red Bull energy drink,
repacked my duffel, and blasted out into the predawn darkness. I arrived
in Dam Neck, a small base on the shores of the Atlantic Ocean a few miles
south of Virginia Beach with less than a half hour to spare.

The HUMINT course started at full speed as soon as I took my seat
in our windowless classroom. The three-month course consisted of mod-
ules on three skill sets, any one of which could take a lifetime to master:
interrogations, counterintelligence, and human-source operations. In the
first month, we studied the Geneva Conventions and learned more than a
dozen sanctioned approaches to military interrogations. The approaches
seemed reasonable and well thought out. They had self-explanatory
names such as "We Know All," "Fear Up," and "Fear Down." So-called
stress positions and other forms of physical coercion were forbidden and
looked down upon as the unreliable tools of terrorists and thugs. Professionals relied on intellect and preparation.

Much of what we learned was classified, and shortly after the course
started the government granted me a full Top Secret/Sensitive Compartmentalized Information clearance. A security officer explained that
sensitive compartmentalized information meant that I could be given access to special, isolated government programs on a need to know basis.

The "need to know" was at the heart of all intelligence operations. It was a world that operated in compartments. I understood why this was important, but I wasn't sure how I would conform to the culture. My tendencies were to share information, not to guard it.

There wasn't much time to reflect. I conformed because I had to, and without complaint. HUMINT was where I wanted to be, and the training was fascinating. It required reservoirs of physical and mental stamina and pushed us far outside our comfort zones. It had an elemental quality that I found attractive as well. No matter how much technology we had at our disposal, HUMINT would always matter. We relied on it to isolate the enemy, to protect our own forces, and to minimize death and injury to noncombatants.

While the course material challenged me, it complemented some of my strengths and occasionally overlapped with my other world. Successful interrogators typically built rapport by "mirroring" body language. Although I had never heard the term *mirroring* before, I had adopted the technique subconsciously while fund-raising. When donors spoke, I often found myself adjusting my demeanor to match their dispositions. The longer people talked about things that mattered to them, the more likely it seemed to be that they would contribute, even if their personal interests were tangential to CFK's goals.

Of course, on some level the circumstances couldn't have been more different. In battle, we interrogated suspected enemy combatants who were often stunned by the shock of capture. My fund-raising meetings were typically in fancy restaurants. Yet the principles were similar. At the heart of it, both fund-raising and interrogation were about persuasion, the art and skill of convincing people to do things they wouldn't otherwise do. There was an element of manipulation in both worlds that felt uncomfortable, and I wrestled with that reality. With donors, it became even more complicated because my relationships often evolved into friendships that I valued far beyond financial contributions to CFK.

ONE MORNING TOWARD the end of interrogation training, I woke up feeling restless. The little clock in the corner of my laptop read 0200 hours. The first e-mail in my in-box was a five-page diatribe titled "Salim must go." Sent from an alias account, the e-mail was addressed to a few of our

Kenya board members, Tabitha, and the CFK Listserv, a group e-mail account with three thousand people, including our most generous donors and influential leaders, such as the U.S. ambassador to Kenya, the president of the Ford Foundation, and Dr. Jendayi Frazer at the White House. We managed the list tightly, sending out only two carefully written updates each year. The rubber band inside my chest stretched as I read the e-mail's content. Excerpts included:

(A) We demand immediate resignation of the project manager (Salim). He is not a Kibera resident. He has therefore taken up an opportunity and many other opportunities from our community.

(B) We are also taking over the running of the organization.

(C) We have included Kash on board.

(D) We also consider Kassim as part of us that is the youth representatives.

(E) We have taken over the office with immediate effect.

We request immediate response from you since we believe this a hallmark of good management.

God bless you, and keep in touch

From C.F.K Youth Representatives / Kibera Community

I checked the Listserv settings. As the Listserv's administrator, I had the power to approve or reject every message. I rejected the message and paced around my room. My instinct was to come to Salim's immediate defense, though I was also angry at being caught off guard. Salim was at an Internet café in Nairobi reading the youth representative letter when I caught him on the phone minutes later.

"Yo, man, what do you make of this?" I asked.

"This thing really pisses me off."

"Did you know it was coming?"

"Not really. I mean, I knew something was up."

"But you didn't want to talk with me about it?"

"What do you mean?"

"I mean, I feel blindsided by this."

"You feel blindsided. How do you think I feel, mista?"

"Well, that's why I'm asking."

"If you think I was hiding something, I don't know what to say."

"No, no," I backtracked. "Sorry, man. I'm sorry I said that."

"You know what this is about?"

"No, what?" Maybe I should have seen it coming. In the previous weeks I had an e-mail exchange with Kassim about our budget after he suggested CFK needed more transparency. I agreed with Kassim and was frustrated that Salim and Tabitha were so guarded with financial information. We created CFK to be a collaborative organization, and I had hoped that the youth representatives, as unpaid volunteers, would set part of the budget for the sports program. That struck me as an innovative structure that could ensure community input and build local capacity. Salim and Tabitha, however, resisted my suggestions. They wanted to go slower and thoroughly test each youth representative to determine who among them could be trusted. I appreciated that we needed to treat financial information confidentially until we had the right processes in place. But it had been almost a year and a half, and I thought we should be ready to reveal our budget to the youth representatives. They were our ambassadors in the community.

"It started when you told them the budget," Salim shot back.

"Me?"

"Yes, Rye, you remember you told Kassim we spend twenty-two thousand dollars a year."

"Well, we do, don't we?"

"We do, but I don't think, honestly, you know, it was not a thing to do. To them it sounds like a lot of money." In a place where $26 could transform lives, it was difficult for anyone, no matter what age, to imagine $22,000.

"So can't we show them the budget without the salary info? That way they understand more of the costs. I mean, our rent alone is five thousand dollars."

"Then they'll want to change it."

"Well, that's the point. We want their input."

"Rye, they will want to change it to give themselves stipends. That's what this thing is about, stipends, not community." Even if the budget was large enough to manage such payments, Salim, Tabitha, and I were united in our opposition to stipends. The power of CFK was in its volunteer

ethos. We didn't want the sports program to become an easy employment opportunity for youth in Kibera. We wanted to use sports to equip
young people with the skills they needed to become leaders and contribute to their communities, and we wanted to do this with the smallest
administrative footprint possible.

"I get that," I reacted. "Our selection of the reps was screwed up. Hell,
half of them came from Jumba, the micro-credit guy." We had finally
formed a group of fourteen representatives, young men and women who
were ethnically diverse and respected in their communities. They had
become more than colleagues. They were friends. "But some of the reps
are really talented, and they've been with us from the beginning," I added.

"That thing [the youth representative council] was set up before I got
here." Salim was getting more frustrated. "Some of them feel like Kash
did, like it's for them to run CFK because they were there first. They
want this thing for themselves. But there are other ways to do youth empowerment."

"Salim, they need more responsibility."

"So they can do what they just did? No, me, I don't think so. Honestly,
it's not right. Trust takes time. We need youth reps who Tabitha and me
can trust." The youth representatives were attempting a coup, and Kash
was probably behind it. Salim's voice cracked. "What I'm hearing you saying is that Salim is the problem. If that's it, fine. I'll go. It's never been
about me."

"No, man, don't be crazy." His words shouldn't have surprised me. I
knew that Salim was extremely sensitive to criticism.

"No, really, I can. Maybe that's better."

Salim was a man of honor. If he felt slighted by CFK, he would leave.
Even if he didn't have another job lined up, he would leave. That was
Salim's way. He would rather fight back and lose everything except his
dignity than to submit to something he knew was wrong. Tabitha shared it
as well, and it was rare. Kenya and much of Africa was plagued by bad leadership. The problem wasn't simply government neglect. The culture of
corruption reached nearly every facet of life. It started with government
graft, from the rookie policeman on the street right up to the Office of the
President. By one measure from the global watchdog organization Transparency International, urban Kenyans paid an average of more than eight
bribes per month. Even if most bribes were relatively small, they added up

to a lot of money and hardship, particularly for the poor. Corruption was a way of life, and maybe that was part of what motivated the youth representatives to send their letter. Although I didn't know the full story, I knew what made Salim and Tabitha exceptional. It was their inability to be corrupted. Theirs was the kind of leadership that could change the status quo.

"Salim, we'd be nothing without you," I said emphatically. "You know that. I know that. These youth reps don't get it. I'm not arguing for them. They need to go, like you said. We can't put up with revolt. But what I'm saying is we have to figure out our structure. I'm not comfortable with where we are at right now."

"I agree." Salim, Tabitha, and I didn't have formal management training. We were struggling to keep up with the administrative demands of our fast-growing organization.

"Well, let's talk about it."

"Please, I don't want to talk about this now."

"Good point." I, too, was emotionally exhausted. "I don't either. Should I call tomorrow?"

"Yeah, okay." We never booked specific times to talk. I called Salim when I could. He always picked up the phone, even if it woke him, and I tried my best to be just as responsive.

"Salim," I stopped him before he hung up. I didn't want to leave us hanging on such a note. "You know I'm with you."

"I know, bro."

TEN OF THE fourteen CFK youth representatives went to Tabitha the following day and told her that they wanted Salim to be fired. She received their information with a poker face. That evening, Salim discovered a handwritten note under his door in Fort Jesus. The note, signed by the same youth representatives, informed Salim that he had two weeks to leave Kibera "or else."

Tabitha and Salim retained an attorney the following day and drafted a terse reply: "Be advised that you are no longer part of the leadership of CFK. It would be illegal and improper to carry out any activity on behalf of CFK. You are also advised not to transact any business or activity using CFK's name. If the requested is violated, legal action will be taken."

Tabitha discovered that Kassim and Kash had collaborated with the ten youth representatives. I began to worry about Salim's security. Kassim had helped lead the Nubian youth in the 1995 ethnic clashes, and Kash had spoken with Nate about a dark period in his life when he had been in dozens of street fights.

Early one morning I woke up from a nightmare that Salim had been shot in the head. I immediately reached for the phone. Salim picked up.

"I'm sorry, man," I said. "I shouldn't have told Kassim the budget, or even discussed it with him before talking to you. I don't want you to get hurt."

I squashed the phone's receiver to my ear. Even when he was upset, Salim spoke softly. "It's okay, Rye. You can talk to whoever, but thank you anyway. Thank you anyway for apologizing."

"I'm worried about your safety. Kash, Kassim, these are tough guys."

"No, no, don't worry about me. Let them try. Honestly, let them try anything. I don't fear these guys. You know, I have friends here, too. Some of my brothers and sisters from the children's home live in Kibera. They know these guys and they keep their eyes out. Even me, I am from Kibera. I know this place."

"You mean because you live in Fort Jesus?"

"No, not that. Fort Jesus isn't really Kibera. When I was at the children's home, there was a family in Kibera who used to let me stay with them between school sessions. That's why also I know a lot of these people. I remember them and they remember me."

"But Kassim and the youth reps think you're from outside. Even Taib, who sent those letters. You never told me this."

"It's not like I was hiding it. The thing is, it was only for a couple of years. I was like six, you know. So for these people, I wasn't from Kibera because I wasn't living my whole life here. But what's 'from Kibera' anyway?" Salim was extremely guarded with personal information, and it took many years for me to get a full sense of his life history. His discretion wasn't simply a safety mechanism. It was a matter of pride. Salim didn't want his past to typecast him as an orphan who grew up on the streets. He wasn't looking for pity. He would prove himself on his own merits.

"So, is that why you never said anything?" I asked.

"Is what why?"

"Well, because it doesn't really matter. The reps, they tried to make being 'from Kibera' an issue because they had nothing else. The issue isn't being 'from Kibera.' It's do you understand what it's like to live in poverty, and do you, CFK's leader, understand communities like Kibera."

"Yeah, sort of. I don't have to justify myself to them. If they want to be part of leading CFK, then it's them to prove themselves to us, and to the community. That's why I don't say anything. Believe me, they know I spent time as a child in Kibera. Definitely, they know that. That's not the point."

"I hear you. I'm just sorry I didn't do more to back you up. I didn't realize how my communication with individual reps was being misinterpreted and complicating things."

"It's okay. It's just different now than when we started."

Again, Salim was right. The truth was that I had trouble drawing the line between friends and professional colleagues. My role had changed, but I hadn't changed with it. I was no longer Omosh, the playful, unpredictable *mzungu* student who lived in a shack in Kibera and bonded with youth leaders and tough guys. Residents knew CFK, and my public identity had changed to a person with access to resources, power, and influence. I needed to step back and support Salim and Tabitha as we developed our management skills. I needed to be persistent but patient as we structured CFK together and helped build local leaders.

Military intelligence provided me with a framework. It all had to do with compartments. I needed to do a better job of separating my professional and personal lives. That was obvious. The larger insight, however, pertained to the balancing act between my two worlds. I had searched for overlaps between CFK and the Marine Corps and found a few. I would soon be done with my training and needed to figure out a way to manage my responsibilities in both spheres, a way that wasn't based on good luck or circumstance and could endure trials by fire. Compartmentalizing was the answer. It seemed so simple. Yet it had taken the youth representatives' revolt and a Top Secret clearance for me to realize it.

TOWARD THE END of the HUMINT course, the general in charge of Marine Corps intelligence arrived from the Pentagon for the graduation ceremony of a class of enlisted Marine intelligence analysts. Standing ramrod straight, with icy eyes and a chiseled jaw, the general skipped the graduation clichés and gave a classified war briefing. Days earlier he had been in Kuwait with the lead Marine division preparing to invade

Iraq. He described our military might there as "awesome," "incredible," and "ready for trigger-time."

I believed we were rushing into war, and I had opposed the doctrine of preemption until Colin Powell, the secretary of state and the former chairman of the Joint Chiefs of Staff, convinced me otherwise. I trusted Secretary Powell when he delivered his United Nations speech and made the case for war based on the "facts and conclusions" from "solid intelligence" that Saddam possessed weapons of mass destruction. Secretary Powell's team, I assumed, had an intelligent, detailed plan for how to transition Iraqi governance once Saddam fell.

"We'll move so fast Saddam won't have time to react," the Marine general concluded, karate-chopping the air. "This will reduce the risk of mass casualties from chemical weapons."

We had been doused with tear gas and taught about chemical weapons at the Basic School. We had carried our gas masks in drop pouches on our thighs and drilled repeatedly with mock alerts. "*Gas, gas, gas,*" the alarm would sound. We'd drop our gear, don our masks, and get into fighting positions.

Despite this familiarity, for some strange reason I hadn't realized what the high probability of being gassed actually meant for our Marines on the ground in Kuwait, until that moment. As the general spoke, my mind returned to an image of a soldier dying from a chemical weapons attack in the poem "Dulce et Decorum Est" (It Is Sweet and Right) by Wilfred Owen, an infantryman killed in action in World War I.

> *He plunges at me, guttering, choking, drowning.*
> *If in some smothering dreams you too could pace*
> *Behind the wagon that we flung him in,*
> *And watch the white eyes writhing in his face,*
> *His hanging face, like a devil's sick of sin;*
> *If you could hear, at every jolt, the blood*
> *Come gargling from the froth-corrupted lungs,*
> *Obscene as cancer, bitter as the cud*
> *Of vile, incurable sores on innocent tongues*

I didn't remember the whole stanza, only those tongues plagued by "vile, incurable sores." It was among the most indelible images of war's horror. What a degrading, miserable way to die. Vile, incurable sores. Those tongues haunted me. And yet they weren't enough to purge the pull I felt to go to battle. Days later, in our windowless classroom, we watched the Iraq invasion on television. Two other lieutenants were in my class. We spoke frequently with each other about our envy of the Marines on the front lines. It wasn't only bravado. We wanted to be there. Duty, honor, and courage played their parts. But for me, there was something else, something subconscious. It had to do with a dark corner of my psyche that mingled with a sense of service and led me to fantasize about what Owen called "the old lie" in his famous last lines:

> My friend, you would not tell with such high zest
> To children ardent for some desperate glory,
> The old Lie; Dulce et Decorum est
> Pro patria mori [It is sweet and right to die for your country].

By the time we graduated at the end of March 2003, our ground forces were assaulting Baghdad. A week later, they took the city. As the general had predicted, our military assaulted Iraq with such force and speed that Saddam hardly had time to react. Years later, we would discover that he also didn't possess the weapons of mass destruction that had been used to justify the war.

The base was a ghost town by the time we returned to Camp Lejeune with our new credentials. Our company was nearly deserted apart from a handful of Marines who were unable to deploy due to medical issues, training conflicts, or family matters. Although I was still hoping to go to Iraq, our mission with NATO to Bosnia needed replacements in less than three months, and I was the only officer who was deployable. Once the choice mission in the company, Bosnia had become the detritus of a forgotten war.

My initial disappointment faded after a few conversations with mentors. Colonel Greenwood, who was still a director at the National Security Council, put the mission into a larger context. While our involvement in Bosnia had tapered off substantially since the initial intervention in 1995, the mission was an opportunity for me to see a mature, multinational military operation and learn firsthand about the U.S. military's evolving experiment with nation building. NATO in Bosnia focused on peacekeeping, though with an important element that Colonel Greenwood referred to as "manhunting." He suspected that my Marines and I would be heavily involved in that work. Among other indicted war criminals, we would hunt Radovan Karadzic and Ratko Mladic, the two Bosnian Serbs who helped mastermind and execute the ethnic-cleansing campaigns and civil war that killed more than two hundred thousand people between 1992 and 1995. Professor Kohn predicted that the low visibility of the mission could improve our chances of doing high-impact work. Peter Whaley, who had served in the region, wrote a one-line e-mail: "Get the bastards."

Three Marine sergeants were assigned to my team. We spent two months preparing to attach to NATO's first-ever multinational HUMINT battalion, a unit that consisted of dozens of military intelligence professionals from the United States and six other European countries. I focused on getting to know my team. Two of my sergeants were single. The other, Sergeant David Thompson, had a wife and two young children, one of whom was fighting a serious heart defect.

Sergeant Thompson exemplified the high caliber of some of our Marines. Orphaned on the streets of New York, Sergeant Thompson had boxed semiprofessionally, sold used cars, and driven cabs for New York's Gambino crime family until a recruiter enticed him to the Marine Corps with details about the GI Bill and other opportunities to advance his education. Within five years, he had deployed as a nuclear, biological, and chemical weapons specialist and earned a master's degree in information systems from Boston University. When he applied to join CI/HUMINT, one of the warrant officers who interviewed him remarked afterward that there was no better training for HUMINT than selling used cars.

THE NIGHT BEFORE we deployed to Bosnia for six months, Tracy joined me at the campground. Although she wasn't fond of the camper and frequently reminded me of its moldy carpets and lumpy bed, she loved being near the ocean. We took a long walk on the beach and said good-bye as the sun began to appear over the Atlantic. I was excited about the mission and didn't realize how difficult my departure was for her.

Later that morning, while driving back to graduate school in Greensboro, she called me in tears.

"It'll be all right," I tried to console her. Bosnia was much safer than

Iraq. We probably wouldn't even see gunfire. What I didn't realize was that every time she turned on the television or radio and heard about a Marine casualty, she would think of me.

"But what if it isn't? What if something happens?"

"It won't."

"Promise?"

"Yes. And, Tracy . . ."

"What?"

"I love you." I said it for the first time. Believing that it was better to show love than to say it, I rarely used the L-word.

"I love you, too." I was taken aback by how good it felt to say and hear those words.

Our NATO BATTALION commander, a U.S. Army lieutenant colonel, assigned me as his operations officer. The billet was intended for a major with over eight years of HUMINT experience. My aptitude played no part in his decision. The battalion's key leadership billets were assigned by country, and I was the only American officer in the battalion with the right training for the job. As Professor Kohn had predicted, I found myself as a young lieutenant in a position of significant responsibility. My duties included directing a platform of dozens of intelligence collectors from NATO bases spread across Bosnia and Croatia. I detached my three Marines with linguist support to the most strategically important bases.

My Marines were older professionals, and I believed I could learn as much or more from them as they could learn from me. I maintained a similar attitude toward the foreign military members in the battalion. My job was to give clear directions, support the collectors in the field, and evaluate their performance. I took a hands-off approach. While there was plenty to worry about, from land mines to automobile accidents, we didn't face a significant threat of direct hostile fire. I encouraged our collectors to be aggressive and "push the envelope."

The region and the work was so complex that I could easily have filled twenty-four hours a day in front of my classified computer reading reports and speaking to our collectors in the field over secure lines. But I felt like a fraud giving operational advice without any real experience. After a few weeks, I identified some sources and set up meetings in Sarajevo and the surrounding region. With interpreter support, a Land Cruiser, and a concealed pistol, I began to operate.

At first, my meetings only took up a small fraction of my time. However, the work was so fascinating that I started taking on too much of it. As I stretched to keep up with my duties, the compartments I had established for CFK and my family and friends became more important, and they seemed to be holding firm. I didn't speak about CFK on the job, and I tried to block it out of my mind, apart from one hour at the end of every day. Prior to sleeping, I scribbled some notes in my journal and used my e-mail account to stay connected with CFK, Tracy, and other friends and family. By the end of my deployment, workdays stretched to nineteen hours. I wasn't getting enough sleep. Yet every time I approached a point of collapse, something new and time-sensitive came up. The work was too important to slow down.

PLEASED WITH OUR performance, my boss, the Army lieutenant colonel, supported my request to nominate my Marines for one of the highest military awards authorized by the command, the Defense Meritorious Service Medal. After I drafted their citations, I learned that the colonel had also nominated me for this distinction. The recognition felt great, and I was disappointed the six-month deployment was coming to a close. Although Radovan Karadzic and Ratko Mladic were still on the run, our battalion had produced valuable intelligence, some of which assisted in the capture of lower-profile war criminals. In recognition of Sergeant Thompson's efforts in particular, President Bush placed a personal call to him on Christmas Eve. Our team had made significant contributions in a mission to punish the perpetrators of extreme ethnic violence.

One of the benefits of the NATO mission was a block of leave. On her first trip outside the United States, Tracy met me in Sarajevo. I turned in my pistol at the armory and picked her up in a tiny, two-door rental car. We spent the night in Old Town, Sarajevo, near the spot where Gavrilo Princip assassinated Archduke Franz Ferdinand and sparked World War I. I thought I was being romantic. Tracy didn't mind, though she had no interest in taking a military-history tour on our first evening together.

Setting off before sunrise, we made our way west toward the small fishing port of Vela Luka on the Croatian island of Korcula. It was the birthplace of my maternal grandfather, an entrepreneur who had emigrated to the United States with his parents before World War I. Frank Barcott had eventually settled in Washington State and started a paint store in Everett, a town on the Puget Sound. Decades of cigarette smoke and lead-based paint fumes destroyed his lungs, and he had died of cancer shortly before I was born. I knew him only from faded photos and the memories of the people he loved. Vela Luka would bring me closer to his spirit, and I wanted to share that moment with Tracy.

We rested for a night before a long ferry ride from Split, Croatia's largest port. An elderly couple sat next to us on the ferry. I greeted them in Serbo-Croatian, and we struck up a conversation in English. They, too, had family in Vela Luka. When I told them about my ties to the town, the man exclaimed, "Then you are a Croat! *Dobar dan*. Welcome home, son."

My personal life was my third compartment. I rarely discussed it with others during my deployment. For the first time since arriving in the Balkans, I was telling someone about my ties to the region. The man's enthusiastic response surprised me. When he asked if some special occasion had brought me back home, I let my guard down some more and told him I worked for NATO in Sarajevo.

"What's taking them so long, this NATO?" He furrowed his dark, heavy brows. His wife averted her eyes. "NATO is not a serious organization. Serious people would have those bastard Serb war criminals by the balls. It's been eight years since Dayton. Eight years and nothing."

"Yes, sir, we're workin' on it," I replied deferentially. Although I knew the challenges of manhunting missions firsthand, it baffled me that Karadzic and Mladic were still free.

"You should work harder."

"You know we have one Croat war criminal left on the list, too?" I said without thinking. I didn't mean to be provocative.

"No, no, boy. You're wrong." He stuck his finger at my face like Oluoch. His wife looked at me with pursed lips. "As a Croat you should know better. There are no Croat war criminals. This happened because of the Serbs. It's those blood-hungry dogs, those barbarians, not us."

Tracy gripped my hand. I should have walked away, but the man had struck something deep. "You're wrong," I snapped, throwing my finger back at his face. "And your country will be worse off for your attitude."

"Who are you to talk to me this way? What do you know of it? Have you seen combat? Have you ever lost a child? No, because you are a child. You should be ashamed. This isn't the way Croats speak."

Our exchange drew the awkward attention of other passengers. Tracy and I excused ourselves and walked out to some benches at the bow of the boat. Vela Luka was a brown dot on the turquoise horizon. Tracy's strawberry-blonde hair flickered in the wind, gracing the back of my neck.

"You didn't have to make a scene." She turned to me. She was right. I had lost my cool. After only five short months as a NATO peacekeeper, I thought I had real expertise about a culture and a place that could take a lifetime to understand.

"I'm sorry." Two of my three compartments had momentarily clashed.

As much as it bothered me that I had argued with the old Croat man, his comment about war struck a deep nerve. At one level, I hated when people called me boy. I interpreted those comments as efforts to discredit me because of my age. More important, the man was calling me out on my military experience. I hadn't seen combat. In Bosnia I felt like a police detective. The work was important; peacekeeping was important. But it wasn't everything that a Marine should be, not when a real war was under way and our brothers and sisters were doing the fighting and dying. As meaningful as my time in Bosnia was, it was missing something essential. I was missing something essential, and it was an intensely personal thing, a thing at the base of my life's Marine Corps compartment.

CHAPTER SIXTEEN

Grass, Flower, and Wind

Camp Lejeune, North Carolina

WINTER 2004

THE COMPANY RETURNED FROM THE IRAQ invasion without a single Marine killed in action. After five years of service, our commander decided to leave the Marine Corps to attend Stanford Law School and pursue a career in the private sector. Lieutenant Dubrule was promoted to the rank of captain, took over as our commander, and selected me to be the company executive officer, his deputy.

We had less than six months to regroup and take most of the company back to Iraq. There was too much to do: combat training, gear check, medical updates, weapons qualifications, language lessons, specialty schools, intelligence briefings, staff meetings, and many other issues that arose as Marines tried to readjust to life out of a combat zone. Additionally, as the ever-changing whiteboard in the commander's office illustrated, we continued to dispatch small teams to elite military training schools and missions in other parts of the world. These missions in places such as the Horn of Africa and Afghanistan often placed a heavy emphasis on unconventional operations, such as civil affairs and military-to-military training. The non-Iraq missions were in high demand among the Marines, many of whom were looking for something different after their first deployment to the Middle East. They were interesting assignments, and I thought the U.S. military needed to be more focused on operations that could prevent violence. But I wanted to go to Iraq.

Captain Dubrule's leadership embraced the Colin Powell philosophy that "perpetual optimism is a force multiplier." When we were tired and stressed-out from the training, the captain reminded us through his words and actions that we were all fortunate to be in one of the best jobs in the Marine Corps. No one in the company worked longer hours than he did. He set high standards and lived by them. He kept us grounded and focused on the priorities. On his first day after his return from Iraq, he briefed the unit on his command philosophy and posted a three-page overview at the entrance to our team house, where it remained for his fourteen months of command. The introduction read:

> I challenge anyone to show me a group who works harder to successfully collect timely and immediately usable intelligence and in the places where it is the most dangerous and difficult to do so. Undoubtedly, many of our brother Marines are alive today and our nation's enemies dead or captured because of your efforts. You should be duly proud of yourselves, this Company and the Battalion. Here is what drives me.

He listed four bullets: "Marine first above all else, personal accountability, initiative, and ownership." Under "ownership" he concluded with the words, "This is your house, your Company. Is it everything it can be? What more can you do to make it better? I am challenging you to take this very personally. Take a step back, take stock of the situation and then strive to leave your mark on this place. It's yours after all."

It took leaders to inspire and constantly refresh a sense of ownership. In this respect, Captain Dubrule's leadership resembled some of the qualities of Tabitha and Salim in Kibera. Tabitha liked to say that the community owned CFK. Salim spoke about ownership in terms of perception and empowerment. It was a spirit and a belief that could exist at individual and collective levels. Once it took root, as it had at CFK and in our HUMINT company, it elevated organizations to new heights.

Leadership at CFK and our HUMINT company was critical at the time. CFK was about to suffer one of its greatest losses, and our company was preparing to go back to a controversial war. There were no weapons of mass destruction. The U.S. government disbanded the Iraqi Army and stood aside as many of its soldiers joined the insurgency. Our daily stream of intelligence reporting indicated that sectarian violence was on the rise, Iraqi government agencies were nonexistent, and the insurgency was metastasizing.

I opposed many of the administration's decisions, and I thought the neoconservative idea of springing a democracy on Iraq through a pre-emptive war was reckless. It was an idea without historical precedent, and it was filled with the type of hubris my father had often described as the Marine Corps' greatest vulnerability. At one point, I became so frustrated that I sent my first campaign donation to a presidential candidate. On the job, however, I kept my mouth shut. Professional military officers didn't broadcast their political views. We had a war to prepare for. Regardless of how we ended up in Iraq, we were there.

MOST MORNINGS CAPTAIN Dubrule and I caught up on the company's business in the weight room. He was a great lifting partner. Although I was about ten years younger than he was, we were close to the same strength, and he worked out hard. We used our workouts to discuss the company's challenges, many of which involved personnel decisions. A key part of Captain Dubrule's leadership was putting together teams for specific missions.

One morning we spoke about our Africa counterterrorism mission. Our team in Djibouti, a tiny country at the northern tip of Somalia, supported a multinational task force with military training, civil affairs, and Special Forces units in Yemen and four countries in the Horn of Africa. Although the mission rarely appeared in the news, it was complex and needed to be led by an officer who could represent the Marine Corps to numerous government agencies and foreign militaries. It was a more independent assignment than the one I had recently completed in Bosnia, because the team leader in Africa was the highest-ranking HUMINT specialist in the fifteen-hundred-person task force. Unfortunately, our most seasoned officers were already attached to specific Marine infantry battalions for the upcoming Iraq deployment. None of the officers who were available seemed to be the right fit for the job.

We finished our workout without a solution and sprinted a quarter mile back to the team house, where I followed Captain Dubrule to the

whiteboard for more brainstorming. Decisions that impacted lives forever were sometimes made in minutes in front of that board, and the
captain was the triggerman. He picked up his dry-erase marker and wrote
Lt Barcott under the acronym HOA (Horn of Africa).

"Rye, I need you to take it," he said in a way that indicated his delib-
erations were complete.

"Sir?" I had not seen it coming. Despite my background in the region
and relevant language expertise, I assumed Captain Dubrule would want
me in Iraq with him.

"I know you want to come with us to Iraq. Believe me, I want to take
you. But if an officer needs help in Iraq, the command is there to fix
things. In Africa, you're on your own, and I know you can handle it."

There was nothing else to say. "Roger that, sir."

Later that day I bumped into another intelligence officer, a captain
whom I knew from a few staff meetings. I saluted him and we made some
small talk. I told him the news of being selected to take over our
HUMINT team in Djibouti.

"Well, I guess you don't have to worry about the Marines screwing the
locals." He sounded as if he were joking, though I wasn't following his
punch line.

"You know, unless your guys have jungle fever or something. Don't
they still live in trees there?"

I didn't respond. For all the officers as gifted and thoughtful as Captain Dubrule and Colonel Greenwood, we still had our share of dolts
with no business leading Marines anywhere. Fortunately, most of these
officers were plugged into relatively harmless staff positions where they
could ride out their tours, and sometimes their careers.

"So, you all going to go undercover?" he asked. Although he had been
briefed many times, the captain had no clue how tactical HUMINT
worked. "Dress up like missionaries or somethin'?"

"No, it's nothing like that." I apologized for being in a rush.

"Oh, I see, if you tell me, you'll have to kill me," the captain chuckled as
I walked away.

THAT NIGHT I was feeling disappointed when I called Tracy. Her upbeat
attitude caught me by surprise. She was happy that I wouldn't be going to

Iraq, even though it could mean that I would be gone nine months instead of the standard six. "Honey," she added, "this mission was meant for you. It's what CFK prepared you to do."

That was part of the problem, though. How could the fire walls I had built in my mind to separate the military and CFK withstand such a deployment? Tracy was a private person. As a clinical psychologist in training, she kept a healthy distance between her clients and her personal life. She understood my concern when I explained it. But she encouraged me to think more broadly about how I divided my life. No one could isolate parts of his or her life completely, she argued. Separation was good in moderation, though I was taking my need to compartmentalize to the extreme. Tracy thought that I could deploy to the Horn of Africa and still keep CFK separate enough, while also using the knowledge I had gained in Kibera to help improve the military's efforts at capacity-building and community development. Her perspective made sense. My primary mission was still intelligence collection, not development. My identity would be as a HUMINT team leader who spoke Swahili, not as the founder of an NGO.

As she so often did, Tracy assuaged my fears. Soon I was excited to take on the Horn of Africa mission with a team of five noncommissioned officers. While Bosnia felt like the tail end of an engagement from a distant era, our counterterrorism task force in Djibouti was at the forefront of a fresh frontier of military thinking called distributed operations. The idea was that the U.S. military could prevent terrorism in volatile parts of the world by surging small teams assembled from Special Forces, intelligence, and civil affairs units. These teams used soft-power tools, such as repairing local health care and education infrastructure, providing medical and veterinary care, and helping train African militaries. It was a significant departure from the typical military emphasis on what was called kinetic operations, also known as "hunting and killing bad guys." The distributed operations doctrine took a long view and appeared to be battling the root causes of terrorism, which included poverty and poor governance.

AT CFK, THE pace hadn't slowed down. Kim Chapman, who was beginning her master's degree in public health at UNC, managed our undergraduate student volunteers. These students kept CFK active on campus, and they provided a leadership pipeline for the organization. We attracted some of the university's top students, and Kim enjoyed working with them. That year we selected an undergraduate named Peter Dixon to be one of our summer volunteers. Peter wanted to join the Marines after he graduated from UNC, so Kim naturally steered him my way for mentorship.

Peter and I met in Chapel Hill one weekend and bonded over a run. His gung ho attitude and sense of adventure reminded me of my own not-so-distant college days. By the time Peter landed in Kibera for the summer, my team and I were about to deploy from Camp Lejeune to Djibouti. Peter called me after he had his first cup of chai at the Mugumeno Motherland Hotel, where he had passed my regards to the no-nonsense matron.

"I'm in love," Peter announced.

"With the matron?"

"No, no." He laughed. "A puppy."

The puppy, a rambunctious mutt that vaguely resembled a Labrador, had been following Peter around Kibera. Peter gave him food and a Swahili name for friend—Rafiki. When Rafiki fell ill, Peter took him to a veterinarian, who remarked that he had never before treated an animal from the slums. From then on, Rafiki traveled everywhere with Peter.

One day in an Internet café in Nairobi's city center, an attractive American lady noticed Rafiki sitting on Peter's lap. She struck up a conversation. The woman was looking for a partner to film a music video called "World on Fire." The following day, she arrived in Kibera with Peter and Rafiki.

When I told Tracy the news of the serendipitous music video, she asked me about the musician.

"I don't know, Sarah something," I replied. Tracy often teased me for having a horrible lack of pop-culture knowledge. "McLachlan, Sarah McLachlan."

"You mean you don't know who Sarah McLachlan is?" Tracy laughed. "Well, she's great, and she's one of my favorite artists."

We pulled up a Web site with a link to the song. Wind swept off the Atlantic, shaking my camper's thin walls. We were thinking about the same thing. Soon I would be gone again, and nine months sounded like an eternity. Tracy put her hands on my shoulders as Sarah sang, "The world's on fire and it's more than I can handle."

ONE OF THE few Vietnam veterans left on active duty, the Marine general in command of the task force welcomed my team to Camp Lemonnier, Djibouti. We were a high-value asset, the general told us. He believed our intelligence collection was critical for the security of our civil affairs and military training teams located on the far frontiers of the war on terror. My Marines were eager to get out into the field and immediately picked up on the value of the general's support.

Although most lieutenants in the Marine Corps reported to captains, my boss at Camp Lemonnier was a colonel, an old-timer from the reserves who had built a thirty-year career as an intelligence officer. The colonel understood our business and took a hands-off approach. A few days after our arrival, the general called him for a meeting. The colonel invited me to join him to brief the general. In the hyper-rank-conscious Marine Corps, it was as rare for lieutenants to brief generals as it was for them to directly report to a colonel.

When I finished my briefing, the general informed us that his intent was to "push the envelope." It was a phrase that I liked to use, and it was a good signal. In such a command climate, we could shape our intelligence collection based on our views of evolving key priorities, and there were plenty of ongoing operations from which to choose. The task force had too many civil affairs and military training teams spread out across five countries for us to support directly. Since the main effort at the time was in Ethiopia, I decided to dispatch four of my five Marines with interpreter support to the Ogaden region, the vast hinterland on the Somali border.

It was exciting work, and at first the mission appeared to be on the right track. The task force was building dozens of wells, repairing schools, and fixing clinics in a troubled part of the world, and we were doing it for relatively little cost. During our welcoming briefing we were told that the price tag for our task force's annual operations was about equivalent to what the United States spent every hour in Iraq, or every day in Afghanistan.

It took a month for me to deploy my team, catch my bearings, and establish a rhythm for managing daily communications, editing intelligence

reports, and attending planning and liaison meetings. Before long I was
itching to get out and operate. As I had done in Bosnia, I began by cultivating local sources around the capital city and keeping my eyes open for
opportunities to make a more direct impact. One of the first opportunities I identified certainly pushed the envelope. Since nearly half the task
force's resources went to military-to-military training, I proposed that
we initiate military intelligence training with the Ethiopian Army.

My colonel supported my idea and arranged another meeting to brief
the general. The general thought the proposal was "forward thinking,"
though he cautioned us to handle the exploratory meetings with a high
level of discretion. He didn't want to read newspaper headlines about the
U.S. military collaborating with Ethiopian intelligence, which had an
even poorer human rights reputation than the Ethiopian Army. One of
the goals of the task force was to ease the heavy-handed approach of the
Ethiopian Army through constructive engagement.

Within days of briefing the general, I was off with my interpreter in a
Land Cruiser stacked with gear, food, ammunition, and spare tires. We
blasted across Djibouti's volcanic plains into the Ogaden Desert and toward the green hills of eastern Ethiopia's highlands.

A captain from Ethiopian military intelligence, my counterpart, met
me in the back room of a bar down a narrow cobblestone street. We were
in the old-town section of Harer, an ancient walled city that was once East
Africa's center of Islamic culture and religion. Although we were indoors,
the captain wore wraparound sunglasses similar to my own and a white
Panama hat that looked like something out of *Miami Vice*. His gray
blazer concealed a nine-millimeter, Soviet-era Marakov pistol. My own
nine-millimeter Beretta was locked and loaded in a concealed holster
beneath my safari shirt, close to the pocket where I clipped my new Spyderco knife.

Our meeting had been arranged through back channels. I was concerned about who might be watching us and with what intentions. For
decades the Ethiopian government had been waging a low-intensity
counterinsurgency campaign against a separatist faction of the Oromo,
Ethiopia's largest ethnic group. The U.S. military wanted no part of that
dispute. Unfortunately, the captain chose our meeting point, and the city
of Harar was near an area considered to be a stronghold of Oromo resistance. I knew little about these long-standing ethnic tensions apart from

the fact that Ethiopian intelligence had interests in using the U.S. military presence for reasons beyond simply preventing the spread of international terrorism.

The captain removed his sunglasses and extended his hand.

"Nice hat," I remarked.

"Thank you." He smiled with pursed lips. "Like *Chinatown*."

My interpreter looked at me and shrugged his shoulders.

"The movie," the captain clarified. "Jack Nicholson. *Chinatown*." He tipped the brim of his hat.

"Ah, yes, great movie." It happened to be one of my father's favorite films. We built rapport for a while by talking about other famous American movies. With one thumb tucked into his belt, the captain spoke in a smooth Amharic, Ethiopia's official language. We concluded our introductions with a discussion of *The Godfather*. It was among my favorite films. The captain admired that I was a Marine, "like Michael Corleone."

"You've been to Iraq?" he asked.

There it was again, that irritating question. "No, not yet."

The captain looked taken aback. It was the same awkward hesitation that I received in the States. Marines deployed to the front lines. Why was I in Ethiopia if the fighting was in Iraq?

"Iraq's next."

"Humph." The captain nodded, and with that we got down to business. The captain began by remarking that he was happy the United States knew how to interrogate its enemies "creatively."

"What do you mean?" I asked.

"Abu Ghraib." The captain combed his mustache with his index finger.

His response rattled me. Months earlier, the press had released ghastly photographs of abuse and torture at Iraq's Abu Ghraib prison. I didn't understand how American military men and women could perpetrate such evil, and I was shocked that the senior levels of the U.S. military command had not been held accountable.

"That's how these people need to be treated," the captain added. I assumed he was referring to members of Al-Itihaad al-Islamiya, the regional terrorist organization in eastern Ethiopia and Somalia, though he might have had Oromo separatists in mind. "They're terrorists. Pigs, all of them."

"No, that's not how we do business. Abu Ghraib was a mistake, a crime."

"You think?" The captain tilted his head.

"Are you an interrogator?" I asked.

"Of course. I wouldn't be talking with you if I wasn't."

"Then you know abuse isn't effective. Anyone will break under torture. The information isn't reliable. Professional interrogators are above that."

The captain eyed me curiously. He had a different impression of his job, and a far different set of life experiences. The gulf was too wide to cross. Nothing of operational value would come out of our meeting, and there would be no future plans for joint training. It was a flop. Beyond that, it disgusted me that our actions at Abu Ghraib could actually serve as inspiration to others. The United States was supposed to be a force for the oppressed, not the oppressors. I launched into a lecture about human rights and the Geneva Conventions.

The captain listened to my rant without affect. At the end of it, he lit a cigarette and nodded. We shook hands. Before I turned away, he added, "You know, I've learned things about interrogation from you."

Was he talking about me?

He took a long drag from his cigarette. *"The Godfather,"* he said with his pursed-lip smile. "Corleone, Don, the father, not the son. Don Corleone, he taught me things."

DESPITE MY DESIRE to be on the frontiers, I spent most of my time at Camp Lemonnier and out and about in Djibouti City, "the ville." My Marines were autonomous and performing well, and I continued to develop a network of local informants to provide us with early indications of threats. Al Qaeda may have considered Camp Lemonnier, a large American military base in a Muslim country, one of its prime targets. But Al Qaeda probably had no presence in the tiny country with a population of less than one million. One American intelligence analyst assessed the situation as such: "If Al Qaeda is ever stupid enough to show up here, the Djiboutian internal services will be on them like flies on poo."

Nevertheless, we couldn't rely solely on Djiboutian intelligence for protection. Since we assumed the slums would be the most fertile recruiting ground for any terrorist organization, I focused my efforts there. I figured my time in Kibera would be good preparation.

During the summer hot season, the temperature in Djibouti City spiked as high as 120 degrees Fahrenheit. Much of the city benefited from a steady breeze coming off the Gulf of Aden. However, the slums were located in what was once a swamp, a natural depression where the winds stalled and the air stagnated.

My interpreter and I took a cab into Djibouti City's largest slum for my first meeting one afternoon. Mosquitoes splattered the windshield. I spotted a tin shack that appeared to be on fire, black smoke billowing out of its front door. A woman emerged from the smoke, tossed a bucket of wastewater into a sump, and walked back into the shack. My interpreter, a Djiboutian American, explained that women made small fires in their homes to "smoke out" the disease-carrying mosquitoes and the persistent hordes of flies. I knew from Kibera that tin roofs intensified the sun's heat, making the slum an especially miserable place during heat waves. Seeing that woman's life in the smoky shack in Djibouti City during the hot season at the hottest time of day was the closest I'd come to witnessing hell on earth.

By the time we arrived at our meeting location, an open-air shack, I was suffering from a serious case of swamp ass. My boxer shorts clung to my rump like a wet swimming suit. We sat down and waited for our source to show up. The stink of rotting fish mixed with the smell of smoke. The waiter didn't bother taking our order. Wearing a tired, bored look, he brought us two cups of steaming tea and bowls of warm spaghetti with red beets, a staple Djiboutian dish inherited from Italian colonial rule in Somalia. My interpreter waved off his tea and spaghetti by pointing to his stomach and watch, a gesture to signal that he was fasting.

The eyes of a dozen patrons turned toward me. A swarm of flies formed a rain cloud around my head. The last thing I wanted to do was eat. I felt like I was back in Kibera with young men sizing me up. So I dove in. Shoulders forward, I dug into the spaghetti with my hands, shoveling fistfuls of noodles into my mouth as if I hadn't eaten in days. Beads of sweat dripped from my forehead into my bowl. When a fly landed in my mouth, I thought about Tracy. She always reminded me to eat with my mouth closed.

The other patrons went back to their business as I devoured my dish.

Salim once told me that it was good to have chai when it was hot out because hot drinks counterintuitively helped cool the body by regulating its
temperature. This may have worked for Salim, but not for me. By the
time I had finished my hot tea and spaghetti, I felt on the verge of becoming a heat casualty, like one of the unfortunate candidates who fell out of
forced marches at Officer Candidates School and took the silver bullet.

My source, a local power broker in the slums, was the type of contact
who might provide nothing for months until he heard something of value
and decided to call because we had an established relationship. That day,
he was rambling on about his nomadic grandfather and a herd of goats
when my cell phone vibrated. Desperate for a diversion, I excused myself.

"May I ask who's calling?" I'd learned from my father never to identify
myself first.

"It's Randy, Randy Newcomb from Omidyar Network." A couple of
weeks earlier, CFK's administrative officer had asked if she could give my
Djibouti cell number to a foundation in California. "I hope I'm not inter-
rupting you."

"No, no, not at all." My source was talking to the waiter. A fly landed
on my nose. A mosquito nibbled into the back of my neck.

"Well, I know you're deployed, and, first, thank you for your service,"
Randy said before telling me that "Pam and Pierre" had watched Sarah
McLachlan's "World on Fire" music video and wanted to make a matching gift. "Would you be willing to take a check for twenty-six thousand
dollars for CFK? You can use it for whatever purposes you need."

We occasionally received random donations for anything from ten to
a hundred dollars, never thousands.

"Yes. Yes!" I exclaimed, and began to tell Randy the story of Rafiki,
the abandoned puppy from Kibera who had attracted the attention of
Sarah McLachlan's videographer. Then my cell phone lost its signal.

Later, when I had downtime back at base, I checked my e-mail and
discovered a note from Randy confirming the donation from the Omidyar
Network. My jaw dropped when I googled *Omidyar*. Pierre Omidyar was
the founder of eBay. The Omidyar Network, led by Pierre and his wife,
Pam, was one of the largest foundations in the world. I immediately
called Salim.

"Now we can really begin building a new clinic," Salim said. He was
always ready for the next big project. The new clinic would give us much

needed space and reduce our rent, our most costly recurring expense after payroll.

Next, I called Tabitha. I blurted out the news as soon as she picked up.

"Omosh, this is a good thing. Good work." Her voice was weak and tired.

"Are you okay?"

"Me, I'm okay. Yes, just a fever." There was some noise in the background. It sounded busy at the clinic.

"Feel better, *mama*. Maybe you can take a nap."

"You know, I cannot. But me, I'm fine." Tabitha was thirty-eight years old and she was building more than just a clinic. She viewed our work as a movement to bring high-quality, locally directed health care to the poor, and to see doctors in and from Kibera.

"*Tuko pamoja*," I said, using the phrase we often placed as the salutation to CFK letters and e-mails. "We are together."

"*Pamoja*. And, Rye . . ."

"Yes?"

"Thank you."

OUR VIETNAM-VETERAN GENERAL looked perfectly at ease. Everyone else in the cargo pit of the C-130 Hercules was pale, sick, and scared. A private sitting next to me uttered a prayer. My interpreter closed his eyes. Sausage and eggs sloshed between my stomach and my throat as our bird twisted, a seventy-five-thousand-pound roller coaster over the sands of Ethiopia. Weeks earlier, the U.S. Air Force pilot in the cockpit had reported that he may have been shot at by a surface-to-air missile in the vicinity of Gode, a small town en route to Somalia.

The Ethiopian Army used Gode, a predominately Somali town by ethnicity, as a key logistical hub. It had the only paved airfield in the region that could support jumbo-jet landings. From Gode, the Ethiopian government had waged counterinsurgency campaigns since 1977, when Somalia invaded Ethiopia and attempted to annex the Somali-speaking Ogaden region. During the mid-1980s, Gode caught a glimpse of international spotlight when relief workers had arrived to fight one of the world's worst famines in recorded history. The commonly cited, though unverified, statistic was that one million Ethiopians died as a result of two years of famine. It was an unimaginable number, a figure so staggering that I found it incomprehensible until I arrived and discovered that Gode was one of the most desolate wastelands I had ever seen.

"What did these people do to piss God off?" our sergeant major said as we stepped off the cargo plane's drop ramp and surveyed the scorched earth.

We had traveled with an entourage to visit the renovation of a local school. A U.S. Army civil affairs team met us at the airfield. They were accompanied by their security detachment, a squad of infantry soldiers from Guam, the U.S. island protectorate in the Pacific Ocean. The American ambassador to Ethiopia arrived with an economic-development specialist from USAID and some other members of her staff. We were the embodiment of unconventional warfare. Our Horn of Africa Task Force convened multiple sources of American power and influence to win "hearts and minds" in a troubled region that we believed was highly susceptible to transnational terrorism. It was an impressive group, and it was what I thought America needed to be doing around the world. Shoot less, give more.

Eventually we reached a hamlet of mud-and-wattle huts and pulled up to a freshly painted concrete building surrounded by a chain-link fence. This was our school, and there wasn't much to see. Our entourage outnumbered the handful of Ethiopian civilians who had turned up for the occasion. The school's rooms were empty. The tour from the local Ethiopian contractor lasted less than ten minutes. No one knew how many kids would attend the school, or when it would open for classes.

My interpreter and I spoke to a few Somali men with high foreheads and distinctly angular faces. The men said our school renovation was good and that they were happy. Another man asked me when we would build him a home. As we began to head back to the convoy, three Ethiopian soldiers pulled a middle-aged Somali man off to the side for no apparent reason. The other Americans were focused on getting into the convoy and handing candy out to a gaggle of children screaming, "GIMME, GIMME!" and "USA NUMBA ONE!"

One of the Ethiopian soldiers drilled the butt of his rifle into the Somali man's stomach, causing his body to buckle and fold onto the dusty ground. I followed them as they dragged the man by his wrists behind the school.

"What are you doing?" They froze as soon as they saw me.

The highest-ranking soldier shrugged. "Nothing."

"What did he do wrong?"

"This man, no good," the soldier replied, walking away and leaving the Somali man in the dust with a bloody nose and fiery eyes.

My interpreter looked at the man and whispered to me, "This is why they hate the army here."

OUR CONVOY DROVE ten minutes to one of the few permanent structures in Gode. While the ambassador and the general went into a cement-block building for official meetings, my interpreter and I took a stroll up a dirt road in search of someone to talk with. We stopped at a mud hut with a sign that read RESTAURANT in Somali. Four men inside were watching Al Jazeera coverage of the Iraq War. They turned around and looked startled. My eyes darted to their waistlines in search of concealed weapons. The men wore colorful *kikoy* wraps that many American soldiers referred to as "man dresses."

"*Ma nabad baa.*" I announced the common Somali greeting with a big smile.

My greeting broke some of the tension. The men laughed and replied in high-pitched Somali, "*Nabad, nabad*" (Peace, peace).

"I prefer CNN." I gestured to the TV, spotting two AK-47s on the tables behind them.

"We don't. But me, sometimes I like Christiane Amanpour," one of the men said, referring to the famous CNN war correspondent. He asked me what I thought of the Iraq War.

"It's bad." My pistol pressed against my stomach. My interpreter didn't carry a weapon. I was outgunned.

"Yes. Bad." The man nodded.

"How 'bout you?" I asked.

"I think it's wrong."

"Well, I agree."

The man raised his eyebrows. He wasn't expecting that response. However, I didn't want a discussion about Iraq. That could go on for hours and wouldn't reveal anything of intelligence value. I changed the topic and asked the man if he knew why we were in Gode.

"You think we're Al Qaeda. But bin Laden is not here." He laughed, and the others joined. "In fact we have no problems with you."

"You have problems with the Ethiopian Army?"

The man tapped the wood table with one finger but didn't respond.

"Have they gotten better since we arrived?"

Suddenly the man became angry. "They're the same as they were during the Dergue. They're fucking dogs. You understand? You understand what they do to us, to our women? Nothing has changed. Only now they wait until you turn your back."

"The Dergue?" I asked. My interpreter hesitated. I had no idea that the Dergue was the Communist military council that ruled Ethiopia from 1975 to 1987, killing and torturing thousands of citizens during a seventeen-year civil war. The U.S. government had once channeled covert resources into the hands of resistance fighters, including Ethiopians of Somali ethnicity. My interpreter's body language was screaming at me not to ask such an ignorant question. I rephrased it: "Yes, the Dergue was bad."

Al Jazeera replayed footage of Iraqi children allegedly killed by an American bomb. The video was graphic, filled with body parts and wailing women.

"You know, we have no problem with the United States," the man finally said. "Our problem is this government. They build military bases, never schools. You come and renovate a school and that we can appreciate. But they're using you to keep us down. They call us terrorists. Terrorists? No, we're not. We're fighting for our rights, you see. Look how we live. We live like animals. You have dogs that live better than we do."

Frank conversations rarely happened in such circumstances. Unfortunately, my radio flashed with a signal. The general and ambassador were ready to leave. I asked the man if he would be willing to have another conversation.

"I cannot," he replied. "I've already told you too much. Just go."

We loaded into our heavily armed convoy to return to Djibouti after less than five hours in Ethiopia. It was still early in our nine-month deployment, and I had arrived in Gode believing that we were pioneers of a new, more effective way of counterterrorism. I left with doubts, and my doubts would only grow deeper with time. Most of the military men and women in the task force were as ignorant of Ethiopia's geopolitics as I was. Our tours lasted six to twelve months, and each of the five countries where we operated had long, complex histories. With the exception of HUMINT and civil affairs, most of the fifteen hundred members of the task force, including its many senior officers, such as my colonel, never interacted with locals.

In 2001, intelligence analysts had suggested that bin Laden and Al Qaeda might attempt to flee from Afghanistan. East Africa was a logical migration point because bin Laden lived in Sudan from 1992 to 1996. In 1998, Al Qaeda had orchestrated the U.S. embassy bombings in Kenya and Tanzania. For whatever reasons, the projected terrorist migration never happened. Three years later, we were still in Djibouti and showing no signs of leaving or scaling back.

Our situation reminded me of Kibera. The slum was rife with external actors such as the United Nations and NGOs. Too often these organizations pushed projects without local leadership and knowledge of what was really happening. Now the tables were turned. I was part of one of the largest external actors in the region—the U.S. military—and it was unclear how our team would effect positive change in any of the countries where we operated.

We didn't have a clue, and it came back to Colonel Greenwood's critique. Long-term U.S. military engagements were often fatally flawed because they lacked continuity and regional expertise. Were we deterring transnational terrorism in Gode? It was tough to tell, in part because the task force never collected data on its impact. Maybe we were building goodwill in Gode; maybe we were resented because of our affiliation with the Ethiopian Army; maybe we were legitimizing a repressive regime. No one knew, and too often by the time our leadership asked the essential strategic questions, they were preparing for the next mission. "Crown rotations" was what one of my buddies called the constant change of command, and with every new commander came new priorities, personalities, and power dynamics. The only thing we were certain of in the Horn of Africa was that none of us would be there for more than a year.

MIDWAY THROUGH MY deployment I called Captain Dubrule on satellite phone. He was at a base in Ramadi, the capital of the largest Sunni province in Iraq. Our Marines were about to surge to Fallujah and begin the bloody takeover of that embattled city. Shortly after he picked up the phone a deafening explosion occurred.

"Mortar," Captain Dubrule calmly observed. I learned later that the mortar had landed directly on a portable toilet, killing a Marine captain.

"You still want to deploy to Iraq?" he asked. He knew my four-year service obligation was coming to a close. His time as our commander would also end before our company would deploy for a third tour to Iraq the following year.

I didn't need to think about my response. "Absolutely."

"And after Iraq?" Captain Dubrule had a hundred other things on his mind as he prepared to lead our company through some of the fiercest fighting of the war, yet he wanted to make sure I was thinking about my career.

"I don't know, sir. Maybe graduate school." While a strong part of me loved being a Marine and didn't want to give it up, I questioned if I could continue my balancing act with CFK and Tracy. The course I was on wasn't sustainable.

"Time goes fast, Rye. I'd encourage you to think about it now and plan ahead. You know we'd love to keep you in the Corps. But you need to do what's right for you."

Our conversation reminded me of my plans over the past year. After returning from Bosnia, I had stitched together something that had resembled a career path, or, at least, a next step. The closer I aged to thirty, the less likely it seemed that I would realize my premonition of an early death. A career in foreign policy, perhaps one day becoming an ambassador or working at the National Security Council, sounded exciting and meaningful. To have such a career, I needed a graduate degree, and law school or a Ph.D. in international affairs seemed to be obvious options.

At the time, Tracy was grinding through a six-year Ph.D. program in clinical psychology. During some months she was so broke she sold her plasma to pay her bills. While I wasn't motivated by a goal of making a lot of money, I didn't want a lack of resources to hold me back from living a life with options. A law degree was quicker, more versatile, and potentially more lucrative than the Ph.D. Once I realized the trade-offs, I had registered for the LSAT and decided to apply for law school, assuming that if I was accepted, I could defer admission until I completed a tour to Iraq.

Tracy supported my law school plan, though I didn't mention the Iraq part. She applied for a psychology fellowship at Yale in anticipation of my admission at Yale Law School, my top choice. Unfortunately, I had scored around the fiftieth percentile on the LSAT. With such a score I didn't have a snowball's chance in hell of getting into Yale. I saw the data, but I had applied anyway. Months later, Yale and every other school sent me regrets.

Wounded by the rejections, I was searching for other options when my friend Andrew Carroll told me about an impressive manuscript he was reviewing for a Marine captain named Nathaniel Fick. The manuscript later became the bestseller *One Bullet Away*, and Nathaniel took time to answer my uninformed questions about his dual business and public-policy masters' degree program at Harvard. I had thought about Harvard's Kennedy School of Government ever since my meeting with Dr. Frazer at the White House. The business half of the degree sounded equally interesting. I believed many nonprofits, including CFK, could be improved by the best practices in business management, and my experience in Kibera seemed to fit with an emerging field called social entrepreneurship.

Once Tracy accepted her fellowship to Yale, she encouraged me to apply to the Harvard dual-degree program, which would keep us within driving distance of one another. My closest mentors thought that the combination of public policy and business made sense. Although I wasn't confident that I could get into Harvard, which was a source of considerable stress, there was a larger issue. I wasn't ready to leave active duty without leading Marines in combat.

THOSE WERE SOME of the personal things on my mind at the end of my call with Captain Dubrule. Weeks later I was blazing through the Ogaden Desert with my interpreter Hussein when he swerved to miss a dik-dik standing like a little reindeer in the middle of the road. That was when we crashed into the ridge and flipped over. Our Land Cruiser totaled, I arranged for an Ethiopian tow truck to haul us back to Djibouti, and nervously anticipated the conversation I would need to have with my colonel.

My mother always said that the worst part of bad news was when it came as a surprise, when it blindsided you. Tabitha didn't sound well on the phone when she called. She had never called me before. I knew she was sick, and her tone suggested that it was more serious than I had initially thought. I needed to see her. I needed to return to Kibera.

Until then, the compartments of Kibera and the Marine Corps had withstood the pressures of my first two deployments. Then, for the first time, my service to Kibera was in direct conflict with my military duties. Nevertheless, I had no choice. I asked my colonel for permission to fly to Nairobi to see Tabitha. The colonel listened to my appeal, fingered the silver cross on his dog tags, and gave me the go-ahead. "God's work" was what he called what we were doing in Kibera. It didn't matter what he called it. I needed to see Mama Tabitha and give her whatever care I could muster.

TABITHA'S STRONG BROWN eyes were stoic and unafraid as I knelt at her hospital bedside. If it were not for her eyes, I might not have recognized her. She had lost clumps of hair and half of her weight. Beads of sweat dotted her forehead. The very effort to speak seemed to cause her pain. She was in one of Nairobi's top hospitals, but she wanted to be treated at her clinic, with her people, in her community.

The attending physician asked me to step out of the room with him. He told me that Tabitha was too weak to endure an ambulance ride back to Kibera. He touched my elbow and apologized. Her appendix had burst, and an infection was spreading through her body and could not be stopped. She would not survive much longer.

I was in shock. I returned to Tabitha and stood quietly by her side before giving her news about things at her clinic. In a soft, strained voice she recalled the week my mother had spent with her years ago nursing patients when the clinic was just getting started.

"Is she well?" Tabitha asked.

"Yes, Mom's well. Still teaching."

"Oh, that's a good thing."

"She loves to tell about when she first came to Kibera. You took her suitcase from my hands. Do you remember that?"

Tabitha nodded.

"You took the suitcase and you carried it on your head, and you took her hand and led her to the clinic. That was the first night. Mom, she loves that memory."

"And the pussy." Tabitha smiled faintly.

"The pussy?"

"The pussycat."

"Oh, yes, yes, it ran on the roof and scared Mom that second night. She was worried but it was just a pussycat. She laughed about it with you the next morning, and Joy and Kevin were there, and Ronnie, too."

"Yes, my children. Will you . . ."

"Yes, I will." I promised her I would make sure her children finished school. Then she drifted off to sleep. I stood there by her side watching the birds in the hibiscus tree in the courtyard outside the window. I thought about the day in the summer of 2000 before I left Kibera for Officer Candidates School—the day that changed our lives forever. Tabitha, in her oversized black leather jacket, had led me to her home and prepared chai. She had taken me into her life and told me about her plan to sell vegetables. Pride and conviction were in her voice. She wasn't looking for pity. She had just needed a boost at a time that was tough by even Kibera standards.

When Tabitha woke up, she touched my cheek. Her fingers were like Vanessa's. They felt like a hot iron. "I have faith in you and the community," she said. "Don't quit pushing this thing."

I promised and kissed her forehead, breaking salty beads of sweat. Her voice began to fade as she recited a quote of some sort with the words *grass*, *flower*, and *wind*. When I leaned forward and asked her to repeat it, she had already fallen asleep.

I stepped out of the room and stumbled down the hall. I made my way out to the courtyard with the hibiscus tree, tears falling down my face. *Why? Why now?*

There was no answer, and early the next morning, with her children asleep by her side, Tabitha passed away. Grass, flower, and wind. Her last words had a beautiful rhythm. She was quoting something, but I hadn't heard the sentences woven between those three words. For years they would remain a mystery.

CHAPTER SEVENTEEN

The Manuscript

Camp Lemonnier, Djibouti

S<small>PRING</small> 2005

I <small>BECAME FAR MORE CRITICAL OF OUR MILITARY</small> mission in the Horn of Africa in my final four months at Camp Lemonnier. Our deployment was considered a hardship post. I could only imagine what Tabitha would have thought if she were alive and saw the hundreds of steak and lobster meals served by Halliburton, one of the world's most profitable companies, or heard that the cost of fuel for one round-trip military flight from Djibouti to Kenya could have covered her yearly expenses at the clinic. Camp Lemonnier was teeming with colonels. Many of these senior officers went their entire deployments without ever having a real conversation with an African civilian. We ran CFK each year for less than the cost of a colonel.

Tabitha never used the word *development*, but in her mind fighting poverty and empowering others required humility and long-term commitment. She often called this "sacrifice." Her approach, and our approach at CFK, was in stark contrast to the haphazard explorations of the military in the Horn of Africa. It wasn't a question of intentions. Most of the military men and women with whom I served wanted to do the right things. They wanted to help local communities develop. But good intentions weren't enough.

The problem wasn't simply our lack of continuity and our ignorance about the communities where we intervened. The larger issue was one that the military couldn't overcome. It was the fundamental impossibility of empowering a community through armed intervention. As long as we wore uniforms and carried weapons, we would be seen for exactly what we were—a foreign military.

These realizations, which occurred over many months, brought me back to the importance of compartments. "Do what you do well" goes the old saw. Institutions have core competencies. The military's core competency was war. Of course, security was a precondition to development, and militaries played constructive roles in establishing and sustaining that security, as we had done in Bosnia. Our military mission in the Horn of Africa, however, had lost focus. While the resources we spent there were insignificant in the larger scope of the hundreds of billions of dollars the Department of Defense consumed each year, it was still millions of dollars of impact lost.

TRACY MET ME at the airport outside Camp Lejeune as soon as my team returned from our nine months overseas. We fell back into our happy weekend routines on North Topsail Beach: long walks, movies, and grilling out. Tracy was pleased that I moved from my camper at Rogers Bay to a one-bedroom apartment farther up the island. The tourist season had yet to begin and we had miles of beach to ourselves. It was glorious.

I waited for a while until I brought up news that I knew would upset her. We were walking along a deserted stretch of sand, talking about the ocean's glassy horizon and the blue sky. "So I've got some news that you're not gonna like. I'm slated for the next Iraq deployment." It was an abrupt transition. I didn't know how to say it other than directly.

"What?" There was a rare sharpness in her voice.

"Yes, babe, I'm sorry."

"How long have you known this?"

"A couple of months, but—"

"A couple of months! What? You've known this that long and you're just telling me now?"

"I needed to tell you in person. I knew you'd be upset."

"Well, you're right about that. When's this going to end? You've been gone for half of the last three years."

I didn't know. Captain Dubrule had recommended that I consider a special program that, after Iraq, could take me into the Central Intelligence Agency. Such a program could allow me to continue collecting intelligence from sources in the field, which was the part of my job that I most enjoyed.

"What's this special program?"

I told her as much as I could.

"I AM SO SICK OF THIS!" she shouted. She never shouted. "I hate these secrets. I hate it that you can never tell me what you're doing, and sometimes you just disappear. Now you're saying this? This sounds worse than the last three years. And when did you think you were going to talk to me about this, this thing with the CIA?"

"Well, isn't that what we're doing?"

"Dammit, Rye." She looked to the ocean.

"It's just an idea." I didn't know what I wanted to do, and I was too self-absorbed to see that the woman I loved wasn't going to wait forever. "It probably won't work because of CFK. There's no way I could stay involved with CFK if I were in the CIA."

"You think? CFK, it's always CFK. How about us? You think I just take second fiddle to everything else?"

"No, no, that's not it at all. Babe, I'm just putting out an idea. If you can't live with it, fine, I won't do it." I reacted before I could think through the consequences.

"Good, because you've done your time. Why Iraq? Why are they making you do it?"

"Well, I volunteered."

"YOU WHAT?! WHAT! I CAN'T . . . WHAT DID YOU JUST SAY?"

"Stop, babe, please." I paused. "Let me explain." I was near the end of my four-year active-duty obligation and could have "dropped my papers." However, if I went that route, the probability was high that I'd be recalled to involuntary duty and stuck in Iraq with a random unit. If I extended my service for another year, I could help lead my company and deploy with Marines I knew and trusted. I didn't want to let my company down and leave them when they were hard-pressed for officers with experience.

Tracy sighed. "And there's something else," I added. "You know when I come back to the States, everyone asks, 'Have you been to Iraq?' Even in the Marine Corps, it's like my tours in Bosnia and the Horn of Africa don't matter as much. They're peripheral. To some Marines, they don't matter at all. And, you know, sometimes I feel that, too. I mean, if I don't go, I feel like I haven't done my part."

"I don't like it," Tracy said under her breath.

Of course there was more to it than simply seeking legitimacy as a Marine. I still wanted to experience war, to see the elephant, as we called it. I sought a baptism by fire. For me, this craving for a taste of combat, which may strike many people as perverse, was more than a rite of passage or the ability to say "been there, done that." Enemy fire was a test of courage, and I had wanted to know how I would react to it ever since I was a child and touched that old smoke grenade behind my father's desk.

"So what's next?" A tear trickled down her face. "After Iraq, you're still thinking about graduate school, right?"

Although Tracy wanted me to leave the Marines, I was tempted to stick around for at least another three-year assignment. There were plenty of options, including ones that would involve fewer deployments. I enjoyed the prestige of being a Marine, the camaraderie, and being a part of missions that could take me to new and challenging places. I knew that I wanted to propose to Tracy after Iraq, and I didn't want to drag her into something that would make her unhappy. Yet I suspected we could still make it work in the military. The CIA was an extreme option. Others were more compatible with family life, I thought.

Nevertheless, I had committed to applying to Harvard for the dual-degree program in business and public policy, so I threw myself into the applications. It was a good thing Tracy and I didn't live together because my work pace was insane. I spent my nights with CFK. Each morning I woke up at 0330 for two hours of GMAT problem sets. I scored poorly on my initial sample tests, and the results made me nervous—but also more determined. I started waking up without an alarm, clutched by anxiety. By 0630 hours I arrived at our company team house for a full day of war preparations.

Captain Dubrule transitioned to a new duty station and handed over the company command to Joe Burke, a Korean linguist with more than a dozen years of intelligence experience. I remained the number two officer, and we immediately hit it off after I spotted his collection of war and espionage books. Captain Burke was forty-two years old, nearly twice the age of the average Marine. His hair was as gray as the smoke from his Marlboro reds, which didn't slow him down. He could outrun nearly everyone in the company. The Marines appreciated his physical stamina, self-effacing humor, and approachability. He was the only commander I knew who signed-off his e-mails to subordinates with his first name.

Half of our company had fought in Iraq, and the Iraq veterans set the tone. In contrast to the eager anticipation that had braced the company before the invasion, the mood was somber and professional. It felt as if we were in the middle of a long, hard slog. Although we were worried, we rarely discussed our fears. We had a job to do and our work was crucial to the fight. HUMINT was at the heart of any effective counterinsurgency. Every week Marine combat commanders deluged Captain Burke with requests for support that we didn't have. We were stretched to the limit and running without brakes.

My own zeal to lead Marines in combat was tempered, though not extinguished, by reminders of war's complexity and cruelty. A brother lieutenant lost his leg in Fallujah. A roadside bomb killed one of our sergeants, and one of our most able interrogators suffered from post-traumatic stress disorder and attempted suicide. My mornings at work began with a stream of classified reports from the front lines. The raw intelligence reporting suggested that we had a poor understanding of our enemy. We were floundering and our intelligence analysis offered no coherent assessment.

Among the lieutenants who had been to Iraq, the consensus was that things were going poorly, but there was no agreement about what to do. Some officers argued that we should ramp up our combat operations to destroy terrorist cells and quell the insurgency through force. Captain Burke and others believed that we were too focused on kicking down doors and needed to shift our efforts to building the capacity of the Iraqi security forces. "We can't kill and capture our way out of an insurgency," he reminded us. His argument made sense to me. It was based on experience and years of studying classic counterinsurgency texts, such as Mao's *On Guerrilla Warfare* and the Marine Corps' *Small Wars Manual*. If we wanted to leave Iraq within the next decade, we needed to build the capacity of the local security forces. Nevertheless, the majority of our intelligence collection in Iraq was focused on targeting the enemy and locating IEDs, improvised explosive devices. Marines were still being killed at high rates, and there appeared to be no resources for broader reporting on "atmospherics."

THE WAR'S MENTAL toll on our Marines reminded me of Peter Whaley. Whaley was trapped in his own wartime trauma when we had first met over calamari in Washington, D.C. I had kept in touch with him over the past six years, and he had remained a loyal and entertaining source of wisdom and advice. I was curious about his thoughts on Iraq. Unfortunately his e-mail was deactivated and his phone number no longer worked. I called the State Department and was eventually routed to a man who identified himself as "an old friend of Peter's."

I told him I was a Marine first lieutenant and a mentee of Mr. Whaley's.

"Oh, you haven't heard?" the man sighed.

"No. No, sir. What is it?"

"Peter died three months ago. I'm sorry. He died of the cancer that he had fought for many years. Such a shame. He was only fifty-four, you know."

His words knocked the wind out of me. "No, I didn't. I didn't know. Cancer?"

"None of us knew. He kept it to himself. That was Peter."

"I only met him in person once. But all these years he helped me out."

"You're not the only one. Peter cared, he gave a damn. If a young person reached out, he answered, always. He pissed off a lot of people. But that's what happens when you speak the truth and the truth is unpopular."

"You said 'he gave a damn.'" I thought I might have misheard him. It was the line from Ted Lord, the student in Swahili class who had guided me with his advice to reach out and eventually a few people, "maybe five percent, will give a damn." Reach out and you might find a Peter Whaley.

"That's right, Lieutenant," the man on the other end of the phone replied, "that's what I said. He gave a damn, and we miss the hell out of him."

I missed him too. I had spent three hours in person with Mr. Whaley that first evening when I was twenty years old with a crazy proposal to attach to the Rwandan military and write a history of their intervention during the genocide. Yet Peter Whaley had made a profound impact on my life. He had always responded to my e-mails and phone calls. Although I wished he had told me about his cancer, I admired his drive to make a difference until the very end. It reminded me of Tabitha. A lot of things reminded me of Tabitha. I thought about her every day.

SALIM AND OUR team were struggling in the aftermath of Tabitha's death. We renamed the clinic in her honor. Her legacy had to live on, and the awesome power of this legacy would bring us through some of our toughest moments to come. Salim had difficulty managing the additional responsibilities of the clinic until he was able to hire a clinic manager with the skills, heart, and community awareness to take over.

Meanwhile, the pace of activity remained high across the spectrum of CFK initiatives. Soon after our new clinic manager joined, we began forming a major partnership with the U.S. Centers for Disease Control and Prevention (CDC), which contacted us in search of a locally led organization with deep ties to the community. With time, it would become an innovative partnership that would further the evolution of my views on research and stand as an example of a responsible way to combine long-term study with action. For our clinic and the residents of Kibera, that action would eventually translate to free medical care for tens of thousands of people. Additionally, our Binti Pamoja Girls' Center published a coffee-table book of first-person narratives and photographs called *Lightbox*. The book would generate thousands of dollars for girls' scholarships. Our sports program was integrating reproductive-health education into its training clinics for coaches and captains, and we launched a new community-based waste-management program called Trash Is Cash (*Taka Ni Pato*).

It was still exciting, though the organization was growing so rapidly that the volume of tasks outpaced our abilities to manage the U.S. office as volunteers. Up until Tabitha's death, CFK was often a source of release for me from the military. Since her passing, however, it began to feel more like a responsibility that kept me captive to a never-ending stream of e-mail and phone calls. When I neared my wit's end, I called Salim. His voice rejuvenated me, and we often talked about our personal hopes and fears. He was one of a handful of friends to whom I could bare a part of my soul.

Our deep friendship was especially important at that time not only because we lost our cofounder, but because of the wars. Salim detested war, and his feelings were especially sharp about Iraq and what he viewed as American aggression overseas. We didn't speak about it frequently, though when we did, we were candid. I respected his opinion and agreed with him on many points. Of course, in certain areas we disagreed. I had a higher tolerance for the use of violence and military hard power to defend a country and its interests. While Salim and I agreed that Iraq was an unjust war, we had a different view about the U.S. invasion of Afghanistan. More important than our specific perspectives was that we discussed them and listened to each other. Had we not spoken openly about it, the wars could slowly have divided us. Salim wasn't happy that I was going to Iraq, but he accepted it as a duty that I had to fulfill. He supported me as a friend.

While our conversations covered a lot of important and sensitive ground, I could never bring myself to speak with Salim about my desire to "see the elephant." That part of me remained in the shadows to all of my friends except a couple of my closest Marine brothers. I didn't know how to explain it to my loved ones who hadn't served in the military. I knew that they would find it difficult, if not impossible, to comprehend.

MY PARENTS FLEW down from Rhode Island in late August the weekend before I left for Iraq. We spent three days together on the beach. Dad was unusually worried.

"I'm sorry to ask this," he said during a long walk. "Have you prepared a will?"

Although it was on my to-do list, I hadn't gotten around to it.

"Well, if you don't mind, tell me about it."

"I'd like to pay off Tracy's debt from grad school, and if there's anything left, put whatever money remains to CFK."

Dad's face twitched a bit below the scar on his cheek. "Why not write it down and send it to Mom and me before you leave. You need to stay focused on Iraq. Never let your guard down. But what are you thinking you will do after?"

I told my father that I was weighing options to stay in the Marine Corps or apply to Harvard for graduate school in business and public policy. My mother thought Harvard was a wonderful idea, "both intellectually and to have you so close to home."

"Those are tough schools to get into, Rye," my father reacted. "You know I got rejected once from Harvard Business School."

"No, Dad, I didn't remember that. You had your Ph.D. in sociology. Why would you bother with HBS?"

"Organizational behavior. They're top-notch at it. You might want to have some backups."

"I'll be competitive." I didn't want to talk about it. It frustrated me that he didn't think I'd get in. I shifted gears to avoid an argument, and I told my father in general terms about the CIA opportunity that Captain Dubrule had suggested before he had handed over company command to Captain Burke.

"Sounds interesting, but what about your lady?"

"Well, that's why I'm not going to do it."

"Good choice, son. What else are you looking at?"

The opportunities ran the gamut from counterespionage operations based out of Washington, D.C., to recruiting duty in Connecticut.

"Why not pick one of them for another three years and then get out after eight?" While he had never entirely objected to me making a career in the Marine Corps, he didn't encourage it either. He hoped that I'd get out, and I knew my mother wanted to see me in a different career. As independent as I sometimes was, the opinions of my parents still meant an enormous amount to me.

Before they left, my father handed me a thick manila folder. We embraced. I hugged my mom and struggled to hold back tears. I knew what was on their minds, though I tried not to think about it.

THE LAST WEEK at Camp Lejeune flew by in a flurry of activity as we made plans for our teams to attach to different combat units and prisons located throughout Al Anbar Province, the war-torn Sunni region about the size of North Carolina located west of Baghdad. Once we arrived in Iraq, Captain Burke would command the company from division headquarters in the provincial capital of Ramadi, and I would take my small team of three Marines and two linguists to the Eighth Marine Regiment in Fallujah.

My gunnery sergeant and I came up with our call sign, Talisman. We would support the Third Reconnaissance Battalion, the same unit with which my father had fought. I would serve as the regimental HUMINT officer. It was a staff job, though I intended to be operational in addition to leading my team and supporting three other teams attached to the regiment's infantry battalions.

Fortunately, I hit the four-year mark days before we deployed. My battalion commander pinned on my captain's bars. After the hasty ceremony, my commander, a lieutenant colonel, pointed to the new silver double bars on my camouflage collar and said, "Congratulations, Captain. Those ought to make your life at the regiment in Fallujah easier."

Captain Burke walked up and shook my hand.

"Sir," I said, "thank you."

"It's Joe now, Rye."

IT WAS USUALLY easy for me to sleep on flights. Most of our Marines were conked out with their rifles in their laps as the commercial Continental airplane carried us from Europe to Kuwait. I had been awake for more than thirty-six hours, the previous day having started with my farewell to Tracy at Camp Lejeune.

"I love you. Stay safe and come back" were her last words.

I felt the stretching sensation inside my chest as I embraced her. "I'll be back soon. I love you," I said, picking up my dad's old duffel and leaving the woman I hoped to marry with a tear falling down her face.

I was thinking about our good-bye when I started flipping through the airline videos. One of my favorite movies was playing, *Kingdom of Heaven*. It was ironic to be flying to war in the Middle East and watching a movie about the Crusades.

My thoughts shifted back to my dad when the knighting scene began. The film's hero knelt as his father spoke on his deathbed: "Speak the truth always, even if it leads to your death. Safeguard the helpless and do no wrong. That is your oath." The father slapped his son across the face, "And that's so you remember it."

The scene shook me. I heard my father's voice and imagined a smack across my face. I stopped the movie, shocked by the realization that I had neglected to read what my father had prepared in the thick manila envelope. Rifling through my rucksack, I discovered a seventy-page manuscript that he had written for me in the months leading up to my Iraq deployment. It was about his year as a Marine counterinsurgent in Vietnam. It began, "My involvement in military life features opportunities gained and lost, variable probabilities, illusions and disillusions, and elusive uncertainties, some of which remain."

Dad's fourth chapter was titled "My First VC (Viet Cong)—or Was He?" The chapter took place during his first month in enemy terrain, where he was in command of a weapons platoon assigned to monitor and defend a mountain pass outside of Danang. Hundreds of villagers moved through the pass each day. Most of them were older women carrying food and walking barefoot. One day, my father noticed that a young man with a bicycle was standing near the pass wearing leather shoes and watching the Marines curiously. Dad confronted the man, searched him, and discovered pencil marks on the inner lining of his jacket. The marks appeared to form a sketch of the platoon's firing positions.

"I stepped back, aimed my 45 [caliber pistol] at his heart, and motioned for him to start walking."

My father walked the suspect Viet Cong to a nearby artillery battery and turned him over to the commanding officer for interrogation. However, he never received any feedback or intelligence about the suspect despite his many follow-up requests for information. Forty years later, Dad reflected, "Uncertainty abounded. Feedback from upper echelons was unreliable and scarce. Members of each unit seemed uninterested in anything but their own primary task. Few officers spent time acquiring and sharing possible new knowledge about the enemy and the nature of our conflict."

I read this with great interest. It surprised me that military intelligence appeared to be so incomplete and one-directional in Vietnam. I didn't read it as a warning. I assumed that Marine Corps intelligence had dramatically improved. We existed to support the Marines on the ground, the warfighters such as my father. Surely we would not let them down.

In the final scene of his manuscript, Dad wrote about the ambush where he was shot in the face and leg. That was the attack in which the old smoke grenade that fascinated me as a child caught an enemy machine gun bullet heading for his heart. It felt like I was discovering a secret as I read:

> After the gunfire died down, I crunched down off the trail and
> tried to figure out what was going on at the ambush site. It was

silent and motionless. Brilliant beams of sunlight pierced down through the tall trees choked with vines. Sunlight and shadows. Lots of deep, concealing shadows. My Marines spread out into firing positions. One of them said, "They were up in the trees, lieutenant." I looked up into the trees, but I couldn't see well. Someone yelled, "Corpsman up. The lieutenant's been hit."

I wondered which lieutenant had been hit. I turned and saw our company executive officer, a strapping, proud, preppy fellow from "Hahvaad," who was looking down at me. A corpsman pulled off my helmet and started swabbing my face and head in search of exit wounds. Then the executive officer grinned and said, "Schwartz, you lucky bastard. You just got yourself a million dollar wound. But you don't look too pretty."

CHAPTER EIGHTEEN

The Elephant and the Velvet Glove

Fallujah, Iraq

FALL 2005

STAY AWAKE, DAMMIT, STAY AWAKE.

My eyes felt heavy. My head bobbed.

I had only been in country for a week. Already I was so tired.

Sweat built up beneath my body armor. The Humvee's air-conditioning roared, churning frosty air into my face. I sucked in a breath and held it, clenching my jaws, grinding my teeth.

They called it the City of Mosques, though from my vantage point on the bridge, I could only spot three minarets standing like chimney stacks in the haze. Everything was brown, dry, and dusty. Our Humvee crossed the Euphrates. A fish leaped, arcing gracefully above the ripples of the olive-green water. Fallujah didn't look like my childhood impressions of a flourishing cradle of civilization.

Blackwater Bridge stood to my left. Known as Old Bridge by the locals, it ran into the most densely populated, volatile part of the city—the Jolan Market. We rarely crossed that bridge. Eighteen months had passed since the charred remains of four U.S. contractors hung from its steel frame. It was an event that had sparked one of the bloodiest battles of the Iraq War—the Battle of Fallujah.

Colonel Berger, the commander of regimental combat team eight, sat in the front seat monitoring his Blue Force Tracker, a computer that charted the real-time location of military units in the region. Although I generally sat behind the colonel, that afternoon I chose the seat behind the driver to get a better view of the market. There, Iraqi children had been tossing grenades from rooftops at our convoys.

"Crossing checkpoint," Colonel Berger said into the radio. We were now in downtown Fallujah.

WATCH THE ROAD! I shouted silently to myself.

We were on patrol for barely three hours. Why was I so tired? This was enemy territory and Colonel Berger was a high-value target. I needed to be alert and on the lookout for improvised explosive devices, IEDs.

COMPLACENCY KILLS read the sign at the exit point of our base.

WAKE UP!

I took in another breath and held it. I'd learned the tactic at the Basic School to prevent myself from falling asleep during PowerPoint presentations. Scouring the pockmarked road, I studied the rocks, upturned earth, and garbage piles. This part of the city resembled photographs of Dresden during the Allied firebombing campaigns of World War II. An IED could be anywhere.

A dozen Iraqi men stood at an intersection ahead. They appeared to be unarmed, though some had cell phones. Cell phones triggered IEDs.

"Fifteen hundred [hours] and these men are out doing nothing," Colonel Berger snarled. "They're up to no good."

A black plume rose from an oil drum. "Smoke up ahead," I said.

"Could be a signal," Colonel Berger replied. "Stay alert. Corporal, you got that?"

"Roger that, sir," the corporal, our gunner, shouted from the turret, and trained the long barrel of his fifty-caliber machine gun toward the smoke. The only men who suffered higher casualty rates than our turret gunners in Iraq were the explosive-ordnance-disposal Marines, the heroic souls who cleared the roadside bombs.

A one-legged man stood near the oil drum on crutches, motionless, a scarecrow waiting for the wind to blow. His cataract-clouded eyes looked like golf balls.

I counseled my Marines to be vigilant, to expect the unexpected. What was my problem?

WATCH THE DAMN ROAD.

I scanned the sidewalks scarred by mortar fire and tank tracks. Three Iraqi schoolgirls in white-collared shirts and colorful shawls strolled up a side street. They stopped smiling when they saw our convoy. Kibera came to mind. There, the schoolgirls also wore pretty uniforms. They looked neat and clean despite the squalor.

BOOM.

My ears rang. We were engulfed by smoke. The corporal collapsed from the turret. I was dazed.

"Marine, you all right?" Colonel Berger turned and seized the corporal's arm.

"Uh, I think," the corporal stammered. "Uh, yes, sir. Yes, sir."

Our Humvee lumbered down Fallujah's main drag on two flat tires. When the smoke cleared, dozens of Iraqi men stood watching us. What were they looking at? I wanted the enemy to shoot at us again so that we could return fire. Colonel Berger wanted to fight as well. I could tell by the tone of his voice and the grimace on his hard face. We knew the enemy were looking at us. Yet all we could do was look back.

We pulled into a forward operating base in the middle of Fallujah. Baseball-size holes peppered our Humvee's armored shell up to its steel turret. Shrapnel had blasted into the undercarriage, slicing through the seat behind Colonel Berger. The gunner was lucky, and I was in a lucky seat. Dumb luck.

"Probably a one-five-five," the colonel said, referring to a 155-millimeter artillery round, the most common ammunition used to make roadside bombs in Iraq.

We reported the IED as one of a dozen significant actions—SIGACTS—that had occurred to our regiment of five thousand Marines and Iraqi Army soldiers in the past twenty-four hours. That was it. If one of us was wounded or killed, we would have been added to the logbook of SIGACTS and become a statistic, another victim of another roadside bomb.

INSIGNIFICANT AS IT was in a long, explosive war, the bomb was the beginning of my baptism by fire. It was the first time someone had tried to kill me, though I wasn't personally the target. It was my uniform and what I represented. That evening, once the shock dissipated, I experienced a rush of ecstasy. It was an extraordinary but brief sensation. Moments later, I was planning that night's operations and thinking about my Marines who were out on dangerous missions.

The IEDs were the worst part of the war. They were excruciatingly difficult to spot from a moving vehicle, and we had little control over them. They drew blood every day, and as the war progressed, the bombs became more catastrophic. Shortly after I arrived, a fellow captain was killed with three of his Marines when a massive roadside bomb with four 155-millimeter rounds exploded, swallowing his heavily armored Humvee in a roar of fire.

"So you've seen the elephant," Captain Burke remarked on the phone the following day.

Yes, I had taken a glimpse, a taste, a touch of a small part of something that was too large ever to fully embrace, let alone understand. Still, it was enough for me to think that I was ready for more if it came my way, and within days, I wanted more. I wanted to fight the insurgents who were trying to kill us. That impulse clouded the theory that I had studied. "The people are the prize," I had read and believed. Yet whom could we trust, and what if we felt no connection to these people?

My reaction surprised me. I had assumed that I would be one of the strongest advocates for a counterinsurgency approach that emphasized building the capacity of local security forces over killing bad guys and kicking down doors. In this regard, the words of one of our most celebrated Marine generals, James "Warrior Monk" Mattis, had served as a guide. The general described the velvet glove approach to counterinsurgency in memorable terms:

> Both the insurgency and the military force are competing for the same thing: the support of the people . . . We will be compassionate to all the innocent and deadly only to those who insist on violence, taking no "sides" other than to destroy the enemy. We must act as a windbreak, behind which a struggling Iraq can get its act together . . . to use the softer forms, focus on lights and water—and go in with small teams to kill the bad guys at night.*

---

* General James Mattis as quoted in Thomas Ricks, *Fiasco: The American Military Adventure in Iraq* (Penguin Press, 2006), p. 318.

"An iron fist in a velvet glove," so goes the saying attributed to Napoléon to characterize a gentle, soft demeanor layered over firm command. The velvet glove made sense when I first heard about it in a briefing at Camp Lejeune. Yet shortly after I hit the sandy soil of the lower Euphrates River Valley, my own thinking shifted. In a city where kids were lobbing grenades at us, everyone appeared to be a potential enemy. Logic could have told me that I was wrong, but my instincts were driving me. I wanted to attack the enemy, not help build the Iraqi security forces, which at the time were by American standards undermanned, poorly equipped, and unprofessional. During my initial months in country, I believed that we needed to kill the terrorists first and worry about the soft stuff later—or have someone else worry about it. What I didn't realize then was that the appropriate levels of force, as well as support, were always difficult to identify because they were based on fluid realities concealed by the fog of war.

General Mattis had called for the velvet glove at the end of 2003, before he returned to Iraq with a division of fourteen thousand Marines. By April 2004, the general had reluctantly removed his glove and swung his iron fist, launching the Battle of Fallujah, one of the largest and most destructive offensive operations since the "shock and awe" bombing of Baghdad began the war. My company had arrived in the fall of 2005. We were trying to rebuild Fallujah and prepare for the first general election under the new constitution. It was again time for the velvet glove, and our senior commanders, including Colonel Berger, were advocating for more capacity building with the Iraqi Army and police. However, the policy and direction coming down from the high command conflicted with our combat-worshipping culture, and it struck many Marines as counterintuitive because insurgent activity was on the rise.

I didn't recognize that we probably needed more boots on the ground, and there was no talk of the possibility of a surge in U.S. military forces, at least not at my level. We were Marines. For the most part, we would make do with what we had. The one critical vulnerability that everyone seemed to agree on was the unacceptable shortage of Arabic interpreters. Most Marine patrols lacked interpreter support, and this severely inhibited our ability to communicate with the population whose support we needed to win.

Because HUMINT was a strategic asset, our teams had enough

contract interpreters. However, there weren't enough of our teams to support all of the combat units. Some Marine infantry platoons went entire deployments without receiving our direct support. With such limited resources, our intelligence collection focused on targeting the enemy and gathering tactical information such as the location of IEDs. We didn't have time to report on atmospherics about local leadership and sentiment, and regardless, that reporting was of less interest to most Marines. Our instincts were to respond to violence with violence. That was how we were trained, and at the heart of it that's what we valued. Marines who had fought in the Battle of Fallujah were the envy of the Corps. Conversely, Marines attached to Iraqi Army units in military transition teams were often perceived as "bottom-feeders," the low performers or staff officers who couldn't find any other way into the fight.

This was the group mentality, and it hadn't changed much since my dad's time in Vietnam. Indeed, it was so ingrained that even the words Warrior Monk Mattis could not shift it fundamentally. The combatants, not the capacity builders, were celebrated. I was a captive to this culture. I conformed to it in ways that, in hindsight, I would find disturbing. All of my experiences in Kibera should have enabled me to break from the clutches of groupthink. When General Mattis's boss commented to the *New York Times* that "our Marines just have to be able to be aggressive and hostile one moment and the next moment be able to play soccer with the kids,"* it sounded like the perfect duty for me. Surely, I had the training and experience to handle this dichotomy. Yet in those initial months in country, I couldn't have imagined playing soccer with Iraqi kids. I was too busy scouring their waistlines for concealed weapons, their pockets for grenades.

Kibera hadn't vanished from my consciousness. It was still there. But I treated it as a separate world, and I didn't think about the inherent contradictions of waging peace while fighting war, especially in the early months. I was still processing the shock of combat and trying to make sense of an environment that often felt like a hurricane. My coping mechanism was to fire wall my life. I wasn't always effective. Events on patrol in Iraq

---

* Lieutenant General James Conway quoted in Michael Gordon, "Leathernecks Plan to Use Velvet Glove More than Iron Fist in Iraq," *New York Times*, December 12, 2003.

triggered powerful memories from Kibera. Occasionally a voice on a call to Kenya made me afraid of dying before our work there was done. However, most of the time I was in Iraq, the walls that I had erected in my mind separated the two worlds.

Kibera arrived in predictable bursts of e-mails and satellite phone calls. I usually had an hour each evening before our night assaults to write to Tracy, scribble some notes in my journal, and catch up on CFK business. This hour came at the expense of sleep, but it was an important outlet. While I often wrote to Tracy and in my journal about the war, Kibera offered an escape. It took my mind away from Iraq, and because of Salim and our team of a dozen Kenyan staff and hundreds of volunteers, the news was generally uplifting.

Shortly after my first IED attack, I received an e-mail from an editor at *Time* magazine. We had met in New York earlier that summer, and the editor had visited Salim in Kibera. He was particularly impressed by our approach to youth empowerment. "Congratulations," he wrote. *Time* magazine and the Bill and Melinda Gates Foundation had selected CFK as a "Hero of Global Health." A month later, the actress Glenn Close presented the award to my friend and colleague Kim Chapman at a black-tie gala in New York City.

"Ultimately, solutions to problems involving poverty are possible only if those affected by it drive development," Kim said in her acceptance speech on behalf of the organization.

That evening would help catapult CFK to the next level. The very thought of the recognition and the possibilities of what could come muzzled the gunfire. We were making an impact, and nothing was more rewarding than that. But, I was in Fallujah, and good news from CFK wasn't enough for me to reconsider my compartments, or my incipient bloodlust.

IT TOOK SIX weeks for me to establish a battle rhythm. My work divided broadly into four areas: leading my Marines; operating; representing our other HUMINT teams at the regiment; and developing liaison relationships with the Iraqi police, U.S. Special Forces units, FBI, and other government agencies. Not surprisingly, I enjoyed operating more than anything else. Some of my most meaningful operational work occurred at the Fallujah city council, with a motley group of recently elected officials whom we hoped would gradually take over from Colonel Berger and govern Fallujah.

The nascent Fallujah city council had many problems. One of our greatest areas of concern was trust and security. We were fairly certain most of the city council members maintained contact with insurgent groups. It would be difficult for them to stay alive if they didn't. Some of the members were heavily connected, while other members, whom we may have been able to trust to greater degrees, faced serious threats from the most extreme factions of the insurgency, such as Al Qaeda in Iraq. My task was a classic counterintelligence mission to identify the members of the council who were connected to the most extreme terrorist groups. One of the members who concerned me most was the chairman, Sheikh Kamal Shakir al-Nazal.

For weeks I watched Sheikh Kamal. I studied his mannerisms from a hidden room overlooking the meeting place of the city council, a dilapidated theater in one of Saddam Hussein's former youth centers. Sheikh Kamal's gray robe draped regally over his body and hung from his arms, winglike, as he made sweeping gestures to convey grief, frustration, and authority. He was a good actor. It was difficult to discern his true passions from deception, and he seemed to relish the moments when the spotlight turned his way. He was a strong man, too, physically large, with heavy hands and a sculpted salt-and-pepper beard. A white kaffiyeh headwrap added a couple of inches to his stature. Colonel Berger, conversely, had a medium build, a shaved head, and a tough, blunt face. When they spoke with one another, the sheikh often held his hands together as a sign of respect.

"He's a scumbag," Colonel Berger's staff intelligence officer, Major J.G. from New Jersey, characterized Sheikh Kamal with his trademark cynicism. "But he's our scumbag."

The lone U.S. State Department representative in Fallujah, Kael Weston, thought differently. Kael, who dropped out of a doctoral program at the London School of Economics to make his way to the front lines, had lived in a forward operating base in downtown Fallujah for more than eighteen months, longer than any other American. A skilled diplomat with a boyish face and a prep-school look that belied his courage and experience, Kael helped set up and convene the locally appointed city council.

"He's a brave man," Kael said of Sheikh Kamal. "Few men were willing to step up and take the job. He's not perfect. No one is, but we need to protect him. He's got one of the most dangerous jobs in Fallujah."

The chairman of the Fallujah city council, Sheikh Kamal had a long title with little power. We controlled Fallujah with an iron fist, though we were beginning to gradually transition authority to the local government. This transition required trust, time, and security. Yet as I had seen in the Horn of Africa, Marine commanders rotated every six to twelve months and often had contrasting styles of communicating with locals. Kael's interactions were unique for their length and character. He cared deeply about Iraqi well-being, and he frequently expressed his compassion and concern. As for our military, some officers thought Kael was naive. I disagreed. It was impossible to live in downtown Fallujah for any extended time and be naive, and without Kael, it seemed unlikely that Sheikh Kamal and other Sunni leaders would have risked their lives by holding public office.

Rumor had it that Kael was considered a rogue political officer in the State Department, where few volunteered repeatedly for such hardship posts. Regardless of how he was viewed by others, there was a severe shortage of foreign service officers near the battlefield, and that was more than unfortunate. It was tragic. Kael Weston was exactly the type of foreign service officer we needed on the front lines. The military filled the nation-building vacuum because we had the economic resources and a can-do attitude. However, we weren't very good at it. My big takeaway from the Horn of Africa was that absent a tectonic shift in our force structure and culture, we would never do nation building well.

The business of rebuilding governments needed to be led by a different part of American foreign policy, not the Department of Defense. Every time Marines spoke at the Fallujah city council, our weapons and uniforms signaled to Iraqis that we were an occupation force, not a transitional one. Nation building had more to do with Carolina for Kibera than the U.S. Marine Corps. We needed the Kael Westons and the Colonel Bergers, but apart from Fallujah, we typically had only an armed, uniformed presence.

The winter of 2005–6 was a turbulent time in Al Anbar Province. Staff officers at the regiment measured and monitored activity in comparison to what we called a baseline level of violence. Activity held steady to the regiment's baseline throughout my deployment at about five to ten SIGACTS per day. Most of the SIGACTS were IED explosions and skirmishes with small arms. We averaged a few casualties each day, and a couple of Marine and Iraqi soldiers killed in action every week.

It was a slow bleed, for the most part. Too often, however, our forces confronted catastrophic IEDs or well-coordinated enemy attacks against our forward operating bases. At these unpredictable moments the levels of violence spiked from the baseline like an electrocardiogram, and because of the injuries more blood was often needed at medical.

December 1 was one of those days. I was in my office swigging coffee and preparing for a sensitive operation with Kael at the next city council meeting when an e-mail marked urgent popped into my in-box. The silent alert called for all hands with type A blood. I wouldn't have seen it in time if the corporal from the intelligence shop had not sounded off: "A POS AND NEG NEEDED AT MEDICAL!"

It was the first time I was in the office for a type A blood call. I darted out the door and ran a quarter mile to the clinic, a unit once called the Cheaters of Death.

A high-back Humvee used to transport troops was errantly parked near the entrance of the clinic, its cargo splattered with blood, sand, and shards of camouflage. In the open hangar a dozen Marines of various ranks and duties sat silently hunchbacked on cots with thin red tubes running from their arms.

A corpsman swabbed my arm and prepared his needle. "What happened?" I asked in a hushed tone.

"Mass casualty. More than a dozen Marines wounded. Many KIA."

The needle went in and my blood flowed out. We all wanted to do more, but we could at least do something. A private who looked sixteen sat next to me softly weeping. He was in the formation with more than fifty other Marines when four bombs hidden beneath the earth erupted.

My blood filled two bags. I began to feel light-headed midway into the second bag when a sudden fear overwhelmed me. It was an amplified version of the anxiety I carried when my small team of a sergeant, a gunnery sergeant, and a linguist were out on reconnaissance missions: *Did something happen to them?*

My gunnery sergeant had a lot of experience and a healthy paranoia. He had fought through the Battle of Fallujah and hunted Al Qaeda with Delta Force. Yet sometimes training and experience didn't matter. Something had happened to them. I was sure of it.

A stretcher passed with a badly wounded Marine. A crimson circle stained the white sheets near his torso. One of his arms dangled over the steel railing. It was heavily tattooed, like my sergeant's arm. *Was it my sergeant?*

The needle ripped from my arm and blood squirted across the floor as I stood and took off toward the stretcher. A corpsman caught me, sliding his body between me and the wounded Marine. He placed his hand up in front of my chest. "Sir?"

"Who's that?" I pointed to the stretcher. "What unit is this?"

"Two-seven," he said, referring to the infantry battalion. I knew that my Marines were with Recon. It couldn't be my sergeant. "Sir, you need to sit down."

I returned to the bloody cot. Soon another corpsman came and told me to leave. They had enough type A for the day.

THE SENSITIVE OPERATION that I was planning with Kael involved Sheikh Kamal, the chairman of the city council. After more than six months of their working closely together, the sheikh had approached Kael and offered to provide intelligence about an important security matter. We planned a meeting for me to debrief him after the next city council gathering. For the sheikh's safety, the meeting would have to be quick and discreet.

The following city council meeting dragged on for two hours. It was another mind-numbing affair. The same issues came up each week: detainees, raids, checkpoints, identification cards, curfews, weapons permits, infrastructure repair, and war reparations. An action-oriented commander with little patience for painstaking political negotiation, Colonel Berger rarely spoke during the meetings. When a question was directed his way, the colonel stood from his chair in the front row and answered directly. If he could do something, he said it. Much of the time, however, he couldn't agree to the demands for security reasons.

I watched as a few journalists from international newspapers took notes. It was rare to have Western reporters attend Fallujah city council meetings. We were curious to see how Sheikh Kamal would behave in their presence. We had warned him ahead of time to be careful with his remarks.

"*La, la, la!*" (No, no, no!) The sheikh slapped the table with his palm and leaped into a dramatic performance that was recorded verbatim by one of our few Marine officers who spoke Iraqi-dialect Arabic fluently:

> In the name of God the most compassionate and merciful, . . . I have been the chairman for six months now, and I feel that I have accomplished nothing. I've done nothing for the city. I feel I have absolutely no real power. I am in deep despair with regard to my duties. We've been complaining about a checkpoint for three months and nothing has been done. We've complained about raids on government institutions, and just yesterday the real estate office was raided. We've talked endlessly about stopping the detention of innocent people. The city council building itself has been attacked more than once. Our clerics have been attacked and ultimately our Mufti Sheikh Hamza was assassinated. We've submitted requests to arm the city council and the imams [religious leaders], and each week this goes back and forth with no results. The fact is, I have submitted my resignation on more than one occasion, but the council members continue to tell me to remain in place. Up to now, my credibility is zero . . . Then, the [local Fallujah] newspaper said I was meeting secretly with the Marines. They insinuate that I'm in league with the Marines, but I'm in such a state that Colonel Berger could very well be ready to arrest me! . . . I have no communication with the resistance [the insurgency]. However, if you press me to answer, I would say, if I were in the resistance, I would be proud to say that I was in it.

After the meeting, councilors began chatting with one another and some of the American military officers, as was custom. With a stern face and angry eyes, Colonel Berger walked out of the room with Major J.G. before an Iraqi could engage him in conversation. The colonel was fed up with Sheikh Kamal. Although it wasn't uncommon for members of the city council to praise the resistance while speaking to Iraqi audiences, this was the first time Sheikh Kamal had made such comments in the presence of foreign press.

Kael made a subtle gesture to the sheikh. I moved through a concealed passage and met them in a locker room that we had converted into an office. Kael excused himself and said he'd be back in ten minutes.

"We've never met. I'm a security officer. What you tell me will be strictly confidential."

Sheikh Kamal looked at my interpreter, who went by the nickname Mike.

"He's American," I said, maintaining my eye contact with the sheikh.

"Not Shiite?" Sheikh Kamal believed that all Shiites harbored loyalties to Iran.

"That's right."

A tall Moroccan American with a great sense of humor, Mike had come to Iraq as a contract interpreter in search of adventure and a larger paycheck. He didn't know until he signed up that our contract interpreters suffered higher casualty rates than most American combat units. We were fortunate to have him. Mike was one of only a few HUMINT interpreters who never complained about being tapped for dangerous missions, and he was an excellent interpreter who had quickly learned the local dialect.

"Not Iraqi?" Kamal asked.

"Correct."

"But he speaks well."

We were losing precious time. "So what is it you've come to share with me today?"

Sheikh Kamal began describing the location of a terrorist safe house less than a half mile from where we sat. He spoke like many Iraqis, circling around the subject with hyperbole and repetition. We didn't have time.

"I'm sorry to interrupt you, Sheikh, but who are these terrorists?"

"They're assassins."

"Assassins?"

"Yes. They are the ones who killed Sheikh Hamza. They'll be there tonight. After that I don't know."

Sheikh Hamza Abbas al-Issawi had been the grand mufti of Fallujah, the most senior religious leader in the city. A few months earlier Kael had encouraged Sheikh Hamza to publicly declare his support for the local Iraqi government because Fallujans had boycotted previous elections. Sheikh Hamza had vacillated until days before the October Iraqi constitutional referendum, when he had made a brave public stand by calling on Fallujans to vote, and "Fallujah's sons" to join the police. It was a consequential moment. Police registration had increased immediately, and the referendum had occurred peacefully, with a remarkably high level of voter participation. Two weeks after the referendum, however, assassins gunned down the grand mufti as he walked to his mosque for morning prayers. His assassination conformed to the modus operandi of Al Qaeda in Iraq and its leader, Abu Musab al-Zarqawi, second only to Osama bin Laden on America's most wanted list. Zarqawi had made the City of Mosques his headquarters until the Battle of Fallujah, when he dressed as a woman and fled in advance of our assault.

Sheikh Kamal believed he was Zarqawi's next target. He claimed his source was reliable and had direct access to the information. "Zarqawi is after me. You understand, Captain? He wants me dead."

I understood, and it was believable. Kael opened the door. I had three minutes left. We needed a target description. Among other things, the sheikh noted that one of the terrorists wore a black watch with Roman numerals and a red dot at twelve o'clock. It was a useful clue. Most Iraqi men preferred silver and gold knockoff Rolex watches.

Kael stepped in. "We really need to go now."

The sheikh and I shook hands. He had a surprisingly light grip and soft skin.

"*Shukran*, Sheikh." I thanked him.

Sheikh Kamal looked me in the eye, and for a moment I sensed the depth of his fears. He had the look of a condemned man, a man out of options.

"KAMAL, THAT SON of a bitch." Colonel Berger stood in his wood-paneled office and spit tobacco into a plastic soda bottle. The office had once been the headquarters of an Iraqi general in command of Iranian dissidents.

"I don't believe him," Major J.G. said after I briefed them on my meeting with Sheikh Kamal.

"What do you think, Captain?" the colonel asked.

I was an attachment to the regiment. Although I didn't report to Major J.G., I was there to support him and the colonel. It was important that I didn't lose their trust, especially in moments when we disagreed professionally.

"I think Kamal believes the information he's telling us is true," I said, "and the threat's credible. AMZ [Abu Musab al-Zarqawi] is after these guys. Kamal knows it. He's scared."

"Good," Major J.G. quipped.

"All right," Colonel Berger concluded. "Captain, you're on the raid. Two-six will hit the target tonight."

I walked out of the colonel's office and prepared my gear: night-vision goggles, red-lens flashlight, notebook, street map, flex-cuffs, and rifle. I spent more than half of my time in Iraq in the safety of large U.S. bases. Having few opportunities to accompany raids, I was eager for the action. There was nothing like the thrill of producing intelligence that drove operations, and I sensed Sheikh Kamal's information was the best chance we had come across to capture the assassins of Fallujah's grand mufti. If we succeeded, it would be a blow to Al Qaeda in Iraq.

Something else made me hunger for the evening's assault. Winston Churchill once said that nothing is more exhilarating than being shot at without result. That was true for me the first time, after that roadside bomb in Colonel Berger's Humvee, and the handful of other times that I had been in IED attacks or shot at. The high was always there, and the frustration, too. Yet while the highs were disconnected bursts of adrenaline, the frustration mounted. It grew both gradually and rapidly depending on forces that often felt out of our control.

The problem, I believed, was that I never shot back. The raid that evening might give me an opportunity to confront the enemy head-on. This impulse to do damage was about retribution as well as courage. It was primal. Yet, it was more than that. The dark element was a curiosity with and attraction to violence. Shooting back and killing were other parts of the elephant, that giant that was too large to ever experience in totality. The elephant was war.

Our actions brought us closer to the very forces of evil and their illusions that we battled. When does violence become evil? When do we cross that line? Is there a line? I didn't know, and at the time I wasn't thinking about the answers. I was too busy with the maelstrom of combat leadership. Soon enough, however, I would be forced to confront these questions.

THAT EVENING MY favorite interpreter, Mike, was preparing for a five-day reconnaissance mission with my team. So I met another interpreter, a Shiite Iraqi American, at the forward operating base next to the youth center.

"Sounds like a hard target," the lieutenant whose platoon was tasked to conduct the raid reacted after I briefed him on the intel. A *hard target* meant a higher probability that we would face resistance. Although there might be a family in the house, we couldn't take any chances. If the assassins were there, we had to be ready for a fight.

We rolled out at midnight in Humvees. The city was still. It was well past curfew. Earlier that evening an F-18 fighter pilot flew over Fallujah and illuminated the target house with an infrared marker. The building glowed like football stadium lights through our night-vision goggles. We stopped in the middle of an empty street, dismounted, and surrounded the house. Each Marine wore more than thirty pounds of inch-thick armor, a helmet, ballistic glasses, fire-retardant gloves, a radio headset, and drop pouches and pockets stuffed with ammunition and grenades. We looked like robots.

I positioned myself at the gate behind the stack, a squad of Marines poised to raid the target. "Good to go, Talisman?" the lieutenant asked over his headset, using my call sign.

Something wasn't right. The gate didn't match Sheikh Kamal's description. The pilot had painted the wrong house. I walked up to the adjacent flat with the right gate. The platoon shifted.

"Now, Talisman?"

"Yes."

A Marine with a battering ram smashed the steel gate open, shattering the night's silence. Two Marines lobbed blank grenades called flash bangs. Explosion. The stack stormed the house, rifles raised, shouting as they cleared the rooms in search of the enemy.

"CLEAR."

"WOMAN, FOUR CHILDREN."

"BEDROOM CLEAR."

"TWO MAMS (military-age males)."

"ON THE GROUND. GET ON THE GROUND. I SAID GET ON THE FUCKING GROUND."

"CLEAR."

"CLEAR."

"ALL CLEAR."

My interpreter and I walked in.

Four children sat next to an older woman on the floor of a living room.

They stared at us with wide, terrified eyes. The oldest child appeared to be a teenage boy, perhaps fifteen years old.

"Sorry for the interruption," I said to the woman, oddly, as if I simply needed to ask her for the time. She looked at me with a blank face. Perhaps she had been through a raid before. Raids like ours occurred throughout Fallujah nearly every night.

"Where do you want them, sir?" a Marine asked, holding a blind-folded man with hands bound behind his back.

"Outside. Keep them blindfolded, separated, and guarded."

As he walked by, I spotted a black watch.

"Hold on, Marine." I inspected its face. Red dot at twelve o'clock. Adrenaline surged through my body. *Got him.*

I made a hasty decision to speak with the teenager hoping that he would provide me with information that I could use against the man with the black watch. Muscular and clean-cut, the boy was shaking as he followed me to an empty room. His T-shirt had a Manchester United logo on it. I removed my helmet and glasses and placed my hand on his shoulder. "It's okay. I'm not going to hurt you. I just need to ask you some questions. You like Man-U?"

"*Naam,*" he responded, relaxing as I made a comment about soccer and asked him some simple questions about his identity. The woman in the other room was his mother. His father had died before the Battle of Fallujah, when Zarqawi controlled the city.

"I'm sorry to hear that," I responded, wondering if his father had fought against us. "Who are the two men?"

The boy hesitated.

"What are their names?"

"Please," he sighed.

"We can leave once you tell me. But I can't leave until then. You can do it."

For twenty minutes I repeated myself, consoling the boy and asking him for the names of the two men. I didn't know whether he would co-operate, and I worried about how much time I was spending with him.

He looked at me with empty eyes until I touched his elbow and asked, "They're in the resistance, aren't they?"

He sighed. "*Naam.*"

"Good. You're doing the right thing. Now what are their names?"

He revealed their full names and *kunyas*, their Arabic noms de guerre. The man with the black watch was the boy's uncle. He showed up unannounced every other month and spent a few nights at the boy's mother's home. Allegedly the uncle boasted about fighting Americans but never spoke specifically about his missions. I couldn't tell how much information the boy was concealing from me, though he appeared to be candid and the circumstances of our conversation made me believe the information that he chose to reveal was probably reliable.

"Do you know who Sheikh Hamza was?"

"Mufti?"

"Yes."

The boy nodded.

"Your uncle was involved with his death."

"No, I don't think that's possible." He looked confused.

There was commotion outside our room. A Marine opened the door. "Sir, we discovered a cache."

I turned to the boy. "Where are the weapons?"

"In the shed."

"You knew about them but you didn't tell me."

"I didn't think about it. They bring weapons with them when they show up."

"What kind?"

"I don't know. Rifles, grenade throwers."

"I'm going to go look. But before I do, is there anything else I should know?"

He looked me in the eyes. "Please, take me to the U.S."

The boy's response stunned me. I placed my hand back on his shoulder. I wanted to encourage him but not lead him on. I couldn't imagine what it would be like to be in his position.

"I can't do that. I don't have that power. But I hope one day I'll see you in the U.S. Just don't join the insurgency. That's a dead end."

"Okay." The boy dropped his head.

A Marine led me to the small shed where we discovered a rocket-propelled grenade and two AK-47 rifles buried under a pile of rubble. Although Fallujah was rife with illegal weapons, it was an important discovery, because without it we had no grounds to detain the two targets for more than twenty-four hours of questioning.

We brought the men back to our forward operating base at the youth center. I began my interrogation at 0300 hours in an empty shipping container. A Marine guard stood behind the man with the black watch, who sat on a box in front of me. He was a short, paunchy man in his late twenties with ruddy cheeks and heavy dandruff.

I began with the "we know all" interrogation approach, suggesting it was futile for him to resist because we had so much information. We knew he was from Baghdad and traveled frequently to Fallujah. We knew he was in the insurgency. We knew his name and many other things.

The man didn't respond. A faint smirk spread across his face as he sat staring at the floor.

"Why are you in Fallujah?"

He claimed that he had come to sell dates.

"Where?"

"In the market."

"What's your relationship to the woman in the house?"

"A friend."

"What's her name?"

He shrugged and muttered a name.

"What's her full name?"

"I don't know." Smirk.

Around and around we went for hours. I moved through different interrogation approaches. The man replied with smirks and shrugs, nothing else.

"So tell me, then, about November twenty-ninth." I was getting angry.

He didn't reply.

"November twenty-ninth. What were you doing in Fallujah on November twenty-ninth?"

"I don't know."

"But you know you were in Fallujah then."

"No." Smirk, shrug.

"Sheikh Hamza. That was the day you killed him."

"No."

I launched into the "fear up" interrogation approach, shouting at him and pointing my finger in his face. "YOU KILLED HIM!"

"No, you did."

"WHAT? YOU'RE KILLING YOUR OWN PEOPLE. WHO SET YOU UP TO THIS?"

"I did nothing."

"YOU WERE SET UP. WHO SET YOU UP?"

"NO!" He shook his head like a boy in a temper tantrum.

"You're going to prison."

Smirk, shrug.

"Other prisoners will know you killed the grand mufti."

"No."

There was nowhere else to go, and I was wearing myself out and losing my cool. I wanted to wipe that smirk off his face with the butt of my rifle. But I subdued the impulse. That wasn't how we interrogated detainees. We had to hold ourselves to higher standards, and that was so much easier to say back in the United States than it was to believe at 0600 hours in a shipping container in Fallujah eyeball to eyeball with a man who I was convinced would kill me if he had the chance. Yet it was the only way. It was the only way for the practical reason that there was no evidence that coercive interrogations provided more reliable information. And it was the only way for the just and more important reason that morality exists on a slippery slope and we as individuals, and as a nation, are nothing without our principles.

I loathed the feeling of impotence. I had given that three-hour interrogation everything I had, and I suspected that subsequent interrogators, all of whom were overworked, would have a low probability of getting anything valuable out of him. He clearly had resistance training. We knew from our raids of terrorist safe houses that many insurgents had heard about our unclassified military intelligence manuals, including the book that detailed all of our interrogation approaches, from "we know all" to "fear-up." According to our regulations, we would have two weeks at Camp Fallujah to interrogate the man and his friend before deciding whether or not to send them to Abu Ghraib. If our two weeks at Camp Fallujah revealed no additional information, it was highly unlikely that the men would be in custody for more than three months. Our prisons in Iraq were overloaded with more than fifteen thousand detainees, and illegal small-arms possessions were among the weakest of offenses. It was possible, and perhaps probable, that we had caught the assassins of Fallujah's grand mufti only to turn them back to the streets in less than three months. Then they would be armed with more information about our capabilities and probably all the more eager to kill us and the brave Iraqis like Sheikh Kamal who were stepping up to repair their broken nation.

The raid that night was a turning point for me. It was near the midway mark in my six-month deployment. As frustrated as I was with my failed interrogation and the fact that the man might be back on the streets in a short time, it was the teenager in the house who made me question my fundamental assumptions about our war effort. He was one of the first boys I spoke with in Iraq, and he reminded me of Kash. The boy was muscular and stood out among other Iraqi teenagers. He had poise that was similar to Kash, and he wanted me to take him to the United States. We had stormed his home, shouted at his mother, threw him to the floor, and detained his uncle. And yet, the boy was still enamored by the idea of America. For all our flaws, we were still envied by much of the world for our resources, our power, and maybe even some of our values.

Why weren't we capitalizing on such goodwill? The boy's perspective baffled me. If I were he and a foreign force had invaded my home, I cannot imagine feeling anything but hatred, a hate so deep that it could lead me to a cause I didn't understand or believe in simply to fight, to lash out, and to restore my honor. Maybe that boy was somehow above such base reactions. Others were not, and the more doors we kicked down, the more ill will we engendered.

There was no clear solution now that we were there. Of course we had to go after terrorists such as Zarqawi. However, those extreme factions were a small part of a much larger, highly fragmented insurgency that we didn't understand. Nearly all elements of that larger insurgency drew strength from our presence. Were our actions persecuting a small group of extremists helping to spawn the next generation of jihadists? Even if we could restore order with a velvet glove and a thousand Kael Westons, was it sustainable? Was it worth the price?

CHAPTER NINETEEN

Eleven Years Old and His Life Is Already Behind Him

Fallujah, Iraq

WINTER 2006

A SOURCE MEETING AT A BLOWN-UP WAREHOUSE in downtown Fallujah consumed the morning. The knots between my neck and shoulders expanded with relief as I removed my body armor back at base. Sweat had soaked so thoroughly through my fatigues that their thick cotton clung to my skin like spandex. I could tell from the carrot color of my urine that I was dehydrated again, though I needed coffee more than water. Earlier that morning my subteam departed on a seven-day mission, and I had stayed up all night to see them off. The hours before my Marines left on dangerous missions always made me the most anxious.

The mug with our team's call sign, Talisman, and an imprint of silver captain's bars sat next to the coffeepot. The day-old, lukewarm coffee poured like syrup and tasted like dirt. I took a gulp and sat down in front of my two laptops, one for classified communication, and the other. I wasn't looking forward to the eight hours of report writing, e-mails, and phone calls ahead.

One of fifty new e-mails was marked urgent. It read that an Iraqi woman was in critical condition at the medical clinic. The woman had been shot during a night raid, and she was requesting to speak with someone about a security issue. As they often did, my plans changed abruptly. More than half of my time in Iraq was spent reacting to unforeseen events.

Both my interpreters were out with my subteam, so I asked the lieutenant in charge of the document-exploitation unit for support. The lieutenant and I maintained a good rapport, in part because I never pulled rank on him. He told me that he would give me his best interpreter and returned minutes later with a white-haired Iraqi man wearing gold-framed glasses. The interpreter, Dr. B., was a medical doctor and American citizen of Iraqi descent. As a twenty-seven-year-old, it felt strange to be temporarily in charge of a gray-haired medical doctor with more knowledge of Iraq than I would absorb in a lifetime. As we walked to the clinic, Dr. B. told me that although it was difficult for him to leave his family and medical practice in the United States, he felt that he didn't have a choice. "It is my duty to be here."

The clinic smelled of disinfectant. I passed a Marine missing one leg. A corpsman escorted us to the woman's room.

She had sunken cheeks and dark, brown eyes. The gaping hole in her back, we were told, was from one of our M16 rounds. Enemy AK-47 fire at such close range would have left a larger exit wound. Bile lined the bucket at the edge of her bed. I could smell it.

I looked at Dr. B.

"Not good," he said.

"My name is Captain Rye and this is Doctor B. He's an Iraqi American and a medical doctor."

The woman gave a slow, slight nod as Dr. B. translated my introduction.

"You're a doctor?" she asked.

"*Naam*."

"Oh, that is a good thing," she said. Tabitha had once used that line. My memory returned to Tabitha and her strong brown eyes. According to the card above her stretcher, the woman was thirty-eight years old, the same age Tabitha had been when she passed away. Sweat lined her forehead. It appeared to cause her pain to speak.

"*Mama*, you do not need to speak to us. It's better that you just relax and recover."

"Mama?" Dr. B. raised his eyebrows.

"No, sorry, don't translate that."

Dr. B. touched the woman's hand and encouraged her not to speak.

"No," she replied. "I called you because there's something I must say. I must say it now." I was taken aback by how forward she was. Iraqi women rarely approached us with information.

The woman looked at Dr. B. and spoke rapidly for two minutes before the doctor calmly raised his hand and turned to me. "She's smart, but she's not an educated woman, the wife of a farmer I suspect. She began by telling me that times were better under Saddam, people were safer, which makes sense of course because she's from a Sunni town." Dr. B. was Kurdish by ethnicity. "She said she doesn't like us, the Americans, but that the terrorists are worse. She wants to tell us what happened so we can leave her country."

"Please, tell us what happened," I said.

"The terrorists, they come to our homes and threaten our families. They took a knife to my son's throat and told me they'd kill him. He's only seven. He doesn't understand. These are evil people." The woman looked at Dr. B.

"I'm sorry to hear this. When? When did they come?"

"Four weeks ago. I've been feeding them for four weeks until you came."

"What were they doing in your town?"

"I don't know. They wore their black masks and didn't speak around me. But they made lots of demands. They did terrible things." She looked to the floor.

"Such as?"

Her eyes conveyed immeasurable pain. She didn't respond.

"Did you hear any of their names?"

"They were all *kunyas*: Abu Abdul, Abu Bakr, Abu Ahmed."

"Iraqi?" Contrary to press reporting at the time, the majority of terrorists were Iraqi.

"I think, yes."

"Did they have a name for their group?"

"I don't know."

"What happened during the attack?"

"You came. It was fast and very late. You came from the sky."

"Helicopters?"

"What?"

"She doesn't know what helicopters are," Dr. B. clarified.

I would've known about a Marine helicopter raid. The raid must have been conducted by one of our most elite units, the Joint Special Operations Command.

"We appreciate this information. It's helpful. Is there something else you want to tell us?"

The woman looked at Dr. B. I couldn't shake the image of Tabitha in my mind. She had the same proud countenance, the defiance, the grace. She reached for the doctor's hand. He leaned forward, and she whispered a piece of information that would launch an onslaught of raids that night.

I asked follow-up questions. When I was done, I wanted to give her something in return. "Can we do something for your son?" I asked. On Tabitha's deathbed, I had promised to find the means to send her children to school. *Maybe I could do something similar for this woman?*

She locked her eyes onto mine and whispered something.

The doctor hesitated.

"What did she say?"

"She said, 'Stay away from my son.'"

IN HIS MANUSCRIPT my father encapsulated his time in Vietnam with a single sentence: "Uncertainty abounded." I can think of no better two-word summary for Iraq. Uncertainty defined our experience. At times it felt as if it were the only constant, the only thing that we could, paradoxically, be sure of. Most of our encounters were fraught with unknowns. They were like the raid in Fallujah with the man with the black watch and the irritating smirk. We didn't receive any additional information of value from him. Eventually, he was sent to Abu Ghraib, where we lost track of him because our prisons were too overwhelmed to function adequately. We didn't discover who killed the grand mufti of Fallujah, either. We probably never will.

The Iraqi woman survived and was escorted back to her village by an Iraqi Army convoy. Her last words to me shocked me not simply because I had wanted to help her son, but because of their candor. I wasn't used to such truth in my interactions with Iraqis. I didn't fault them for what I viewed as a culture of deception that had come to define a central part of their existence. After all, deception was a survival mechanism from decades of oppression under a vengeful, paranoid dictator. Nevertheless, it forced me to filter everything I heard from our Iraqi sources through a lens of probability. The security information that the woman provided to us about the terrorists in her village was probably true. Her hospital room was an isolated place where no other Iraqis could have heard what she said. My interpreter, Dr. B., was an American without local ties, and the woman claimed to have been tormented by the enemy. She wanted revenge, which was among the strongest of all motivations that led Iraqis to cooperate with us. Yet, there was still some doubt. There would always be doubt. Her description of the enemy was vague, and we had to be cautious of personal vendettas and local feuds with complicated histories. The only thing that I was sure of was the truth of her last line: "Stay away from my son." I knew it from her eyes.

All of the great military theorists wrote about uncertainty, from Sun Tzu to Clausewitz with his famous phrase, the "fog of war." When I read these classic texts in college and at basic training, I had thought I understood them. But I had no real awareness until I was in Iraq. Our job in military intelligence was to cut through the fog so that our combat forces could take the fight to the enemy. In absolute terms, ours was an impossible task because we would never see clearly through the haze.

My "come-to-Jesus moment," as my gunnery sergeant called it, was more of a process. Real awareness didn't arrive until sometime in the second half of my deployment. I figured out then that there was no way I could lead my teams effectively, support my command, and operate while also digesting all of the HUMINT reporting and analysis that our regiment produced on any given day. I began stepping back from the daily barrage of raw intelligence reporting and took deep dives into a few threads of information that had the potential to address larger security questions. Each thread involved at least one prominent target and a convergence of reporting that we could analyze, corroborate, and use to build operations.

My new focus on depth over breadth in Iraq resembled the CFK approach to leadership development. Roughly half of Kibera's population was under the age of fifteen. The size and scope of our youth engagement programs through sports, health care, girls' empowerment, and waste management was significant. It involved an active membership of almost twenty-five hundred young men and women. From those twenty-five hundred young people, we spent most of our time and effort developing the top one hundred leaders. These were young people who volunteered constantly with the organization and proved themselves to be among the best and the brightest in Kibera. As Salim often said, we could do only so much with our scarce resources. It made sense to focus on the young people who could make the greatest positive impact in Kibera, and beyond.

So it was that during my final three months in Iraq I invested heavily in a half dozen of the most promising intelligence threads. To the best of my knowledge, the majority of these threads amounted to nothing. A couple of them, however, traced to larger tapestries that with time and work revealed new secrets of strategic importance. I focused most of my energy on the demise of Sheikh Kamal, the charismatic head of the Fallujah city council. His fall led to my most profound revelations.

THE CHIEF OF Fallujah's police, Brigadier General Salah Al Ani, met us at the entrance to the youth center with his swagger stick and dark blue flak jacket. A former Iraqi Special Forces officer who had participated in the initial deep reconnaissance of Kuwait in 1990, General Salah appeared ready for a military mission, not another Fallujah city council meeting.

"*Salaam alaikum*, Colonel Berger." General Salah saluted.

"General." Colonel Berger nodded.

"I have good and bad news. Kamal is dead. The good news is we have caught the assassins. They're with our intelligence now."

"Captain." The colonel turned to me.

"Roger, sir. I'm on it."

My interpreter Mike and I walked fifty yards to the police station, a dismal two-story concrete stack surrounded by puddles of stagnant green sewage. I had been in the building many times to meet with the head of a small Iraqi intelligence cell, a captain with a decade of experience as a spymaster in the Mukhabarat, Saddam's principal intelligence agency. The U.S. military had declared 2006 the "Year of the Iraqi Police." Although my relationship fell under the umbrella of capacity building, it was more confrontational than cooperative. I assumed my counterpart viewed me as an amateur. Just like Kenyans, Iraqis expected deference to age and experience. The Iraqi captain was old enough to be my father.

"Captain Rye, so good to see you," the captain greeted me, with his phony smile. He was slender and cleancut. He wore a black mustache and had a long pinkie fingernail. His brown patent leather shoes were immaculate and shiny despite the filth surrounding us. A lightbulb dangled from the ceiling of his windowless office in the bowels of the police station. The compact space was barren, furnished with only a wooden desk and a small black-and-white television tuned to a channel playing high-pitched Arabic music. One of his deputies sat on the sofa in civilian clothes fingering prayer beads and watching me.

"*Salaam alaikum*, Captain." I placed my hand over my heart. "May we have a word together?"

"*Wa 'alaikum as-salaam.*"

"Alone, please."

The captain nodded at his deputy, who stood and walked out, closing the steel door behind him with a clank. "My office is your office." The captain smiled.

"You've been busy this morning, Captain. How are you doing?"

"*Naam.* Busy, very busy. No time for kebabs." He chuckled. Fallujah was famous for its giant grilled meat kebabs "as big as a child's arm." I frequently opened my source meetings with a proclamation of love for the city's signature dish.

"Are you interrogating them?"

"Not yet."

"Where are they?"

"They're here."

"In this building?"

"*Naam.*"

The captain didn't offer information. I asked for it. Although I never caught him in a lie, our interactions were filled with illusion. He was a professional case officer. He backstopped well.

"May I see them?" It wasn't a question. We controlled the city.

"*Naam.*"

The captain took me to the adjacent room. A rat scampered across the floor as we opened another steel door, flooding the dank room with sunlight. It was an old, abandoned bathroom with filthy white tiles and the stench of excrement.

There was a whimper. The captain pointed to a stained mattress propped against the corner of the room. He walked up and shifted the mattress flat to one side of the wall, like he was opening the side door of a Dodge Caravan. In the corner a small person knelt, hands bound behind his back, blindfolded and sniveling.

"Stand up," the captain ordered.

It wasn't a man. It was a boy, a kid with a face full of acne, a mound of black, lice-infested hair, and an oversized T-shirt. He looked no older than thirteen and reeked of stale sweat.

"This is one of the assassins?" I was too surprised to conceal my disbelief.

"*Naam.*"

"How old?"

"Fifteen."

"And the other?"

"*Naam.*"

"Is he here?"

"*Naam.*" The captain glanced to a mattress in another corner of the room. Behind that mattress an even smaller boy crouched above a puddle of urine with a large wet spot at the crotch of his jogging pants. The captain placed one hand under the boy's armpit and lifted him like a sack. The boy was so short that the top of his head hardly reached my chest.

"How old?"

"Eleven years."

"No. Really?" The rubber band in my chest was about to snap. I lost my breath. *Could boys be assassins?*

"*Naam.*"

The boy overheard our conversation but remained expressionless. I told the captain to move him to another part of the room away from the urine. I could tell from the captain's face that he hated when I told him what to do. He moved the boy and escorted us out of the room.

The captain led us to the getaway car in a parking lot for confiscated and blown-apart vehicles. I assumed the car would be something small and ordinary, perhaps an Opel, one of those box-shaped four-door imports from Germany that were ubiquitous in Iraq. Instead, the captain pointed at a slick, black 700 series BMW.

Mike and I had worked together closely enough in tough situations that we could read each other's reactions instantly. We didn't believe the captain. We doubted the kids had killed Sheikh Kamal, and we didn't know what to think of the BMW.

"How'd they do it?" I asked.

"Drive-by. Shot out of the window."

"Where's the weapon?"

"In my office," the captain replied. I knew the game, but it still frustrated me that I had to ask.

Mike noted the Baghdad license plate number on the BMW and we returned to the captain's office, where I inspected the AK-47 and wrote down its serial number. On my request, the captain brought the eleven-year-old boy to his office and left us alone. Mike removed the boy's blindfold. He squinted as his eyes adjusted to the harsh light of the bare bulb dangling from the ceiling. I would've begun with condolences and comforting words were it not for the boy's calm, self-assured look. *Maybe he did kill Sheikh Kamal?*

"What's your name?" Mike translated to Arabic.

The boy's body language conveyed a defiance that was completely out of place for his small body.

"Do you know why you're here?"

"No." The boy looked at Mike.

"Please, look at me. Is the older boy your brother?"

"No."

"Who is he?"

He didn't respond.

"Who is he?"

"A friend."

"What were you doing in the BMW?"

"Nothing." He answered in a flat tone, neither belligerent nor convincing.

"So you were in the BMW but doing nothing?"

He hesitated.

"Yes?"

"No." He looked to the floor.

"Then how did the police arrest you?"

He hesitated again. "I don't know."

"Son"—I touched his shoulder and sounded like my father—"look at me."

He looked up, a man's eyes in a boy's body.

"I need to know why you're here. Tell me about how the police arrested you and your friend this morning."

Just then the steel door opened and the captain's brown dress shoes clicked against the floor. The captain apologized for the interruption and informed me that Colonel Berger was at General Salah's office and had requested my immediate presence. Frustrated though feigning indifference, I thanked the captain, blindfolded the boy, and walked out with Mike.

Colonel Berger was speaking with a handful of officers outside General Salah's office. When he saw me, he broke from the group.

"Captain, what do you know?"

"Well, it's going to take some time, sir."

"Salah mentioned they were young. What ages?"

"Eleven and fifteen, sir."

"Eleven?"

I nodded.

Colonel Berger released a deep sigh.

"Yes, sir. It's pathetic."

He paused. "Yes, Captain, it is. What else do we know?"

I distilled what I knew and briefed the colonel in less than a minute.

"So do you think they did it?"

"I don't know, sir, maybe." The manner in which the eleven-year-old answered my questions filled me with doubt.

The colonel sighed and shook his head. "Eleven years old and his life is already behind him."

At a certain point most soldiers and Marines made mental transitions and blocked out pain and surprise to function effectively. Emotions could be dealt with later, if at all. I can't speak for the colonel, but I had reached such a point. We needed to stay focused on the next decisions because they were coming rapidly and were about things that we could affect. For Colonel Berger, his next decision challenged him to balance our desire to empower the Iraqi police against the reality of their often brutal tactics, especially when they knew we weren't watching. Many Iraqis didn't differentiate between interrogation and torture. When the topics came up in meetings, a number of my Sunni Iraqi sources had told me a story of Saddam allegedly ordering a bottle to be shoved into a suspected defector's rectum and shattered with a bat. It was hearsay, but the fact that it was believed and passed on by Sunni Iraqis hinted at the context of fear in which they lived. In such a world, human rights had little meaning.

Colonel Berger decided to let the police take custody of the kids for the rest of the day after warning General Salah that they were to be treated humanely. "This will be a test," the colonel concluded, "we'll see if they get any useful information."

I agreed with Colonel Berger's decision. With a warning to General Salah and such a short time of custody, the likelihood that the boys would be abused was low. The colonel was already viewing the boys as part of the enemy apparatus, and I had begun to see them that way as well.

While waiting for nightfall at the old youth center, I spent some time with Kael Weston from the State Department. Shaken by the assassination, Kael told me he felt some responsibility for Sheikh Kamal's death, even though the sheikh knew that he was stepping into one of the world's most dangerous jobs. Kael handed me Sheikh Kamal's identification card, bloodstained with a bullet hole through the center. "His brother brought it to me this morning," Kael said, choking up.

Although Kael may have been the only American who grieved Sheikh Kamal's assassination, most senior officers with whom I spoke realized its significance and worried that it would intimidate other Iraqis from taking public office. We didn't know it then, but the brazen attacks against Iraqis such as Sheikh Kamal and Grand Mufti Sheikh Hamza were backfiring. Sunni public opinion was turning in our favor, and the seeds of what would later be called the Al Anbar Awakening were taking their roots. Iraqi nationalists, such as General Salah, forged closer relationships with the United States in order to battle Al Qaeda, with the hope that they would be included in the new Iraqi power structure forming in Baghdad.

Dusk came and the muezzins sounded their final calls to prayer from the minarets of Fallujah's many mosques. I returned to the office of the Iraqi intelligence captain.

"You look good. The interrogation must have gone well." I painted a smile across my face. The captain appeared as polished and fresh as he had eight hours earlier.

"What do you mean?"

"The interrogation, you were questioning the boys, right?"

"No, not me. My men."

There was a pause.

"Oh, well, how'd it go? How'd they do?" It was annoying that I had to ask.

"Not well. The boys, they're stubborn."

"Stubborn?" It was a curious choice of a word.

"Yes, they didn't say anything."

"Are you sure they were the ones?"

"*Naam*."

"May I see them?"

"*Naam*, but they aren't here. They're coming."

"You didn't interrogate them here?" We didn't know of another police facility in the city.

"No."

"Where?"

"Somewhere else."

"Please show me." I looked him in the eye and took out my laminated map with satellite imagery of every building in Fallujah. If nothing else, I would take that piece of information from him.

The captain placed the tip of his long pinkie fingernail on a square roof deep in Hai al-Shuhada, the Martyrs' District. I detected a scowl beneath his thick black mustache. It was the first true emotion I may have elicited from him.

"Thanks, Captain. *Shukran*."

THE BOYS DIDN'T show any signs of abuse when I dropped them off at our detention facility back at Camp Fallujah with our interrogation team. Captain Joe Burke had recently moved with the division headquarters from Ramadi to Fallujah. He met me at the chow hall for a midnight dinner.

"*Habari soldja?*" I greeted a strapping Ugandan guard in a creased khaki uniform outside the chow hall.

"*Mzuri, Captain. Jambo*," he replied, popping to attention.

Joe was fluent in Korean. He found our Swahili exchange amusing. "That comin' in handy?"

A year earlier a suicide bomber had attacked an army chow hall in northern Iraq and killed fifteen soldiers. The military reacted by sending private security contractors to every large chow hall in Iraq. Lured by the relatively high pay, our chow hall guards had been among the Ugandan military's most capable soldiers. I spoke with them from time to time about the Lord's Resistance Army, a terrorist group in northern Uganda known for conscripting child soldiers and mutilating civilians.

"Sounds like we could use them in the field instead of checking IDs," Joe said, half-joking. The Ugandan guards were professional and vigilant, though they may have followed a more repressive approach to counterinsurgency.

"One more way to outsource this war," I replied. By some estimates there were as many contractors in Iraq as U.S. military members. Unlike our Ugandan guards, most of our contractors worked in jobs that weren't directly related to security. Contractors ran our laundry service, the barbershop, and all the other stores on base. They served as mechanics and translated documents. Most of the contractors were foreigners who worked for the U.S. conglomerate Halliburton, which made a nice profit on each employee it hired from Bosnia, Ethiopia, the Philippines, and other developing nations. It would have helped economic development if the jobs went to Iraqis. Unfortunately, insurgents aggressively targeted the few Iraqis who had access to U.S. bases, especially our local interpreters. Joe and I had supervised numerous counterintelligence investigations on Iraqi employees blackmailed by threats to their families.

We sat down with our trays of food and griped about the chow hall. Proud of our ability to do without, we shared a disdain for the place. The all-you-can-eat buffet with Baskin-Robbins ice cream, a dozen flat-screen TVs, and other amenities was excessive. We felt guilty sitting there as most of our Marines were in the field conducting high-risk night operations and living for weeks on packaged military meals specially manufactured to induce constipation.

I gave Joe an update on Sheikh Kamal's assassination and mentioned the Iraqi captain's line about the boys being stubborn.

"It's true," Joe reacted, "eleven-year-olds can be stubborn. Who's taking them into the booth?"

"Sergeant A.B." He was one of our best interrogators.

"Good. We'll find out. May take time, but he'll get the info. You okay?" Joe asked, nudging me with his elbow.

"Yeah, yeah. I'm fine. I mean, just need some coffee."

"So, what's next?"

"What do you mean?"

"I mean after Iraq?" Joe, like his predecessor, Mike Dubrule, was a great commander. He cared about his Marines, and he took an active interest in their career development.

"Oh, yeah, that. Looks like grad school." My decision was set days earlier when I received e-mails from Harvard. Tracy had been ecstatic when I called with the news. My excitement, however, was tempered by everything around me. I didn't have the mental capacity, time, or energy to build another psychological compartment and think about what came after Iraq.

Joe congratulated me and said that I'd be missed within our HUMINT community. He thought the graduate school program, which we had spoken about in the past, would be a good way to read and reflect on our wartime experience. His opinion meant a great deal to me. Some commanders would have held it against me for not making the Marine Corps a career, but not men such as Joe Burke and Mike Dubrule. They were leaders who would support what was best for their men, even if that was something that wasn't necessarily in the short-term interests of the Marine Corps.

SERGEANT A.B. AND another of our skilled interrogators spent hours with the two boys each day for two weeks. They learned their movements and mannerisms. They confirmed their identities and carved out contradictions in their stories. By the end of the second week, Sergeant A.B. was convinced that the boys had killed Sheikh Kamal. But he didn't have a confession.

A general approved our request to delay the boys' transfer to Abu Ghraib for a third week. On the twentieth day, our team made a breakthrough. It was the eleven-year-old's sweet tooth that did him in. Sergeant A.B. and his partner had tried many different incentives on the boys, including every type of candy available on base. However, when a guard detected that the younger boy craved a boxed grape drink served with dinner, Sergeant A.B.'s partner took a case of the sugar water into the interrogation booth. Surprisingly, hours later, he walked out with a confession. The boy admitted to driving the BMW. His foot had barely reached the gas pedal. With his confession, the older boy buckled and admitted to having pulled the trigger. The fifteen-year-old claimed that a member of the city council had coerced them to kill the sheikh.

It was a startling discovery, and we needed to continue the interrogation to extract all of the details. Unfortunately, we weren't permitted another extension. The following day, the boys were transferred to Abu Ghraib prison.

WE CALLED ABU Ghraib "the black hole" because it was so difficult to receive information from the massive prison that two years earlier had shocked the world. Our detainees went to Abu Ghraib and disappeared in an ocean of nearly five thousand prisoners. We rarely received intelligence from follow-up interrogations, and we often weren't notified when suspected terrorists were released after hasty trials at the dysfunctional Iraqi Criminal Court. E-mails and phone calls to Abu Ghraib went unreturned. On one occasion, a sheikh from Fallujah had died in the prison. Incredibly, his body couldn't be found for Kael Weston to return it to Fallujah's leaders for proper Muslim burial.

Days after the boys were transferred from our custody at Camp Fallujah I caught a helicopter to Abu Ghraib. I needed to secure approval for Sergeant A.B.'s partner to continue his interrogation, and I was also hoping to initiate a better relationship between the prison and my regiment.

The prison's stench hit me as our helicopter hovered over one of its many well-lit landing pads. The foul smell resembled the funk from re-used, sweaty socks. For years to come similar odors would trigger vivid memories of my thirty-six-hour visit to this infamous place.

The following morning, a major greeted me at his cubicle in the Abu Ghraib intelligence shop, a bunker with meat hooks still lodged in the walls from Saddam's time. The major was the Marine Corps' liaison officer to Abu Ghraib. His bloodshot eyes and pale face gave the immediate impression of an overworked staff officer on the verge of collapse. He listened as I briefed him, then he cut straight to the point: "So we need to locate the two boys and get the approval for your sergeant to spend some time here?"

"Yes, sir." We sorted through some paperwork and routed a formal request to the general in charge. Afterward, the major called a guard to show me where the kids were being held. The guard, a barrel-chested sergeant with bloated cauliflower ears, was in a Florida National Guard infantry unit. He had never received training to work at a prison. As we left the major's office I asked him about the pervasive sock stench.

"Yeah, I don't even notice it no more," he responded. "No one really knows what it is. There's speculation, some superstitions. My theory? My theory's that Saddam ripped one on this place right before we bombed his sorry ass. Then that smell just hung here, Saddam's last fart." He chuckled and then lowered his voice. "But there are ghosts here, sir. They creep this place out, I tell ya. Some of the prisoners believe Saddam's still around. Not here, but watchin'. Especially the Shiites. They believe this. This place has bad memories, like over there."

The sergeant pointed to a block of white buildings that looked like the rest of the cement rectangles zigzagging across the prison. "In there, that's where it happened. That's where they did those things to those prisoners. Section 1-A. Ya want to see it?"

"Yes."

It was eerily quiet as our boots clapped down the halls. Soon we were in parts of the prison that had never seen sunlight. The smell of urine and body odor overpowered the sock stench. Orange-suited prisoners languishing in cells eyed us as we passed. No one spoke.

Section 1-A looked similar to other parts of the prison except there were no prisoners. It was a small area. I wouldn't have recognized it from my memory of the notorious prisoner-abuse photographs. Its yellow walls had been cleansed of the blood smears, the makeshift torture games having long been disassembled and removed. No physical reminder remained of what had happened. Yet there we were.

The photographs that were released to the press were bad enough. There were, however, others that were never made public. I had seen many of them on our classified intranet. The graphic images returned to my mind as I stood there. I saw the blood on the walls, mutilated prisoners on leashes, covered with feces, sodomized by truncheons, stacked into naked pyramids, the terror, the trauma, the fear, the fear so pure it was nauseating. A howl echoed through the halls. It was so sharp in pitch I wanted to cover my ears. Suddenly it stopped, and I was panting like a dog.

"What was that?"

"What was what, sir?"

"That noise?"

"Noise, sir? There was no noise."

"Really?"

"Yes, sir."

"Oh."

"I don't know how it happened." The sergeant said, "How could we have done this."

"Done what?" I was flustered from the howl. I could have sworn it was real.

"The torture, the abuse. I mean, it's despicable. We're Americans. We're better than that."

How AND WHY were the questions I had asked myself as a fifteen-year-old when I saw Rwandan boys my age on television murdering a man with machetes and clubs spiked with nails. Those questions remained unanswered, as did the one that I had found even more disturbing: What would I have done if I were born to the majority ethnic group in Rwanda and was told to participate in genocide? That question haunted me in part because I grew up believing a clear line existed between good and evil, and that people could freely choose to be safely on one side or the other. My experiences in the Marines and in Kibera suggested to me that a long, wide spectrum lies between these two poles, and that most people are capable of doing evil things, including myself. I had never been at the other extreme of the spectrum, near a point of pure goodness, and I knew few people who existed in that space. Tabitha and Salim were there, or they were close. I was not. For most of my life I was somewhere in between, and in five short months in Iraq I had moved far closer to the dark end than I would ever have imagined.

My combat experiences were nowhere near as intense, tragic, and terrifying as many others'. But they allowed me a glimpse into the abyss and its seductive, slippery force. It didn't take long for me to begin to move down the slope. Within weeks in Fallujah I experienced moments of bloodlust, the impulse to destroy for destruction's sake. Much of our training was geared to control these impulses, and our training was generally effective. But how long could I keep my morality intact and not act on these violent, misplaced urges? I didn't know. Maybe months. Maybe years. It would certainly depend in part on the circumstances I faced, my moral luck. Eventually, though, a place as toxic as Iraq's Sunni Triangle in 2006 would take me farther down the levels of the inferno.

There I was standing in Abu Ghraib 1-A, a place that had once been at the far evil end of the spectrum when three years earlier a group of young Americans went beyond the point of no return and shamed us all. For whatever reasons, they became outliers at a volatile, confused time. These men and women, these American soldiers, were without the proper resources, training, or leadership. They were part of a broken system that fed negative thoughts and tolerated cruelty. At one point, most of them were probably decent people who never imagined what they would become. While these circumstances mattered and dispersed responsibility, they still weren't enough.

What would I have done if I was so unfortunate to have been in the guard force of Abu Ghraib prison in 2003? So many things in our lives were outside of our control, and yet we had choices to make and decisions to own. In this extreme circumstance, the answer was clear. It was clearer to me than Rwanda because the context was more sharply defined and I could relate to parts of it more readily. While I may have had the capacity to do evil things, nothing could have seduced me into participating or witnessing as a bystander what had happened at Abu Ghraib. It would never happen.

My upbringing, the opportunities I had been given, the second chances, and something spiritual deep inside me gave me the strength to say "never." We existed to guard the defenseless against such sadism. I would lose everything, including my life, before I relented to that horror or ever gave up fighting it. It was too far down the spectrum. I knew this. What I didn't know was at which level of the inferno I would eventually stop, and what it would take to push me that far.

Not all Marines felt such a pull toward the primal and elusive powers of darkness as I had, though many of us did, and we resisted because of our training, leadership, and values. Nevertheless, the more destruction and killing one experiences, the harder it becomes to ward off evil. Marines in combat are often called to operate at the very rim of the abyss, the point at which the spectrum is a blur. We flirt with the darkness and attempt to control it. But few people, I believe, can control it forever, and this was part of the reason why we constantly rotated units in and out of combat zones. Burnout happened at various degrees on three levels: physical, mental, and spiritual. I believed I witnessed that last level in its extreme manifestation with the Ethiopian military intelligence captain who admired Don Corleone, the sly Iraqi captain in Fallujah, and there, at that moment, with the specter of American soldiers in a dungeon at Abu Ghraib. It was the burnout of the soul.

We exited 1-A and stepped outside to rows of tents where detainees were kept on cots, twenty to thirty prisoners per tent.

"This is our Boy Scout camp." The sergeant pointed to a small dirt patch at the end of the row of tents. "That's the day care. Looks like it's playtime."

Some kids in orange jumpsuits were in the middle of a soccer game. We stepped up to the sidelines. The sweaty sock funk was so pungent I wondered if it slowed the kids down. Two helicopters roared overhead, adding to a breeze across the dirt patch. A field of date trees stood time-lessly behind the base's glimmering razor wire. The dull *thunk-thunk* of mortar fire sounded in the distance.

"Ya see 'em, sir?"

The boys were playing together on the shirtless team. Their brown chests were as flat as their backs. The eleven-year-old took a forward, offensive position. He hustled, though his ballhandling was poor. Soon his teammates were cutting him out of the action. As he became more and more frustrated, the eleven-year-old abandoned his position and chased the ball up and down the field. The fifteen-year-old, on the other hand, took a midfield position and stuck to a defensive game. His approach was strategic and restrained. He studied the field for the right moments to exert bursts of energy. He had better ball control than his younger accomplice, though his step was flat-footed and ungainly.

The eleven-year-old finally caught up with the ball and took off toward the sweeper, a skilled defender who looked to be at least sixteen years old. The small boy didn't stand a chance until his friend and accomplice sprinted ahead, lowered his shoulder, and crashed into the sweeper.

The young boy continued toward the goal. He didn't have the ball

control to change his course when the goalie charged. A split second before contact, the boy thrust his leg back and toed the ball into the goal as
the goalie crushed him in a head-on collision.

Squirming out from beneath the goalie, the boy bounced up and
threw his open hands in the air. *"ALLAHU AKBAR!"* he shouted. "GOD
IS GREAT!"

Not until I saw the boys on that dirt patch playing soccer did it really
hit me. As troubled as I was by the boys' situation, I had still viewed them
as the enemy. Now, they had confessed and were playing soccer, and I
was seeing them again for who they were. Kids. They were just boys.
They still knew how to laugh. They could still afford a smile.

What would Salim think? He would be surprised to see me there in my
body armor looking like a robot. Once he got over that, if he could, he
would see the potential in those kids trapped in an impossible situation. I
had tried to convince myself that the boys at Abu Ghraib were guilty, yet I
couldn't help but feel sympathy and sadness as I stood there thinking about
Salim and Kibera. Those boys were smart and capable. They had foiled
our best interrogators for more than two weeks. They were kids caught in
the cross fire, born to circumstances they couldn't control. They didn't
have great mentors, a quality education, or safety. They didn't have second
chances. A powerful Iraqi man who sat on the city council had coerced
them to commit murder. *Were they really guilty? What would I have done as
an eleven-year-old in that boy's place, or when I was fifteen and angry at the
world?*

Kibera and the Marine Corps. I had separated them neatly into isolated
compartments in my head and convinced myself that with discipline and
perseverance I could live two lives. Yet here they were again, my compartments crumbling and clashing, falling apart as they always did. The walls
were, after all, figments of my imagination. It wasn't possible to keep them
separate, and I had never really viewed them as distinct. They were different means toward the same goal: peace and stability in a violent world. In
Kibera, I could feel the impact directly. Our annual budget that year was
less than what the United States spent every minute in Iraq. Surely we
would always need a strong military, though there had to be a better way
toward peace than this, our detention at Abu Ghraib of two kids almost
half my age. At a fundamental level it was like Kibera. It shouldn't happen.
It wasn't right.

Could the eleven-year-old be rehabilitated or was his life truly behind him? Salim would say yes, the boy could be rehabilitated, but it would take some work and the boy would have to want it. The battle-hardened Marine colonel said no. Some people may think that the colonel was jaded; others may see him as a realist. Standing there at Abu Ghraib as the boys were celebrating their goal, I had to believe the answer was yes. Yes, they could still have a healthy and productive life. Something in my soul needed to believe this, and I didn't want to lose that hope, as much for the boys' sake as for my own.

CHAPTER TWENTY

Impact

Camp Lejeune, North Carolina

SUMMER 2006

"KASH WAS KILLED."

"What?"

"I called Nate already," Salim said. His high-pitched voice cracked at the end of each sentence. "I tried you earlier. I couldn't get through."

"How?" Stunned, numb, I needed more information. We were all about the same age. Kash was in perfect health when I had last seen him in his UNC basketball shirt in front of Tabitha's Clinic.

"He was shot. Not that late. Maybe eight at night. Thugs came. Outside the clinic. They, they shot him in the stomach."

"Robbery?" Eight P.M. was early. Kibera bustled in the evenings. There must have been witnesses, and with witnesses, the specter of mob justice.

"No, they didn't take his things. All they took was his life."

"All and everything."

Salim exhaled. My eyes swelled. A prickling heat shot across my back.

"Did anyone see?"

"Yes, but they haven't any suspects. The thugs, they must have come from outside Kibera."

"How'd Nate take it?" Nate was living in New York City waiting tables at high-end restaurants.

"Not so good, man." Although Nate and I never spoke openly about it, he still believed we should have given Kash a second chance.

Salim and I stayed on the phone, sharing memories. Kash had helped keep my mother safe when she slept overnight at the clinic. Mom loved to tell the story about how he studied French while listening to Edith Piaf. Salim recalled the 2001 riots, when Kash defended the clinic from marauding thugs while Tabitha treated streams of patients. I told Salim about the first time Nate and I discovered Kash's handmade gym with its hand-welded bars and scrap-wood bench tucked in an alley next to a pit latrine. We were so sore after our first day of lifting with Kash that we couldn't raise our arms over our heads to flag a *matatu* minibus heading downtown.

Salim laughed.

"And his smile, man."

"Yeah, his smile. It could make you feel good." Salim remembered how Kash's Hollywood smile had electrified the room full of donors at the Peacocks' house.

Eventually Kash appeared to rebound, yet again. He helped start a girls' education program with Ali's charismatic friend Kassim. Afterward, Kash launched a "slum tourism" company that had some initial success until he found employment at a Western-owned safari company. Kassim told me that before he died Kash had a *mzungu* girlfriend and was "really doing well."

When we had seen each other in Kibera in the years that passed since he had left CFK, Kash and I still exchanged fist bumps. But there was always a tension. It frustrated me that Kash had never apologized. Yet I still cared about him. He was the closest friend I knew who had died from gunfire. I wanted to bring his killer to justice, and I imagined that doing so might help somehow restore my memories of him to only the happy ones.

Kash embodied the best and worst of Kibera, its talent and its temptations, its promise and its spoil. We never found out who killed him.

BACK AT CAMP Lejeune, my departure from active duty was bittersweet. One moment I would find myself embraced by nostalgia and oblivious to the world. Minutes later I would be brooding about the past, worrying about the future, and struggling to contain inexplicable, violent urges.

"What's next, sir?" enlisted Marines sometimes asked me. I had spent four and a half of my most formative years departing and coming back to our team house and the patch of grass outside where Sergeant Mo had leveled me during our flak-jacket pickup game. A large part of me wanted to stay with them.

Graduate school was the last thing I wanted to discuss with enlisted Marines. I always felt terrible and terribly privileged, even though most Marines didn't seem to pass negative judgment. The men were going back to war, and I was heading to one of the most elite institutions in the world. It was easier to share plans with the other junior-grade officers, many of whom were preparing to leave the Marine Corps after four years. The standard career track looked frighteningly dull to many of us. It involved becoming staff intelligence officers and facing years of analytical and administrative duties far from the front lines. In my cohort of a dozen officers, a handful chose to pursue law or business school degrees, while most transitioned with relative ease into the FBI or CIA, where they would continue to fight in the global war on terror.

On my last day at the company Captain Joe Burke joined me for a lunchtime beach run. We took my Green Bean from the team house to Camp Lejeune's Onslow Beach. Joe commented on my whitewall tires, which pleased me because I took pride in keeping them shiny with steel-wool pads and Armor All protectant. He thought it was hilarious that I had additional adhesive safety reflectors stuck to my rear bumper.

"Safety first, that's what my dad always says." I laughed, recalling how my father had stuck the reflectors on my bumper one day without asking me first.

"Your father, he's a Vietnam vet, right?"

"Sure was."

"Infantry?"

"Yes."

"Well, then, as far as I'm concerned, he can say whatever the hell he wants about safety."

"No doubt." I didn't mind the reflectors. They added some more color to the old Caravan and gave me a reason to talk about my father with a friend like Joe.

We started running at a moderate pace, which was good because it was noon and Joe wanted to go on a long run. As one of the few undeveloped points on the southeastern seaboard, I imagined the beach resembled the same stretch of wide, flat sand two hundred miles north along the Outer Banks where a century earlier the Wright brothers had made their first flight. A half mile inland the air was so humid you could taste the swamp in it. But on the beach it was breezy and cool.

Nostalgia returned, overpowering my senses. When I had needed escape during deployments and trips to Kibera, I returned in my mind to these beaches and the memories of long, barefoot walks with Tracy, hand in hand, sometimes talking, sometimes dreaming, often just listening to the ocean and the rhythm of its release.

Joe and I talked shop as we ran, as always. I brainstormed with him about our strongest and weakest Marines, and how to man future teams. We talked about training, and we griped about higher headquarters. By the time we finished our eight or so miles, I was winded, thirsty, and struggling to keep up. As we walked to the Green Bean, Joe removed a pack of Marlboro reds from his sock. The smoke seemed to take his mind to a deeper place.

"Ya know why I joined the Marine Corps?" he asked. We had never spoken about his decision, though I knew a bit about his childhood growing up in a depressed part of East St. Louis. He once told me that after college he had planned to go into the Peace Corps.

"Why's that?"

He took a hard drag on his cigarette. "To make a difference. Ya know, it's all about impact."

"That's what I fear I'll miss the most."

"Yeah, maybe. But you won't miss the staff meetings." Half of our days were consumed by meetings with staff officers Joe called "oxygen thieves."

"Or the awards board," I added. We spent countless hours crafting awards citations and fighting administrative battles.

Joe shook his head. "Well, I'm glad we got you yours before you left. I once received an award for a deployment two years after I returned."

Days earlier I had received a medal Joe had nominated me for. Its citation read *Captain Barcott's engagement of theater and national-level intelligence organizations, detention facility interrogation teams, and Iraqi intelligence and security personnel led to the capture of numerous high value individuals.*

When I reread the citation my mind flipped to Abu Ghraib and the fifteen thousand detainees in our custody in our prisons across Iraq. That's where those "high value individuals" ended up. They went to our prisons and sat like Boy Scouts in tents, where they could plot future attacks and recruit new blood from the thousands of other detainees. Then, in most cases, the detainees were released because many of them were innocent, our priorities were elsewhere, and our prisons themselves were badly overcrowded. In 2006 we were told the average time of detention at Abu Ghraib was three to six months. It had been five months since we sent the man with the black watch and the smirk to Abu Ghraib. More likely than not, he was back on the streets trying to kill Americans and brave Iraqi leaders, the next Sheikh Kamals. The two child assassins came to mind as well. I would never know what happened to them. There was so much we would never know. Six months in country, then we were gone. "My involvement in military life features opportunities gained and lost, variable probabilities, illusions and disillusions, and elusive uncertainties, some of which remain," my father wrote about his war before I experienced mine.

"So, Joe, let me ask you something. Did it meet your expectations?"

"What d'ya mean?"

"Do you feel like you're makin' that difference?" I suspected his answer was yes, but I was curious because Joe and I were both pessimistic about the trajectory of Iraq. The country appeared to be on the verge of civil war.

Joe took another long drag, drawing the embers of his cigarette down to its butt and pinching it out with his tar-stained fingers. "Most days I don't know and don't think about it." Sweat dripped from his gray brows. "There's a lot that sucks. But that's life. Yeah, I do. That's why I stayed in. Plus, what would I do in the real world?"

"Play the blues?" Joe had once told me that he had spent a couple of years in his twenties as a vagabond musician strumming a guitar in smoky jazz clubs in New Orleans.

Joe shook his head and opened the door to the Green Bean. It was time to get back to work. There were less than four months to prepare the company for another Iraq deployment, its fourth in four years.

That afternoon we had a good-bye gathering at Hooters for the handful of us who were changing duty stations or leaving the Corps. We joked and told war stories. It was a good group, some Marines more scarred than others, all struggling with the transition from war to the banality of American life.

When I drove out of Camp Lejeune's main gate past the streams of homemade WELCOME HOME WARRIOR banners, a young private spotted the blue officer's sticker on my window and popped to a crisp salute. He wasn't saluting me. He was saluting my rank. He was saluting our Corps. What Joe said was true for most Marines. We volunteered for military duty to make a difference, and to be part of something larger than ourselves.

Had I made enough of a difference?

I HAD TO admit the truth: I didn't know. I knew I was blessed to have served under exceptional commanders and to have returned from dangerous places with all of my men physically intact. I had proven myself, seen part of the elephant, fulfilled a dream, and grown considerably. Yet, things were missing.

At one level, it was important to me that the greatest value of my military experience wasn't simply my personal development. I wanted clear results that I could point to and say, "We did that, and that mattered because of _____."

Maybe it was presumptuous to think that I would be able to measure the impact of our actions. We were, after all, small teams, and I was just one Marine in a military with nearly three million active and reserve members. In my five years of service, my Marines and I had operated in eleven countries, and that was part of the challenge as well. Near the beginning of my active-duty service, my mentor Colonel Greenwood had warned me that, in his opinion, lack of continuity was the Achilles' heel of the U.S. military. Part of the reason I couldn't discern what impact we had made was because our transfer of knowledge was dysfunctional. At the time, my sentiments may have been different if we were on more stable courses in Iraq, Afghanistan, the Horn of Africa, and elsewhere in the world. But even still, it would have been difficult to identify any specific contributions of lasting value. We were temporary, limited parts of an enormous organization, and that, like most things in life, had many trade-offs.

No one in CFK or the Marine Corps ever asked me which form of service mattered more to me. Salim, Nate, and Tabitha never asked. Colonel Greenwood, Captain Burke, and Sergeant Thompson never asked. Yet this was one of the most frequently asked questions I received when I spoke on behalf of CFK. My colleagues knew that it was impossible for me to choose. Each world was special and important in its own right. In Kibera I could feel our impact directly. It was clearly identifiable, and, to a certain extent, it was measurable. We had built CFK into a unique organization from scratch. It was ours, and we had to fight to keep it alive and thriving. In the Marine Corps, I was part of a historic institution that would last regardless of me or any one person and would be respected long after I died. It was noble and called for extreme sacrifice. Both worlds cultivated leaders and celebrated actions over words. Both served. Both mattered.

Yet the dichotomy remained. CFK focused on preventing violence; the Marines employed it. I understood and respected that for some, such as Salim and my mother, this divide was not reconcilable. I certainly wrestled with its inherent contradiction, especially before I had begun deploying as a Marine and built firmer compartments between my worlds. My fundamental view, however, remained the same. It came down to the fact that we lived in a volatile and violent world. Despite its misuse in controversial wars, the Marine Corps, like the rest of our armed forces, existed to protect the United States and, in some cases, enhance the safety of other parts of the world. Our military forces were rather blunt instruments for reducing threats to our national security, but they were also extremely effective in the most urgent and precarious situations. The military didn't decide our nation's wars; it executed them on the command of our elected leadership. This tenet of civilian control is a pillar of our Constitution, that great body of ideas and ideals that my father and I swore to defend with our lives. Of course, that wasn't the only answer. The military was flawed, too, and bureaucracies had tendencies to perpetuate themselves far beyond their useful lives. So much in the end came down to leadership, at home and abroad, and in and out of uniform.

Elephants aside, this was the rationale that enabled me to volunteer for a war that I knew was unnecessary and severely flawed. My father held similar beliefs even though he distrusted war and almost died in one that was also unnecessary. *Would we fail in Iraq as we had in Vietnam?* I didn't know, though at the time it looked probable, especially if we continued to rely on military might instead of the more sophisticated soft-power instruments in our deep reservoir of resources outside the armed forces.

So it was that my thoughts returned to my father as I pulled out of the main gate at Camp Lejeune. He was wounded more profoundly by his war than the bruising that I had taken in mine. Vietnam defined much of his generation and probably a lot more of him than he realized. The failures there, the needless wasting of so many Vietnamese and American lives, disturbed him in ways that I suspected could still be as raw and as agonizing as they had been forty years earlier. For many reasons, including his love, my experience reintegrating into society would be far less arduous. Yet it was still difficult, and my first coping mechanism was to turn to the one place where I knew I could still make an impact—Kibera.

WORKING FIENDISHLY, I packed my schedule for the three summer months before starting at Harvard: three weeks in Kibera; fund-raisers in London, California, and New York; a conference on poverty at the Aspen Institute in Colorado; a meeting at the National Security Council in Washington, D.C.; a weekend with my parents in Rhode Island; the move to Cambridge; and then the grand finale—two weeks in Morocco, where I would propose to Tracy at the home of my interpreter and friend from Iraq, Mike.

Tracy, who didn't know about my proposal plans, thought I was nuts for wanting to do so much during the first large chunk of free time since graduating from college. She realized, though, that my staying busy was therapeutic. The daily barrage of news from Iraq was grim, and I grew irritable and difficult when I had too much time on my hands.

As before, fund-raising was a large part of my work with CFK. We were struggling to generate the scarce resources needed to keep pace with our growth in the community. We landed a breakthrough opportunity when one of the most recognizable figures in international development decided to pay us a visit. Unfortunately, we didn't know who she was before her arrival one morning to our youth center. She traveled under the cover of a U.S. embassy delegation. Salim welcomed her and gave an overview of CFK with some members of our Binti Pamoja Girls' Center and local mothers from a self-help group.

Afterward, the woman walked into our small office and spoke in a soft, humble manner to our staff. She apologized for the inconvenience that her presence caused and asked some thoughtful questions about CFK's model of participatory development and youth empowerment. Before she left, Salim begged her pardon and asked her to sign one of the chai-stained pages of our guest book. It was good manners for hosts to offer their guest book, though he still had no idea who she was.

Happily, she signed her name. *Melinda Gates.*

Instantly recognizing her name, Salim took a deep breath. Whether he was speaking with a street child high from huffing glue or one of the most affluent women in the world, he was quick on his feet. "Missus Gates, thanks again for coming to see us. Now you're part of our community, and you're welcome anytime."

"Well, thank you, Salim. You're doing impressive work." She smiled graciously.

"Um, do you have a card?"

"Oh." She laughed. "No, I don't carry one. But, I think you can reach me through my assistant here."

In a *Newsweek* article about her visit to Kibera, Melinda Gates wrote:

> A few months ago, on a trip to Africa, I met with a group of women in Kibera, the biggest slum in Kenya. These women ranged in age from 16 to 45 but had one thing in common: AIDS had devastated their lives . . . Through our foundation, my husband, Bill, and I are working to develop tools that can put the power to prevent AIDS into the hands of women.*

Our Binti Pamoja Girls' Center worked in concert with the sports program and the Tabitha Clinic to prevent AIDS and gender-based violence, and so began a courtship with the Bill and Melinda Gates Foundation.

---

* Melinda French Gates, "What Women Really Need," *Newsweek* May 15, 2006.

DURING MY FIRST week back in Kibera that summer, we hosted a U.S. congressional delegation. Kibera had become as much a stopping point for celebrities seeking a glimpse of poverty as Fallujah had become a destination for politicians and senior officers searching for war stories. Salim and I were cynical of most visits. They rarely resulted in tangible benefits to the community, and their press coverage often amounted to glib photo ops geared to Western audiences. I was more interested in being with our team than giving slum tours. Nevertheless, this delegation was an exception, because it was led by the senior congressman from North Carolina, a former professor of political science at Duke University and a gracious Southern gentleman named David Price. Representative Price's district included Chapel Hill. He was a fellow UNC graduate, and he had sent me a handwritten, heartfelt letter when I was in Iraq.

Salim and I welcomed the congressman and his team to our office. We gave them a brief overview of our work and a tour that included walking through the mud to an eighth-of-an-acre mound of dirt, the future site of the new Tabitha Clinic. We needed to raise more than $150,000 before we could begin construction of what we hoped would become one of the few permanent buildings in Kibera, a two-story, ecofriendly clinic built by and for the community. After the tour, Representative Price chatted with a few UNC student volunteers and some of our staff at our youth center. He asked thoughtful questions about the history of poverty, local politics, and the challenges we faced.

"What can I do to help you?" Representative Price asked me. I should have been prepared for the question. We didn't seek USAID program support because of the strings attached with it, including, potentially, a loss of local ownership.

"What do you think, Salim?" I turned to my cofounder. Salim didn't miss a beat. He never did. He asked if the congressman could help us raise funds to build the new clinic in Tabitha's honor. As Representative Price explained the unfortunate restrictions of U.S. government funding for capital expenditures overseas, I spotted a copy of the *Daily Nation*, Kenya's largest newspaper. The cover had a photograph of U.S. senator Barack Obama. I didn't know much about Senator Obama, but I was amazed by the press coverage he was receiving in advance of his first official visit to Kenya in August 2006, long before he was being considered as a serious candidate for the U.S. presidency.

"Sir, is there any chance you could help us arrange a visit for Senator Obama during his upcoming trip?" I asked.

Representative Price responded enthusiastically, and, months later with help from the congressman and many others, Barack and Michelle Obama arrived at CFK. Thousands of residents clogged the streets, chanting, "Obama has come! Open the way!"

The Obamas' first stop was our youth center, where they met with Salim and some young leaders from Kibera. After listening to a young girl speak about HIV/AIDS prevention, the Obamas inquired about health care in Kibera. Salim told them Tabitha's story and our vision to build a new Tabitha Clinic.

"Impressive!" Michelle Obama exclaimed.

I STARTED SPENDING my mornings with Jane Atieno, Tabitha's best friend and former neighbor. She was the first resident of Kibera I had met after arriving to Oluoch and Elizabeth's house in Fort Jesus as a twenty-one-year-old eager to make a difference through research. At CFK, Jane did more than prepare chai and keep the office and the clinic clean. She was part of the soul of our organization. She was in charge of Tabitha's home-based-care program, providing food and love to widowed mothers battling AIDS, many of whom were abandoned by their friends and family because of the stigmas associated with the disease. Antiretroviral medication was prohibitively expensive, and without proper treatment, half of the group's two dozen members had passed away in the year and a half after Tabitha's death.

On our first morning together, I accompanied Jane on some home visits. She met me with her radiant smile.

"Mama Jane!"

"Omosh!" She always called me by my African nickname. We hugged. I reached for the twenty-pound bag of beans she was carrying.

"No, no. This, I have."

I insisted and took the sack. Jane led me zigzagging through the mud toward the river. As we walked, she updated me on Tabitha's four children. Jane had become a surrogate to them. She felt it was the least she could do for her best friend. She recalled when she and Tabitha were unemployed and "really struggling." Tabitha's husband had passed away, and Jane's husband was out of work. They teamed up to search for employment. Tabitha did most of the talking because "she was educated and had the English. She was educated, but she never held that thing above others. She was never too proud."

"That was before you met Oluoch and Elizabeth?"

"Same-same time. I took the job and Tabitha she kept looking. You heard about Elizabeth?"

"No, what?" Elizabeth and I hadn't communicated in a long time. The orange van that Oluoch had purchased with our loan sat for years outside their flat in Fort Jesus, one block away from Salim's apartment.

"Sorry, Omosh."

"What? What is it?"

"Elizabeth, she passed."

"No!" She wasn't that old, perhaps fifty. "How?"

"She was sick, an ulcer. That's what they say."

During my first summer in Kibera, Elizabeth had told me that she was getting old and didn't have much time left to pursue her dream of starting a nursery school for orphans. She was twice my age. The sound of urgency in her voice had struck me.

"And her school?" The last I had heard, the school was educating fifty children.

"It passed with her." Jane said that Elizabeth had taught until she began losing weight.

"Oluoch?"

"You know, he's not her husband." It was another secret that I had never known. Elizabeth was separated from her husband. Her family owned the house in Fort Jesus, and a nasty feud between them and Oluoch erupted as Elizabeth's health began its rapid decline. It was painful, bitter news, all of it. Elizabeth was a good person. She deserved a more dignified departure from this world, and, as I felt with Kash, I regretted not reaching out and reconciling our relationship.

OUR FIRST HOME visit was to a woman named Achieng. Achieng was a friend and patient of Tabitha's whom I had met years ago but couldn't remember. We turned past the empty plot where we planned to build the new Tabitha Clinic. It was on the same path where Tabitha had spotted me five years earlier, grasped my hand, and led me to her first clinic.

Achieng was cleaning laundry in a bucket outside of her mud shack. She looked up and greeted us with a warm smile. It bothered me that I didn't recognize her.

Achieng welcomed us to her sofa, a metal cage without padding, and she made us chai. *Kiroboto*, bedbugs, darted everywhere. A few bounced onto my head and burrowed into my scalp.

"You don't remember me, Omosh?" Achieng asked. She was thick-boned and tall, with striking white teeth.

"Sorry, *mama*." I handed her some beans from the bag we'd brought.

"Oh, thank you. It's okay that you don't remember. I looked different then, isn't it?" She turned to Jane.

"Oh, yes," Jane agreed. "Very different. You know for a time, Achieng, she was struggling to get out of the bed."

Achieng turned and pulled back the *kanga* that separated her bed from the rest of her home. She reached into a plastic bin.

"This, this was what I looked like when you saw me last."

She placed a grainy photograph on the table and slid it in front of me. There was no resemblance, in appearance or spirit. It was a photograph of a skeleton: sunken cheeks, clumps of hair missing, skin clinging to the bones, and eyes so swollen they looked like they were going to fall out. As she spoke, I thought about Vanessa. My eyes swelled and I leaned back against the sofa's metal frame, struggling to contain myself.

Achieng and Jane didn't know how to react. They were showing me a miracle, something to rejoice about. Months earlier, President Bush's Emergency Plan for AIDS Relief had reached Kibera and made antiretrovirals available free of charge. Achieng and thousands of people like her suddenly had new lives.

Jane touched my knee. "Omosh, what's wrong?"

"I'm sorry," I said, raking my fingernails through my hair to kill the *kiroboto*. "I'm sorry. It's just, never mind. This is, this is incredible. What happened, Achieng? I mean, how did you recover?"

"I'm a power woman." She burst out laughing with Jane.

"Yes, yes, you are!" I exclaimed.

"Jane is, too. You know about power women?" she asked.

I didn't know what Achieng was talking about, and wondered if I was misunderstanding her Swahili. "Yes. Powerful women. Yes. Survivors."

Jane and Achieng laughed some more.

"Omosh! No, no, no, Omosh. We mean this, our group," Achieng explained. "We're called the power women. There are twelve of us."

"These twelve women, they all knew Tabitha. She cared for them. There were others, but they passed on," Jane added.

"They were all HIV-positive?"

"Yes, we are." Achieng replied, confidently. "All except our leader, Jane."

"They are widows with children," Jane said. "Together we're starting businesses, making jewelry. You'll see. Omosh, even you, you can buy. We want you to take power women beads back to the U.S. and help us sell them."

"Yes, whatever you need."

"Do your level best, Omosh." Achieng reached for something in a box under her bed. She placed a folded purple *kanga* on the table. Jane put her hands over her mouth and took a deep breath as Achieng unfolded it.

"You remember this?" Achieng asked.

I cracked the door open to let more sunlight into the room.

"Jane told me the story," she added.

The Swahili aphorism on the *kanga* read: *Mawingu ya dunia ufanika wajane.*

"It was like the *kanga* you gave to Tabitha, same saying," Jane said. "Now it's our motto. Power women motto."

The clouds of the earth cover the widows.

I'LL NEVER KNOW if Tabitha was HIV-positive when we first met in the summer of 2000. As a nurse she must have known her condition before the time of her death in December 2004. Yet she never revealed it. Had the doctor not told me her status as she was dying of an infection from a burst appendix, I would never have known. Even her children were unaware.

Salim had been confused when I told him that Tabitha was HIV-positive. "Why'd she not tell us?" he had asked. We were partners after all, a trio. Perhaps we could have helped prolong her life or planned for the clinic's longevity without her.

We were frustrated, especially by the challenge of keeping the clinic running after Tabitha's sudden departure. But Salim and I also sympathized with her. The stereotypes surrounding HIV/AIDS were venomous. Myths spread rapidly about the killer virus, badly distorting public awareness of the truth. By some estimates, the virus infected as much as 15 percent of the adult population in Kibera. Although our Binti Pamoja Girls' Center was doing a lot of work to educate the community, there was a dangerous lack of knowledge about how HIV was transmitted. Tabitha was wise. There were reasons for keeping her secret from everyone, including her children.

The blessed reunion that Jane had arranged for me with Achieng reminded me of a duty that I had not yet fulfilled. I felt obligated to reveal to Tabitha's children that their mother had died of HIV-related complications. They deserved to know, and I regretted not telling them immediately after she passed away.

Perhaps stunted by years of poor nutrition, Tabitha's oldest son Kevin had not grown much for an eighteen-year-old. He wore glasses that he called "specs," and he was shorter and thinner than Salim. His mannerisms exuded caution, and he rarely spoke unless he was asked a direct question. One day we met for a lunch of pilau and then returned to his humble ten-by-ten. It reminded me of his mother's shack in 2000 when we had first met. There was a wood cross on the wall hanging next to a photograph of his mother in her clinic, her hair pulled back in short braids.

I didn't know how to say it other than directly. I hoped he wouldn't be angry with me for waiting so long to reveal the secret. I apologized and told him the truth.

"Oh." His eyes opened wide. He took a quick breath.

"I know, and I'm sorry I didn't tell you sooner. You didn't know, did you?"

"No. You know, with Mom, there's so much she didn't tell us."

"I'm sure she did it to protect you."

He nodded.

"She did it to protect the clinic, too, I think."

"Yes."

We sat in silence. "You think your dad may have had it?"

"That's what I'm thinking. My dad, he was not so good."

"I never heard much about him from your mother." Apart from the time that I had asked her directly about him, Tabitha had never spoken about her late husband. She had only told me that he was a welder and had died unexpectedly of an illness. After Tabitha's funeral, I was aware that most of her extended family had ostracized her, ostensibly because she refused to obey the Luo custom and marry one of the brothers of her late husband.

"Dad, he hurt Mom." I remained quiet as Kevin took me deep into his life. His face was blank as he told me that his father frequently slept with other women. His promiscuous behavior was a source of bitter conflict with Tabitha, who refused to be treated in such a way. One night, when Kevin was nine years old, Tabitha took him and his five-year-old sister Joy and left the man.

Kevin's father eventually found them at a relative's house. He drew a pistol and pointed it at Tabitha. She fled in haste, leaving Kevin and Joy behind. Her husband chased after her until she reached a *matatu* minibus on Kibera Drive.

"My husband's going to kill me. Go. Please go now!" Tabitha pleaded to the driver. He stepped on the gas as her husband sprinted in pursuit.

Kevin's father returned that evening, mixed rat poison into a glass of milk, and killed himself in front of his only son and youngest daughter.

I put my arm over Kevin's shoulder. We wept. How can anyone ever recover from such trauma?

"Life became so, so hard from there." Kevin recalled how some relatives began accusing his mother of murder. Tabitha shifted homes to a different village in Kibera, where she became neighbors with Jane. Shortly after, the government reduced its health care expenditures. Tabitha lost her job as a nurse. When we first met in 2000, she had been unemployed for more than two years.

In some ways, Kevin's story of his father felt like a central piece to an intricate puzzle that I would never complete. No wonder Tabitha was so cautious, methodical, and guarded with information. She protected her secrets because she realized the damage they could cause. While she was alive, I respected her privacy and the knowledge that her life was very different from mine. She had no obligation to tell me about the nightmares of her past, or even her HIV-positive status.

"Nobody could have known I was facing difficulties," Tabitha once told me, "but I personally knew it was a hard life."

Tabitha was my partner and colleague, my mentor and guide, and I loved her like a mother. The fuller picture of her life made our work at CFK all the more relevant and urgent. She was the model, and she was always the first to make the point that she was not exceptional. There were other Tabithas in Kibera, and in slums and war-torn areas world-wide. The future Tabithas were among the five thousand members of our youth sports program. They were meeting every Sunday at our Binti Pamoja Girls' Center to fight for women's rights. They were creating sustainable businesses in our waste-management program and working at the Tabitha Clinic. They were the next generation of leaders, groomed by CFK and inspired by the life of Tabitha Atieno Festo.

TABITHA'S FINAL WORDS to me were barely audible. She had looked me in the eyes and recited something. It was a passage. But her voice was so soft and pain stricken that I had only caught three words of it: *grass, flower,* and *wind.*

For years I carried these three words with me as an unsolved riddle. During the week of Veterans Day in November 2008, near the fourth anniversary of Tabitha's passing, I attended a service at Harvard's Memorial Church. I was a student again, and I loved listening to the witty, engaging sermons of the Reverend Peter Gomes. He was a masterful orator. That day, however, I didn't hear a word he said. I sat in the pew paralyzed by the psalm before the day's sermon:

> *As for mortals, their days are like grass;*
>   *they flourish like a flower of the field;*
> *For the wind passes over it, and it is gone,*
>   *and its place knows it no more.*
> *But the steadfast love of the Lord is from*
>   *everlasting to everlasting.*

Epilogue

ALL OF MY PEERS who left active duty spoke about the shock of losing leadership responsibility. Few other jobs in the world placed so much onto the shoulders of young men and women as the Marine Corps in combat. In addition to the loss of leadership, it was jarring to be cut out of the flow of information about the war and our former units, many of which felt like extended families.

Although I struggled with adjustment, I was lucky to be in a good place at Harvard's Kennedy School of Government, where I began the first of my three years of graduate school. The school had an impressive convening power. Any given day featured multiple guest lectures by decision-makers, from generals to cabinet members, senators, ambassadors, and foreign dignitaries. Some of these lectures were large, though many were held in small rooms with off-the-record discussions. It was heady stuff.

The topics that we discussed were strategic and geopolitical. Few of our speakers had any exposure to what was happening on the ground in places such as Fallujah or Kibera. Through these interactions in my first month in Cambridge, I realized that I could make contributions based on my experiences. My mentor from UNC, Professor Kohn, encouraged me to write. In his opinion, knowledge rarely came from experience without

periods of intense, prolonged study, and writing was one of the best ways
to force serious reflection. His comment made sense. The past six years
felt like a prolonged blizzard. I had thousands of observations, powerful
emotions, and few conclusions.

Professor Kohn connected me to his colleague Ernest May. A member
of Harvard's faculty for a monumental fifty-three years, Professor May
graciously took me under his wing. He was a man of few spoken words,
and his advice was simple: "Just write. Write while it is still fresh and
relevant, and while you have the time." Over the next year, my writing
ballooned into a 150-page manuscript, an article for a military professional journal, and written testimony about the debacle of our detention
process and prisons to the Iraq Study Group, a bi-partisan commission
that Congress appointed when public opinion about the war was particularly low.

It was a monkish period of my life. I needed space and silence to sort
things out. During the weekends, I drove to New Haven, where Tracy
was finishing her postdoctoral fellowship at the Yale Child Study Center.
On Saturdays, we turned to wedding planning.

That previous summer, shortly after I had returned from Iraq, Tracy
and I had taken a two-week vacation to Morocco. Mike called me on a
satellite phone from Baghdad a day before we flew to Casablanca. Unfortunately, his flight out of Iraq was canceled due to a military operation.
Without Mike, we couldn't hold a traditional Moroccan engagement
ceremony at his mother's home. It was a Marine Corps "improvise, adapt,
and overcome" moment. Two days later, on a balcony overlooking a sunset over the ocean in a town called Essaouira, of which neither of us had
ever heard but instantly loved, I proposed.

Tracy and I had been a couple for five years before we were engaged.
We had buried grandparents together and helped each other fulfill parts
of our childhood dreams. She supported me through three long deployments and put up with my camper, Caravan, and cleaning habits, which
included washing dishes without soap. I was ready for her two cats, even
though they didn't like me. Tracy promised to let me keep what she
called my "wall of man"—a collection of fighting knives from around the
world—even though she loathed it. We understood each other better
than anyone else, and I couldn't imagine living without her.

Nevertheless, our marriage couldn't have happened if I hadn't changed.

The closer I aged toward thirty, the less I believed my childhood premonition by the pond would come true, and it wasn't simply because of time passing. Something deep within me had shifted. I had gone to Kibera and sought combat for many reasons, from a desire to serve and make a difference to a quest to prove myself and something else that I had never admitted to others or come to terms with myself. That something was a curiosity about evil and a fixation with death, particularly my own death. I wanted to die doing something intense and memorable, a blaze of glory in a righteous battle, and I wanted it badly enough that I took risks that many would view as extreme. Along the way, I fell in love, and over many years, and having survived combat, I changed—not completely, but enough to realize an essential selfishness within what I had long viewed as sacrificial and, at times, close to divine. It was love, and Tracy was a part of it, the largest part, and that's why I needed to marry her. But there were others too, other giants: Tabitha and Salim, my parents, my mentors, and Kibera. These were the forces that showed me the way.

TRACY AND I weren't planning to have a large wedding. We were saddled with debt and didn't mind doing something low-key with our closest friends and family. Since we had met in Chapel Hill and Tracy's family was all in North Carolina, our alma mater was the obvious choice as the place to hold the special day.

Sometime during the fall we traveled back to Chapel Hill for a CFK meeting. My mentor Jim Peacock and his wife, Florence, let us stay at their elegant Southern home where we had held our first major CFK fundraiser. During the day, I spent time with our board of directors while Tracy searched for wedding venues. One evening we joined Jim and Florence outside in the garden behind their house. We were talking with them about Morocco when Florence surprised us and offered to host our wedding at her home. Thrilled by their incredibly generous offer, we immediately accepted. Florence loved hosting special events for her friends and family, and the setting felt perfect. As far as guests were concerned, she and Jim encouraged us to "fill the garden." We changed our plans and invited hundreds of family and friends.

THE YEAR PASSED quickly, and soon enough we were standing on the porch overlooking our family and friends gathered in the Peacocks' garden. It was a hot July evening. Many of the guests were using the hand fans Florence had added to the welcome basket of favors. Although summer storms were crackling across the state, there was a pocket of clear sky above Chapel Hill.

Nate, who was studying to become a physician's assistant, stood by my side. He would later begin his best man's speech with "Ladies and gentlemen, this isn't the first time today that I've stood up from a warm seat with white paper in my hand." Our parents and surviving grandparents were in the front row as the writer Andy Carroll, one of my groomsmen, read part of a letter I had written to Tracy from Iraq, and Jim Peacock read excerpts from the Bible's Song of Solomon and Ecclesiastes 3.

Seeing everyone gathered brought back strong memories from my two worlds. My Marine mentors and brothers showed up in force. Colonel Greenwood was there. The colonel and I had reunited in Fallujah, when he was leading the training of Iraqi security forces for the Marine Corps. After thirty years of service, he was about to retire and teach at Georgetown University. Captain Mike Dubrule had arrived from Virginia Beach with his family and commented that our wedding looked like a United Nations gathering. Soon he would again deploy to Afghanistan, as would my friend and first Marine mentee Lieutenant Peter Dixon, whose adopted dog from Kibera, Rafiki, had since passed away at his family's home in northern California. Sergeant David Thompson, who was working as an instructor in a counterintelligence course for another government agency, drove down from Washington, D.C. After our Bosnia deployment, Sergeant Thompson had served with distinction in Afghanistan and Iraq. Unfortunately, my friend and final company commander, Joe Burke, had a military obligation that prevented him from joining us. His second deployment to Iraq as company commander that year was difficult. Three of our Marines were killed by IEDs.

Salim joined us from Kibera and brought greetings from our team on the ground. He spent most of the evening with his mentor Dr. Mary Ann Burris, the former Ford Foundation program officer who had since started her own organization to promote indigenous culture and health based in Nairobi. Kim Chapman had been recently married and joined us with her husband, a fellow Tar Heel. They were expecting their first child. Soon,

Kim would transition to being a regular board member and hand over the chair position to Jennifer Coffman. Jennifer had arrived from James Madison University with her family. She was teaching anthropology and ran a top-notch study abroad program in Kenya. The first donor I had ever asked directly for support, Alston Gardner, was there, as was Ted Lord, who nine years earlier had inspired me in Swahili class with his advice, "reach out to a bunch of people and eventually a few will give a damn." Ted was finishing his medical degree at Harvard.

Hundreds of other special people were with us that day in person and in spirit as we said our vows. They were all great people, people of integrity and upstanding character, and, in the end, that was what mattered most. It's what matters in life, regardless of one's pursuit. It's what made CFK possible.

AFTER A SHORT honeymoon, Tracy moved to my small apartment in Cambridge and started a psychology fellowship at Children's Hospital Boston, while I began my first year at Harvard Business School. The time we had together during the evenings and weekends was wonderful, though there was far less of it than either of us had expected. Life's pace was once again frenetic, and I struggled to keep up with CFK, friends, family, and the most demanding academic course load I had ever faced. Additionally, I was searching for work in renewable energy, an industry that appealed to me because it was relatively new and had wide-ranging social and economic ramifications. Tracy had always been supportive of CFK, but we both knew that we would need to find a new balance in our life together.

The tension came to a head in late December 2007. We had been living together for five months, and I was planning on returning to Kibera for two weeks during winter break with Dr. Melanie Walker, a senior program officer from the Bill and Melinda Gates Foundation, and Jennifer Coffman. Tracy didn't like that I would be away for such an extended time, but she accepted it because she knew how important the visit would be for CFK. It was our first serious opportunity for funding from the Gates Foundation since Melinda Gates had visited Kibera nearly a year and a half earlier. We had invested a lot of time and effort cultivating the relationship.

On December 27 Kenya held a presidential election. The incumbent

Mwai Kibaki, a Kikuyu, appeared to be trailing the lead opposition candidate, Kibera's very own member of Parliament, Raila Odinga, when the election was abruptly declared to be over and Kibaki was sworn back into office in a private ceremony. Five years earlier, at the end of 2002, Salim and I had been at Kibaki's swearing in ceremony in Uhuru Park. Fueled by Kibaki's strong anticorruption rhetoric, expectations had soared across the country. In the five years that had passed, however, little had changed. Kenya consistently ranked among the world's most corrupt nations.

Kenyans were fed up heading into the 2007 election, and the apparent rigging of the results by Kibaki and his henchmen sparked violence. Kibera, an ethnic faultline with a history of clashes, was among the first places to erupt.

Our clinic remained open to assist hundreds of victims needing emergency care. I held on to my plane ticket as the initial news unfolded. Each time I spoke to Salim the situation sounded worse. Dozens of Kikuyus had been killed by roving bands of Luo men called "youthwingers." There was talk of retaliation by an underground Kikuyu gang called Mungiki. Dr. Walker at the Gates Foundation called the day before we were scheduled to leave and canceled her visit. It was the right thing to do, but I wasn't sure whether we would ever have another opportunity to showcase our work. Of course, that was only part of the reason I held on to my ticket. It all came out at dinner that night with Tracy.

"So you've canceled your flight, right?" she asked matter-of-factly.

"Not yet, babe."

"Well, what are you waiting for?"

"I don't know." I wanted to be with Salim and our team, helping people, defending CFK, moving to the sound of guns.

"What's going on?" she asked.

I tried to explain it honestly. I apologized.

"So you're not going?"

"I don't know."

"Babe." She raised her voice, "No."

"But—"

"No, don't do this." Silent tears streamed down her face.

I was no longer a roving soldier gambling my life with high-risk missions in hopes of big-impact paydays. This change was excruciating. The only reason it happened was that I eventually felt a greater pull toward a future with Tracy's love and support of peaceful work than to a past holding my father's grenade. My responsibilities in life were changing. They weren't greater or more important; they weren't smaller or less significant either. They were just different, and I was still figuring out and coming to terms with what that all meant.

THREE MONTHS LATER, after the violence had subsided and with Tracy's blessing, I returned to Kibera for spring break. A charcoal odor overpowered the typical pit-latrine stench as I reentered the slum. Stands that had once bustled with hawkers at the *matatu* minibus stage had been reduced to ashes on the sidewalk. The stained-glass windows on the church above Kibera were shattered. Its steeple was charred.

More than fifteen hundred Kenyans had died in the clashes by the time the former United Nations secretary-general Kofi Annan and a team of mediators managed to cobble together a fragile power-sharing agreement. That agreement created the position of prime minister for Raila Odinga and left Mwai Kibaki with the crown jewel, the highly centralized and powerful office of the Kenyan presidency. No one viewed it as a lasting solution.

The specific circumstances that had led to the 2008 postelection violence were superficially different from the events behind the clashes of 1995 and 2001 in Kibera that Kassim and other sources-turned-friends had dissected for me when I was a college student. The root causes, however, were the same, and they had little to do with ethnicity. They were political and economic. Real and imagined differences were manipulated to control resources from land-tenure rights in Kibera to the Kenyan national-security budget, an area that was particularly rotten with self-enrichment. As time passed, ethnic polarization seeped into the root causes and fed them like rainwater.

The 1995 and 2001 clashes in Kenya were largely contained within Kibera and a few other pockets of violence. In 2008, however, the fighting exploded with a depth and breadth that was unprecedented in Kenyan history. It took everyone by surprise. Hundreds of thousands of Kenyans were displaced, and the nation became more torn by ethnic differences than it had ever been before. Difficult conversations between warring ethnic groups needed to happen. If they didn't, the tensions would be bottled up, and that would mean that the next outbreak of violence could take Kenya beyond the brink of civil war.

CFK WAS CONVENING some of these difficult conversations in Kibera. Abdul "Cantar" Hussein met me at the mud-hill pulpit near Kibera's entrance to lead me to a peace forum the morning after I arrived. Cantar was a friend of my initial point of contact to the Nubian youth community, Ali Khamis Alijab, who was now an Arabic teacher at a local mosque. Quiet and patient, Cantar had attended the first focus group discussion that Nate and I held on a dirt field overlooking Kibera in the summer of 2001.

Cantar found his voice and became a leader in CFK. After our youth-representative revolt in 2003, he was the only one of the fourteen representatives who hadn't demanded to be paid for his volunteer service with CFK, and soon afterward he was hired as CFK's first sports program officer. About half of the other fourteen representatives eventually came back to CFK as volunteers, while many of the others became leaders in other organizations. Together and with hundreds of volunteers and a dozen staff members, Salim, Cantar, Binti Pamoja's Carolina Sakwa, Tabitha, and Jane had built an organization that was more than a sports association, girls' center, waste-management program, and large health clinic. They created a holistic leadership program that was owned by the community and created opportunities for more than five thousand young people each year.

The peace forum we attended that morning was part of a reconciliation campaign funded largely by Pam Omidyar's organization Humanity United. CFK mobilized youth from different ethnic groups, some of whom had participated in the fighting, and used drama and community meetings to confront the stereotypes behind the violence. The forum brought me back in contact with Rashid Seif, the captain of the winning team during CFK's first soccer tournament. Since then Rashid had helped launch a community self-help group to create a sustainable waste-management business in collaboration with our Trash Is Cash program. I also reconnected with John Adoli, a leader in our sports program who had protected a young Kikuyu boy after thugs had torched the boy's shack and chased his parents away. John, a Luo, gave this boy shelter in his own ten-by-ten even though that action jeopardized his own security. Fatuma Roba was also at the forum that morning. When I had first met

Fatuma through our Binti Pamoja Girls' Center years earlier, she was too shy to speak with me. During the ethnic violence, Fatuma covered the events in Kibera for the United Nations as a paid reporter. She would go on to create an aid organization for women who were victims of rape and war in Sudan.

LATER THAT MORNING I left the CFK peace forum to meet Salim at the new clinic. The route to the clinic was so familiar that I strolled it casually. I passed the old Mad Lion Base, which had mysteriously gone out of business shortly before Tabitha had passed away. The face of the lion with its fiery eyes was still spray pointed on the forest green wall. When I approached the alleyway that led to my old shack, I thought of Dan, who had since married and moved to Fort Jesus after cofounding a successful AIDS relief program with an American medical doctor. Passing the Mugumeno Motherland Hotel, I poked my head in and greeted the tough matron with the gap in her top row of teeth. She smiled and greeted me, "Where have you been lost, Omosh?" My favorite bumper sticker was still posted to the thin tin wall: OUR CUSTOMERS ARE SPECIAL, SERVICE IS FREE.

Across the dirt alley from the Mugumeno there was a community toilet donated by the crew of the Hollywood film *The Constant Gardener*. It was a modest and worthwhile contribution. The construction of community toilets had in recent years reduced the number of flying toilets clogging the sumps, river, and Nairobi Dam. Nearby, however, a gaunt dog slurped in a sump of sewage, and a small boy was defecating onto a sheet of paper. The dog and the boy reminded me of Tracy's reaction after her first day in Kibera years earlier. "I know there's hope and what you're doing is important," she had said. "You want to show the good side to these places, too. But to live in such conditions would be like hell to me."

I was thinking about Tracy's comment in light of what we had accomplished over the years and how much more there was to do when I recognized a water vendor named Owiti. He was one of Kash's best friends. We had worked out together once many years ago in Kash's gym. Veins protruded from his thick neck. He recognized me with a nod. We hadn't spoken since Kash had been expelled from CFK in 2002.

"*Vipi, Owiti*," I greeted him.

He didn't respond. When I stepped closer, I noticed his glare was fixed on something behind me. Suddenly, he leaped from his stand and collided with a body. I spun around, hands raised to defend myself.

Owiti hovered over a thin man with wild eyes. A rusty, scrap-metal bar hung out of the sleeve of the man's coat. Owiti swung his leg like a sweeper clearing a soccer ball downfield. He drilled his foot into the man's gut.

"No, no!" the man pleaded, holding his hands above his head as Owiti wound up for another kick. There was a cracking sound. The man wheezed and spit up blood.

"*Mwizi,*" Owiti said flatly, turning to me. "Thief."

I pointed to my chest. *Was I the target?*

Owiti nodded and returned to his business. A woman was waiting for him to fill her jerrycan with water.

An image of Kash came to my mind. Kash had helped keep Nate and me safe when we launched CFK. He had put out the word to his friends to watch our backs. Without him, we would almost certainly have been attacked.

I believe that Owiti the water vendor didn't protect me because of CFK. He didn't come to my aid because of who I was or what I had done for his community. He intervened in a burst of violence for Kash, his friend, a friend so close he was family. And in Kibera, and in the Marines, and in most if not all dangerous places in the world, family meant everything.

SALIM MET ME at the entrance to the new clinic along the route where Tabitha had first spotted me during our second summer. Strands of rusty rebar jutted toward the cloudless sky. A thick stone wall surrounded the three-story foundation, where a half dozen workers, all of whom were residents of Kibera, labored. It was my first time at the construction site since the tour with Congressman Price, when it had been nothing but an empty plot of dirt the size of an average American house.

The clinic that we were building would be like nothing else in Kibera. It would provide high-quality health care with medical doctors, a full laboratory, nurses from the community, and an X-ray room. It had taken four years, hundreds of community forums, donor letters, meetings, and calls to hammer through government bureaucracy that seemed to always stand in the way of doing the right thing. But we wouldn't be stopped, and it wasn't just Salim and me. It was Kim and the rest of the board back in the States and dozens of Kenyan and American volunteers and staff pouring their lives into it.

"What's up, mista?" Salim greeted me with a fist bump. He was wearing a stethoscope over his T-shirt.

"What's this, *daktari*?" I tapped the silver coin at the end of the stethoscope. "*Daktari* Mohamed."

"Our first donation to the new Tabitha Clinic. What do you think?"

"Incredible. You're a developer. Look at this place!"

Salim rolled his eyes. "Man, don't even tell me about it." The clinic construction had grown from a $75,000 project in 2004 after our $26,000 donation from the musician Sarah McLachlan to a full-service, $350,000 health care facility designed free of charge by one of Kenya's top architects.

Salim inspected the work at the construction site. He handled a brief negotiation with the foreman, a hefty man who was nearly twice his size and age. We walked up a flight of stairs to the second story and stood on what would become a balcony overlooking a stretch of Kibera.

"I make this trip two to three times a day," Salim said.

"Keeps you in great shape. You're lookin' good."

"Yeah, I don't have to go running anymore. But actually I like it. It keeps me close to the community."

"Awesome to see the progress."

"It is, but it's killing me." Never one to trust quickly, Salim retained full control over the construction, and it had worn him down.

"You know, it's amazing you've made it this long," I said.

"What do you mean?"

"You've been doing this for a long time. You've been with CFK when we were broke, through the youth rep revolt, clashes, all this. Seven years, man. Most people couldn't last a week in your job. The best maybe make it a couple of years before burnin' out." There were the death threats, too. I didn't mention them because they were still a source of major stress. Salim had received more than seven credible threats to his life since we had started.

"You know, my brother, what we do, it's not work," Salim said. "It's not a job. But even still, you're right. I need a break."

"So what do you think?"

"I don't know." Salim was too busy thinking about others to make plans for himself.

"Maybe more school, that Manchester program?" We spoke about additional education often. Salim wanted to attend college, but he couldn't fathom taking three to four years off work to pursue a degree. The only program that looked as if it might work was a unique master's degree in social development at the University of Manchester in the United Kingdom, where occasionally social entrepreneurs from the developing world were accepted without an undergraduate degree. It was an ideal fit for Salim if he could get accepted and raise enough money to cover his tuition and fees.

"I'd really like that."

"You can do it, man, and I'll help. It'll be tough for CFK to see you go." We could never replace Salim as our executive director. But we would try when he was ready for the next challenge.

"Don't worry. Me, I'll always be with CFK. It'll always be a part of me. You too, isn't it?"

"No doubt."

Salim laughed as he remembered the first time we met: "You came into my office at MYSA, and, man, you were so dirty, mud all over your pants, those boots. I mean, who wears the same outfit every day? No one, not even the street kids."

I laughed with him and imagined myself walking into his office as a twenty-one-year-old. "Did I smell?"

"Not really. You were just funny-looking, and you had those candies."

"Creme Savers!"

"Yeah, they're horrible."

"You didn't take one when I offered, but you gave me your time."

"Mista, I had no choice. You wouldn't leave."

"Oh, come on, you liked some of it. I remember you said that great line about youth being the present and the future leaders. We even talked about doing something together in Kibera, and that was just our first meeting."

"You know, Rye," Salim corrected me, "I had so many conversations with people from the outside wanting to learn this and that. You can spend all your time with them but with no results."

"You didn't think you'd hear back from me?" I grinned as I said it, thinking of the thousands of hours he and I had talked since that day.

"Noooo. Are you kidding? You were just this guy. I mean, when you said you were a college student I was like, how is this guy going to get this money to establish such a thing? I just thought you were lost in the sauce."

"Lost in the sauce." I laughed. It was another phrase that I had adopted from the Marine Corps and brought to Kibera.

"You're still lost in the sauce," Salim teased me, pointing at my chest. "Just look at your shirt."

"You remember this shirt?" I was wearing the baby-blue, short-sleeve, button-down shirt Salim had given me in 2002 after I was jumped during the presidential inauguration.

"Of course, that's my shirt."

"Did that boy who jumped me ever join our soccer league?"

"Not really, but what we said to him, it was good. Maybe he learned something that day."

I looked down at the shirt. "I love this thing. It's perfect. Breathes easy, lots of pockets, Carolina blue. Why change if you have a good thing?"

"It doesn't look that good."

"Hey, you bought it."

"Well, it looks okay on me." Salim grinned.

"It's big on me. This thing would be like a dress on you."

"You're crazy."

"Hey," I said on a whim. "Let's check out the roof."

"What do you mean, go up on it?"

"Yeah, come on." I stepped over the balcony onto a ramp that led to the roof. Salim followed me. From on top we could see the expanse of Kibera, the brown salamander, an ocean of mud and rust strung with make-shift electric wires and dotted by blue gum trees and tin roofs shimmering in the sun.

"You remember that day? It was a crazy day," I recalled, returning to the memory of the 2002 inauguration, when Moi stepped down in what felt like the dawn of a new era. "There were such high expectations for Kibaki, the end of corruption, of tribalism. That's what people thought was coming."

"And it's only gotten worse," Salim sighed.

"Do you feel safe?"

"In Kenya?"

"In Kibera, I mean, as a Kikuyu and all?"

"You know, I don't really. But if I let that stop me, then I'm just making the tribalism worse, isn't it? It has to stop somewhere."

"It's stupid."

"What do you mean?"

"Nothing," I said, but I was thinking, *What are we really doing here? What if Salim is killed? How could our work ever justify such a loss?* They were the same type of thoughts that had haunted me when I sent my Marines out on missions.

Salim looked out over Kibera to the south toward the soccer field where we held our first focus group discussion and beyond it to the green hills of Nairobi National Park. "You know what I think?" he asked.

"What?"

"I think it's love."

"Love?"

"Yes, love. We need more love. Mama Fatuma taught me that at the Children's Home, my grandmother, too."

"Love, yeah, man, I hear you."

"That's what this is about." Salim tapped his foot against a clay tile.

"The clinic?"

"Yeah, during the violence, the thugs, they came here for it." Salim painted the scene. There, outside the front gate, a roving gang of a dozen men with machetes showed up to loot the construction site. It was late in the afternoon and many of them were drunk on bloodshed and moonshine, stumbling about as they pounded on the metal gate and tried to break in. The lock wasn't strong and wouldn't have held them back for long had the neighbors not heard the clamor and come out to investigate. The neighbors—men, women, grandparents, and children—formed a human wall and faced the thugs.

As Salim spoke, I imagined myself there, standing with the neighbors, facing the thugs who might attack and kill us all. I looked down to my hands for a weapon, but found nothing, no machete, no pistol, no hammer. Even my Spyderco was missing.

"What are you thinking about?" Salim asked.

"I wish I had been there, with them."

"No, that would not be good. This isn't your fight, not even mine. It's theirs, the community's. That's the only way. The community came because they knew the Tabitha Clinic is theirs."

I tried to visualize the community during the clashes. I saw Kibera burning and a band of residents outside the shell of our half-constructed clinic, rebar reaching toward the sky, shouts, chaos, a people facing machetes and making a stand. A human wall.

"That's it, isn't it? It's the community's," I said. "And Tabitha, she felt that way, too. Imagine if she were here with us now."

"But, Rye, she is."

I closed my eyes. The sun's rays felt warm and good against my face. Salim was right. I turned to him. "Before she passed, Tabitha said, 'Don't quit pushing this thing.' We won't quit."

"No, my brother, we won't." Salim placed his hand on my shoulder and looked into the community. There in the crisscrossing alleyways *mamas* balanced jerricans of water on their heads; children kicked soccer balls made of plastic bags and twine; and men hauled the bricks and mortar to what would become the largest clinic in Kibera. "We won't quit pushing because they won't."

Acknowledgments

A book, like a nongovernmental organization, takes a community, and this book would not have been possible without the steadfast love, help, and encouragement of my family, friends, and colleagues. My deepest gratitude goes to my wife, Tracy, who showed me the way with her strength and grace. I love you.

Philip Caputo once wrote that the challenge of memoir is to write well, straight, and true. I agree, and I endeavored here to present an accurate and honest portrayal of often chaotic events as I and others experienced them. Along the way I benefited tremendously from nostalgic conversations with friends, many of whom are "characters" in this book. I'm indebted to my father and the writer Andrew Carroll for repeatedly encouraging me to keep a journal. My journals, as well as countless hours of film coverage that producer, friend, and CFK volunteer-extraordinaire Beth-Ann Kutchma coordinated over the years, were invaluable.

The following people believed in this book before there was a "there there." These friends and mentors helped me shape the proposal and find a way into the publishing industry: Max Anderson, Aaron Charlop-Powers, Dr. Al Chase, Professor Bill George, Professor David Gergen, Colonel Thomas Greenwood, Linda Harrar, Michael Kleinman, Professor Richard Kohn, Professor Ernest May, Tom Rielly and the TED community, Jack Sallay, Second Lieutenant Nicholas Taranto, and authors Bruce Barcott, Rod Beckstrom, Andrew Carroll, Claire Dederer, Nathaniel Fick, George Harrar, Michael Holman, Bryan Mealer, Glenn Rifkin, and Michela Wrong.

A tremendous thanks to my squad of readers who stuck with this through multiple drafts: Tracy Barcott, Yaniv Barzilai, Tyson Belanger, Aaron Charlop-Powers, Professor Jennifer Coffman, Captain Brad Fultz, Linda and George Harrar, Beth-Ann Kutchma, Salim Mohamed, Nathan Nelson, Jonathan Reiber, and my parents T. P. and Donna Schwartz-Barcott.

A mentor of mine suggested that I reach out early to a broad base of advanced readers. I'm glad I followed that sage advice. Each reader made this a better book by revealing new insights and valuable interpretations. To my advanced readers, thank you for your time and candor: Yaw Agyenim-Boateng, Ryan Allis, Jason Arthurs, Jane Atieno, Karen Austrian, David Baker, Leann Bankoski, James and Mary Barcott, Alison Beckwith, Jason Berg, Peter Bisanz, Beth Braxton, Captain Jason Brigadier, Betsy Brink, Matthew Bugher, Diana Bullington, Heather Burke, Major Joe Burke, Anthony Burton, Dr. David Callaway, Andrew Carroll, Canon Chris Chivers, Annie Clark, Zach Clayton, Mary Louise Cohen, Mark Derewicz, Kate Di Pietro, Betsy Dixon, Matt Dougherty, Deborah Dubrule, Diane Frazier, Amit Garg, Melanie Gerber, Professor Hannah Gill, Sammy Iregi Gitau, Judy Gration, Eli Griffis, William Grumbles, Lynda Goldberg, Blake Hall, Tripp Hardy, Roger Dean Huffstetler, Abdul "Cantar" Hussein, Taylor Jo Isenberg, B. Jamison, Semaj Johnson, Judith Kaufmann, Alex Kehl, Danielle Kehl, Gil Kemp, George Kogolla, Professor Richard Kohn, Lynne Kohn, Carin Krasno, Major Jason Ladd, Michael and Christine Lee, Peter Levesque, Donald Lichay, Lieutenant Tyler Lippert, Alex Loizias, Carrie Majer, Erin Marubashi, William and Sara McCoy, Laura McCready, Professor Kathleen McGinn, William McKinney, Esteban and Dana McMahan, Professor Eric Mlyn, Ambassador George Moose, Ben Mshila, Lisa Mullins, Mary Jo Myers, Joseph Nganga, Kevin Festo Odongo, Dorine Okoko, Michelle Osborn, Lisa Price, Dr. Mary Rowe, Barbara Ryan, Professor John Sanders, Nancy Serrurier, Captain David Stapleton, Professor Niklaus Steiner and the UNC Center for Global Initiatives team, Doc Skelly, Christian Sutherland-Wong, Professor Nancy Tewksbury, Chris Tomlinson, Ian Thomson, Shawn Turner, Emily Verellen, Kate Wattson, and Aleta Williams.

Thanks, too, to the following people who helped along the way in other ways: Jackie and Mike Bezos, Shantha Bloeman, Sam Bond, Brett Bullington, Donovan Campbell, Ronica Cleary, Dr. Alan Cross, William Grumbles, Donald Dixon, Captain Peter Dixon, Thomas S. Kenan III, Jason

Kutchma, Jane Kilonzo, Barb Lee, Susan Linnee, Wes Moore, Craig Mullaney, Randy Newcomb, Peter Olson, Pam Omidyar, Kim Chapman Page, Matt Pottinger, Bradley Inman, Ginger Sall, Lara Santoro, Sophie Schmidt, and Jean Woodward.

Photographers Francesco Broli (cover photo) and Jason Arthurs, and graphic designer Lindy Dobbins, generously gave their extraordinary work. Beth-Ann Kutchma created the book's superb Web site and trailer. Her husband, Jason "J-Kutch" Kutchma, wrote and recorded the kick arse song "Arms Around the World" for the trailer. Ladye Jane Vickers went above and beyond the call organizing and executing the twenty-six city tour for the hardcover release. Roberta Bowman, Jim and M. A. Rogers, and many other colleagues at Duke Energy gave their time and good ideas to make our book launch a success.

To my publisher, Bloomsbury, thank you for the opportunity to realize a dream. I will be forever indebted to Anton Mueller, a brilliant "old school" editor and new friend. Production editor Nathaniel Knaebel went far above and beyond the call of duty. Copy Editor Steve Boldt was so good he caught typos in Swahili. Assistant editor Rachel Mannheimer's attention to detail and hard work consistently improved the book, and Publisher George Gibson offered valuable input at pivotal moments. Founder and CEO Nigel Newton generously gave his time. My agent Heather Schroder at ICM is a tireless confidante and font of great ideas. Her assistant Nicole Tourtelot also has a keen literary eye and will one day be a great agent in her own right, if she so chooses. I'm lucky to have worked with such professionals.

Large chunks of the initial manuscript were written in four places, each of which was overly generous with their hospitality: High Rise Bakery on Concord Avenue in Cambridge, Owen's Bagel & Deli in Charlotte's South End, Caffe Driade in Chapel Hill, and Nairobi's Java House at Adams Arcade.

Lastly, thanks to Ken Okoth, the Bezos Scholars, the students of Carrboro High School and their teacher Matt Cone, Tyson Belanger, and Caroline Scott for helping to create three engaging study guides.

THE END OF this book is not the end of our story. Twenty-six percent of proceeds from sales of this book go to CFK. The hardcover price was listed at $26. It's the same amount of money that Tabitha took to begin creating what's now the Tabitha Clinic, where more than forty thousand residents each year receive care from a staff of dedicated Kenyan doctors and nurses in the heart of Kibera not far from Dan's shack, the old Mad Lion, and the river.

In 2011, CFK proudly celebrated its tenth anniversary. We marked this happy milestone with the release of this book and the creation of a feature-length documentary produced by Beth-Ann Kutchma and directed by Jason Arthurs. As we pause to reflect on our past accomplishments, our eyes remain fixed on the future. There are Tabithas and Salims in every struggling community, and with them those of us born in more privileged places can multiply our impact, and learn a lot, too. The future of fighting poverty and preventing violence lies in the hands of those who experience it every day. That's the essence of participatory development. With long-term investment in local leadership, communities will transform themselves.

We thank you for helping our cause, and we invite you to do more. If reading this story has meant something to you, please consider taking action. Help us spread the word about CFK and this book, and take the twenty-six day challenge at www.thepowerof26.org.

Rye Barcott
Charlotte, North Carolina

Questions for Discussion

26 Questions for Military Readers and Families

26 Questions for Book Clubs

26 Questions for Students

26 Questions for Military Readers and Families

"Captain Belanger, report to Colonel Greenwood."

It was early summer 2006 and near the end of my fifth deployment as a Marine officer. During that tour, I had helped develop Iraq's local police forces in Anbar Province. Upon my return home, I planned to leave active service and begin a Ph.D. at Harvard University. I felt a duty to investigate how democracies should mix "carrot and stick" strategies to improve war outcomes. When I met with Colonel Greenwood, he thanked me for serving on his staff, expressed interest in my research, and urged me to stay in touch. He also said he hoped to introduce me to a remarkable former Marine intelligence officer named Rye Barcott. Three months into my school year, and before Colonel Greenwood had a chance, another mutual Marine friend, Nathaniel Fick, introduced us.

Rye amazed me. Personally, I had always felt inclined to do just one thing at a time. It was hard for me to imagine how good service happened any other way. That was before I met Rye. Somehow, Rye balanced many lives and lived them all well. When we swapped stories about being Marines, his diverse service experiences in Bosnia, Djibouti, and Iraq impressed me. Later, I met Tracy. She is exactly as gracious, kind, and "angelic" as Rye describes. I was in awe of how Tracy and Rye's strong love had overcome so much for so long. Then, in 2008, I visited Kenya and had a chance to learn more about Rye's life with Carolina for Kibera. Local members of the CFK team inspired me with their self-confidence. The new Tabitha clinic hummed with activity. CFK's interethnic soccer teams thrived. I felt proud to know Rye, and I wanted to help. So when he asked if I could read drafts for this book, I jumped at the opportunity.

We should embrace brave souls who serve and then share their personal stories. They give America and the world a triple gift: their deeds, their writing, and the deeds they inspire. Rye's writing opened deep conversations between us, and he welcomed my views even when we saw things differently. As he prepared the book's paperback version, he asked me to join him in posing military-related questions for readers. The idea was to help readers reflect on the book and relate it to their own lives. Here are twenty-six of our best questions.

—Tyson Belanger
Cambridge, Massachusetts

1. Rye felt influenced by many books about human security, military service, and strategy. Which ones affected him the most and how? Which books have meant the most to you? Are books more or less important today than they were in the past?

2. About 8 percent of Americans have served in the military. How did Rye's father feel about his service as a Marine in Vietnam, and how did his example affect Rye? Do you know someone who served in the military, and have you spoken with them about their experiences?

3. About 2.3 million men and women now serve in the active and reserve components of the U.S. military. What is the mission of the Marine Corps? How does the U.S. military support and defend American democracy? How has 9/11 affected the military's duties?

4. The Marine Corps has three official values: honor, courage, and commitment. What are some of the unofficial values of the Marine Corps? Have you ever been a member of a group with strong values? What is it like to be part of a cohesive family, team, tribe, or community?

5. Since 1973, the U.S. has had an all-volunteer military. Tabitha described Rye as a "guardian," and Rye saw her as one (150). Why did Rye volunteer to join the military? How do people with a guardian ethos serve others? Are there other kinds of service ethos?

6. Rye's Reserve Officers Training Corps scholarship application asked him to describe himself with one word, and he wrote, "Determined" (30). What personal qualities make a good prospective Marine officer? If you were to describe yourself in one word, what word would you use?

7. Colin Powell believed, "Perpetual optimism is a force multiplier" (230). How important was optimism and confidence to Rye in becoming a Marine and succeeding during his deployments? Has optimism ever harmed your ability to overcome a challenge?

8. What is the mission of human intelligence? What skills help people persuade other people to share information? What did Rye think of torture? Do you agree that it can be counterproductive for American values and interests?

9. Describe Rye's relationship with his enlisted Marines. How might this be similar or different from officer and enlisted relationships in other military occupations within the Marine Corps and in other branches of service?

10. Are you surprised that Marine commanders granted Rye permission to go to Kibera? To what degree should the Marine Corps support a Marine pursuing an initiative like CFK while on active duty? Would where you work now support you if you proposed to journey to Kibera?

11. What is participatory development? How does it compare with the economic-development operations Rye supported as a Marine in Ethiopia? How is participatory development compatible or not compatible with military interventions and operations?

12. Can we compare Rye's service and risks in the Marines with his service and risks in Kibera? How did Rye diffuse dangers and help resolve conflict in Kibera? Would these techniques have succeeded in Bosnia, Djibouti, and Iraq?

13. Marines in combat have responsibilities for using lawful force and enduring mortal danger. In what ways was Rye eager and not eager for combat? How do you believe others in the military approach these difficult responsibilities?

14. Rye earned the Defense Meritorious Service Medal in Bosnia, a highly esteemed award, and still he felt he did not yet done his part until he served in

Iraq. What was Rye searching for in Iraq? What does it mean to "see the elephant" and what is the attraction to seeing it (253)?

15. Rye said that, when he was younger, his greatest fear was living an ordinary life. How did Rye respond to risk and danger? Have you ever experienced a situation in which you could have died because you did something risky for the sake of making a difference?

16. Dangerous and stressful circumstances often push people to do what they might not otherwise do. When does Rye ask what he would have done if he was in someone else's place? How much do you believe people's morality and behavior depends on their circumstances?

17. Rye agreed with the core principles supporting the "three-block war" (183) and General James "Warrior Monk" Mattis's counterinsurgency strategy (265). What were the key components of each? For Rye, what was most difficult about implementing these strategies, especially as an intelligence officer in Iraq?

18. Rye had a lot of respect for Kael Weston. Who was he and why did Rye respect him? What should the role of the State Department be during counterinsurgencies? How can diplomacy and development overcome the challenges of local instability and corruption?

19. Colonel Greenwood said Marine operations suffered when they lacked continuity (245). When did Rye encounter discontinuity, and what did he say about the benefit of rotating Marines? Have you seen failures of continuity in groups, organizations, or businesses you have been in?

20. Rye's father described his service in Vietnam with the phrase, "Uncertainty abounded" (286). How does uncertainty affect the way service members feel about their sacrifices? How important is it for people to know and feel, with certainty, that their efforts were worthwhile?

21. Did Rye initially support the Iraq war? Whose testimony changed his mind? Why did he ultimately oppose it? In Rye's experience, did Marines talk much about politics? How much does it matter whether people agree with the policies and causes that they implement?

22. Rye concluded that, if he had not changed, he could not have married Tracy. How did he change? Could you ever see yourself marrying someone in the military? If you are married to a member of the military, how have you overcome the challenges of being a military spouse?

23. Compare the responsibilities of being a Marine, leading a nonprofit, graduating from college, and starting a family. Which is harder to begin? Which is harder to do well? Which is harder to complete? How might someone's experience in one affect his or her efforts in the others?

24. Marines say, "Once a Marine, always a Marine." Why did Rye ultimately leave the Marine Corps? Why did Captain Joe Burke prefer to stay in? What does it mean to be a Marine veteran? When did Rye receive mentorship or assistance from Marine veterans?

25. The dedication to the book reads, *"Talent is universal; opportunity is not."* How did the Marine Corps connect Rye's talents with opportunities he might not otherwise have had? Could military service connect your talents with opportunities? If so, how? If not, why?

26. *"Harambee"* is a Kenyan motto that means "we all pull together" (142). Some translate the Marine phrase "gung ho" as "work together." Have you ever "pulled together" with people outside your family? Do you think we as a society pull together more or less today than in the past?

26 Questions for Book Clubs

Book clubs come in many guises and sizes. They can be anything from a gathering of neighbors to a Skype group across the globe. Whatever their makeup, book clubs inspire, inform, and have fun. In rare cases—when the chemistry between book and club strikes a special chord—the discussion can translate to deep reflection and then action. *It Happened on the Way to War* is a book that sings, and I hope this study guide helps make that chemistry possible for you and your club.

On a more personal note, the book affected me deeply in three significant ways. First, it made me more aware of the impact sports have had on my own life . . . Not only have I met many friends through playing sports, but I have also cemented life-long friendships on the bleachers while watching my children participate in their athletic events. I have visited many countries around the world, and even in the most disadvantaged countries children can be seen playing some kind of pick-up game with nothing more than the resemblance of a ball. Sports transcends race. They can inspire teamwork, instill discipline, promote health, and, of course, create friendships. I would love to see this book act a catalyst to promote sports in other communities, especially where there is unrest, unemployment, and a large youth demographic.

Secondly, this book has given me an appreciation of the lives of Marines. We hear about them and see them and admire them, but this book underscored the challenges and even ambivalence many of our servicemen and women face. The military is not a vacuum. It's a complex organization filled with diversity and talent. I am humbled by the dedication and service of our veterans.

Finally, this book emphasizes the power of the human spirit. Most of the people of Kibera own virtually nothing. But some of them have been able to rise above their circumstances and achieve greatness. It is heartwarming to read about the good people of Kibera, and it reminds me that material things are not nearly as important as we tend to think they are.

—Caroline Scott
Chapel Hill, North Carolina

1. What moments in the book made you laugh?

2. The phrase *"Talent is universal; opportunity is not"* is on the book's dedication. How does this statement connect with your own life experiences?

3. Chapter 1 opens with the statement "My father was the main reason I was a Marine" (17). However, we soon realize that Rye's father was ambivalent about this decision, and his mother was even less enthusiastic about the military. Would you ever encourage your children to join the military? How did this book connect to your own views on parenting?

4. Rye travels to Kenya with his parents when he is thirteen years old. What are your own thoughts on giving young people international experiences? Would you ever let your own child travel to Kibera alone? If so, at what age and under what circumstances?

5. As a college student on his way to Kibera to do research, Rye asks himself if poverty makes people less trustworthy. What do you think?

6. Carolina for Kibera was originally founded as a way to prevent ethnic violence and develop youth leaders through sports. Do you agree that sports can help prevent violence? What roles have sports played in your own life?

7. Would you have given to Carolina for Kibera when Rye was forming it with Nate as a college student? What would it have taken for you to contribute? How much would you have given and why?

8. Who would you have invested with in Kenya if you were in Rye's shoes: Taib, Tabitha, Jumba, Oluoch, Kash, Elizabeth, Salim?

9. What happened to Kash? Do you sympathize with him? Do you agree with Salim's and Rye's decisions and actions? Why or why not?

10. Is anyone in the book selfless? Are people inherently selfish?

11. When Rye is deployed overseas he is challenged by the two seemingly opposing forces of his life: Kibera and the Marines. How can he be a champion for peace in Kibera while at the same time seek to kill enemy combatants in Fallujah? How is the violence advocated by the Marines different from the ethnic violence in the slums of Kibera? Who determines when violence is "just"?

12. What are your impressions of the relationship between Tracy and Rye? How does it impact the events described in the book? Was Tracy too patient? Was she not patient enough?

13. Rye believes in finding local leaders, and then empowering them through participatory development. How was this successful in Kibera? Do you think this kind of collaborative leadership could work in other situations? What are the drawbacks?

14. Have you ever met a Tabitha? A Salim?

15. Are the youth of today "the present and the future leaders" (69)?

16. There is a description of the ideas behind Rye's assignment to Djibouti called distributed operations. He calls this a new way of thinking about counterterrorism, and it is currently employed by our armed services around the globe. What is your concept of appropriate counterterrorism?

17. Why does Rye spend so much time discussing compartments? What compartments do you keep? How have they changed over time? What's the best way to manage our life's compartments?

18. What is the significance of the elephant metaphor? Can you relate to the desire to "see the elephant" (253)?

19. The wars in Iraq and Afghanistan have affected hundreds of thousands of American families. What do you think of the way that Rye dealt with his experiences? Who do you know who has been affected by these wars?

20. Did this book alter your views of the U.S. military? If so, how?

21. Which character in the book would you most like to meet and why?

22. Who were Rye's most important mentors and what characterized those relationships? Who have been the most important mentors in your life? How are you "paying it forward" (110)?

23. Why has CFK been successful? What makes it unique from other nonprofits and nongovernmental organizations, if anything?

24. What role does faith play in this story? How did the book relate to your own spirituality?

25. What was the most memorable scene to you and why?

26. What can you buy for $26?

26 Questions for Students

Living in extreme poverty stinks. Living in violence stinks. It stinks. It's foul. And it's the type of deep, under-your-skin stench you just can't shake.

I know because I was born in a 10-by-10 shack not far from the old Mad Lion, the tracks, and Tabitha's first clinic. As a teenager I remember when goons hired by government cronies barreled into my community with bulldozers, whips, and clubs. They destroyed all of the homes near the railway line. In an instant my family—Mom, Dad, and my five siblings—and I lost everything. Our community lost everything. In the aftermath, we reunited, and we rebuilt. Although there was some competition between ethnic groups, back then we mixed and mingled fluidly. Friendships crossed ethnic lines, and our tastes did too. The best sausage and roasted *nduma* (arrow roots) came from the Kikuyu villages like Gatwekera. Tin shack restaurants in Luo villages were the destinations for fish of all sizes—sardines, tilapia, nile perch—and of course the maize meal *ugali*. We trekked down the tracks to the Makina and the Nubian villages for iftar delicacies during Ramadhan, or warm *mandazi* (African donuts), strong tea, and samosas.

Yet poverty and tension between ethnic communities grew more intense in the late 1980s and 1990s after World Bank and IMF Structural Adjustment Programs and economic liberalization eliminated the thin safety nets that had existed in rural and urban Kenya. The government introduced cost-sharing in health care and education and privatized many industries, resulting in a dramatic spike in unemployment. The floating of the Kenyan shilling resulted in massive inflation and further inhibited the development of a middle class. People flocked to the cities with high hopes but often little education and minimal skills. They landed in Kibera and the other slums that surround Nairobi.

It was also around this time that another tsunami struck. It was a force twisted by stereotypes and misunderstanding. We never mentioned it by its true name. HIV/AIDS stole our friends, relatives, and teachers. So many people in my church congregation died from the virus between 1988 and 1997 that I stopped attending funerals and questioned the existence of God. Children landed in orphanages, became street kids, or were adopted by relatives who were often as likely to abuse them as they were to nurture them.

This is the Kibera that Rye comes to and captures vividly as a college student seeking a research project for his senior thesis. It is a Kibera of hope in the face of despair. It is a Kibera where talent is clearly universal, but opportunity is not. My mother and teachers had emphasized that only a good education could lift me out of Kibera and allow me to pursue my dreams. As a boy I started to believe that I had to leave to save myself. I caught my first big break in January 1992. Through hard work and perfectly timed strokes of luck, I was awarded a full scholarship to Starehe, one of Kenya's premier boarding schools. I sold newspapers on street corners for two years after high school before stumbling across my second big break: a rare opportunity to attend St. Lawrence University in the United States. Years later I earned a master's degree in international relations from Georgetown University and began teaching history at the Potomac School near Washington, DC.

I first encountered Carolina for Kibera on a brief trip home to Kenya in 2005. The organization buzzed with activity and positive energy. It was connecting talent with opportunity. It was creating role models. Even my brother had been impacted. Although he had dropped out of high school, he proudly showed me a certificate he had earned from CFK after participating in a workshop on small business management and entrepreneurship. Soon it became common for people in the U.S. who knew I was from Kibera to ask me if I knew CFK and its cofounders, Salim, Tabitha, and Rye.

Rye and I eventually connected over e-mail and he agreed to come speak to my students at the Potomac School about his life as a Marine and a social entrepreneur in Kibera. His words elevated our students' expectations of what was possible. Although he was not as tall as I had imagined, to me, Rye embodied a certain American spirit. There is something special about America—from the pioneers who settled the West, to the generation who liberated Europe from two World Wars, to the developers of space travel and moon landings. In the twenty-first century, this century, our generation of American leaders will have to find ways to eliminate extreme poverty, promote human dignity, peace, environmental preservation, and more. It is possible, and the actions of people like Rye, Salim, and Tabitha illustrate that nothing is insurmountable if we confront our fears and participate together.

You don't have to grow up in a slum to understand that talent is universal, but opportunity is not. Just read this book. Then use it as a call to action for whatever cause you care about. That's what I intend to do with the students I now teach in the United States and in Kibera.

—*Tuko pamoja*
Ken Okoth
Kibera

1. How was Rye influenced by the trip to Kenya he took with his parents when he was thirteen, and what did he do about it? **(Ch 1)**

2. How is Kibera viewed in Kenya? To what extent are these views accurate? **(Ch 2)**

3. What did Kassim tell Rye about the ethnic clashes in Kibera? What were the root causes of these clashes, and how did they influence politics? **(Ch 3)**

4. Why did Rye give away the $26 to Tabitha when he had refrained from giving freely otherwise? **(Ch 4)**

5. What are the positive and negative attributes of Marine Corps boot camp? How do these attributes influence leadership development? Can they be improved? **(Ch 5)**

6. What does it mean to be a doer? Are there downsides to being a doer? Are you a doer? **(Ch 6)**

7. Throughout his studies and his work with CFK and USMC, Rye relies on both friends and those he terms as "mentors" to provide him with help and advice. How do the two positions of "mentor" and "friend" differ? Is it possible for a person (such as Tabitha) to play both roles? Is one role particularly better than the other? **(Ch 7)**

8. With a mix of good fortune and skill, Dan lived the so called "Kibera Dream" (123). He moved to Kibera as an eighteen-year-old, despite the dangerous circumstances, in search of a job and opportunity. Within five years he

stepped into a new economic class and experienced new quality of life. How does his experience compare to that of early twentieth century immigrant's coming through Ellis Island in search of the "American Dream?" What are similarities? What are differences? **(Ch 8)**

9. When Rye talks to a journalist about covering youth in Kibera, he says that he's only covered violence from the slum because, "If it bleeds it leads" (138). What do you think this outlook to poverty in the media does to influence our perception of poverty? Do you think it contributes to action or inaction? **(Ch 9)**

10. The emcee speaks of Tabitha with admiration, "She turns no one away. I can say she's like the Red Cross, here in Kibera, where you know even the Red Cross, it is afraid to come" (145). As illustrated by this quote, both Tabitha and Rye are risking their lives in Kibera. Do you think that Rye's premonition about an early death and Tabitha's illness make them better able to serve their communities? Why or why not? **(Ch 10)**

11. Do you think that there is a long term solution for cleaning up Kibera? **(Ch 11)**

12. How would you have reacted to the scenario with Oluoch? Would you have sent the letter? **(Ch 12)**

13. What does "talent is universal; opportunity is not" mean (193)? Do you agree with the statement? How does it relate to Kibera and to the Marines? How does it relate to your own life? **(Ch 13)**

14. How would you have handled Kash's situation if you were Salim, Tabitha, or Rye? What were the key decisions that they made? Were they good or bad decisions? What would you have done if you found yourself in their positions? **(Ch 14)**

15. Do you think there is glory in dying for your country? Explain. **(Ch 15)**

16. Should the U.S. military be involved with humanitarian work? Why or why not? **(Ch 16)**

17. What are Rye's views concerning the use of violence and military hard power used to defend a country and its interests? Do you agree or disagree with him? Was the Iraq war just? **(Ch 17)**

18. Rye thinks about the boy in the home they had raided. He says "We had stormed his home, shouted at his mother, threw him to the floor, and detained his uncle. And yet, the boy was still so enamored with the idea of America" (282). Why do you think the boy is still so interested in America? Why do you think he did not join a terrorist organization? **(Ch 18)**

19. What would you have done if you were in the position of the prison guards when the mutilation of prisoners took place? Does anybody have the right to be treated that way even if they are terrorists? **(Ch 19)**

20. At the end of the book, Rye finally hears the quote that Tabitha said before she died. Why do you think she chose this to say? What does it mean? **(Ch 20)**

General Questions

21. Do you think that by starting CFK Rye made a bigger difference than he would have made by donating to preexisting nongovernmental organizations (NGOs)? In a larger sense, when and why is it necessary to start a new NGO?

22. Is there an object or place, like Rye's father's grenade, that holds a seemingly magical spell over you? Explain how that object or place makes you feel?

23. After completing this book, could you picture yourself working at an NGO? If so, what specifically encourages you to do so?

24. How do you think corruption can be stopped? Does the solution rely solely on the authority figure(s)?

25. Rye's mother studied anthropology and conducted research in Peru. What did Rye's mother believe about the U.S. military, and how did this affect Rye's beliefs about it? Do you know people who have lived independently overseas, and have you spoken with them about their experiences?

26. Rye learned to balance and compartmentalize his Marine, Carolina for Kibera, and family lives. When did these lives work together or come into conflict?

A Note on the Author

RYE BARCOTT cofounded the nongovernmental organization Carolina for Kibera with Salim Mohamed and Tabitha Atieno Festo while he was an undergraduate at the University of North Carolina at Chapel Hill. He served in the Marines for five years then earned master's degrees in business and public administration from Harvard University, where he was a Reynolds Social Entrepreneurship Fellow. A World Economic Forum Young Global Leader and TED fellow, he works in the sustainability office at Duke Energy and lives in North Carolina with his wife and daughter. This is his first book.